SUPERVISING POLICE PERSONNEL

SUPERVISING POLICE PERSONNEL

THE FIFTEEN RESPONSIBILITIES

Second Edition

Paul M. Whisenand, Ph.D.
California State University, Long Beach

George E. Rush, Ph.D.
California State University, Long Beach

REGENTS/PRENTICE HALL
Englewood Cliffs, New Jersey 07632

Library of Congress Cataloging-in-Publication Data

Whisenand, Paul M.
   Supervising police personnel : the fifteen responsibilities / Paul
Whisenand and George Rush. – 2nd ed.
     p.   cm.
   Includes bibliographical references and index.
   ISBN 0-13-878331-4
   1. Police–Supervision of. 2. Police–Supervision of–United
States. I. Rush, George E. (George Eugene), 1932– . II. Title.
HV7936.S8W48 1993
350.74′068′3–dc20   92-35834
                                 CIP

Production Editor: *Adele M. Kupchik*
Acquisitions Editor: *Robin Baliszewski*
Cover Design: *Mike Fender*
Copy Editor: *Andrea K. Hammer*
Prepress Buyer: *Ilene Levy-Sanford*
Manufacturing Buyer: *Ed O'Dougherty*
Editorial Assistant: *Rosemary Florio*

 ©1993, 1988 by REGENTS/PRENTICE HALL
A Division of Simon & Schuster
Englewood Cliffs, New Jersey 07632

Printed in the United States of America

10 9 8 7 6 5 4 3 2 1

ISBN 0-13-878331-4

Prentice-Hall International (UK) Limited, *London*
Prentice-Hall of Australia Pty. Limited, *Sydney*
Prentice-Hall Canada Inc., *Toronto*
Prentice-Hall Hispanoamericana, S.A., *Mexico*
Prentice-Hall of India Private Limited, *New Delhi*
Prentice-Hall of Japan, Inc., *Tokyo*
Simon & Schuster Asia Pte. Ltd., *Singapore*
Editora Prentice-Hall do Brasil, Ltda., *Rio de Janeiro*

For our Children and their Children.
Love Dad and Granddad
Paul and George

Contents

Preface   *xiii*

OVERVIEW
Characteristics of Responsible Supervisors   *1*

Total Quality Leadership 2
Fifteen Responsibilities 5
Universal Mission Statement 7

PART ONE   Know Your Job   *9*

RESPONSIBILITY ONE
Values: Understanding Ourselves and Others   *11*

Values: An Overview 12
Values: Understanding and Respect 12
Definition, Sources, and Changing of Human Values 13
Values: What Do They Do for Us? 17
Value Clarification 20
Police Supervisor as Value Driven 22
At the Center 24
Prologue to Responsibility Two 27
Key Points 28
Discussion 28
Structured Experiences 28

RESPONSIBILITY TWO
Ethics: Professional Standards and Conduct   **33**

Ethics and Ethos   33
Hard Choices   34
Ethical Decision Making   35
Strategy for Fostering Integrity   37
Ethics Training   39
Key Points   44
Discussion   45
Structured Experiences   45

RESPONSIBILITY THREE
Leadership: Combining Values and Ethics into Vision   **47**

Authority and Power   47
Formal and Informal Leaders   49
Three Theories of Leadership   50
Police Leadership Challenge   54
Police Department: Voluntary Organization   56
Goals: Departmental and Personal   57
Self-Management and Leadership of Others   58
Leadership Paradigm   58
Leadership Defined   65
Key Points   65
Discussion   66
Structured Experiences   66

RESPONSIBILITY FOUR
Communications: Sharing the Vision   **68**

Communications: Leadership, Decision Making, and
Trust   68
What Is Communication?   69
What We Know about Communications   70
Types of Communication Channels   72
Methods of Communicating   75
Communications: Down, Up, and Lateral   78
Messages: Volume and Types   81
Communication Networks   86
Flip Side of "Information Age"   87
Barriers to Effective Communication   89
Removing the Barriers   90
Conclusion: A Challenge   93
Key Points   93
Discussion   94
Structured Experiences   94

RESPONSIBILITY FIVE
Time Management: Focusing on Values, Ethics,
Leadership, and Communications   **98**

A Couple of Questions for You 99
Our Mission 99
People, People, People 99
Time Dimension 100
Time and Productivity 100
Overloads 101
If It's Worth Doing, It's Worth Doing Poorly 102
Four Generations of Time Management 102
On Becoming a Category II Police Supervisor 105
Key Points 110
Discussion 111
Structured Experiences 111

PART TWO Know Your Staff   **115**

RESPONSIBILITY SIX
Motivation: Inspiration and Perspiration   **117**

Role of the Police Supervisor 117
What Is Motivation? 118
School of Motivational Thought Based on Needs 120
School of Motivational Thought Based on Process 123
Motivation, Work Performance, and Job Satisfaction 128
Morale 129
Job Satisfaction: Causes and Consequences 129
In Search of Job Satisfaction: Some Suggestions 130
Inspiration and Perspiration 133
Key Points 133
Discussion 134
Structured Experiences 134

RESPONSIBILITY SEVEN
Goal Setting: Supervising by Objectives   **138**

Role of the Police Supervisor 139
Goal Setting 139
From Goal Setting to Planning 141
From Planning to MBO 143
Supervising by Objectives 148
Obstacles to MBO 151
Key Points 152
Discussion 152
Structured Experiences 153

RESPONSIBILITY EIGHT
Performance Evaluation: Feedback —
The Making of Winners   **156**

Getting Quality Results through People   156
Role of the Police Supervisor   157
Performance Evaluation Defined   158
Complex Process   158
Variety of Purposes   159
Key Points   184
Discussion   184
Structured Experiences   185

RESPONSIBILITY NINE
Employee-Oriented Supervision:
I. Empowerment and Participation   **190**

Em-power-ment   190
Delegation   191
Participation   197
Quality Circles   199
Getting the Quality Out of Quality Circles   204
Supervising Effective Police Work Groups   206
Teamwork = Participative Supervision   207
Key Points   208
Discussion   209
Structured Experiences   209

RESPONSIBILITY TEN
Employee-Oriented Supervision: II. Conflict Resolution   **213**

Resolving Our Conflicts the Inupiat Eskimo Way: The Song
Duel   213
Keep in Mind . . .   213
Role of the Police Supervisor   214
Conflict: The Internal Consequences   215
Problem Employees: Worker Relations   218
Problem Employees: Citizen Relations   220
Phase 1: Complaint Receipt   223
Phase 2: Investigation   228
Phase 3: Adjudication   229
Preventing the Problem Employee   229
Most Often . . .   230
Negotiations: Getting to Yes   230
General Approach for Negotiating Differences   231
Seven Steps You Can Take for Getting to Yes   234
Summary   238

Key Points 238
Discussion 238
Structured Experiences 239

RESPONSIBILITY ELEVEN
Stress: A Choice for Wellness   **245**

Stress: The Demand for Change 246
Role of the Police Supervisor 246
Stress as a Demand for Change 248
Sources and Forms of Stress: The Stressors 250
Detecting One's Stress Level 254
Converting Stress into Wellness 260
The Good News 263
Key Points 264
Discussion 264
Structured Experiences 265

PART THREE *Putting Ourselves to Work*   **269**

RESPONSIBILITY TWELVE
Teamwork   **271**

A Paradigm 272
Role of the Police Supervisor 273
What Is Perception? 273
How Perception Works at Work 274
Perceptual Shortcuts 277
Perception and Teamwork 277
Role of the Police Supervisor 278
Training Goals 279
Training: The Process 280
Effective Training 281
Team Building 287
Simply Do It! 290
Key Points 291
Discussion 292
Structured Experiences 292

RESPONSIBILITY THIRTEEN
Community-Oriented Policing: A Focus on Effectiveness   **296**

More on Effectiveness 296
Universal Mission Statement 297
Some Specific Mission Statements 298
Central Mission 298
Case for Quality 302

Who's Really Responsible? 302
Why COP? 303
Will COP Happen? 304
COP Implementation 305
Who Benefits 308
Concluding Remark 309
Key Points 310
Discussion 310
Structured Experiences 311

RESPONSIBILITY FOURTEEN
Problem-Oriented Policing

312

Departmental Strategy 313
Problem-Oriented Policing 313
Why POP? 315
Example of POP 316
Basic Components 321
Identification of Problems 326
Analysis of Problems 327
Options 327
Concluding Thought 328
Key Points 328
Discussion 329
Structured Experiences 329

RESPONSIBILITY FIFTEEN
Total Quality Services: A Focus on Excellence

331

Some Background and Direction 331
Accent on Excellence 332
Alignment 334
Development of Action Plans for Excellence 339
Building of Excellence 339
On Your Way: The Excellent Supervisor 342

Preface

You will soon see that this book on police supervision is comprised of fifteen responsibilities and not chapters. You'll likewise see an overarching responsibility. "Supervision is a responsibility for getting total quality results through people." Basically, we're saying that **being a supervisor is being responsible**. In this case, it is being responsible for getting total quality work out of people. Note the terms "total" and "quality." When you're able to do that as a supervisor, excellence follows.

Due to our many years of teaching, training and working within police agencies, we were able to hear and observe what the successful supervisors were doing as compared to those who were marginal in their jobs. We concluded that the responsible supervisor is, in reality, performing fifteen interdependent responsibilities.

Being a police supervisor does indeed make very high demands on a person. It demands that they be truly competent in fulfilling their responsibilities. It demands that they take their work seriously. Being responsible at times is a harsh taskmaster. To demand it of others without demanding it of oneself is futile—in fact it is irresponsible.

Nothing quenches motivation as quickly as a slovenly supervisor. Police employees have the right to expect that supervisors will empower them to do a good job and work productively. A leader may not be the best *liked* boss, but he or she always inspires confidence, and always commands respect. The job of police supervisor demands the acceptance of responsibility for making human strengths effective.

We may have written a most unfashionable or unpopular book. It does not talk about rights. It stresses responsibility. Its focus is not on doing one's own thing, but on **total quality performance**.

While reading the fifteen responsibilities, keep in mind that people supervise. Every success (or failure) of a supervisor is the success (or failure) of a human being. Hence, our book concentrates on you, me and everyone else who wants to supervise and who wants to do so successfully.

We're not looking for logic as much as we are arguing for quality results. This book grew out of practice and it **centers on practice**.

We thank the thousands of supervisors we've trained, talked to, and observed at their work. They gave us the fifteen responsibilities and now we present them to you. We also thank Adele Kupchik, our production editor, for the "quality" she added to this effort.

Paul Whisenand and George Rush
San Clemente, California
1993

SUPERVISING POLICE PERSONNEL

OVERVIEW

Characteristics of Responsible Supervisors

Supervision is a responsibility for getting total quality results (TQR) through people.

When accepting the job of a police supervisor, an individual automatically inherits the overarching responsibility of getting TQR through people. It doesn't merely come with the job—it is *the job*! This job, likewise, encompasses other characteristics or subresponsibilities. Together they furnish the means or vehicle for getting results.

Imagine a police supervisor driving a patrol car full of police officers in a particular direction—one that seeks certain results. The various parts of the vehicle are interdependent and specifically designed to assure that the supervisor and officers arrive on time and effectively perform their duties. The supervisor steers the course, the interdependent parts cooperate and move the vehicle forward.

With the cornerstone responsibilities in mind (TQR), we have isolated fifteen discernible characteristics or subresponsibilities (subsequently referred to as responsibilities) of people who are successful supervisors. The fulfillment of these responsibilities not only characterizes effective supervisors, but they also serve as signs of progress for all of us.

Each one of the fifteen responsibilities plays a vital role in getting TQR. If one or more is dysfunctional or weak, it slows progress—delays or blocks needed results.

Soon you'll be studying and, we hope, practicing the fifteen responsibilities. Remember, if you're a police supervisor, quality, results, and people are critical to your success. Further, acting on a few of the responsibilities and ignoring the others won't work. Doing the fifteen responsibilities is not easy—but, after all, if supervising were easy, everyone would be doing it.

TOTAL QUALITY LEADERSHIP

The movement toward TQR as the operating model for organizations large and small, manufacturing and service industries alike, is increasing at an exponential rate because quality is widely seen as the key to American economic survival and success.

Under whatever variation adopted, the principles and processes of TQR represent far more than a passing fad or trendy quick-fix solution to what ails us. TQR represents the century's most profound, comprehensive alteration in supervisory theory and practice. Yet, many police agencies are failing, at least not fully succeeding, in their quality improvement efforts. Growing frustration and cynicism mark the milestones thus far along our police organization's path to TQR.

Our first edition of this book was subtitled, *Back to the Basics*. We meant by this a return to greater effectiveness. And, naturally, effectiveness included "quality." Wrong!

The icon kicker, Tom Peters, has bluntly stated, "Quality and flexibility through skilled labor have never been an American custom." He acknowledges that we are great at mass producing goods and services. Regretfully, quality has not been a prominent part of our national game plan. Who made your car, television, VCR, FAX, etc.? When you think of quality, do you comfortably accept an American-made product or service? The private sector needs to join the quality movement. So does the government. And, *so do the police.*

Total Quality: Leadership and People Paradigm

Ironically, the primary elements of TQR — leadership and people — as espoused by W. Edwards Deming himself, have somehow been lost in the forest of quality. (Dr. Deming is an American who coached the Japanese on how to whip most of our major industries.) Police executives have focused on the leaves of quality, bottom-line statistics, while ignoring its roots, leadership and people.

How many departments follow a TQR program assembled from some combination of the following components?

Computer hardware	Quality-control circles
Hard work	New facilities
Making people accountable	Management by objectives
Merit systems	Incentive pay
Work standards	Management information systems

"Wrong!" says Deming. "All Wrong!" None of the preceding represents TQR! But, if hard work, quality-control circles, management by objectives (MBO), management information systems (MIS), and computers are not TQR, what is?

Although some of these elements may contribute to TQR (and others undermine it), they by no means assure it. Herein lies the essential understanding of what TQR is and how to achieve it. Deming realizes that TQR resides effectively in the eye of the beholder—it is what the agent of quality believes it to be. Thus, for the police officer quality may be pride of workmanship; for the chief, decreasing crime; and for the citizen, reasonably priced police services that protect and help him or her.

Ultimately, however, the result of quality is what the citizen determines it to be. No other stakeholder of a police agency—city council, police chief, officers, neighborhood watches—can long survive while ignoring the demands of the judge of quality, the citizen. Thus, all quality initiatives must be customer focused. Quality is what consumers judge it to be by contributing their tax dollars.

But how do we achieve quality in the judgment of consumers? Dr. Deming contends that quality, the result, is a function of quality, the process. And the fifteen responsibilities that follow provide the principles and application tools necessary to activate the two ingredients most essential to this quality process: leadership and people.

Transformation of Supervision

TQR is primarily a paradigm (a way of looking at the world) concerning leadership and people. Overlooked so often in Deming's work is his central premise: The single most important requirement to halt the decline of Western industry and for America to regain worldwide industrial competitive advantage is "to fundamentally transform the Western style of management." And what is the primary transformation that must occur? "The job of management is not supervision, but leadership," says Deming. "The required transformation of Western style of management requires that managers be leaders." This holds true for police supervision as well.

The purpose of TQR is to bring to the community desirable and continually improving police services at ever-increasing value, as judged by consumers, thus providing a securer life. The purpose of a police supervisor is to empower officers to achieve their worthwhile objectives, in essence to become more effective at whatever they do.

TQL = Empowerment of People

Police supervision must change fundamentally, and transform its attitudes, mind-set, basic paradigms, before total quality can become a reality. We're talking about the way in which police supervision views itself, its role, and its relationship to employees and to all other stakeholders, especially customers.

Our current leadership paradigm is that people are things, "commodities." Give them a fair day's wage, and they will return a fair day's labor. Human relations and human resource philosophies have added little of substance to this theory: If we also treat people kindly and ask their opinion once in a while, they will respond more completely with heart and mind as well as substance, thus improving their labor's output.

Police management has given lip service to tapping the potential of its most important resource—its people. "The greatest waste in America is failure to use the abilities of people," laments Deming. The first fundamental transformation of thinking required of police management is to develop new basic attitudes toward the intrinsic dignity and value of people, of their "intrinsic motivation" to perform to their maximum capabilities.

Police supervisors must empower their people in the deepest sense and remove the barriers and obstacles they have created that crush and defeat the inherent commitment, creativity, and quality service that police officers are otherwise prepared to offer. To receive joy and pride in one's work is the right of all. And it is supervisory practices that prevent it! To achieve total quality, supervisors must become leaders, drawing from their people their greatest capacity to contribute ideas, creativity, innovative thinking, attention to detail, and analysis of process and product to the workplace. In other words, police supervisors must become empowering leaders.

Foundation for Transformation

Although Deming's body of total quality theory explains the "what" to do and gives a partial explanation of "why" it should be done, there is little practical development of "how" it can be done. The fifteen responsibilities supplies the missing "how to do it" component of TQR.

The fifteen responsibilities reflect timeless, fundamental principles of effective human interaction. They are not easy, quick-fix solutions to personal and interpersonal problems. Rather, they are foundational principles that, when applied consistently in countless specific practices, become behaviors enabling fundamental transformations of individuals, relationships, and organizations.

The fifteen responsibilities are integrated, interdependent, holistic, and sequential. They build, one on the other, providing a practical, cohesive basis for successful interpersonal relationships and for organizational effectiveness.

Because the fifteen responsibilities focus on basic, fundamental principles and applicable processes, genuine, deep transformation of thinking and character can transpire. Profound, sustainable cultural change can occur within a police department (such as commitment to TQR) only when the individuals within the organization first change themselves from the inside out. *Not only must personal change precede organizational change, but personal quality also must precede organizational quality.*

For instance, classes in communication skills to foster team building may have little sustainable benefit when police supervisors retain the attitude that their subordinates must be constantly checked and controlled or they will produce inferior services, or that too much police employee empowerment or initiative could threaten the supervisor's job.

Suppose, however, that police supervisors develop a new paradigm that employees are capable and desire to make a quality contribution, and that empowerment enhances the supervisor's overall effectiveness. In using the fifteen responsibilities, supervisors can assist police employees to achieve their potential. With these underlying paradigms exercised within aligned systems and structures supporting high-trust levels, teaching the skills of productive communication can be effective over the long term.

Internalizing the fifteen responsibilities results in the transformation of people and organizations. It is just this transformation that is the key—for many, the missing key—to successful TQR.

FIFTEEN RESPONSIBILITIES

To develop momentum toward TQR, you must

- Know your job.
- Know your staff.
- Put yourself to work.

Each one of these three arenas includes four or more of the fifteen responsibilities. As a police supervisor, you're responsible for getting forward movement on each one of them.

Know Your Job

It may seem like a paradox that *to know your job you must first know yourself.* This means you must understand yourself—your values, interests, and drives. Once you are aware of what makes you tick, you're in a position to comprehend the workings and people that comprise your job purview. Responsibility One is devoted to *values.*

The next step involves ethics and professional standards—the "dos" and "don'ts" in your organization and in your profession. Where are the integrity lines drawn? Can you fully recognize absolutes and courageously condemn the bad and champion the good? Responsibility Two focuses on *ethics.*

We're now able to take values and ethics and blend them into a vision. The vision sets us up to be a potential leader. "I can see where we ought to be going, let me show you how it looks, follow me. I'll empower you." With a vision comes Responsibility Three—*leadership.*

To share a vision you must communicate it to others. Leaders know and fulfill Responsibility Four—*communications.*

All of the preceding requires time. Not just mere time but top-priority time. And we all know that time is tough to come by or control. "Oh, if I only had more time," is a common complaint. Either we manage it, or it manages us. Thus, Responsibility Five is *time management.*

Know Your Staff

The first five responsibilities have set the stage for you as a supervisor to know your staff. Remember, they're the people who will, or won't, get TQR for you and your police agency. This section will show you how to make five individual efforts into what appears to be the efforts of fifty. This is referred to as "synergy." Basically, synergy is adding one plus one and coming up with six, sixty, six hundred.

Why know your staff? You wouldn't be able to free up their motives if you didn't. Motivation and inspiration are partners. The prefix "in" means inside or within. Inspiration then translates into helping someone letting what's within, without, and then guiding it. Simply put, Responsibility Six is *motivation*.

If you haven't a distinction in mind, any route will get you to where you're going. We need to know where and why we're moving in a particular direction. We need goals! Many years ago Peter Drucker conceptualized the process of MBO in the late 1950s. We've modified it here for our purposes and refer to it as supervision by objectives (SBO). A goal is a desired end, a hoped for result. SBO supplies that plus some means for getting results. Hence, Responsibility Seven is *goal setting*.

After goals are set in place, measuring their attainment becomes critical. Goals are most often achieved by brain power and physical energy. In measuring goal fulfillment, we're actually evaluating the individual efforts of police officers, cadets, civilian dispatchers, corrections officers and more. Thus, Responsibility Eight is *performance evaluation*.

The next characteristic focuses on making everyone feel and behave as though they're 100% responsible for their work output. Two methods are available for building individual accountability. First, empower people to do their work. Second, ensure that they participate in decisions that affect them. Responsibility Nine is employee-oriented supervision or *empowerment and participation*.

Each of us enters into jobs, relationships, and situations with certain unspoken expectations. And one of the major causes of "people problems" in police organizations is unclear, confusing, or unfulfilled expectations. Conflicting expectations regarding rules, roles, and goals cause most of us pain and problems, adding stress to working relationships. Responsibility Ten is likewise employee oriented—*conflict resolution*.

Despite all the "wellness" literature to the contrary, there is no easy way of coping with stress. Stress is change. Stress or change is natural. It is going to happen. How we handle it is up to us. We have a choice. We can choose our response to any circumstance or condition. When stress impacts us, we choose to unleash within ourselves a winning or whining response, a growth or grinding experience, a healthy or harmful reaction. Responsibility Eleven is *stress management*.

Put Yourself to Work

Putting yourself to work has two dimensions: *quality* and *commitment*. Quality comes from the heart, commitment from involvement. Commitment and quality produce results—TQR.

By this point in the book you'll know how to know your job; you'll know how to know your staff; and, thus, it's time to go to work. Basically, you'll be applying all of the previous eleven responsibilities in a pattern of behavior that is value driven, results oriented, and quality conscious.

Have you noticed that we're the least trained for some of the most crucial roles we play and responsibilities we assume? For example, how many of you took classes on birthing, parenting, planning family finances, or being a spouse? We know of police agencies in which the officer is actually performing police work *before* he or she receives classroom instruction. Similarly, there are police supervisors who are working without any prior supervisory training. Responsibility Twelve is to develop your staff and yourself constantly — or *training*.

For decades our police managers hammered on their staffs to be more efficient (doing things right, bottom-line statistics). The supervisors conveyed their expectations by demanding more and more quantity of services from the line officers. "Lower the crime rate; move, move, move; faster, faster." The late 1960s saw a reaction to such policies and practices. The reaction was labeled, "police community relations." Later other titles were applied such as "team policing" and "neighborhood policing." With only slightly differing approaches, these programs sought to link the police to their community better. Underlying all of these programs was a nearly unrecognized hope to produce quality services. Responsibility Thirteen is *community-oriented policing* (services).

Related to community-oriented policing is a parallel endeavor, only its focus is more on the problem (traffic problem, gang problem, robbery problem, drug problem, etc.). Some police agencies are attempting to be problem driven as compared to call driven. They're seeking to attack the root of the problem, and not some evasive and random set of occurrences. Responsibility Fourteen is *problem-oriented policing* (efficiency).

The final responsibility is one of continuous improvement in professional development, interpersonal relations, supervisory effectiveness, and departmental productivity. We present it as a value. A value that drives individuals. If you, your officers, don't have it personally, you won't get it organizationally. The value we're referencing is quality (TQR). All quality initiatives must be customer or citizen focused. Responsibility Fifteen is *total quality services.*

UNIVERSAL MISSION STATEMENT

Steve Covy has conceptualized a universal mission statement that is intended to serve leaders of organizations as an expression of their vision and sense of stewardship. It attempts to encompass, in one brief sentence, the core values of the organization. We believe that the fifteen responsibilities, when internalized and practiced, will help fulfill it.

Our universal mission is to improve the economic well-being and quality of life of all stakeholders.

Part One

KNOW YOUR JOB

RESPONSIBILITIES:

- *Values*
- *Ethics*
- *Leadership*
- *Communications*
- *Time management*

RESPONSIBILITY ONE

Values: Understanding Ourselves and Others

More than anything else, we are what we believe, what we dream, what we value.

Arnold Mitchell*

Find a quiet place to read and think about the next few paragraphs. Make a conscious effort to project yourself into the following situation.

Picture yourself driving to a retirement dinner for a co-worker who is also a close friend. You park your car and walk inside the restaurant. You locate the assigned ballroom and enter. As you wander in, you notice the banners and flags. You spot the smiling faces of your co-workers and their spouses. You sense gaiety and happiness in the room.

As you approach them, you look up at the head table and see your name card on it. You also see the name cards of your wife and three children. Overhead on a banner is printed in large letters your name and, "Congratulations for Twenty-Five Years of Service." Below that banner is another that reads, "A Happy Retirement to You." This is your retirement! And, all of these people have come to honor you, to express feelings of appreciation for your work.

You're escorted to the head table where your wife and children join you. You're handed a program. There are five speakers. The first is your wife. The second is one of your children. The third speaker is your closest friend. The fourth speaker is an employee who is currently working for you. The final speaker is your boss. All of these people know you very well but in differing ways.

Now, think carefully. What would you expect each of these speakers to say

*Arnold Mitchell, *The Nine American Lifestyles* (New York: Macmillan Publishing, 1983). Reprinted with permission.

11

about you and your life? What kind of spouse, father, and friend would you like their words to reflect? What kind of supervisor? What kind of a subordinate?

What values would you like them to have seen in you? What contributions, what achievements would you want them to remember? Look carefully at the people who have gathered to wish you well. What difference would you like to have made in their lives?

Take a few moments and write down key values that you think they would attribute to you.

VALUES: AN OVERVIEW

> *What lies behind us and what lies before us*
> *are tiny matters*
> *compared to what lies within us.*

—Oliver Wendell Holmes

Our values play a crucial role in our professional and personal lives. Basically, a *value* is something for which we have an enduring preference. As a police supervisor, one could be expected to value supervising and police work. Although associated with other concepts, such as needs and attitudes, values differ from them and are much more fundamental.

Values serve a variety of purposes, including acting as filters, generation builders, individual distinctions, standards of behavior, conflict resolvers, signs of emotional states, stimuli for thinking, and forces that cause one to behave. Our values are primarily derived from the early, formative years. Values change over time, and we have a choice as to what we will value and its priority in our value system.

We are what we value, and thus will supervise ourselves and others accordingly. *Moreover, values become the beliefs that guide a police organization* and the behavior of its employees. Responsibility One focuses on individual value systems. Later in Responsibility Thirteen we'll look at organizational values.

VALUES: UNDERSTANDING AND RESPECT

The ability of the police supervisor to perform his or her role successfully is directly linked to an understanding and respect for the values and attitudes of assigned personnel. With this understanding and respect, the supervisor is fortified to influence and lead others in the accomplishment of their assigned duties. The focus must be twofold, however. The supervisor must first comprehend his or her values and attitudes. Once accomplished, the supervisor is in a better position to accurately understand those possessed by other employees.

We Are What We Value

Human values are important to us, because they *are* us. Simply stated, our past values have determined who we are and what we are pursuing in life; our present values are likewise shaping our life today, and our futures will be primarily shaped according to the values that we possess at each coming point in time.

It is vital for the police supervisor to know and appreciate human values because they serve as a destiny (an end or a goal) and as a path (a means or guide) toward reaching that destiny. In summary, then, each of us should know his or her own values because they underpin one's character, personality, and supervisory style and performance. This chapter assists you in clarifying your own value system so that you can eventually apply it in a way that will support, rather than detract from, your responsibility for being an effective police supervisor.

Worker Attitudes

Our human values, in conjunction with the organizational setting and our personal lives, shape for each of us work-related attitudes. We would underscore the "personal side" because what we feel and think about our job is very much influenced by personal or private events, and vice versa. Even if we do not want this connection or spill-over from one arena to another, it happens. This is simply a manifest reflection of our holistic nature. An understanding of attitudes, attitude formation, and attitude change is important for several reasons.

1. Attitudes can be found in every aspect of police work. We have attitudes about most things that happen to us, as well as about most people we meet. In view of this universal characteristic of attitudes, an understanding of their nature is essential for supervisors.

2. Attitudes influence behavior. Much of how we behave at work is governed by how we feel about things. Therefore, an awareness of attitudes can assist supervisors in understanding human behavior at work. Changes in police employee behavior can be expected to the extent that supervisors can change or control employee attitudes.

3. Bad attitudes on the job cause problems. Poor job attitudes can be reflected in subsequent poor performance, citizen's complaints, equipment abuse, turnover, and absenteeism, all of which result in direct costs to the police agency.

DEFINITION, SOURCES, AND CHANGING OF HUMAN VALUES

The modern individual is assailed from every angle by divergent and contradictory value claims. It is no longer possible, as it was in the not too distant historical past, to settle comfortably into the value system of one's forebears or one's community and live out one's life without ever examining the nature and the assumptions of that system.

—Carl R. Rogers
Lecture, University of Southern California, October 13, 1971

The term *value* has a variety of uses. For example, one may value one's family, value one's leisure time, value one's reputation, value one's position as a police manager, or value jogging. Each of these five values is different in several respects. One is a goal-oriented value: one's reputation. Another value, jogging, is a means to another desired state: one's physical and mental health. Yet another value, one's position as a police supervisor, is temporal; that is, it is a temporary position. We have a tendency to forget that what some persons may value highly, others may not. (For example, you may place a high value on the promise of a promotion, while someone else, satisfied with his or her present job, may not.) In fact, people are alike or are different due to the commonality or the incongruence of their professional, personal, and societal values.

Values Defined

A *value* is an enduring belief that a specific mode of conduct or end-state of existence is personally or socially preferable to an opposite or inverse mode of conduct or end-state existence.[1] Because each of us possesses more than a single value, it is essential that we think in terms of a *value system*, which is an enduring organization of beliefs concerning preferable modes of conduct or end-states of existence in a hierarchical ranking of relative importance.[2] Hence, a value is an enduring but changeable belief that a particular means to a particular goal is to be preferred over an option. However, one should not be deluded into thinking that there is always a one-to-one connection between a means and a goal. One usually has approximately eighteen end-state values (goals) and sixty to seventy modes of conduct values (means).[3]

Sources of Our Values

The process of value creation may actually begin long before birth, as argued by many sociobiologists and popular authors such as Carl Sagan in *The Dragons of Eden* and Desmond Morris in *The Naked Ape*. Many experts suggest that *some* behavior patterns in our primitive ancestors might have been encoded in the DNA, which in turn now guides *our* behavior patterns. Whatever the degree of genetic input, for our purposes it is enough to assume that genetics shape broad patterns of human behavior. Our concern is with behavior patterns that are learned from the moment of birth forward.

[1] For more on values see Milton Rokeach, *The Nature of Human Values* (New York: Macmillan, 1973), pp. 33–65.
[2] Rokeach, *The Nature of Human Values*, pp. 33–65.
[3] Rokeach, *The Nature of Human Values*, pp. 33–65.

Our value-programming periods can be divided into three periods: imprinting, modeling, and socialization.[4]

Imprinting. During the first six to seven years of age, in addition to *physical* behavior development, a tremendous amount of *mental* development takes place. The popular analogy, "As the twig is bent, so the tree shall grow," is perhaps so obviously simple that we frequently fail to apply it to children. The early years of childhood may be compared to the foundation and frame of a building. The foundation determines the quality and strength of the structure that goes on top. The completed structure depends on its base, even if additions are built. The foundation of a person is the child as formed in his or her early years. The key figures here are Mom and Dad and a few others. Even though real "formal" learning does not start in the preschool period, there are many important stages that determine how, how much, how well, and what the child will learn as she or he develops. The question that we must answer and comprehend is "By *whom*, and *how* were we (or they) imprinted in our formative years?"

Modeling. From seven or eight to thirteen or fourteen years of age, the process of identification—initially with the mother, then the father and important "others" around the child—expands. The child shifts into intense *modeling*, relating to family, friends, and external "heroes" in the surrounding world. People the child would "like to be like" are carefully observed. As a result, our initial close models give way to more expanded contacts. Soon, group membership begins to exert its influence. We identify not only with play groups or gangs as a whole, but also with certain "important" individuals within them. New values and behavior patterns are combined with the ones we absorbed from our family. Once in school, the process of identifying extends to the heroes of history and fictional stories. Furthermore, our increasing involvement with media during this period will bring in characters from movies and television as additional heroes. We use these models to construct our internal ego ideal, the person we would like to become. We are now a complex composite of absorbed inputs. The programming accelerates.

The hero models in our lives are very critical people. They are the people we try to behave like, the people that we want to be like when we become adults. The modeling period is a critical period during which we absorb values from a diverse selection of models. Do you remember your own modeling activities? When you were ten years old, whom did you want to grow up to be like? Whom did you secretly look up to, try to imitate in the way you talked, the way you walked, the way you dressed, the way you wanted to be? What about your co-workers? Who were their potential role models at the age of ten or eleven?

Socialization. From thirteen or fourteen to around twenty years of age, our social life becomes structured primarily in terms of our friends. This

---

[4]This typology is based on Morris Massey, *The People Puzzle: Understanding Yourself and Others* (Reston, Va.: Reston Publishing Company, 1979).

intense *socialization* with one's peers results in people of common interests (values) grouping together for reinforcement. During the period of adolescence, we are in the process of defining and integrating values, beliefs, and standards of our particular culture into our own personalities. It is during this period that we achieve full physical maturity and a dominant value system. This system determines our basic personality. During this period of socialization, we engage in experimentation, verification, and validation of our basic life plan. From about twenty years on, our value system programmed during childhood and adolescence locks in, and we then repeatedly "test" it against the reality of the world.

People of like interests, behavior, and developing value systems associate intensely with one another and reinforce each other in their development. Who were your friends? What was your "best friend" like? What did you talk about? What about sex? Were you a leader or follower, a joiner or loner? Did your friends have a nickname for you? What did you do together? How long have your friendships lasted? These same questions should be addressed about your co-workers.

Changing Our Values

Our values, while enduring, can be changed. This transition can ocur in one of two ways. The first is a traumatic or significant emotional event (SEE). The second revolves around major dissatisfaction. Let us look at each condition more closely.

Significant emotional events.   The common denominator of SEEs is a challenge and disruption to our present behavior patterns and values. In job situations or family relationships, such challenges might be artificially created (e.g., being fired or promoted), but, more likely, SEEs occur in an unplanned, undirected manner (e.g., being seriously injured, or winning an athletic contest). We must be careful to distinguish between SEEs, which actually change our gut-level value system, and external events, which simply modify our behavior. For example, a departmental order imposed on us may demand that we pay attention to the needs of the employees. Our behavior may change accordingly, but our values remain the same. The closer such events occur to our early programming periods, the more likely significant change will occur. The less dramatic the event, the longer we hold our programmed values, and any change in values will occur more slowly, if at all. It is possible to "teach an old dog new tricks," but the learning is much more difficult than for the younger animal. SEEs are neither good nor bad. Their frequency, type, and how we cope with them determine if they are positive or negative for us.

Profound dissatisfaction.   To be successful in this most difficult of transitions—psychological growth—requires a special combination of inner and, to a degree, outer circumstances. These are set forth with splendid simplicity by psychologist Clare Graves.[5]

[5] Adapted from Clare W. Graves, *On the Theory of Value*, mimeographed paper, 1967.

Graves says that a person must possess three attributes if he or she is to make a substantial psychological step forward:

1. The individual must be deeply dissatisfied. Otherwise, why change?
2. The individual must possess much psychological and physical energy. Few things are harder to break than old bonds, old views, old prejudices, old convictions, old loves.
3. The individual must have or acquire the psychological insight to know what will slake the driving dissatisfaction. Without this, the effort to change will be directionless, ceaseless, and pointless.

Only when all three of these factors are present simultaneously will a person have the motivation to change, the drive to act on the motivation, and the foresight to know where to go and when he or she has arrived. See Figure 1-1, which graphically describes this section.

VALUES: WHAT DO THEY DO FOR US?

In a general sense, values tell us much about who we are, as individuals, as citizens, as consumers, as a nation, and as a police supervisor.[6] As you examine the remainder of this section, keep in mind the following:

- The total number of values that each person possesses is relatively small (thirty to sixty is a flexible range).
- Everyone everywhere has the same values, to different degrees.

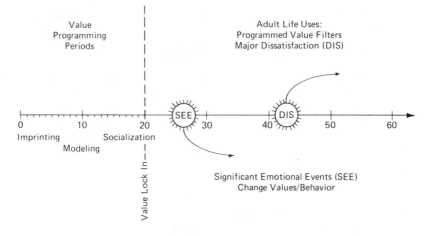

Figure 1-1 Value Programming Periods and Change

[6]A recent and well-documented scientific study of our current and emerging value systems can be found in Arnold Mitchell, *The Nine American Lifestyles* (New York: Macmillan, 1983).

- Values are organized into value systems.
- The origin of human values can be traced to one's formative years, culture, institutions, society, and—to some limited extent, perhaps—one's unique genetic makeup.
- The consequences of one's values will be manifested in virtually all that one feels, thinks, and does.
- A large part of a police supervisor's effectiveness, or lack of it, is dependent on his or her value system.
- Enhanced or continued effectiveness is directly linked to a police supervisor's awareness of his or her values *and* the values of co-workers.

Filters

Literally everything is sifted through the fundamental value systems operating in each of us. Values are our subjective reactions to the world around us. Although some items are purely functional and can be viewed rationally and objectively (chalkboards, picture books, light bulbs, rulers, etc.), most items involve a subjective reaction, especially when our feelings come into play. Gut-level value systems automatically *filter* the way we view most of the things around us. Your filters operate in degrees and shades of good/bad, right/wrong, normal/not normal, or acceptance/rejection.

Generation Gaps

In recent decades, the acceleration in the rate of change of technology, legal dimensions, social behavior, education, and economic systems has created vastly diverse programming experiences between generations. The differences in these experiences have created a spectrum of widely varying value systems within our society. Recently a popular label was "the generation gap"—but it is much more. In volumes of material, people have attempted to reconcile differences between generations that, in reality, are irreconcilable—perhaps *understandable*, but *nonnegotiable*. The fundamental value systems are, in fact, dramatically different between the generations that presently exist simultaneously in our society. Police organizations can reflect as many as four or more generations within their employees. Obviously this can, and usually does, present a problem for the supervisor.

Individual Differences

Value programming is not simply a process of indoctrination. Nor is the behavior of people the result of a series of processes that simply overlay a particular culture on the biological core of individuals. Rather, society shapes a person's inherited temperament, but it does not transform that person into a complete opposite of his or her own basic nature. We each emerge with somewhat distinctive ways of behaving, despite the influences in our generation's programming. Our basic physical and mental abilities are influenced by a wide range of inputs. In broad categories, the major sources of programming experiences for all of us were (1) family, (2) educational experiences of a formal nature, (3) religious inputs, (4) the media, (5) our friends, (6) where we grew up geographically, and (7) the amount of money that provided a base for these other factors.

Standards

A value system acts as a set of standards and thus guides our conduct. It causes us to take a position or to abandon one previously adopted, predisposes us to accept or reject certain ideas or activities, gives us a sense of being right or wrong, aids us in making comparisons, acts as a basis from which we attempt to influence others, and affords us an opportunity to justify or rationalize our actions. Thus, our value system is, in effect, our individual "code of conduct."

Conflict Resolvers

We frequently find ourselves in conflict with another person because of individual value system disparities. In an intrapersonal way, however, value systems more often than not support us in making choices. "I prefer blue over brown" or "I choose to allocate my police personnel in a crime-prevention program over a crime-specific program" are illustrations of this. Briefly, one's value system assists in making decisions. Nonetheless, when individuals possess different values, they are apt to conflict with one another.

Emotion Indicators

Most people give the value of "fairness" a high rank. As a consequence, when seeing or experiencing wrongful personnel practices, one's emotional threshold is normally breached and one becomes angry, depressed, or threatened, or a combination of all three. If one has been the perpetrator of the unjust act, then the emotion of guilt is probably triggered within oneself. The police supervisor who disciplines an errant employee with reasonable cause may feel some sadness because of his or her value for the family unit, feeling that the employee well deserved being disciplined, but also feeling sorry for the employee's spouse and children.

Thought Provokers

If we value being an effective police supervisor, does it not make sense that this value should provoke us into thinking about what means (e.g., enhancing one's job knowledge) would best achieve the desired outcome (success)? Fortunately, there are techniques for the recording and exploration of one's thoughts in a meaningful way so that we can put these thoughts to use. The techniques range from keeping a diary to following planned exercises. We will cover a number of such techniques later; in the meantime, remember that values generate thoughts as well as guide them.

Motivators

The terms *motivation* and *motive* denote desired or actual movement toward an identified end. A person's value system motivates him or her to choose one path (means) as compared to any others. Thus, one can feel or see one's motivations by inspection of or introspection on one's behavior. What moves a person to act, or to want to act, in a particular manner stems from his or her own value system. In essence, one's values underpin and generate one's motives. As a result, if you value supervision, it is reasonable for you to be motivated to become a police supervisor. This sense of being motivated further serves as a motivation for acquiring the skills, knowledge, and abilities necessary for supervising a group of police officers.

Your value system determines how you relate to your family, what products you buy, and how you vote. It dictates your leisure-time activities, what information you absorb, and your religious convictions. Of relevance here is that your values decide how well you perform your job as a supervisor. Figure 1-2 summarizes this section.

VALUE CLARIFICATION

This is the paradigm: bureaucratic values tend to stress the rational, task aspects of the work and to ignore the basic human factors which relate to the task and which, if ignored, tend to reduce task competence. Managers brought up under this system of values are badly cast to play the intricate human roles now required of them. Their ineptitude and anxieties lead to systems of

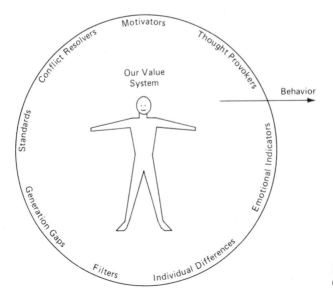

Figure 1-2 How Our Values Affect Our Behavior

discord and defense which interfere with the problem-solving capacity of the organization.

—Warren G. Bennis and Burt Nanus
Leaders: The Strategies of Taking Charge (New York: Harper & Row, 1985), p. 2

Select any one of your values (e.g., your job), and if you can answer each of the following questions with a yes, you have identified and confirmed one of your values.[7]

In terms of a particular value, are you

1. Choosing freely?
2. Choosing from options?
3. Choosing after thoughtful consideration of the consequencs of each option?
4. Prizing being happy with the choice?
5. Willing to make a public affirmation of the choice?
6. Doing something with the choice: performance?
7. Using the choice in a pattern of life?

Choosing Freely

The values that are chosen freely are those that one will internalize, cherish, and allow to guide one's life. Society or one's physical environment may impose a value, but it does not necessarily become one's own.

Choosing from Options

It follows that, if there are no options, then there is not a freedom of choice. One would be hard-pressed to convince someone that he or she valued employment with a specific police department when in fact it was the only one that would hire him or her.

Choosing after Thoughtful Consideration

A value must be *freely* chosen after a careful review of the consequences of each option. In other words, the consequences must be known to whatever extent possible. After all, if we do not realize the consequences of a particular alternative, we do not know what is likely to occur and therefore cannot have freely chosen that alternative.

Prizing

Briefly, a value is something that we cherish, respect, and show pride in.

---

[7]Adapted from L. E. Rath, M. Harmon, and S. Simon, *Values and Teaching* (Columbus, Ohio: Charles E. Merrill Publishing Co., 1966), p. 30.

Public Affirmation

If one values a person, an object, or a concept, it seems only reasonable that one would profess it openly. Are you pleased and proud to tell others that you are a police supervisor or not?

Performance

What one does reflects one's values. The importance of a particular value (such as acquiring a college education) can be assessed in line with how much time is spent on it (such as taking three units a semester rather than nine). There is an obvious difference between thinking about a value and acting on it. Thinking about a value (such as losing ten pounds) may be an early indication that one is forming a specific value, but it is in performing the value (an actual loss of weight) that one can attest to its being a full value.

Pattern of Life

Values, because one acts on them, become a dominating influence in one's life. They establish patterns in thought and deed. Consequently, they motivate us to attend church or not, to get married or not, to have children or not, and to *supervise effectively* or not. It is interesting that we frequently think that we possess a value that, in reality, we no longer hold. We assume that because we once held a particular value that we continue to hold it, and we may be shocked to find that it is no longer a value, or at least no longer an important one. There are two value-clarification exercises at the end of this chapter to assist you in analyzing your value system.

POLICE SUPERVISOR AS VALUE DRIVEN

Figure 1-3 shows the supervisor's job environment as being a highly normative (value-laden) process. Following is an explanation of each of the boxes.

Position and Person

The position of the police supervisor serves best as a starting point. This component is value free. The position of police supervisor alone does not contain values. Obviously, it may be valued by someone. Once a person is inserted into a position, it takes on values. Once staffed, it will not only reflect the individual supervisor's preferences but also those of the agency and the community (organizational and environmental preferences). Hence, we find a human being who chose to be a supervisor and possesses a unique value system inserted into the position, and his or her value system is supported or challenged by incoming external values to varying degrees.

Organizational-Environmental and Resources

Next, the organizational and environmental values component acts on the police supervisor and determines, to a large extent, the amount and types of

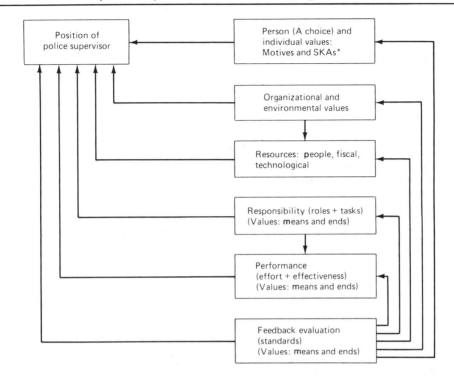

*SKAs = skills, knowledge, and abilities

Figure 1-3 The Police Supervisor: Value Driven (Paul Whisenand, *The Effective Police Manager*, © 1981, p. 57. Reprinted by permission of Prentice-Hall, Inc., Englewood Cliffs, N.J.)

resources the supervisor will have to administer. Certainly, the input resources will significantly constrain or promote her or his ability to perform effectively and achieve results. The type and amount of resources are evidence of an agency's values.

Responsibility

Figure 1-3 identifies responsibility as a key supervisory value. The responsibility component subsumes the role concept (job behavior) and various tasks (such as planning, communicating, morale, control, etc.). Here is where values can operate in a dual sense. To illustrate, the value of assuming responsibility for effectively supervising a police unit has a futuristic connotation or *end-state*. Simultaneously, acting responsible is a daily phenomenon and thus is more of a *means* toward a given purpose.

Performance

In being and acting responsibly, the police supervisor expends effort to perform effectively. Again, many value considerations crop up in the performance component, for example, the questions of how much effort should be given to the job of supervising compared with being a spouse and parent, or how much emphasis should be placed on organizational output compared with individual officer job satisfaction.

Feedback

Finally, we arrive at feedback. To be valid and reliable, feedback must be related to standards of performance and to methods for program and individual evaluation. What one decides to measure is largely determined by what one values. The setting of standards is similarly linked to the police supervisor's individual (internal) value system as modified by the agency's and the community's (the organizational and environmental) respective set of values.

AT THE CENTER

What you are speaks so loudly
I cannot hear what you say.

—Ralph Waldo Emerson

Does the organization you work for have a mission statement? Have you paid attention to the mission statements of other organizations? What do they reflect? Can you see one or more values contained in them? Tom Peters and Bob Waterman discovered that *excellent companies vigorously uphold and precisely adhere to a few core values.*[8]

There are some people that have developed a *personal* mission statement, or philosophy or creed. The statement commonly focuses on what they *are* or wish *to become* (character) and what they *have done* or *wish to do* (achievements). They are loaded with values or principles on which being and doing are based.

Responsibility Five contains examples of both organizational and personal mission statements. In the meantime, think about why they're located under "time management."

As we start probing for our driving forces or central values—those values that comprise our life's mission—we typically discover that whatever they are, they serve as *the source of our security, guidance, wisdom, and power.* Our values drive, therefore, our security, guidance, wisdom, and power. These four can be referred to as "supervalues" in that our other values underpin and drive them.

Security

Security represents your sense of worth, your identity, your emotional anchorage, your self-esteem, your basic personal strength or lack of it. Because *self-*

---

[8] Thomas J. Peters and Robert H. Waterman, *In Search of Excellence* (New York: Harper and Row, 1982).

esteem plays a vital role in our overall sense of security, we'll take time here to review it in more detail. By spending more time on this supervalue, we would not want you to think it is more important than the other three. Space permits us to discuss in detail only one of the four.

As the world becomes more complex, competitive, and challenging, self-esteem is more important than ever. The shift from a manufacturing- to an information-based society and the emergence of a global economy characterized by rapid change have created growing demands on our psychological resources.

Self-esteem defined.   Despite the abundance of books, studies, workshops, and committees devoted to the subject of self-esteem, there is little agreement about what it means. We believe self-esteem has two essential components.

Self-Efficacy.   Self-efficacy is the confidence in one's ability to cope with life's challenges. Self-efficacy leads to a sense of control over one's life.

Self-Respect.   Self-respect is experiencing oneself as deserving of happiness, achievement, and love. Self-respect also makes possible a sense of community with others.

Self-esteem is a self-reinforcing characteristic. When we have confidence in our ability to think and act effectively, we can persevere when faced with difficult challenges. The result is that we succeed more often than we fail. We form more nourishing relationships. We expect more of life and of ourselves.

If we lack confidence, we give up easily, fail more often, and aspire to our goals less. The result is that we get less of what we want.

What self-esteem is not.   Self-esteem is a *necessary* condition of well-being. But it's not the only one. Its presence *doesn't make life problem free.* Even people with high self-esteem may experience anxiety, depression, or fear when overwhelmed by issues they don't know how to cope with.

Self-esteem can be considered as the *immune system* of consciousness. A healthy immune system doesn't guarantee you'll never become ill, but it does reduce your susceptibility to illness and can improve your odds for a speedy recovery if you do get sick.

The same is true psychologically. Those with strong self-esteem are resilient in the face of life's difficulties.

It's impossible to have too much self-esteem. People who are arrogant or boastful actually show a lack of self-esteem! Those who are truly comfortable with themselves and their achievements take pleasure in being who they are — they don't need to tell the world about it.

Becoming successful, powerful, or well liked does not automatically confer good self-esteem. In fact, talented and powerful people who doubt their own core values are usually unable to find joy in their achievements, no matter how great their external success.

What I think of me.   Self-esteem has to do with what I think of me, not what anyone else thinks of me.

The highly touted use of affirmations is also ineffective, or at best of marginal help, in raising self-esteem. Telling yourself you're capable and lovable accomplishes little if you are operating irresponsibly in key areas of your life.

Roots of self-regard.   Genetic inheritance may have a role in a person's self-esteem—it's conceivable, anyway. Parental upbringing can also play a powerful role.

Parents with strong self-esteem lay the foundation for that value in their children. They raise them with plenty of love and acceptance, believing in their competence and setting reasonable rules and expectations.

Yet, there are exceptions that we still don't understand. Some people who have these positive factors in their backgrounds become self-doubting adults, whereas others who survive seemingly destructive childhoods grow up with a strong sense of self-worth.

Strengthening self-esteem is not a quick or easy process. We can't do it directly. Self-esteem is a consequence of following fundamental internal practices that require an ongoing commitment to self-examination. We'll refer to these practices as the five habits for healthy self-esteem.

Living Consciously.   The first habit involves paying attention to information and feedback about needs and goals. It also entails facing facts that might be uncomfortable or threatening, and refusing to wander through life in a mental fog.

Self-Acceptance.   The second habit is being willing to experience whatever we truly think, feel, or do, even if we don't always like it. In addition, it involves facing our mistakes and learning from them.

Self-Responsibility.   The third habit is establishing a sense of control over our lives by realizing we are responsible for our choices and actions at every level. It involves the achievement of our goals, happiness, and values.

Living Purposefully.   The fourth habit involves setting goals and working to achieve them rather than living at the mercy of chance and outside forces. It also entails developing self-discipline.

Integrity.   The fifth habit is the integration of our behavior with our ideals, convictions, standards, and beliefs. It is acting in congruence with what we believe is right.

More of us are taught from an early age to pay far more attention to signals coming from other people than those from within. We are encouraged to ignore our own needs and wants, and to concentrate on living up to others' expectations.

Self-esteem requires us to listen to and respect our own sensations, insights, intuition, and perspective. Ghandi, the great Indian leader, remarked that, "No one can take away our self-esteem. But, we can give it away!" It depends on who you listen to and what they're saying. For all of us, developing the habits of self-esteem is a life-long—and worthy—challenge. Later on you'll cover this subject again in Responsibility Five. You'll find that positive self-regard (self-esteem) is one of the cornerstones of becoming a leader.

Guidance

Guidance means your source of direction in life. Encompassed by your map, your internal frame of reference that interprets for you what is happening out there involves standards or principles or implicit criteria that govern moment by moment decision making and action. Making this value a reality for you will help in fulfilling many of the responsibilities that follow.

Wisdom

Wisdom is your perspective on life, your sense of alignment, your understanding of how the various values and principles apply and relate to each other. It embraces judgment, discernment, comprehension, and maturity. Knowledge is the accumulation of facts. *Wisdom is the application of truth.* Maturity can be defined as "emotional wisdom." Goodness knows, police organizations are looking for mature supervisors!

Power

Power is the faculty or capacity to act, the strength and potency to accomplish something. It is the vital energy to make choices and decisions. It also includes the capacity to overcome deeply embedded habits and to cultivate higher, more effective ones. An old poem aptly speaks about power.

> *Man is the master power that molds and makes.*
> *And man (woman) is mind and evermore he takes*
> *The tool of thought and shapes what he (she) wills.*
> *He (she) brings forth a thousand joys, a thousand ills.*
> *He (she) thinks in secret, and it comes to pass.*
> *Environment is but his (her) looking glass.*
>
> —Author Unknown

PROLOGUE TO RESPONSIBILITY TWO

The four supervalues provide protection for those few values that we hold as ethics. All ethics are values, but not all values are ethics.[9]

As you proceed with the next responsibility of a supervisor, keep in mind the role of the supervalues. First, our security helps us to resist fads, trends, and frequent change. We're secure in knowing that our ethics do not have to change. Wisdom and guidance help us discern the way things really are. We are able to make several decisions using correct information. Power gives us the

---

[9]W. Bennis and B. Nanus, *Leaders* (New York: Harper and Row, 1985), p. 33. Reprinted with permission.

capacity to choose our circumstances most of the time and choose our reaction to circumstances all of the time.

KEY POINTS

- We supervise ourselves and others according to our value system.
- A value is a means or a goal, or both.
- Our values stem from three periods in our life: imprinting, modeling, and socialization.
- Although enduring, our values can be modified.
- Our values play eight significant functions in our personal and professional lives.
- Our values can be clarified, and it is important that we do.
- There are four values that can be considered as "supervalues": security, guidance, wisdom, and power.
- The supervalues protect those particular values that so vitally serve as our ethics.

DISCUSSION

1. How does the phrase "we are what we value" pertain to the police supervisor?
2. Indicate what was the most significant input to your value system during each of the three value-programming periods.
3. Has anyone had a SEE lately? What did it do to your value system?
4. Identify a value—any value (e.g., "personal safety"). Discuss how this value acts as a filter, reflects generation gaps, produces individual differences, creates standards, resolves conflicts, triggers emotions, provokes thoughts, and motivates us.
5. What is your evaluation of the "supervalues"? Do you agree with our premise or not? Why do you concur or question it?

STRUCTURED EXPERIENCES

1. Ten of Your Values:
Two Value-Clarification Exercises

Let us take the next few minutes and explore some of your individually held values. The following two exercises can be accomplished either alone or in a group setting.

To begin with, complete the Value Indicator List by quickly writing down the ten things that you enjoy (value) doing in your professional, social, or personal life. In other words, of all the things you do in your life, list the ten that you enjoy the most.

Value Indicator List

Rank	Value	Symbol
_____	1. _____	_____
_____	2. _____	_____
_____	3. _____	_____
_____	4. _____	_____
_____	5. _____	_____
_____	6. _____	_____
_____	7. _____	_____
_____	8. _____	_____
_____	9. _____	_____
_____	10. _____	_____

Paul Whisenand, *The Effective Police Manager,* © 1981, p. 53. Reprinted with permission of Prentice-Hall, Inc., Englewood Cliffs, New Jersey.

Now study your list and rank your values on the left side of the list in order of priority. 1 indicates the most valued, 2 the next most valued, and so on. Next, where they apply, place the following symbols on the right side of the list.

1. Put a "$" by any item that costs thirty dollars or more each time you perform it. (Be certain to look for hidden costs.)
2. Put a "10" by any item that you would not have done ten years ago.
3. Put an "X" by any item that you would like to let others know you do.
4. Put a "T" by any item that you spend at least four hours a week doing.
5. Put an "M" by any item that you have actually done in the last month.
6. Put an "E" by any item that you spend time reading about, thinking about, worrying about, or planning for.
7. Put a "C" by any item that you consciously choose over other possible activities.
8. Put a "G" by any item that you think helps you to grow as a police supervisor.
9. Put an "R" by any item that involves some risk. (The risk may be physical, intellectual, or emotional.)

In looking at your list, the more markings you have put next to an item, the more likely it is that the activity is a value for you. This list is not necessarily a compilation of your values; rather, it may be an indication of where your values lie. Count the number of marks next to each item—the activity with the most marks being first, and so on. Now compare your first ranking (left side) with your second ranking (right side) and note the following:

1. Do your rankings match? ˙
2. Is your highest value in the first ranking the one that has the most marks next to it?
3. Can you see any patterns in your list?
4. Have you discovered anything new about yourself as a result of this activity?
5. Is there anything you would like to change about your preferences as a result of this exercise?

If you are studying as a group, you may want to divide into subgroups of four or five members each and share what you have learned about your values.

Let us take another approach that may prove to be somewhat more supervisor oriented. Complete the Supervisor Value Priority Rankings form in Figure 1-4 by assigning 1 to the highest priority, and then in descending rank order, 2, 3, and 4.

As with the first exercise, if possible, form groups of four to five members each for the purpose of discussing individual rankings. The groups can create a single group response by consensus.

2. Supervisor Value Priority Rankings

1. I think that the best police supervisor is one who:

    _____ tells you what should be done.

    _____ consults with you on important issues.

    _____ persuades you to live up to your ideals.

    _____ facilitates a consensus on important issues.

    _____ other: _____

2. For recreation, I prefer:

    _____ conversation in a small group.

    _____ doing something together in a group.

    _____ watching TV.

    _____ reading the newspaper.

    _____ other: _____

3. In my role as a police supervisor, I like to:

    _____ work by myself.

    _____ work with others.

    _____ delegate responsibility to others.

    _____ other: _____

4. I like to use my free time to:

    _____ be by myself.

    _____ visit my friends

    _____ catch up on work.

    _____ other: _____

5. In my retirement, I would want to:

    _____ work on my hobbies.

    _____ travel.

    _____ take a part-time job.

    _____ other: _____

Figure 1-4 Supervisor Value Priority Rankings (Paul Whisenand, *The Effective Police Manager*, © 1981, p. 55–56. Reprinted by permission of Prentice-Hall, Inc., Englewood Cliffs, N.J.)

6. For my professional future, I should:

   _____ stay just as I am.

   _____ take on new interests.

   _____ renew present interests.

   _____ drop some of my present interests.

   _____ other: _____

7. With police supervisor colleagues, it is best to:

   _____ keep quiet about yourself and your work.

   _____ ask for help, advice, or consultation when you need it.

   _____ be friendly, but not talk about personal or important
   business matters.

   _____ tell them about yourself and your work.

   _____ other: _____

8. Does this list leave out any important areas? If so, add other
   areas below, including possible approaches to that area, and then
   rank them as above. With the first exercise, if possible, form
   groups of four to five members each for the purpose of discussing
   individual rankings. The groups can create a single group response
   by consensus.

   _____

   _____

   _____

   _____

Figure 1-4 **(Continued)**

RESPONSIBILITY TWO

Ethics: Professional Standards and Conduct

Everyone is called to one common human vocation — that of being a good citizen and a thoughtful human being.

Mortimer J. Adler[1]

Imagine that you are a police officer and you're at roll call training. Your newly assigned sergeant starts the training by introducing himself and then adds, "If you have any doubts about how I want you to treat our citizens, treat them *exactly* the way I treat you!"

Now imagine that you're a police sergeant and you've just introduced yourself to your newly assigned shift officers. One officer raises her hand and asks, "How do you expect us to treat the citizens?" What is your reply? On a sheet of paper or in the margin of this page write down your response.

ETHICS AND ETHOS

Certain types of values are *ethical values*. Values and ethical values are a branch of philosophy. Ethics is concerned with *moral duties* and how we *should* behave regarding both ends and means. Police work is an intrinsically practical service enterprise that judges its employees and acts only in terms of the effective use of power and the achievement of results.

Ethos is the distinguishing character, moral nature, or *guiding beliefs* of a person, group, or institution. What are your guiding beliefs, those of your work

---

[1] Mortimer J. Adler, *Six Great Ideas* (New York: MacMillan Publishing, 1981), p. 9. Reprinted with permission.

group, those of your department? Does the ethos support or conflict with the ethics? For example, the following are ethical values:

- Honesty
- Fairness
- Trustworthiness
- Integrity
- Respect for others
- Law abidingness
- Loyalty
- Accountability
- Thoughtfulness

Let us assume that you possess the preceding values. Now, do your ethos or guiding beliefs agree? Further, do your acts reflect them? There are three vital steps to ethics:

1. Knowing what is right.
2. Totally believing (committed) in it.
3. Doing it.

HARD CHOICES

Over the years we have seen and read about officers, supervisors and managers wrestling with some "hard choices" and some not-so-hard choices. It is important to recognize that there is a constant conflict between the practical realities of politics, personal ambition, and the democratic ideal of selfless public service. Ethics and the "real world" place very different demands on us that are not easily reconcilable. Are we in an ethics vacuum in this nation? Do you perceive a "sleaze factor" in our society? Is there a materialistic excess that has spawned a "me era"?

Public office (e.g., police sergeant) is a public trust. This axiom, supported by the related idea that participatory democracy requires public confidence in the integrity of government, lays the very foundations for the ethical demands placed on police personnel and the laws establishing baseline standards of behavior. Laws and rules are especially useful concerning choices on brutality, stealing, perjury, and bribe taking. Although the choice here is not always easy, it's clear and straightforward. Laws are needed to define *minimum* standards of conduct.

Referring to such laws and rules as "ethical laws" or "ethical standards" is misleading and actually counterproductive. It is misleading because the laws deal only with a narrow spectrum of ethical decisions facing police employees. It is counterproductive because it encourages us to accept only existing laws as ethics. We accept narrow technical rules as the *only* moral criteria of conduct.

Hence, if it's legal, it's ethical. It would be like using the penal code as a substitute for the Bible, Talmud, or Koran.

One reason ethics is much easier said than done is that the legal kind of unethical behavior has become so very ordinary, as we can see from these generic examples.

- Embellishing claims
- Scapegoating personal failures
- Shirking distasteful responsibilities
- Knowingly making unreasonable demands
- Stonewalling questions
- Acting insincerely
- Reneging on promises
- Covering up
- Making consequential decisions unilaterally
- Loafing and loitering

None of these behaviors is scandalous. But each, nonetheless, violates a sense of what is the morally correct behavior (e.g., the behaviors of personal responsibility, honesty, fairness, etc.), increases cynicism and distrust, undermines integrity, and can be a stepping stone to wrongful behavior.

Though laws can secure compliance within limited margins, they are far too narrow or minimum to act as a substitute for ethics. One authority on ethics put it this way, "We expect too much from laws and demand too little from people." (Jim Farley).

The easy choices typically involve clear-cut laws and rules. You take a bribe, the choice may result in the obvious—you're fired and go to jail. The hard choices deal with moral issues and ethical considerations such as a discretion, rule infractions (e.g., sleeping on duty), deception in police investigations, the use of deadly force, the use of physical force, off-duty behavior that may or may not be job related, and so on.

Ethical decisions—the hard choices—are much more difficult than we would like to think. It is not simply a matter of character or upbringing. Ethical decision making requires an alert and informed conscience. It requires the ability to resist self-deception and rationalization. It requires courage and persistence to risk disapproval of others and the loss of power and prestige. Finally, it requires the capacity to evaluate incomplete or confusing facts and anticipate likely consequences under all kinds of pressure.

ETHICAL DECISION MAKING

Ethical decision making is a skill that can be learned. The first step is to know what the ethics are. Figure 2-1 presents an ethical code—if you're a law-enforcement officer (public and private), you should know it. Take a few

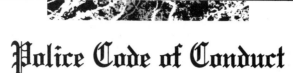

Police Code of Conduct

All law enforcement officers must be fully aware of the ethical responsibilities of their position and must strive contantly to live up to the highest possible standards of professional policing.

The International Association of Chiefs of Police believes it important that police officers have clear advice and counsel available to assist them in performing their duties consistent with these standards, and has adopted the following ethical mandates as guidelines to meet these ends.

Primary Responsibilities of a Police Officer

A police officer acts as an official representative of government who is required and trusted to work within the law. The officer's powers and duties are conferred by statute. The fundamental duties of a police officer include serving the community, safeguarding lives and property, protecting the innocent, keeping the peace and ensuring the rights of all to liberty, equality and justice.

Performance of the Duties of a Police Officer

A police officer shall perform all duties impartially, without favor or affection or ill will and without regard to status, sex, race, religion, political belief or aspiration. All citizens will be treated equally with courtesy, consideration and dignity.

Officers will never allow personal feelings, animosities or friendships to influence official conduct. Laws will be enforced appropriately and courteously and, in carrying out their responsibilities, officers will strive to obtain maximum cooperation from the public. They will conduct themselves in appearance and deportment in such a manner as to inspire confidence and respect for the position of public trust they hold.

Discretion

A police officer will use responsibly the discretion vested in his position and exercise it within the law. The principle of reasonableness will guide the officer's determinations, and the officer will consider all surrounding circumstances in determining whether any legal action shall be taken.

Consistent and wise use of discretion, based on professional policing competence, will do much to preserve good relationships and retain the confidence of the public. There can be difficulty in choosing between conflicting courses of action. It is important to remember that a timely word of advice rather than arrest—which may be correct in appropriate circumstances—can be a more effective means of achieving a desired end.

Use of Force

A police officer will never employ unnecessary force or violence and will use only such force in the discharge of duty as is reasonable in all circumstances.

The use of force should be used only with the greatest restraint and only after discussion, negotiation and persuasion have been found to be inappropriate or ineffective. While the use of force is occasionally unavoidable, every police officer will refrain from unnecessary infliction of pain or suffering and will never engage in cruel, degrading or inhuman treatment of any person.

Confidentiality

Whatever a police officer sees, hears or learns of that is of a confidential nature will be kept secret unless the performance of duty or legal provision requires otherwise.

Members of the public have a right to security and privacy, and information obtained about them must not be improperly divulged.

Integrity

A police officer will not engage in acts of corruption or bribery, nor will an officer condone such acts by other police officers.

The public demands that the integrity of police officers be above reproach. Police officers must, therefore, avoid any conduct that might compromise integrity and thus undercut the public confidence in a law enforcement agency. Officers will refuse to accept any gifts, presents, subscriptions, favors, gratuities or promises that could be interpreted as seeking to cause the officer to refrain from performing official responsibilities honestly and within the law. Police officers must not receive private or special advantage from their official status. Respect from the public cannot be bought; it can only be earned and cultivated.

Cooperation with Other Police Officers and Agencies

Police officers will cooperate with all legally authorized agencies and their representatives in the pursuit of justice.

An officer or agency may be one among many organizations that may provide law enforcement services to a jurisdiction. It is imperative that a police officer assist colleagues fully and completely with respect and consideration at all times.

Personal-Professional Capabilities

Police officers will be responsible for their own standard of professional performance and will take every reasonable opportunity to enhance and improve their level of knowledge and competence.

Through study and experience, a police officer can acquire the high level of knowledge and competence that is essential for the efficient and effective performance of duty. The acquisition of knowledge is a never-ending process of personal and professional development that should be pursued constantly.

Private Life

Police officers will behave in a manner that does not bring discredit to their agencies or themselves.

A police officer's character and conduct while off duty must always be exemplary, thus maintaining a position of respect in the community in which he or she lives and serves. The officer's personal behavior must be beyond reproach.

THE INTERNATIONAL ASSOCIATION OF CHIEFS OF POLICE

Figure 2-1   Police Code of Conduct (Reprinted with permission of the International Association of Chiefs of Police.)

minutes to read it now; you'll find it loaded with ethical values that are much broader than a set of criminal laws. Because many police organizations directly or indirectly report to a city or county manager, we thought their code of ethics worthy of your attention (Figure 2-2). More and expanded ethics training for police employees is a discernible trend of the 1990s and beyond.

Ethics in the workplace cannot be left solely to each officer's conscience for two obvious reasons. First, temptations and pressures in the workplace may overcome conscience. Second, a person's unethical behavior invariably affects other officers. Ethics, therefore, must be a departmental as well as an individual responsibility.

Most police personnel want to do the right thing. In fact, this desire is so compelling that some will unintentionally engage in rationalizations to justify ethically doubtful behavior. Building on this tendency, it is possible to increase the likelihood that police employees will act more ethically more often if they're taught how to do it.

We know a police manager who taught himself ethical decision making. When asked how he did it, he replied, "Simple. Every time I have a hard choice to make, I imagine my Dad standing in front of me and looking into my eyes. At the same moment, I imagine my ten-year-old daughter looking over my shoulder. With this picture in my mind, a hard choice converts into an easy one for me."

STRATEGY FOR FOSTERING INTEGRITY

The third edition of *Local Government Police Management* (International City Management Association) contains a chapter entitled, "Fostering Integrity." It focuses on corruption (law violations) and "other misconduct (ethical violations)." It noted that in the 1980s drug trafficking surpassed gambling as the most lucrative opportunity for graft. The chapter emphasized the "misuse of police authority for personal gain" as the most frequent form of corruption. Mention is also made of police brutality (excessive force) and other illegal acts. We would only add—a police employee can be dishonest, break commitments, and be unfair and unaccountable (e.g., the abuse of sick leave) without breaking the law.

Why the concern for building a strategy to combat unlawful or unethical conduct? First, wrongful conduct reduces public confidence in the police and thus inhibits citizens from cooperating in crime prevention and control. Second, it enhances criminal activity. After all, if the police are corrupt, others may decide to follow their example. Third, it destroys effective police management and supervision. Finally, departmental morale goes down the drain.

We propose a five-point strategy for fostering integrity as follows:

1. *Live it.* The chief, command staff and supervisors must, minute by minute, speak integrity and act with integrity. Line personnel do pay careful attention to what their bosses think and do!

ICMA
CODE OF ETHICS

THE PURPOSE of the International City Management Association is to increase the proficiency of city managers, county managers, and other municipal administrators and to strengthen the quality of urban government through professional management. To further these objectives, certain ethical principles shall govern the conduct of every member of the International City Management Association, who shall:

1 Be dedicated to the concepts of effective and democratic local government by responsible elected officials and believe that professional general management is essential to the achievement of this objective.

2 Affirm the dignity and worth of the services rendered by government and maintain a constructive, creative, and practical attitude toward urban affairs and a deep sense of social responsibility as a trusted public servant.

3 Be dedicated to the highest ideals of honor and integrity in all public and personal relationships in order that the member may merit the respect and confidence of the elected officials, of other officials and employees, and of the public.

4 Recognize that the chief function of local government at all times is to serve the best interests of all of the people.

5 Submit policy proposals to elected officials; provide them with facts and advice on matters of policy as a basis for making decisions and setting community goals, and uphold and implement municipal policies adopted by elected officials.

6 Recognize that elected representatives of the people are entitled to the credit for the establishment of municipal policies; responsibility for policy execution rests with the members.

7 Refrain from participation in the election of the members of the employing legislative body, and from all partisan political activities which would impair performance as a professional administrator.

8 Make it a duty continually to improve the member's professional ability and to develop the competence of associates in the use of management techniques.

9 Keep the community informed on municipal affairs; encourage communication between the citizens and all municipal officers; emphasize friendly and courteous service to the public; and seek to improve the quality and image of public service.

10 Resist any encroachment on professional responsibilities, believing the member should be free to carry out official policies without interference, and handle each problem without discrimination on the basis of principle and justice.

11 Handle all matters of personnel on the basis of merit so that fairness and impartiality govern a member's decisions, pertaining to appointments, pay adjustments, promotions, and discipline.

12 Seek no favor; believe that personal aggrandizement or profit secured by confidential information or by misuse of public time is dishonest.

ICMA, the professional association of appointed administrators serving cities, counties, regional councils, and other local governments

This Code was originally adopted in 1924 by the members of the International City Management Association and has since been amended in 1938, 1952, 1969, 1972, and 1976

Figure 2-2 International City Management Association Code of Ethics (Reprinted with permission of ICMA [International City/County Management Association].)

2. *Accountability.* Poorly managed and supervised departments are breeding grounds for slimy behavior. Every police manager and supervisor must be, first of all, answerable for their conduct as well as the conduct of their staff.

3. *Moralistic discretion.* The decisions by the police must be compatible with the overarching values of society and especially their community. All police activity should be subjected to the light of truth—this light is a combination of legal constraints and ethical propositions.

4. *Outside help.* Gaining the backing of the city manager, city council, and board of supervisors is of help. Much of their support would manifest itself in them speaking about and acting with integrity. Other criminal justice agencies (the prosecuting attorney and criminal courts) are also important in pushing integrity.

5. *Ethics learning.* Values can be learned, leadership can be learned, public speaking can be learned, and so on. Most crucial, ethics can be learned. A police department program that does nothing more than keep behavior legal, while no small accomplishment, would not be a bona fide ethics program. It would be more of a "law-enforcement" program. Laws and regulations are not the answer to keeping behavior above the bottom line of ethics. Training is. . . .

ETHICS TRAINING

All of us have been trained to read, write, and calculate numbers. We've been trained to operate a computer, FAX machine, an automobile. We've learned how to protect ourselves from being victimized. We learned many, many more things. How many of us, have you, taken a course on ethical conduct? Ethics training for police employees has been nonexistent or superficial. This is changing. There is, fortunately, an accelerating trend to train ethics.

It is possible for police agencies to create a positive ethical culture consciously that nurtures and rewards moral behavior and discourages bad conduct. There are four ways to enhance ethics.

1. Inspiration
2. Collaboration
3. Education
4. Integration

Inspiration

Inspiration is fostered by the following:

Leadership by example. *We preach a better sermon with our life than with our lips.* We've heard sergeants comment with detectable frustration, "The officers don't pay attention to me." Nonsense. They do pay *careful* attention to their supervisors and managers. For most officers, leadership either occurs or not based on their relationship to their sergeant and, to a lesser extent, the middle manager. They rarely have direct contact with the administrators. Essentially, they see them on occasion and basically know them second-hand through what the sergeant may have to say about them. We're aware of some supervisors who imply that "management is the enemy." Little do they realize that the officer is likely to take such a warning one step further—"If they're my enemy, you're best not trusted either." Remember, *your staff does pay careful consideration to what you say and what you do!*

Value orientation. *Assure that everyone, especially newcomers, knows and understands the laws, rules, and values that should guide their hearts and behavior.* This establishes a culture of ethics. If your agency has a mission statement, a code of ethics, or a set of goals, periodically review it with your staff. Reinforce it with the decisions you make—live it minute by minute.

With all cultures there are countercultures. Some countercultures may be good (e.g., a group of officers who refuse to accept bribes when others do so). Alternatively, we may see an agency striving very hard to provide high-quality services, whereas a counterculture of officers is advocating that the public (or most of it) is the enemy.

Culture building is not a one-shot endeavor. It takes time and a lot of reinforcement. People want to know the rules, the laws, the goals, and the values that guide and measure their activity. Far too often we've been told by officers (sometimes by sergeants and higher-command personnel), "I do not know what our mission is here. I do not know if we have a set of goals. I really have a sense of aimlessness." The answer, if there isn't a mission statement or set of values or goals, is—create them for your staff. Use the International Association of Chiefs of Police or the National Sheriffs Code of Ethics as a start. Remember, one of your responsibilities is to build a culture that is value laden—especially with ethical values.

Limitations of laws and rules. *The technical compliance with laws is necessary but not always enough!* A person can be dishonest, break commitments, be unfair and unaccountable without breaking the law. Laws cannot replace the need for a sensitive conscience or free one of the moral duty to adhere to traditional *ethical principles.* To encourage good faith acceptance of the moral obligation to abide by both the letter and spirit of the law, every opportunity must be used to (1) clarify the reasons for the rules; and (2) emphasize the importance of the "appearance of wrongdoing" test.

Good ethics are expected and appreciated by supervisors. The line personnel are no different—good ethics are expected and appreciated by them, of their supervisors. Those supervisors who use the legal "dos" and "don'ts," who impose the "should" and "should not" of rules are missing their main power source—ethical values.

Collaboration

Collaboration can be achieved by the following:

Unifying the group.   *Unify individuals behind the traditional ethical values.* One way is to appeal to the common interest all personnel have in ethical behavior of every individual. All should be informed that it is to everyone's advantage that police personnel (sworn and civilian) be, and be perceived to be, ethical. The goal here is shared esteem for duty and honor, and where it is obviously unacceptable for any member to place self-interest (e.g., taking extra rewards such as free meals) above the public trust.

We've listened to a sheriff admonish his staff about not accepting gratuities. "Not one dime, not one cup of coffee," he asserted. Later, he signed a permit to "carry a concealed weapon" for one of his key campaign donors. Something doesn't jibe here. A colleague of ours had the courage to tell a story on himself. He sermonized a group of newly appointed sheriff's sergeants on the virtues of honesty. For thirty minutes he extolled them on morality. He then proceeded to play a pirated VCR tape. Naturally, the duplicated tape was politely called to his attention by members of the group. He was embarrassed, he blushed, he was speechless. He learned a lesson, however. If you're going to preach something, you'd darn well better be practicing it.

Identifying situations.   *Identify situations in which those values are likely to be tested.* Typically, those in the best position to anticipate value challenges are supervisors. After all, they've recently experienced identical or similar hard choices. Any ethics program must be custom built by and for a particular agency. What may be an ethics problem for one agency may not be for another.

Members of an agency should be surveyed to discover ethical problems and issues. Once the critical concerns have been spotted, then training scenarios and simulations can be constructed. Similar to a finely tuned and expertly trained athlete, all of us can be conditioned to make, when necessary, the right choices, which frequently are the hard choices.

Specifying guidelines.   *Specify guidelines and approaches for deciding on hard choices.* This task involves the development and pronouncement of minimum standards of behavior for various situations. It also involves guidelines for coping with the totally unanticipated circumstances.

We recall a police sergeant that reprimanded one of his officers for poor performance with, "Maynard, you've only given the minimum here since I've been your supervisor!" Maynard snapped back, "Sergeant, if the minimum wasn't acceptable, it wouldn't be the minimum!" Either the "minimum" had not been conveyed, or it should be elevated. Hard choices require known guidelines.

Education and Training

Ongoing educational programs focusing on *issue spotting,* reasoning, and other decision-making skills are vital ingredients of an ethics program.

No sermonizing.   *Moralizing about ethics is not very effective in sustaining or changing attitudes and behavior.* Traditional lectures on ethics should be scrapped and replaced with group discussions. We're confident that if police personnel were asked in the early 1980s, "Where might our major vulnerability for corruption be?" The answer would have been, in most cases, "Drug money and drug usage." The officers knew this but, regretfully, few administrators asked them.

Anticipating and recognizing ethical issues. *People should be educated and trained in early detection of ethical issues.* They should be sensitized to the four factors that tend to defeat ethical instincts.

- Self-interest
- Self-protection
- Self-deception
- Self-righteousness

Self-interest tends to impede one's ethical awareness. When our personal interests subordinate our professional code of conduct, objectivity is next to impossible. In such cases, there is a tendency to push the importance for the questionable conduct.

An example of this occurred when a bright and respected police chief we know submitted an application for a nationally recognized award for his department—not himself. The award involved no monetary gain for anyone. Someone disclosed that the department had not met the requirements for the award, and the chief knew it. He resigned. He apologized and emphasized that his action was not for his "self-interest." He deceived himself and lost his job as a consequence. If he'd only spoken to a few, trusted associates, they would have likely caused a "reality checkpoint" for him. He might have heard, "Don't do it! You're deceiving yourself."

One means for determining if you're becoming a victim to the preceding four factors is asking yourself or your work unit to review the following:

- "Ethics is not performance."
- "Ethics is behavior, and behavior and results are the two parts of performance."
- "Ethics is too subjective to be measured."
- "Ethical behaviors can be appraised."
- "It's an overseeing big brother."
- "Not if done right, like self-appraisal with exceptions."
- "It makes ethics confrontational."
- "Unethical behavior needs to be confronted."
- "We hold people accountable in other ways."
- "What ways and how well?"
- "It's implicitly understood."
- "Ethics and its communication are too important to be left to mind reading."

Ethical competence. *Seeing "ethics" is easier than doing "ethics."* The first involves *consciousness* and the second emphasizes *commitment.* We must learn how to better evaluate facts and make reasoned decisions on ethical conduct. There are some people who overestimate the costs of being ethical and underestimate the "costs of" compromising ethical values. Decisions that include deceit or coercion often cause secondary risks that are not seen or properly evaluated. If you wonder what we mean by this last statement, merely scan the front page or business section of a daily newspaper.

An ethics course should attempt to build competency in creative, realistic problem solving. This can be accomplished by helping others to identify optional approaches for staying on the "high road" and avoiding the lower one.

Integration

Basically, this step involves combining *inspiration, collaboration,* and *education and training* into a comprehensive package that daily becomes a viable influence within our lives and our organizations. Unfortunately, exercising moral restraint does not ensure that others will do likewise. On occasion it places the ethical person at a disadvantage in competing with persons who are constrained by ethical principles.

Do you agree, or not, that it is better to lose than to sacrifice integrity? One person quipped, "The trouble with the rat race is that even if you win, you're still a rat." We cannot turn moral commitment on and off as it suits us or the situation. An ethically based person cannot win by being dishonest, disloyal, or unfair anymore than one can truly win a tennis match by cheating.

Should upon. No one likes to be "should upon." We've attempted to avoid doing that here. If we fell prey to sermonizing, we apologize.

Our intent here is to emphasize

- Ethics as a subset of values
- What ethics are all about
- Ethical standards at times makes for hard choices
- Ethics can be trained
- Supervisors often make decisions involving ethical matters
- Individual acts of moral courage are never wasted—each instance of ethical fortitude provides a lasting example that teaches and inspires.

What we know about ethics. Literally, our past centuries have vividly shown us that those who use the hard choices as opportunities to construct their reputations and character will live to fight on other battlefronts—frequently, the stronger for their convictions. Those who resist temptation, refuse to trash or bend ethical values as conditions seem to dictate, or lose their honor and self-respect by handing over their moral autonomy to others of lower aspirations and weaker character.

Many years ago the National Advisory Commission on Criminal Justice

Standards and Goals (1973) produced a bench mark monograph *Police*. Standard 19.6 reads as follows:

Positive Prevention of Police Misconduct

The chief executive of every police agency immediately should seek and develop programs and techniques that will minimize the potential for employee misconduct. The chief executive should insure that there is a general atmosphere that rewards self-discipline within the police agency.

- Every police chief executive should implement, where possible, positive programs and techniques to prevent employee misconduct and encourage self-discipline. These may include:
  a. Analysis of the causes of employee misconduct through special interviews with employees involved in misconduct incidents and study of the performance records of selected employees;
  b. General training in the avoidance of misconduct incidents for all employees and special training for employees experiencing special problems;
  c. Referral to psychologists, psychiatrists, clergy, and other professionals whose expertise may be valuable; and
  d. Application of peer group influence.

What would police work look like today if every chief, sheriff, police administrator had adopted and *enforced* this standard?

Criminalizing more unethical behavior is clearly not the answer to making ethical behavior more habitual in police work. Police leaders can achieve most of this goal by implementing a comprehensive ethics program that addresses the basic personal and situational causes of unethical behavior.

Some of us overestimate the costs of being ethical and underestimate the costs of compromise.

—Michael Josephson

KEY POINTS

- Ethics focuses on moral duties and how we should behave.
- Ethos is the distinguishing quality, moral nature, or guiding beliefs we hold.
- Certain values serve as ethical values.
- Obeying the law is an easy choice as compared with an ethical decision that can be a hard choice.
- Self-deception and rationalization will cause us difficulty with hard choices.
- Ethics training involves inspiration, collaboration, education, and integration.

- No one appreciates being "should upon."
- Individual acts of moral courage are never wasted; each instance of ethical fortitude provides a lasting example that instructs and inspires.

DISCUSSION

1. Develop a group setting. Identify and rank order what you as a group believe to be the seven most important ethical values that a police supervisor should hold. Next, rate yourself against each value with a number of one (low) to seven (high). Discuss your highest and lowest ratings with your associates.
2. What does *ethos* mean to you? Cite a guiding belief that *you* believe represents your police agency.
3. Relatively, obeying the law is an easy choice. Making ethical decisions is a hard choice. Why? Do you have examples?
4. Identify a recent motion picture that portrays "moral courage." Describe an act or activity. Why did you select it? What does it tell us?
5. What has this responsibility not covered? Where did it push or sermonize? Where did it seem uncertain or lacking?

STRUCTURED EXPERIENCES

Exercise: How to Deal with Citizens

1. Please return to the start where we asked that you deliver a roll call briefing. Imagine that you've urged them to treat others as you treat them. One officer asks, "How do *you* treat others? I'd like to know." What is your response?
2. The late comedian/actor, W. C. Fields, instructed that on his gravestone be inscribed, "If it's all the same to you, I'd just as soon be in Philadelphia." We read of an ancient king that passed on, and his subjects saw fit to write, "King Jehoram reigned for eight years; he expired without being mourned." Now, what do *you* want printed on your marker? Think carefully. Is it one word or a few sentences? Write it down. Study it. Do the words reflect, or not, your values? How? Why?
3. There are numerous films that either directly or implicitly deal with the subject of ethics. Annually, Hollywood cranks out many films that are entertaining, and often they involve ethical considerations. Rent one, and stop and start it at key ethical points. One film we've used with a lot of success is *The Parable of the Sadhu* (Coronet/MTI Film and Video; 800-621-2131).
4. Some of the following comments are signposts of ethical wrongdoing. Have you heard, or are you now hearing, them in your organization?

Denying or trivializing its significance

- "Show me a victim."
- "It's not illegal."
- "You can't legislate morality."
- "It's just a technicality."

Invoking the double standard

- "Morality is a personal matter."
- "I don't mix business with my personal feelings."

Arguing necessity

- "It's cutthroat out there."
- "If I don't do it, someone else will."
- "It's my job."
- "It will save some jobs."

Arguing relativity

- "It's not illegal elsewhere."
- "In the United States, ideals are turned into laws."
- "No act is inherently illegal."
- "We are no worse or better than society at large."

Professing ignorance

- "I wasn't told."
- "Ethics is a gray area."
- "The rules are inscrutable."

RESPONSIBILITY THREE

Leadership: Combining Values and Ethics into Vision

The dominant principle of organization has shifted, from supervision and management in order to control an enterprise to leadership in order to bring out the best in people and to respond quickly to change.

John Naisbett and Patricia Aberdene

This is not the "police leadership" officers so often call for when they really want a father figure to take care of all their problems. It is a participative yet demanding leadership that respects people and encourages self-management, autonomous teams, and problem-oriented policing.

There is a big difference between supervision and leadership. Leaders and supervisors differ in orientation, mission, assumptions, behavior, organizational environments, and ultimately results.

Leadership is the process of moving police personnel in some direction, mostly through their willingness to go. Supervisors are more short term, control oriented, and report focused. Leaders think longer term, comprehend the relationship of larger realities, think in terms of renewal, have social perception, cause change, emphasize values, and achieve unity.

There is nothing wrong with being a supervisor. Clearly, we've needed them in the past and will do so in the future. Our hope here is for *the police supervisor to also take on the mantle of a leader.*

AUTHORITY AND POWER

Leadership can and ought to be a logical addition of a paramount strength to the position of police supervisor. As you have perhaps seen or surmised, not all supervisors are leaders. Alternatively, not all leaders are supervisors. Supervision and leadership can occur together, which is highly preferable, or they can operate separate from one another. The single linking pin between the two functions is *influence.*

47

Authority

Once, in a police agency, we noticed that the police chief "managed" and that his assistant chief managed and "led." Briefly, the chief used the *authority* of his office to gain compliance and provide direction for *achieving results*. Authority is the "right" to command. The assistant chief had the same right and executed it at times. However, he most often relied on his leadership, or his individual capacity for managing. Although both were successful managers, the assistant chief demonstrated more *effectiveness* in achieving results than did the chief.

Authority is the *right* to command. All police supervisors have it. As a police supervisor, your authority originates in your *position*. Your position grants you the right to reward and sanction the behavior of those who work for you. In other words, all three—position + rewards + sanctions—provide you with authority. And, when you exercise your authority, you are attempting to influence the attitudes and behavior of others. If they comply, then your authority is working well.

Position. By its very definition, your position is to command or influence the acts of others. The statement of your duties, your stripes, your salary, your training, and so on, attest to the responsibilities of job.

Rewards. Your authority to reward is based on the right to control and administer rewards to others (such as money, promotions, or praise) for compliance with the agency's requests or directives.

Sanctions. Your authority to sanction is based on the right to control and administer punishments to others (such as reprimand or termination) for noncompliance with the agency's requests or directives.

Power[1]

Men may doubt what you say, but they will believe what you do.

—Lewis Cass

Supervisors, because of the responsibilities of their position, acquire the right or the authority to command. With this right or authority goes influence. Hence, police supervisors are strategically located for moving an agency toward goal attainment. It is the effective supervisor who develops his or her talent for leading others, and consequently possesses a significantly enhanced influence (authority + power) for achieving results—for *achieving results effectively*.

Fundamentally, your power is person based as compared with position based. Your power to lead others is derived from your *expertise* and *example*. Both combine to attract others to follow you.

Expertise. Expert power is based on a special ability, skill, expertise, or knowledge exhibited by an individual. For example, a new police sergeant may

---

[1]The books on the subject of "power" could fill a small library. One in particular deserves your attention. Anthony Roblins, *Unlimited Power* (New York: Random House, 1986).

have some questions regarding the functioning of a piece of equipment. Rather than ask the lieutenant, the supervisor contacts the individual who previously held the sergeant's position for assistance because of his or her previous knowledge or expertise with the equipment.

Example or referent. Referent power is based on the attractiveness or the appeal of one person to another. A leader may be admired because of certain characteristics or traits that inspire or attract followers (charisma is an example). Referent power may also be based on a person's connection with another powerful individual. For example, the title of "assistant" has been given to people who work closely with others with titles such as sheriff or police chief. Although the title of assistant to the sheriff may not have reward or coercive (or legitimate) power, other individuals may perceive that this person is acting with the consent of the boss, resulting in his or her power to influence. The sheriff's assistant is perceived as the sheriff's alter ego. Many will wonder if the assistant is acting for the sheriff or on his or her own. Rather than take a chance, one typically opts in favor of the former possibility.

More important, there are specific attitudes and behavior on the part of a supervisor that usually result in leadership regardless of the situation. They are optimism, perception, goal emphasis, work facilitation, communications facilitation, supportive relationships, conflict resolution, and a sense of humor. More will be said about each one later. Keep in mind that *power is the capacity to command.* All police supervisors have it. Not all police supervisors use it. Hence, only some police supervisors are leaders.

FORMAL AND INFORMAL LEADERS

Not all police leaders have sergeant's stripes or lieutenant's or captain's bars. For a number of reasons, there are informal leaders. These people surface in all organizations to fill a one-time or ongoing need. For example, if a particular expertise is required, then the person who possesses it will provide leadership. This could occur if the victim of a crime can only communicate in Spanish. A Spanish-speaking officer thus may temporarily lead in an investigation. Another occurs when the supervisor fails to establish followership because of either inadequate expertise or a poor example. The work group will commonly fill this void by creating an informal leader.

The reasons for an informal leader emerging determine if it is helpful or harmful to the work group. Informal leaders are a normal phenomenon in an organization. They can be extremely useful to a supervisor if they act in concert with and support of the group's goals.

Leadership Defined

Leadership is a relationship between two or more people, in which one attempts to influence the other(s) toward the attainment of a goal or goals. Figure 3-1 summarizes the relationship between power, influence, and leadership.

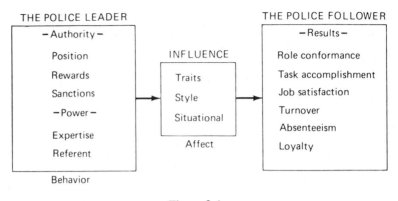

Figure 3-1

The key to the concept of leadership is to look at it as an influence process. It is a process that includes the elements of the *power base* of the leader and of the degree of acceptance with the characteristics, needs, and decision role of the subordinate(s).

THREE THEORIES OF LEADERSHIP

Three major theories of leadership will be examined: the *trait theory*, the *behavioral theory*, and the *situational theory*. The basic foundation of each approach is summarized in Table 3-1.

Trait

During my basic (preentry) police training, platoon leaders were selected by the cadre. Each was one of the tallest members of our sixty-six-person academy class. Being only average in height, I was excluded from consideration. Appar-

TABLE 3-1 Major Theories of Leadership

Theory	Emphasis
Trait (1940s–1950s)	There exists a finite set of individualized *traits* or characteristics that can be used to distinguish successful leaders from unsuccessful leaders.
Behavioral (1950s–1960s)	The most important aspect of leadership is not the traits of the leader, but what the leader does in various situations. Successful leaders are distinguished from unsuccessful leaders by their particular *style* of leadership.
Situational (1970s)	The effectiveness of the leader is not only determined by his or her style of behavior, but also by the *situation* surrounding the leadership environment. Situational factors include the characteristics of the leader and the subordinate(s), the nature of the task, and the structure of the group.

ently, leaders are tall (Alexander the Great, Napoleon, and Hyman Rickover) or psychologically powerful (Franklin D. Roosevelt, Helen Keller, Mohandas K. Gandhi). Although the results of these trait considerations appear to be helpful in identifying certain salient characteristics of leaders, little has been provided for understanding or predicting leadership effectiveness. The list of important leadership traits is endless, and grows with each passing year. It has not yet been shown that a finite set of traits can distinguish successful from unsuccessful leaders. Although such aspects as personality do appear to be significant factors, they are only a few of the many factors that can contribute to leadership effectiveness.

Also, focusing on individual traits does not show what a police manager actually does in a leadership situation. Traits can identify who the police leader is, but not the behavioral patterns he or she will exhibit in attempting to influence subordinate actions. The trait theory has ignored the police subordinates and their effect on leadership. The effectiveness of leadership depends to a large extent on the situation within the environment of the leadership or influence process: A particular leadership pattern may be effective for a group of uniformed police officers, but may be totally ineffective for a group of detectives. Interactions among the many factors of the situation must be examined before any predictions about leadership effectiveness can be made.

Behavioral

During the 1950s the dissatisfaction with the trait theory of leadership led behavioral scientists to focus their attention on the actual behavior of a leader —what leaders do and how they do it. The foundation for the style-of-leadership approach was the belief that effective leaders applied a particular style to leading individuals and groups to the achievement of certain goals, resulting in high productivity and morale. Unlike the trait theory, the behavioral theory focused on *leader effectiveness*, not on the emergence of an individual as a leader.

A number of definitions of leadership style were developed. Although many terms were assigned to the different leadership styles, two factors were emphasized in each approach: task orientation and employee orientation. *Task orientation* is the emphasis that a leader places on getting a job done by such actions as assigning and organizing the work, making decisions, and evaluating performance. *Employee orientation* is the openness and friendliness exhibited by a leader and the leader's concern for the needs of his or her personnel.

In their search for the most effective leadership style, the researchers' findings suggested that a universally accepted "best" style was inappropriate for the complexities of modern organizations. For a supervisor's leadership style to be effective, other situational factors must be considered.

Situational

During the late 1960s, researchers recognized the limitations of the behavioral theory and began to develop a new theory of leadership, focusing on the more complex situational factors. The work of the trait and the behavioral style theorists provided a significant foundation for the study of leadership within organizations, because the results of these researchers strongly suggested that the most effective way to lead is a dynamic and flexible process that adapts to particular situations.

One of the most important functions of a manager's role is to diagnose and evaluate the many factors that may have an impact on the effectiveness of his or her leadership. Diagnosis involves the identification and understanding of the influence of factors such as individual differences, group structure, and agency policies and practices. A careful study of each situation is a crucial process for leaders contemplating the application of a particular style. For example, a group of uniformed police officers working under conditions of extreme stress to control a riot will require a different type of leadership style than would a group of detectives who routinely investigate the properties of a criminal event. The accurate diagnosis of a situation requires an examination by a manager of four important areas: (1) managerial characteristics, (2) subordinate characteristics, (3) group structure and the nature of the task, and (4) organizational factors. These factors are summarized in Figure 3-2.

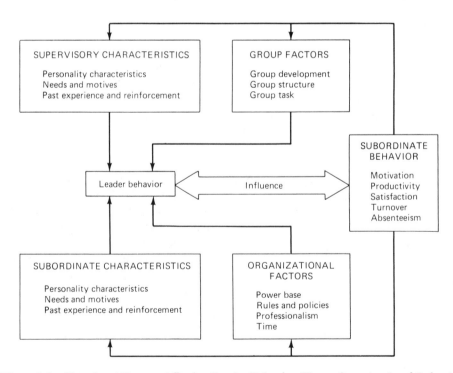

Figure 3-2 Situational Factors Affecting Leader Behavior (From *Organizational Behavior and Performance* by John M. Ivancevich, et al. Copyright © 1977 by Scott, Foresman and Company. Reprinted by permission of HarperCollins Publishers.)

1. *Supervisory characteristics.* The leader's behavior in any given environment is dependent on the forces or characteristics of the individual. The important factors include
   a. Personality characteristics
   b. Needs and motives
   c. Past experience and reinforcement

2. *Subordinate characteristics.* Before a police leader decides on a particular leadership style, he or she should assess the individual characteristics and behavioral patterns of the staff. The staff members, like the police supervisor, have internal factors that may affect their behavior. Some of these factors include
   a. Personality characteristics
   b. Needs and motives
   c. Past experience and reinforcement

3. *Group structure.* Groups are a prominent feature in society and organizations. The particular characteristics of the group usually have a significant impact on a police supervisor's ability to lead his or her personnel. Some of the important group factors include
   a. Group development stage (Where the group is in its development can influence the effectiveness of a particular leadership style. The supervisor's behavior during the orientation stage may not be appropriate during the internal problem-solving stage, in which conflict resolution is a frequent occurrence.)
   b. Group structure
   c. Group task (The nature of the task has an important impact on the success of any leader's influence activities. For example, groups working on ambiguous tasks may require a completely different type of leadership than groups involved with routine tasks.)

4. *Organizational factors.* Among the most crucial yet least understood factors in the leadership situation is the type of organization. Some of the most important considerations are
   a. Influence base (What is the foundation of a police leader's influence base? Does it consist of authority, reward, coercion, expertise, and referent power, or some subset?)
   b. Rules and procedures (Agencies vary in the manner in which rules, policies, standards, and procedures are used to guide the work of police employees. Many police departments have developed extensive policy systems, such as manuals and standard operating procedures, that may dictate the type of police-leader behavior required.)
   c. Professionalism (Highly trained police professionals, such as criminal investigators, may depend more on their educational backgrounds or experiences than on the police leader to guide their work, which may limit the ability of the leader to influence them.)
   d. Time (If an immediate decision must be made, or if there is a high level of tension and stress, the involvement of personnel may be difficult, if

not impossible. However, there is usually ample time to elicit the opinion of those who will be affected by the pending decision.)

POLICE LEADERSHIP CHALLENGE

We can cite a long list of challenges the police leader faces. In our opinion, the number one challenge today is *people*. Granted, the department's budget for equipment, technology, and facilities is important. But it is the people who work for the agency that can make or break it. To harness their power, leaders inspire commitment and empower employees by sharing authority. Responding to labor shortages with flexibility, they enable their departments to attract, reward, and motivate the best officers and civilian personnel.

We'll cover the following emerging characteristics of the police work force: *education, loyalty, gender and ethnicity, type, selection, and "ladders."*

Well-Educated Work Force

Because we so often lament the overall decline in education *standards*, it is easy to overlook the dramatic increase in educated people in the past twenty years.

One-quarter of the work force aged twenty-five to sixty-four consists of college graduates or better, *twice* the percentage twenty years ago. Another 20 percent has one to three years of college, more than double the old ratio. That means nearly half—45 percent—of the work force is college educated. In addition, 40 percent are high school graduates.

The police supervisor must be prepared to lead an ever-increasing, better-educated employee. This requires that he or she be a step ahead in knowledge and training. The supervisor's capacity for leadership depends on being an example of a "well-educated work force."

Loyalty

Many police managers and supervisors are realizing that police personnel do not reflect the same loyalty to their departments that was the norm in the 1950s. Police employees are indicating that professional growth should precede loyalty. Lateral entries and open promotions are fueling it. Besides moving around within the police profession, many police employees will change jobs —not careers—at least three times.

Survey research results convinces us that greater loyalty is interdependent with improved leadership. The driving force is that leaders expect loyalty, and they operate in such a style to inspire it. Bluntly, *they earn it.*

Gender and Ethnicity

We assume you've noticed that the composition of the work force has changed. The all-male work force is history. Sameness of sex and ethnicity is out, and differences are in.

In sheer numbers women dominate the information society. Eighty-four percent of working women are part of the information-service sector. Of the people whose job title falls under the category of "professional"—versus clerical, technical, laborer—the majority are women. Forty-four percent of adult working women (ages twenty-five to sixty-four) are college educated, compared with 20 percent in 1965. Further, six out of ten joining the work force right now are female. And, by the year 2000 it is estimated that parity of gender will exist in our work force.

Daily we see the ethnic composition of our police agencies come nearer to mirroring the racial makeup of our society. Some of our newer Americans are seeking a career in law enforcement. With their employment is attached new values, different cultures, and varying mores.

Police supervisors will have to be especially adroit in leading a more diverse work force. We would urge that all supervisors recognize the enormous power that is unleashed by a diverse work force. In our opinion, it is one of this nation's paramount strengths, and this should hold true for its police agencies.

Type: Sworn and Civilian

In the past, most police agencies were composed of primarily sworn personnel. The casual civilian employee was usually a typist-clerk or, at best, a specialist such as a criminalist. This is not the case today.

Civilians have invaded police organizations in significant numbers. Some departments are now comprised of 30, 40, indeed, 50 percent civilians. We see them working in all divisions and bureaus. We also see them as supervisors and managers, and top-paid technical specialists. Police divisions (and even a few police departments) are being commanded by civilian personnel.

Years ago civilian employees were considered short-term employees (most were female) and not really involved in providing services. This has drastically changed and, currently, civilians either directly or indirectly deliver police services. (The para-professional or community service officer is one example.) Further, many are long term and actively seeking career enlargement and advancement in police organizations.

Civilian personnel are expecting to participate in decisions that affect them. They're expecting to be treated as equal members of a team of people devoted to giving citizens top-level police service. No second-class or low-order treatment is tolerated. Everyone has a position of importance. Everyone stands to benefit from sworn and civilian employees functioning as a team. *The police supervisor as a leader must cause this to happen.*

Selection

Since 1950 we've been hearing from police supervisors, "We're not getting the talent that we used to." Such comments probably predate the 1950s. We have watched spit-and-shine recruitment teams encourage individuals to join their ranks. We have seen expensive media blitzes do likewise. Some agencies are offering their personnel rewards (money, time off with pay) for bringing bodies into the basic training academy.

The baby bust generation will be eligible for police employment in the next few years. The number of police jobs will have increased at least in line with our growing population. The point being, there'll be fewer potential officers with a greater demand for them.

There are numerous solutions being thrown at this paradox—one of which is money. We believe that until everyone in the agency becomes an earnest recruiter, the problem will persist.

A few years ago a group of university criminal justice majors went to twenty-six local law enforcement agencies (the agencies ranged from 21 to 1,800 employees) seeking information about working there. In summary, they were politely turned away by: "Fill out this card, and we'll letcha know when we're hiring"; "Stop back in a couple of months and we can talk with you then"; and "I'm not responsible for hiring—phone our business office and they'll talk to you." One person was told by a front desk officer, "Why in the hell would you want to work here? This is a miserable department." Three of the twenty-six agencies set in motion a proactive recruitment and selection process.

Your success as a supervisor is dependent on those leaders. *If you're not recruiting the best available police talent, obviously your job as a supervisor is going to be extremely tough.*

Ladders

Management is doing things right; leadership is doing the right things. Management is efficiency in climbing the ladder of success; leadership determines whether the ladder is leaning against the right wall.

The difference between the two can be seen if you'll for a few moments imagine a group of police officers concentrating on the problem of burglaries. Their thinking and their patrol tactics are exclusively focused on combating burglaries. The supervisors are assisting them by deployment, overtime, technology, and other resources. They're always there and always behind them.

It is the leader who carefully analyzes the crime problem and then has the guts to yell, "It's not a burglary problem; we've got a drug enforcement problem." This police leader has said, "Stop, we've got to move the ladder to the proper wall." Some officers and sergeants will respond, "Be quiet; we are getting success here." It is the responsible leader who creates a new destination on the road map. His or her inner compass provides us with the new direction.

Leaders live out of their imagination instead of their memory. They tie themselves to their infinite potential instead of their limiting past. It's incredibly easy to gall into the activity trap, in the busy-ness of police work, to work harder and harder at climbing the ladder of professional success only to discover it's against the wrong wall. It is possible to be busy as a police supervisor —very busy—without being effective.

POLICE DEPARTMENT: VOLUNTARY ORGANIZATION

Authority is bottom up! If you really do not want to work for an organization anymore, you can quit. You have that freedom of choice. (There are a few select organizations, such as prisons, where quitting is not an option.)

When you commence working as a police officer, you temporarily loan the department over you. If they abuse it or foul up in some way, you can merely take it back. As Johnny Paycheck sings, "You can take this job and shove it. I'm not working here anymore." Granted, finding another job may be difficult. The fact remains you do have a choice.

Supervising through raw authority is impossible. The supervisor must win loyalty, achieve commitment, and minute-by-minute earn respect and trust.

Paradoxically, employees who are free to leave, who are independent thinkers, who question established approaches are a leader's best source of accurate information and the key hope for providing top-drawer police services.

GOALS: DEPARTMENTAL AND PERSONAL

Earlier, we discussed ladders, or vision. To be of use, the vision and its goals must be communicated (Responsibility Four) to others. If they do not comprehend the big picture, they're unable to do their fair share of painting it.

We're surprised when a police manager or supervisor criticizes a line employee (in some cases one another) for "not seeing the big picture." Our first reaction is—were they ever informed? Second, is the leader daily reinforcing the vision by what he or she thinks and does?

The police work force will assist the organization to achieve its goals if it can achieve its own personal goals as well. This is a plus for both parties—if the personal goals include achievement, security, creativity, and rewards. Obviously, there are personal goals that should be rejected such as self-aggrandizement, doing as little as possible, and advancement at all costs.

The overarching vision must encapsulate both organizational and personal goals. By doing so, the leader is in a much better position to sell it to others. And, it is the "others" who get the job done.

Front-Line Bias

Loyalty, commitment, respect, and trust of the front-line officer is gained by the supervisor

- Emphasizing their welfare
- Giving them top priority in everything
- Rewarding staff personnel on how well they support the line people

Review your actions at the end of each work shift. Have you made your bias for the front line—and those on staff who vigorously support them—convincingly clear? The axiom "patrol is the backbone of police work" is a wasted platitude. Most police managers and supervisors look on and treat front-line employees as necessary cogs in a wheel. (There are some exceptions such as motorcycle officers, vice officers, and other specialized and prestigious assignments.) Front-line police work suffers from a distinct lack of care and nurturing. This malady must be cured, and the police leader is responsible for seeing to it.

SELF-MANAGEMENT AND LEADERSHIP OF OTHERS

Six premier writers and thinkers play a major role here: (1) Peter Drucker for *Action and Results*; Warren Bennis for *Scientific Evidence and Self-Expression*; (3) John Naisbett and Patricia Aberdene for *Change and Trends*; (4) Tom Peters for *Appreciating Chaos and Excellence*; and (5) Steve Covey for *Vision and Communication*. Their works contain all of the subjects listed and much much more.[2] Their individual emphases vary, however. They unanimously agree that leadership skills are possessed by a majority but used by a minority. It's something that can be learned by anyone, taught to everyone, denied to no one. Nonetheless, Bennis has asserted that leadership is like the Abominable Snowman whose footprints are everywhere but is nowhere to be seen.

The problem with many police organizations, and especially the ones that are deficient, is they tend to be overmanaged and underled. Management and leadership are equally important. Managers do things right, and leaders do the right thing. The first concentrates on efficiency, and the second requires effectiveness. (Please reread this paragraph—it's fundamental to everything that follows.)

We are convinced that leadership is *the* pivotal force causing ordinary organizations to be successful organizations.

LEADERSHIP PARADIGM

A few years ago, Bennis committed two years of his professional life to investigate leadership. He conducted ninety interviews, sixty with acknowledged successful business chief executive officers (CEOs) and thirty others. From corporate boardrooms to sport coaches to public officials, he ardently inquired of these people: "How did you become a leader?" His research led to their *four strategies for leadership*, which follow:

1. Riveting one's attention via vision
2. Creating meaning via communication

---

[2]If interested in more information on the subjects mentioned, consult the following: (1) Peter F. Drucker, *Management: Tasks, Responsibilities, Practices* (New York: Harper and Row, 1974); (2) Warren G. Bennis, *On Becoming a Leader* (Reading, Mass.: Addison-Wesley Publishing Company, Inc., 1989); (3) John Naisbett and Patricia Aberdene, *Megatrends 2000: Ten New Directions for The 1990s* (New York: Morrow, 1990); (4) Tom Peters, *Thriving on Chaos: A Handbook for a Management Revolution* (New York: Knopf 1987); (5) Steve Covey, *The Seven Habits of Highly Effective People* (New York: Simon and Schuster, 1989).

3. Building trust via positioning
4. Deploying yourself via positive self-regard and trying[3]

The preceding strategies form a cause-effect equation. If I create a vision, the effect will be your attention. If I convey communications, the effect will be meaning. If I position myself (knowing who I am), the effect will be trust. And, if I manifest high regard for myself plus (to the best of my ability) do my job, the effect will be experiencing me as a dedicated police supervisor.

Attention through Vision

Vision *grabs*. At first it grabs the leader and, if effectively projected, it convinces others to get on board. The leader's vision is intended to be magnetic. Winning coaches transmit an unbridled clarity about what they want from their players. If coaches can do it, so can police supervisors—if they want to.

The first thing you do with your vision is to *convey* it to others. Your staff has to know what you see. Second, they must *understand* it. The understanding may be vague or incomplete, but they have at least a fundamental concept of what you're proposing. Third, the people must be convinced that the vision is of *paramount importance*, even if it initially appears impossible. It excites people and drives them. Fourth, the leader pays close *attention* to the vision and uses it as transaction between himself and his followers. It becomes a subtle link that forges the leader and follower as one. Coach and team. Sergeant and officers.

Once the preceding steps have been taken, the leader must

- Closely live the enabling vision
- Use it to prioritize (quality first, quantity second, etc.)
- Adapt to vision of changing needs and new opportunities

If you understand your values, the values of your department, and the values of your profession, then visioning is possible for you. You merely allow your *imagination* and *conscience* to take charge. Through imagination, you can visualize the uncharted wealth of potential that lie within *yourself* and *others*. Through conscience, you can compare your ideas with universal laws or principles as well as your personal standards.

We'll take a few moments here to illustrate the preceding process. Captain Jim Nunn, his department, and his profession hold "quality" as a cornerstone value. He is currently in command of one of his sheriff department's nine patrol stations. The area served will soon incorporate as a city. The city will either form their own police agency or contract for police services with the sheriff. His imagination causes him to envision the newly elected city council

---

[3]This section is adapted and modified from two of his works that pertain to Bennis's research: *On Becoming a Leader,* op cit.; and in conjunction with Burt Nanus, *Leaders: The Strategies for Taking Charge* (New York: Harper and Row, 1985).

opting to contract for sheriff coverage. His vision also included an approach to furthering this goal—provide top-quality police services. Nothing less than the very best! He conceived a rather risky motto, "Treat those that you serve exactly the way I treat you." Finally, he foresaw a comprehensive training program that would ignite the interest, and secure the follow through, of his entire staff.

You're Sergeant Ortega and you learn of his vision, see its importance, and make a commitment to its implementation. You present the vision to your line employees with enthusiasm and total endorsement. You likewise adopt the captain's motto. However, you add an energizing concept of your own, "We're 100% responsible for everything that *we* do." Your imagination has locked on to *teamwork*. Consequently, you start training, praising, rewarding, and reprimanding team, not individual, efforts.

Your conscience informs you that *fair play* is a critical principle while introducing a new program. It also tells you that you'll be the example, and you'll set the standards. As you pay close attention to your staff, they'll be paying equal (if not more) attention to what you are doing regarding quality police services. Finally, your inner voice says that every act, no matter how small, counts.

In conceiving our vision, many of us discover nonproductive thoughts, inconsistent guidelines, and unworthy habits. We don't have to live with them. We are "response-able" to apply our imagination and creativity to go beyond our present horizon in search of new opportunities for organizational and personal excellence. *Supervisors realize that they have choices; leaders act on them.*

Meaning through Communication

Responsibility Four that follows provides an expansive coverage of this strategy. We underscore it here because Bennis's research demonstrated that all of the leaders he studied mastered communications. It was inseparable from effective leadership. It isn't just information or facts—it's the *context* of presentation, the overall meaning.

All police organizations depend on the existence of shared meanings and interpretations of reality, which facilitate coordinated efforts. "Meaning" surpasses what is typically meant by "communications." Meaning has little to do with facts or even knowing. Facts and knowing pertain to technique, tactics, with "knowing how to do things." That is useful and often necessary. But thinking is much closer to what we mean by "meaning" than knowing. This is not a subtle difference. Thinking prepares one for what *ought* to be done.

To depend on facts, without thinking, may seem all right, but in the long run, it is dangerous because it lacks *directions*. The distinctive role of leadership (especially in a volatile police environment) is that the "know-why" occurs before the "know-how." This logic shows, once more, one of the basic differences between leaders and supervisors.

Police supervisors primarily engage in a mental process known as problem solving. Problem solving includes a problem, a method, and a solution based on the former two factors. A creative mental process outcrops when neither the problem nor the method, let alone the solution, exists. There's no rule, manual or guru, to turn to. Hence, it's up to the supervisor to discover the *real* problem. Creativity uncovers a "hidden problem"—one that requires attention from the start to the finish. *The highest type of discovery always centers on problem finding!*

Why do people align behind one solution, direction, or vision, and not another? We believe that endorsement of a vision—or any new idea or change—requires that the employees be interested in paying attention to the hoped-for destination.

Let us forewarn you—new ideas of visions are never judged solely by their inherent quality or goodness. (Adolph Hitler had a lot of visions, all of which proved to be disastrous.) Even the prudent ideas are only as good as their capacity to attract attention. Police organizations are by nature unpredictable; they can reject a good vision just as easily as a bad one.

Leadership, by communicating meaning, generates a confederation of learning, and this is what successful police agencies proudly possess. *Lack of clarity makes police organizations little more than simple devices for the avoidance of responsibility.*

We've conducted more than 2,000 team-building workshops for police and sheriff departments. (We've also conducted similar workshops for fire departments, city councils, and a variety of business firms.) With rare exception, the number one issue in the workshop is the failure to communicate with one another. Far too often the participants state with detectable anger, "I never got the word." "Everything moves, but there's no feedback." "I've expressed my ideas before, but they could care less." And the worst one is, "I don't know our priorities, let alone our goals."

If our body's arterial system does not touch base with our cells, they'll eventually die. *Similarly, if our police organizations' communication system does not contact, with meaning, its human resources—the staff may not be dead, but they might as well be.*

Trust through Positioning

Trust encompasses accountability, predictability, reliability, and faith. Technically, it is a noun. But to achieve it, there must be a mental or physical act. Something must happen for me to trust you or vice versa. You tell me that you'll be at work on time, and you are—I start the "trust process."

Trusting involves a trust bank account (TBA). You consistently arrive at work on time, and your TBA prospers. You make many, daily TBA deposits in a variety of ways. You open new TBAs with people that you meet. Depending on your working relationships, family members, and friends, you may have hundreds of TBAs in existence. You could be *trust rich.* Conversely, you could be *trust poor.*

It takes a lot of deposits to build a strong TBA with another person. Making a mistake, for example lying to another person, can wipe out your TBA. It could send you into indefinite, maybe permanent, bankruptcy with the other party. It could also destroy a working relationship, a marriage, a friendship. TBAs take considerable time to build and only one second—in some cases, one word—to dissolve.

Kids have a remarkable memory. A few years ago, one of your authors told his wife that he'd *never* made a promise to their four-year-old grandson that was not fulfilled. As most good spouses will do, she said, "Let's see what his opinion is." I asked, "Derek, Grandpa has always done what he said he would do—right?" The split-second retort was, "No. You said you'd take me fishing. You didn't do it." I do not recall making such a promise. To this day, I'm certain that he was correct. (To the best of my knowledge, I've not made any other withdrawals from my Derek TBA.)

We cannot imagine a police organization that does not have some level of trust among the working personnel. It may be very little, but still it's there. The lower the trust, the weaker the leadership.

Although TBAs are very fragile, they are very resilient at the same time. If we have a healthy TBA, let us assume a trust bank (TB) of 200,000 with others, we can make small withdrawals of TB 5,000 from time to time. Those concerned will understand and tolerate it. For instance, we may need to make a very unpopular unilateral decision, because of time pressures, without involving others or even explaining it to them. In doing so, we make a TB 5,000 withdrawal, leaving TB 190,000 on deposit. Perhaps the next day, we can explain what we did and why we did it, thus redepositing the TB 5,000. Obviously, outright lying and so on to a co-worker can result in a "closed account."

Leaders who are trusted make themselves known and make their positions (e.g., values, principles, vision) known. Followers do not stay with shiny ideals and cute words. *Only relentless dedication to a position on the part of a police leader will engage trust.*

Positioning is a set of actions necessary to implement the vision of a leader. Through establishing the position (by action), the followers are given the chance to *trust—trust in the leader and trust in the position; they're synonymous.*

For a police organization to foster trust, it first must present a sense of who it is and what it is to do—in other words, a position. The police leader is responsible for seeing to it that the position of the department is known to employee and community members alike. This is not easy because people form different perceptions. The police leader may see the position of the department as X, the employees as Y and the citizens as Z. If the three positions are contradictory, then trust is hard to achieve.

The greater the agreement on what the position of the department is, the more one is able to trust it. If I know what you stand for, and believe in it, I'll trust your leadership.

Second, positioning needs courageous patience. The leader has to stay with it. With time, he starts managing trust. Change may occur, and innovations may be needed; thus the position must be carefully shifted and then maintained.

We know of a large-scale local law-enforcement agency that took the position of full stress during basic academy training. This position was trusted and, hence, vigorously endorsed by the leaders. One innovative employee questioned the position of full stress—he didn't trust its results. The results of his research caused a shift in basic training from full stress to modified stress. A new position was identified, and it caused enhanced trust in the training program.

Positions must adjust, as appropriate, to maintain trust. The police leader must recognize when to maintain the steady course or change direction. *Trust in his ability to lead depends on his decision to retain or shift a position.*

Deployment of Self through Positive Self-Regard

The higher you advance in a police organization, the more interpersonal and relational the working environment. This deployment of self makes leading a profoundly personal activity. Such a deployment depends on one's positive self-regard. *Positive self-regard* is a three-sided triangle consisting of (1) competency, (2) positive other-regard, and (3) the Wallenda factor.

Competency. Positive self-regard is not self-aggrandizement, conceitfulness, or ego mania. Essentially, it is confidence in who you are and what you are capable of doing. It is prudent self-esteem and self-respect.

The first step in building positive self-regard is *recognizing your strengths and compensating for your weaknesses.* The next step involves the constant *nurturing of skills.* The final step is astuteness in *evaluating the fit between your perceived skills and what the job requires.* Being good at your job and knowing why sums up one side of positive self-regard. We label this "competency."

Other-regard. Those that have high regard for themselves typically have the same for others. Having positive self-regard is contagious. Potentially everyone can catch it. *Positive self-regard creates it in others.* It seems to exert its force by generating in others a sense of confidence and high expectations.

Positive self- and other-regard encourages the development of five key people skills.

1. The ability to accept individuals as they are, not as you would like them to be. This ability is fundamental to leading a culturally diverse work force.
2. The capacity to approach people and problems in relation to the present rather than the past.
3. The ability to deal with those that are close to you with the same active listening ear and courtesy that you give to citizens and casual acquaintances.
4. The ability to trust in another person's dedication and capabilities.
5. The ability to function without constant approval or even support from others.

Wallenda factor. In his research, Bennis found that the leaders he studied simply didn't think about failure. In fact, they didn't use the term. The closest they would identify with it were through words such as "mistake," "setback," or "error."

Failure to them was like learning to ski. At first you're destined to fall; with persistence and perspiration you'll eventually master the art of skiing. It's the same with leadership. *They used their mistakes as a lesson on what not to do as well as what to do next.*

Failure and mistakes can open you up to self- or other-criticism. It can erode both positive self- and other-regard. The more valid it is, the more bothersome it is to us. The successful leader accepts it, but then twists it into a useful message. Remember, *feedback is the breakfast of champions.*

Karl Wallenda was one of the premier high-wire aerialists. He fell to his death in 1978 while walking a seventy-five-foot-high tightrope. After his fall, Mrs. Wallenda commented that for three straight months before the accident, all he thought about was not falling. He substituted his past successful thinking about walking the tightrope with falling.

Karl Wallenda would likely tell the police supervisor, pour your energies into success (walking the tightrope) and not failing (or not falling). To worry places barriers in the path of clear thinking. An absence of clear thinking can cause *mistakes* for those who possess positive self-regard. An absence of clear thinking can cause *failures* for those that do not have it.

Three sides of positive self-regard. The three sides combined look like the following diagram:

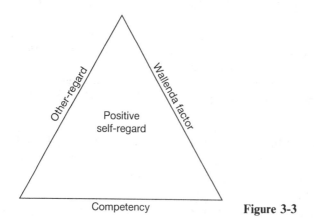

Figure 3-3

Your positive self-regard is a direct derivative of

• Your competency—you have what it takes and you know it.

- Your capacity for instilling it in others by having high other-regard for them.
- Your conviction of an outcome—the expectation of success.

For effective leadership to occur, there has to be a fusion of competency, capacity, and conviction. It is similar to the archer who builds his prowess to the point where the zeal to hit the center of the target is obliterated, and man, bow, arrow and target become one, united. Positive self-regard magnetically attracts and gradually empowers people to join the police supervisor, the police leader, in a quest for quality services that are good for police departments and for society.

LEADERSHIP DEFINED

We've looked at numerous definitions of leadership and have a few of our own. We believe Bennis exposes it when he writes that the leader is the person *who knows what he or she wants, communicates it to others, positions himself or herself correctly, and then empowers others to perform their duties successfully.* If this definition is too long for you, then we'd merely say that *leadership is self-expression.*

KEY POINTS

- Authority is the right to supervise, and power is one's capacity to do so.
- Both authority and power seek to influence the behavior of others.
- There are two types of authority: sanctions and rewards. Also, there are three types of power: position, expert, and example.
- Informal leadership is a natural phenomenon in an organization.
- There are three schools of thought about how leaders emerge: trait, behavioral, and situational.
- There is no one best way to become a leader—but there are ways.
- The police work force is changing by being educated; supplanting loyalty with professional growth; becoming more diverse in composition; having a greater percentage of civilian employees; being more difficult to recruit and hire; and having a greater need than ever before for leadership.
  - The police organization is a voluntary organization, and its goals should complement those of its work force.
  - Many police organizations are overmanaged and underled.
  - Successful leaders demonstrate four common patterns of behavior. They consistently (1) get your attention through a vision they have; (2) create meaning through communication; (3) build trust via positioning; and (4) project positive self-regard.
  - Leadership can be learned.
  - All of us, therefore, are capable of becoming a leader.

DISCUSSION

1. Discuss authority and power. How do they differ? What is their common bond? If you could only have one, which would you choose?
2. Realizing that you, the police supervisor, are a formal leader, how do you explain the likelihood that there are informal leaders in or around your assigned work unit?
3. Give a specific illustration of each theory (trait, behavioral, and situational) of leadership. Try to use an example from your own department.
4. What other changes can be seen in the police work force today? What changes may be anticipated within the next five years?
5. What is meant by positive self-regard? How does one acquire it? Who do you know that has this characteristic?

STRUCTURED EXPERIENCES

1. Is Supervision for You?

A career in police supervision isn't for everyone. Along with authority, challenging work, and financial rewards come responsibilities, performance pressures, and the need to make tough decisions.

A questionnaire follows that can help assess whether or not a career in supervision is for you. Take a couple of minutes to answer the items in this questionnaire and then follow the directions for computing your score.

The results from this questionnaire are not precise predictors. In comparing your score against others, differences of a few points are probably insignificant. However, based on research into the leadership and motivation patterns of successful supervisors, we can say that the higher your score, the more likely you are to fit the role requirements related to a supervisory job.

IS A CAREER IN MANAGEMENT FOR YOU?

Instructions: For each statement, check the response that best represents your feelings.

	1 Strongly Disagree	2 Disagree	3 Undecided	4 Agree	5 Strongly Agree
1. I dislike following somebody else's orders.	____	____	____	____	____
2. I dislike having to compete against others with whom I work.	____	____	____	____	____
3. It is important for me to be liked by the people with whom I work.	____	____	____	____	____
4. I prefer to act in customary ways, to blend in with the crowd.	____	____	____	____	____

IS A CAREER IN MANAGEMENT FOR YOU? *Continued*

	1 Strongly Disagree	2 Disagree	3 Undecided	4 Agree	5 Strongly Agree
5. It is important for me to do things better or more efficiently than it's ever been done before.	———	———	———	———	———
6. I like to assert myself and take charge.	———	———	———	———	———
7. I enjoy giving directions to others.	———	———	———	———	———
8. It doesn't bother me to do routine tasks.	———	———	———	———	———

Compute your score as follows: You get one point for a Strongly Disagree response, two points for Disagree, and so on up to five for a Strongly Agree answer. Add up your score for items 5 through 8. For items 1 through 4, you need to reverse the scoring table. That is, Strongly Disagree becomes 5, Disagree becomes 4, and so on. Using the reverse scoring, add up your total for items 1 through 4 and combine that with the sum you obtained for items 5 through 8 to get your total score.

2. Leadership Characteristics

Warren Bennis discovered four critical characteristics or strategies that proven leaders had. What four would you add to his list? First of all create your own list; then along with your colleagues, get consensus on a joint list of four strategies.

3. Leadership Characteristics

There are several excellent motion pictures that portray leadership characteristics and strategies. The movie *Patton* is one example. Another is *Stand by Me.* Identify a movie that you can borrow or rent. (Be certain the movie depicts an actual leader.) View the movie and analyze it for leadership characteristics. Look for the successes and mistakes that he or she experienced. Record what you see. When the movie is finished, discuss with one another what you saw in the leader's behavior (values, vision, positive self-regard, integrity, etc.).

RESPONSIBILITY FOUR

Communications: Sharing the Vision

The management of meaning, mastery of communication, is inseparable from effective leadership.

Warren Bennis and Bert Nanus

Communication is our most important human skill. Everything that we've done, are doing, and wish to do revolves around it. It's, therefore, axiomatic that everything a police supervisor does involves communicating. Not a few things, but everything! You can't make a correct decision without information. That information has to be communicated. Once a decision is made, again communication must take place. Otherwise, no one will know a decision has been made. The most creative suggestion or the finest plan cannot take form without communication. Supervisors, therefore, need effective communication skills. We are not saying that solid communication skills, alone, make a successful police supervisor. We can say, with confidence, that ineffective communication skills can lead to a continuous stream of problems for the supervisor.

COMMUNICATIONS: LEADERSHIP, DECISION MAKING, AND TRUST

We began Responsibility Four by asserting that "communication is our most important skill." Not one of many, but *the* most important skill. Our ability to communicate effectively and directly determines our success on becoming a *leader*, our success in making accurate *decisions*, and our success in being *trusted*. Let's explore these three dimensions in more detail.

Leadership

Communication is the vehicle for supervisory leadership. In other words, the police supervisor is a key person in building and maintaining effective organizational communications as he or she interacts with subordinates, peers, superiors, and the citizenry.

A communication, or in terms of an organizational setting, a communication system, provides the means by which information, statements, views, and instructions are transmitted through a department. Although one often speaks of the "flow" of communications, this flow actually consists of a series of discrete messages of different length, form, and content. These messages are transmitted through certain channels (or lines of communications), which make up the communication system or network. Each message is sent by a transmitter (an individual, a group, a division, a computer) to a receiver or several receivers. Significantly, the supervisory role and function are filled with a heavy volume of transmissions and receptions.

Decision Making

A police supervisor decides issues based on information received in conjunction with previously developed strategies, procedures, or rules. Consequently, the communication process is necessary because the flow of proper information to the decision points throughout the organization is such a vital requirement for task accomplishment. In fact, if supervision were thought of primarily as decision making and if the decision process were considered essentially a communication process including a network of communication systems, then supervision could be viewed as a communication process. The closer we look at leadership and decision making, the more we become aware of the significance of information exchange.

Trust

Elsewhere we've covered the concept of a TBA. Oliver Wendell Holmes wrote about trust when he penned, "What lies behind us and what lies before us are tiny matters compared to what lies within us." In other words, the most important ingredient we put into any relationship is not what we say or what we do, but what we are. We do this by communicating. How do you react to the person who does not share with you his ideas, values, hopes, and ethical standards? Do you grow to trust him? Probably not. He either refuses or is incapable of making deposits into your TBA. In fact, if this individual persists in being closed, he'll likely make withdrawals from your TBA. *Trust and communications are linked.* For one to be high, the other must be high. You lower one (reduced communication), and you'll lower the other (reduced trust).

WHAT IS COMMUNICATION?

Communication is the transfer of meaning. If no information or ideas have been conveyed, communication has not taken place. The supervisor who is not heard or the writer who is not read does not communicate. For communication to be successful, the meaning must not only be sent, but also comprehended. Therefore, communication is the movement and understanding of meaning. Perfect communication, if such a thing were possible, would exist when a transmitted thought is perceived by the receiver exactly the same as envisioned by the sender.

Good communication is often erroneously defined by the communicator as agreement rather than clarity of understanding. If someone disagrees with us, it's not unusual to assume they just didn't fully understand our position. What happens is that many of us define good communication as having someone accept our views. But a supervisor can very clearly understand what you mean and not agree with what you say. In fact, often when observers conclude that a lack of communication must exist because a conflict has continued for a prolonged time, a close examination reveals that there is plenty of effective communication going on. Each fully understands the other's position. The problem is one of equating effective communication with differences in values, responsibilities, and roles.

WHAT WE KNOW ABOUT COMMUNICATIONS

> *A system of information flow is vital to the decision-making process. Information is the raw material of intelligence activity which touches off the recognition that a decision is to be made.*
>
> —Fremont E. Kast and James E. Rosenzweig
> *Organization and Management: A Systems Approach*
> (New York: McGraw-Hill Book Company, 1970), p. 97

What knowledge exists about communications is scattered over numerous disciplines and fields and is often contradictory. In many ways, what we know about communications has been derived from our failures rather than our successes. Thus it is in the residues of our discovered imperfections that we are better able to predict what might work. Sufficient evidence is now before us to conclude that communications is perception, is experience, makes demands, is related to but different from information, and is suboptimal when one-way. These five premises are explained next.

First, paradoxically it is the recipient who communicates rather than the person who emits the message. (Therefore, the truism—a leader cannot lead until he has a follower.) While the communicator speaks, writes, or gesticulates a message, communication does not occur until the receiver(s) perceives it. Keep in mind that perception is a total experience as opposed to logic. And receivers vary in their sensory and mental capacities to perceive data inputs. Hence the first question that the communicator must ask prior to the sending of a message is, "Can the receiver perceive it?" That is, are the receivers sensorially and cognitively capable of ingesting and conceptualizing the message? The second question concerns the values, attitudes, and emotions of the recipient. Thus the query, "What is the receiver's particular mental set at this time?" The communicator is therefore dealing with psycho-physiological tolerances and conditioning factors that determine *if* the message is received and *how* it is interpreted.

Second, in most instances we perceive what we expect to find in the message. The unexpected or unwanted data are frequently ignored or filtered in line with our expectations. Basically, our human mind seeks to fit incoming data into a preestablished pattern of expectations. Consequently, before we attempt to communicate, we must predict what the recipient expects to hear or see. And we should keep in mind that minor discongruities will probably be rejected or distorted to fit the pattern. Thus, if the data are important, the communicator may find it necessary to apply sufficient "shock" or drive to the message so that it disturbs the pattern and alerts the recipient that the unexpected is occurring.

Third, the prime usage of communications is to influence or control. Therefore, it is always making demands on us to change or continue to do what we are doing, believe or not believe, and act or not act. Usually such demands are gradual or subliminal in that major demands are frequently resisted because they do not comply with the existing pattern of expectations.

Fourth, information and communications, although different, are nevertheless interdependent. Information is formal and logical. Conversely, communication is personal and psychological. Indeed, communications can occur without information. As an example, we can share in an experience while not receiving the logic of information. Also of interest is the difference between effective information and effective communication. The former is specific, terse, and structured. The latter is subjected to varying perceptions, expectations, and demands. It is debatable whether information once freed from these three conditions becomes more informative or whether, on the contrary, it tends to lose its meaning. Am I communicating this thought to you? What is your *perception*?

Fifth, one-way communication typically fails. It is dysfunctional for the obvious reason that we do not know if or how the recipient has perceived the message. Listening is important, but not sufficient to ensure that one has communicated. Moreover, the answer to better communications is clearly *not* more information. Usually more information tends to widen the communications gap between the sender and the receiver (information overload). Are not most of us today in need of more communications and less information?

The solution is threefold: (1) develop an understanding of the perceptions and expectations of the recipient, (2) assess the demands made in your message, and (3) seek feedback regarding the perception and reaction to your message. *Communications is a two-way process.*

TYPES OF COMMUNICATION CHANNELS[1]

The efficiency of a large formal organization is sizably enhanced when its own chain of command or decision or communication is tied into the informal network of groups within the organization, so that the network can be used to support the organization's goals.

—Bernard Berelson and Gary A. Steiner
Human Behavior: An Inventory of Scientific Findings
(New York: Harcourt, Brace & World, Inc., 1964), p. 370

Various channels of communication are available to the police supervisor for exchanging information. Commonly, a communications system is divided into formal and informal channels. We modify this list by dividing the informal communication channels into three subclasses: subformal, personal task directed, and personal nontask directed.

Formal Communication Channels

All organizations develop formal communication channels as a response to large size and the limited information-handling capability of each individual. The formal channels adhere to the recognized official structure of the organization. Accordingly, the formal communication channels transmit messages expressive of the legitimate structure of authority. Hence, one usually sees formal orders and directives, reports, official correspondence, standard operating procedures, and so on. Those persons who emphasize going through channels are doing so in deference to the unity of command principle within the formal hierarchy.

Strict compliance with formal channels can be dysfunctional. These dysfunctions are primarily in terms of time, creativity, and experience. To explain, first, it takes a long time for a formal message from a supervisor in one division to pass to another supervisor in another division. Second, formal messages are on the record and thus restrict the free flow of ideas. As an example, police officers may not want to expose their ideas to their supervisors for the time being, even in rough form; yet any formal communication is immediately routed through the originator's supervisor. Third, in practice a formal communication system cannot cover all informational needs. Informational needs change quite rapidly, while the formal channels change only with considerable time and effort. Therefore, the most urgent need for informal communication channels is to plug the gaps in the formal channels.

Informal Communication Channels

Regretfully, there are some who consider formal communication channels as the only way to transmit information so necessary to the functioning of the

[1]Pages 339–343 are taken from Paul M. Whisenand, *Police Supervision: Theory and Practice* (Englewood Cliffs, N.J.: Prentice Hall, 1976), pp. 311–324.

organization. However, this precept is no longer as sacred as it once was. Not only are we witnessing an interest in acquiring a better understanding of the informal organization, but along with it has come an awareness of its potential use. This interest and awareness quite naturally leads to a different perspective on the structuring of communication flow. In essence, this perspective does not confine organizationally useful communication to purely formal channels. It includes all the social processes of the broadest relevance in the functioning of any group or organization. Consequently, we now treat informal and personal communications as a supportive and frequently necessary process for effective functioning. Furthermore, the unofficial communication channels become a prime means for studying the informal organization. In fact, police supervisors are often expected to seek information through channels not officially sanctioned.

The prevalence of informal channels means that formal channels do not fully meet the important communications needs in a police department. Therefore, it is futile for police administrators to establish formal channels and assume that those channels will carry most of the messages. Ironically, the more restricted the formal channels, the greater is the growth of informal ones. However, while the informal system attempts to fill the gaps in the formal one, the leaders of a police organization can severely curtail the development of the former by simply ordering subordinates not to communicate with each other, by physically separating people, or by requiring prior clearance for any communication outside a certain division. In doing so, the number of meaningful messages is sharply reduced, thus affecting the overall effectiveness of the organization.

We next proceed to an analysis of three kinds of informal communication channels. The first two are task, or goal, oriented, while the third is oriented toward the individual.

Informal communication channels: subformal. Subformal channels carry those messages arising from the informal power structure existing in every police organization. Every member of the department must know and observe informal rules and procedures about what to communicate and to whom. Such rules are rarely written down and must be learned by experience and example, a necessity that causes difficulties for newcomers.

There are two types of subformal communications: those that flow along formal channels, but not as formal communications, and those that flow along purely informal channels. Both types have the distinct advantage of not being official; therefore, they can be withdrawn or changed without any official record being made. As a result, almost all new ideas are first proposed and tested as subformal communications. Significantly, the vast majority of communications in police organizations are subformal.

While in general it has been indicated that subformal channels meet the communication requirements not met by formal channels, they become all the more necessary under certain conditions. First, the greater the degree of interdependence among activities within the department, the greater is the number and use of subformal channels. Second, the more uncertainty about the objectives of the department, the greater is the number and use of subformal channels. When the environment is relatively unpredictable, people cannot easily determine what they should be doing simply by referring to that environment. Consequently, they tend to talk to each other more to gain an improved understanding of their situation. Third, when a police organization is operating under the pressure of time, it tends to use subformal channels extensively, because there is often no time to use the formal channels. Thus, police administrators reach out for information whenever they can get it from whatever channel is necessary. Fourth, if the divisions of a police organization are in strong competition, they tend to avoid subformal channels and communicate only formally. Conversely, closely cooperating sections rely primarily upon subformal communications. Hence, strong rivalry has significant communications drawbacks. Fifth, subformal communications channels are used more frequently if departmental members have stable, rather than constantly changing, relationships with each other.

Informal communication channels: personal task directed. A personal task-directed communication is one in which an organization member deliberately reveals something of his own attitude toward the activities of his own organization. While personal, this communication is also in terms of the goals or activities of the organization. Thus we can refer to it as task directed. It possesses the following characteristics. First, task-directed personal channels are nearly always used for informing rather than for directing. Second, before a person acts on the basis of information received through personal channels, he or she usually verifies that information through either subformal or formal channels. Third, this channel transmits information with considerable speed because there are no formal mechanisms to impede its flow. Fourth, because task-directed personal messages are transmitted by personnel acting as individuals, they do not bear the weight of the position emitting them. To this extent, they differ from subformal messages, which are transmitted by individuals acting in their official capacity—but not for the record.

Informal communication channels: personal nontask directed. As suggested by its title, this form of communication apparently does not contain information related to the tasks of the organization. Note the word *apparently*. Paradoxically, this channel may handle information on occasion far more valuable to the achievement of organizational goals than any other channel, including the formal ones. An example of this channel is the supervisor learning through a friendly subordinate of the reasons for growing job dissatisfaction. A discussion of its characteristics should provide an explanation of its utility. First, nontask-directed channels furnish a vehicle for an individual to satisfy his or her social needs. In doing so, a person experiences a certain degree of need fulfillment that carries over into the job, and, as described in earlier chapters, a person is more likely to remain with an organization if satisfied. Second, this channel provides a way for an individual to blow off steam over things that are disturbing. This pressure-release valve often reduces a person's level of tension to a point where she or he does not engage in acts

injurious to the functioning of the organization. Third, nontask-directed channels frequently supply useful feedback information to the management and
supervisory levels. This feedback is normally comprised of unexpected information not obtainable in any other way. Fourth, personal channels offer the
best medium for a person to become socialized in the organizational setting.
Unwritten standards, group values, and "the way we do things here" are conveniently expressed through nontask-directed channels.

METHODS OF COMMUNICATING

Let's review the various methods that we can use to convey information and
assess their strengths and weaknesses.

Oral

The method most used by people to communicate with one another is oral.
Popular forms of oral communication include speeches, formal one-on-one
and group discussions, and the informal rumor mill or grapevine.

The advantages of oral communications are speed and feedback. A verbal
message can be conveyed and a response received in a minimal amount of
time. If the receiver is unsure of the message, rapid feedback allows for early
detection by the sender and for correction.

The major disadvantage of oral communication surfaces whenever the
message has to be passed through a number of people. The more people a
message must pass through, the greater the potential for distortion. In a police
agency where decisions and other information are verbally passed up and down
the authority hierarchy, there exists considerable opportunity for messages to
become distorted.

Written

Written communications include memos, letters, organizational periodicals,
bulletin boards, or any other device that transmits via written words or symbols.

Written messages have advantages because of the fact that they are permanent, tangible, and verifiable. Typically, both the sender and receiver have a
record of the communication. The message can be stored. If there are questions
concerning the content of the message, it is physically available for later reference. This is particularly important for complex or lengthy communications. A
final benefit of written communication comes from the process itself. More
care is taken with the written word than with the oral word. Written communications are more likely to be well thought out, logical, and clear. After all, they
appear as departmental orders and regulations.

Of course, written messages have their drawbacks. They're time consuming. You could probably say the same thing in ten to fifteen minutes that it
takes you an hour to write. Thus, while writing may be more precise, it also

consumes a great deal more time. The other major disadvantage is feedback, or lack of it. Oral communications allow the receivers to rapidly respond to what they think they hear. However, written communications do not have a built-in feedback mechanism.

Nonverbal

Some of the most meaningful communications are neither transmitted verbally nor in writing. These are nonverbal communications. A loud siren at an intersection tells you something without words. A supervisor teaching a group of officers doesn't need words to tell when the trainees are bored. The size of a person's office and desk or the clothes people wear also send messages to others. However, the most well-known areas of nonverbal communication are body language and verbal intonations.

- Verbal intonations refer to the emphasis someone gives to words or phrases. A pleasant, smooth tone creates a different meaning than an intonation that is abrasive with strong emphasis placed on the last word.
- Body language includes everything from facial expressions to our sitting or standing posture.

Understand first—empathic listening. *The key to influencing another person is to first gain an understanding of that person.* As a supervisor, you must know your staff to influence them. Most of us are prone to want the other person to open their mind to our message. Wanting to understand the other person requires that *we open our mind to them.*

Consider this scenario. Sergeant Ker is speaking to Sergeant Paulson, "I can't understand Officer Hooper. He just won't listen to me." Sergeant Paulson replies, "You don't understand Hooper because *he* won't listen to *you*?" Ker answers, "That's what I said." Paulson remarks, "I thought that to understand another person, *you* needed to listen to *him*!" Ker realized that he didn't communicate with Hooper because he didn't understand him.

When we seek to understand, we are applying the principle of "empathy." *Empathy* is a Greek word. The "em-" part of empathy means "in." The "-pathy" part comes from *pathos*, which means "feeling" or "suffering." Empathy is not sympathy. Sympathy is a form of agreement, a form of judgment. We have empathy, then, when we place ourselves within the other person, so to speak, to experience his feelings as he experiences them. *This does not mean that we agree, simply that we understand the other viewpoint.*

Once we understand, we can proceed with the second step of the interaction: seeking to be understood. But now it is much more likely that we will actually be understood, because the other person's drive to be understood has been satisfied.

- To understand another person, we must be willing to be open to their thoughts.

- When we are open, we give people room to release their fixed positions and consider alternatives.
- Seeking first to understand lets us act from a position of knowledge.
- By seeking to understand, we gain influence in the relationship.
- Seeking first to understand leads people to discover other options.

When we seek to understand, people become less defensive about their position. They become more open to the question, "How can we *both* get what we want?" As they get their position out of the way, they begin to see their values more clearly so that they can use them as guidelines for creating and evaluating other options.

Empathic listening is particularly important under three conditions.

- When the interaction has a strong emotional component
- When we are not sure that we understand
- When we are not sure the other person feels confident that we understand

Under other circumstances, empathic responses can be counterproductive. For example, we don't need to reflect our understanding, nor would it be appreciated, when someone asks us what time is it.

Listening with the Eyes. *To truly understand, we must listen to more than words.* Words are weak compared with the richness and complexity of the ideas that we need to express. They are particularly poor at expressing feelings, for example, and yet feelings are often the thing that people most want us to understand. So when we seek to understand, we must look beyond the surface issues that the words describe, to consider how people feel.

Win-Win. The most vital part of empathic listening is developing a win-win attitude. *Win-win requires a nexus of courage and consideration.* It will give us success even when we are not adept at the skill. As we learn the skill, we will be that much better.

Empathic responses will destroy understanding if the attitude behind them is wrong. The danger of empathic listening is that we may use it because we believe that it "works." We may see it as a tool for getting what we want, or for manipulating people. If we use it with wrong intentions, we corrupt the skill. Empathic listening creates positive results only when we accept it as a useful principle, and use it solely with the intent to understand.

Now to Be Understood. Once we understand, we can then proceed to be understood. This is related to the earlier comment that win-win is a balance between courage and consideration. Understanding the other person shows consideration. Being understood takes courage. Both are necessary conditions for win-win agreements.

If, in the course of being understood, we sense resistance, we have another opportunity to choose again either to be defensive, or to seek to understand. So we may find ourselves moving back and forth between seeking to understand

and seeking to be understood. The process is complete when both parties feel understood, and when their interaction has given them a foundation for discovering other options. *This is what empowerment is all about* (see Responsibility Nine).

COMMUNICATIONS: DOWN, UP, AND LATERAL

Earlier we saw that communications flow in more than a single direction. Traditionally, communication flow was envisioned as being exclusively downward and synonymous with the pattern of authority. The pattern of authority provides, of course, the structure of an organization, but almost invariably it is found to represent an idealized concept of what the organization is like, or what it should be like, and this is why students of organization theory constantly need to investigate the informal structure for other directions of communication flow. The formal and informal channels indicate the three directions of communications in an organization. Furthermore, the content of the message varies with the direction of flow. The three directions possible for a message to flow are downward, upward, and laterally (horizontally). We begin our discussion by a look at the downward flow of messages.

Downward

Communications from supervisor to subordinate are of primarily five types.

1. Specific task directives: *job instructions*
2. Information to produce the understanding of the task and its relation to other organizational tasks: *job rationale*
3. Information concerning organizational *procedures and practices*
4. *Feedback* to the subordinate officer about his performance
5. Information to instill a sense of mission: *indoctrination of goals*

The first type of message is most often given priority in police organizations. Instructions about the position of police officer are communicated to the person through direct orders from the supervisor, training sessions, training manuals, and written directives. The objective is to ensure the reliable performance of every police officer in the organization. Less attention is given to the second type, which is designed to provide the police officer with a full understanding of his or her position and its relation to related positions in the same organization. Many police officers know what they are to do but not why. Withholding information on the rationale of the job not only reduces the loyalty of the member to the organization, but it also means that the organization must rely heavily on the first type of information, detailed instructions about the job. If a person does not understand why he or she should do something or how his or her job relates to other jobs performed by coworkers, then there must be sufficient repetition in the task instructions so that the individual behaves automatically. This problem is dramatically illustrated in the conflict about the information to be given to police officers about their functions. Some city and police administrators are in favor of reducing the police officer's behavior to that of a robot; others want to use the officer's intelligence by having him or her act on an understanding of the total situation. It can be seen, therefore, that the advantages of giving fuller information on job understanding are twofold: If an officer knows the reasons for an assignment, he or she will often carry out the job more effectively; and if the officer has an understanding of what the job is about in relation to the overall mission of the department, he or she is more likely to identify with its goals. Third, information about organizational procedures supplies a prescription of the role requirements of the organizational member. In addition to instructions about the job, the police officer is also informed about other duties and privileges as a member of the police organization. Fourth, feedback is necessary to ensure that the organization is operating properly. It is also a means for motivating the individual performer. However, feedback to the individual about how well he or she is doing in the job is often neglected or poorly handled, even in police organizations in which the managerial philosophy calls for such evaluation. Where emphasis is placed on compliance to specific task directives, it is natural to expect that such compliance will be recognized and deviation penalized. Fifth, the final type of downward-directed information has as its purpose to implant organizational goals, either for the total organization or a major unit of it. Consequently, an important function of a police supervisor is to describe the mission of the police department in an attractive and novel form. For example, a police supervisor may depict the role of the police department as the work of professional officers engaged in a constructive program of community improvement.

The size of the loop in downward communications affects organizational morale and effectiveness. In terms of morale, communications about the goals of the police organization cover in theory a loop as large as the organization itself. In practice, however, the rank-and-file officers are touched only minimally by this loop. Their degree of inclusion within the loop depends mainly upon how they are tied into the police organization. If they are tied in on the basis of being rewarded for a routine performance, information about the goals and policies of the overall structure will be of no interest to them. Therefore, the police supervisor should make every effort to see that subordinates are involved members of the organization. Next, the size of the loop affects the degree of understanding contained in a communication. Messages from top management addressed to all organizational personnel are often too general in nature and too far removed from the daily experiences of the line police officer to convey their intended meaning. To be effective, messages about departmental policy need to be translated at critical levels as they move down in the organization.

Hence, the police supervisor is required to translate a received message into specific meanings for subordinates. This does not necessarily mean that a police officer should get all his or her job directives from a single supervisor, but it does mean that additional supervisors should be used only if experts on a specialized function. To illustrate, the patrol officer, in addition to complying with the orders of an immediate supervisor, on occasion can also find relevant direction from a superior of a traffic, vice, or juvenile unit.

Upward

Communications from subordinate to supervisor are also of chiefly five types.

1. Information about his or her *performance* and *grievances*
2. Information about the *performance* and *grievances* of others
3. Feedback regarding organizational *practices* and *policies*
4. Feedback concerning what needs to be *done* and the *means* for doing it
5. Requests for *clarification* about goals and specific activities

However, there are great constraints on free upward communication for a variety of reasons. Most prominent is the structure itself. Simply stated, bureaucracies or highly formalized organizations tend to inhibit upward informal communications. In doing so, a tremendous amount of important information never reaches the upper-level decision centers. Other factors adversely affecting the upward flow of messages are as follows. Superiors are less in the habit of listening to their subordinates than in talking to them. Furthermore, information fed up the line is often used for control purposes. Hence the superior is not likely to be given information by subordinates that would lead to decisions affecting them adversely. They not only tell the superior what he or she wants to hear, but also what they want the supervisor to know. Employees do want to get certain information up the line, but generally they are afraid of presenting it in the most objective form. Full and objective reporting about one's own performance and problems is difficult. For all these reasons the upward flow of communication in police organizations is not noted for spontaneous and objective expression, despite attempts to formalize the process of feedback up the line. Importantly, it is not a problem of changing the communication habits of individuals, but of changing the organizational conditions responsible for these habits.

Horizontal

Communications between people at the same hierarchical level are basically of four types.

1. Information necessary to provide task *coordination*
2. Information for identifying and defining *common problems* to be solved through cooperation
3. Feedback from co-workers that fulfills social needs
4. Information needed to provide social (not organizational) control for a group so that it can maintain the members' compliance with its standards and values

Organizations face one of their most difficult problems in procedures and practices concerned with lateral communication. In essence, a working balance must be found between unrestricted and overrestricted communications among peers in an organization. To explain, unrestricted communications of a horizontal character can detract from maximum efficiency because too much nonrelevant information may be transmitted. At the opposite extreme, efficiency suffers if an employee receives all his or her instructions from the person above, thus reducing task coordination. Our position here is that some lateral communication is critical for an effective police organization. Police tasks cannot be so completely specified from above to rule out the need for coordination between peers. The type and amount of information that should be circulated on a horizontal basis is best determined by answering the question, "Who needs to know and why?" To put it another way, the information transmitted should be related to the objectives of the various units in the police organization, with primary focus on their major task. An interesting hang-up in horizontal communications occurs when people overvalue peer communication to the neglect of those below and above them. Sergeants talk only to sergeants, and lieutenants only to lieutenants. However, in many instances the really critical information is at levels below or above them.

Finally, as organizations move toward a greater authoritarian structure, they exert more and more control over any flow of horizontal information by outlawing the forms of free communication among equals. Consequently, employees cannot organize cooperative efforts and, in turn, the organization is adversely affected.

MESSAGES: VOLUME AND TYPES

The more communication there is, the more difficult it is for communication to succeed.

—Professor Wiio
Lecture, California State University-Long Beach, October 1979

Communication is costly. Every message involves the expenditure of time to decide what to send, time for composing, the cost of transmitting the message (which may consist of time or money, or both), and time spent in receiving the message. Consequently, the volume of messages in an organization is of real concern to an administrator. Not only do they take time and money, but they can also seriously hamper an individual because they subtract time from the working day. Plainly, the more time a person spends in searching or communicating, the less time there is for other types of activity. Furthermore, every individual has a saturation point regarding the amount of information that can be usefully handled in a given time period. In this case, both the volume and the length of the message can overload an individual beyond the saturation point. When overloaded, a person will be unable effectively either to comprehend the information provided or to use it. All of this means that the particular methods used by a police organization to collect, select, and transmit information are critically important determinants of its success. First, we take a closer look at the volume of messages; second, at the types of messages.

Volume

The volume of messages in a police organization is determined by six basic factors.

- The total number of members in the organization
- The nature of its communications networks (downward, upward, or horizontal)
- The transmission regulations controlling when and to whom messages are sent
- The degree of interdependence among the organization's various activities
- The speed with which relevant changes occur in its external environment
- The search mechanisms and procedures used by the organization to investigate its environment

High message volume usually results in overloading. Attempts are automatically made to reduce any overloading. Police supervisors can react to this situation in one or more of the following ways. First, they can slow down their handling of messages without changing the organization's network structure or transmission rules. This action will cause the police department to reduce its speed of reaction to events, and thereby lessen its output. Second, they can change the transmission rules so that their subordinates screen out more information before sending messages. This reaction also reduces the quantity of the department's output. Third, they can add more channels to the existing network to accommodate the same quantity of messages in the same time period. This reaction provides more opportunities for message distortion and is more expensive. Fourth, they can relate tasks within the organization so that those units with the highest message traffic are grouped together within the overall communications system. This action reduces the volume of messages sent through higher levels in the network and facilitates the coordination of effort. Fifth, they can improve the quality of the messages in order to reduce the time needed for receiving, composing, and transmitting them. Furthermore, besides bettering the content and format of the message, the supervisor can decide on more advantageous methods for handling them. In conclusion, a police organization compelled by its functions to maintain a high volume of messages must inevitably suffer certain disadvantages over a department functioning with a low message volume.

Types

Messages vary in content and form. There are reports, statements, inquiries, questions, accounts, comments, notes, records, recommendations, rejoinders, instructions, and so on. Each message may have a different purpose in control procedures and lead to a different response. Furthermore, messages can be transmitted either formally or informally by one of three media: (1) written communication, (2) oral communication in face-to-face meeting of two or more individuals, and (3) oral communication in telephone conversations.

Written messages.   Samuel Eilon groups written messages into six categories (see Table 4-1): routine reports, memoranda, inquiries, queries, proposals, and decisions.

1. *Routine report.* A routine report is a message that supplies information as part of a standard operation. There are two ways in which a report can be created: (1) time triggered: a report called for at set time intervals (e.g., a police supervisor is required to send weekly reports on the activities of subordinates), and (2) event triggered: a report called for when certain tasks are completed (e.g., a report is to be sent when a case is finished or when certain training has been provided to subordinates).

   In each of these examples, the initiative to make a report does not lie with the supervisor; the circumstances under which a report is issued are clearly specified by organizational procedures. The supervisor is required

TABLE 4-1   Types of Messages in a Communications System

Types	Subtypes
Written	
Routine report	Time-triggered report
	Event-triggered report
Memorandum	Statement, following an inquiry or event triggered
	Comment
	Details on data collection and processing, as follows, may be included:
	Data from available records
	Ad hoc data collection
	Routine data processing
	Ad hoc processing
Inquiry	Inquiry covered by standing procedures
	Inquiry about a novel situation
Query	Query about problems covered by regular procedures
	Query on novel situations or to clarify ambiguities and inconsistencies
Proposal	Proposal about procedures or recurrent events
	Proposal on an ad hoc issue
Decision	Decision on procedures affecting recurrent events
	Decision on ad hoc issues
Oral	
Meeting, the outcome of which may be any or several messages above	
Telephone discussion	

Reprinted from "Taxonomy of Communications" by Samuel Elion, published by Administrative Science Quarterly Volume 13 (Sept. 1968), p. 278, Table 1, by permission of Administrative Science Quarterly.

only to determine that the circumstances conform to the specifications. Frequently, the contents of the report are prescribed, either in the format the report is to take (as in the case of a predesigned form) or in the information it is expected to furnish, although the supervisor can exercise limited initiative as to the content and coverage.

2. *Memorandum.* A memorandum also supplies information, but not as a part of a routine procedure. A memorandum can be (1) *a statement of fact,* submitted in response to an inquiry, to aid in evaluating a problem or to prepare proposals for action; (2) *a statement that is event triggered,* released when circumstances have changed in an unprescribed manner, calling for some initiative by the transmitter in drawing attention of others to the change so that a plan of action can be formulated; or (3) *a comment,* made in response to some other statement to add information or to give a different interpretation of data.

This explanation does not mean that all routine reports are devoid of initiative, whereas all memoranda are not. If a memorandum is made in response to a request, then the initiative for generating the memorandum lies with the requesting individual, not with the person who created the memorandum. And although event-triggered routine reports do not call for any initiative to create them, initiative may be exercised in composing their content, while event-triggered memoranda may not call for a great deal of initiative with respect to content. There is a distinction between a prescribed event, which triggers a report, and an event that generates a memorandum: the first is described by "*When* event such and such occurs, then, . . . ," the second, by "*If* the following event occurs, then, . . . ," The first describes an event that is expected to occur, the second, an event that may occur. This is the basic difference between the circumstances that lead to reports and those that lead to memoranda.

The creation of a message containing information (report or memorandum) may include one or several of the following activities: (1) extracting data from records; (2) processing data, including computations and analysis, on a routine basis; (3) collecting data as needed; and (4) processing data as needed. In the case of reports, activities are generally confined to the first two activities, whereas memoranda may include all four.

3. *Inquiry.* An inquiry is a message requesting information to assist in evaluating a given problem, usually before making recommendations for action. The response to such a request would be a memorandum, which would include a statement with the necessary information and an analysis of the data. An inquiry usually involves information not included in reports, unless the reports are time triggered and the information is required before the next report is due. Relatedly, an inquiry may meet with a comment, which asks for clarification or points out the difficulties in providing certain information in the time specified. Such a comment is usually generated when the inquiry is ambiguous.

4. *Query.* A query is a message defining the characteristics of a problem and asking for instructions or proposals about courses of resolution. A query is

often made by a subordinate concerning problems not fully covered by standing regulations, either because of the novelty of the situation or because of ambiguities or inconsistencies in procedures. Furthermore, a query may also be generated by a supervisor seeking advice and direction from peers or subordinates.

5. *Proposal.* A proposal describes a course of action the writer feels should be taken. It can be the result of several exchanges of queries, inquiries, reports, and memoranda. It may be generated by a subordinate, on her or his own initiative, or at the instigation of a supervisor; or it may be created by a supervisor wishing to test the reactions of peers or subordinates. A response to a proposal may take the form of a comment or a counterproposal. The absence of a reaction to a proposal is usually viewed as tacit approval.

6. *Decision.* A decision states the action to be taken. This message may be of two kinds: (1) a decision that affects recurrent events, which provides direction, not only on how to handle the particular event that caused the discussion prior to the decision, but also similar events in the future (such a decision is made to avoid handling similar problems on an ad hoc basis in the future and to delegate the action for such problems to a lower level in the organization), and (2) a decision on an ad hoc problem, which does not formally affect future procedures.

   A decision can take a number of forms. It may begin with a request to review the causes that necessitate making a decision to resolve certain problems; it may continue by outlining alternative courses of action and explaining the reasons for the rejection of some; it may then specify what has been decided and how the decision is to be implemented; next it may indicate what feedback is expected to keep the decision maker informed of progress in implementation.

Oral messages.   Oral messages are of two varieties: meetings (face to face) and telephone conversations (ear to ear).

7. *Meetings.* A meeting involves a discussion among two or more people. Meetings have four purposes: (1) to provide a means for exchanges to take place quickly, (2) to provide a job environment in which members are stimulated to new ideas by the rapid exchange of views between individuals, (3) to reduce the amount of semantic difficulties through face-to-face interaction, and (4) to get the members attending the meeting committed more strongly to given proposals or procedures than they would be otherwise.

   There are two types of meetings: routine meetings, such as those of permanent committees, and ad hoc meetings, called to discuss particular issues. The difference between a routine and an ad hoc meeting is similar to that between a routine report and a memorandum. Like a routine report, a routine meeting can be either time or event triggered, whereas an ad hoc meeting may either be called in regard to a request to consider a particular problem or be event triggered. Furthermore, a meeting can result in the issuance of any one or several of the messages, listed earlier; a report, a memorandum, an inquiry for further information, a request for instructions, a proposal, or a decision. Significantly, a meeting can also fizzle out and end inconclusively.

8. *Telephone conversations.* Many of the comments made on meetings are pertinent to telephone communications. The distinction made earlier between routine and ad hoc communications may be useful here. There are, however, some noteworthy differences between the two media: (1) a telephone conversation is generally confined to two participants, and (2) it lacks certain unique characteristics of interaction that take place in a face-to-face exchange.

COMMUNICATION NETWORKS

The vertical and horizontal dimensions in departmental communications can be combined into a variety of patterns or into what is referred to as communication networks.

Five Networks

Five common networks are shown in Figure 4-1; these are the chain, Y, wheel, circle, and all-channel. In Figure 4-1, the chain network represents a five-level vertical hierarchy where communications can only move upward or downward. In a police department, this type of network could be found in direct-line authority relations with no deviations. For example, the officer reports to the

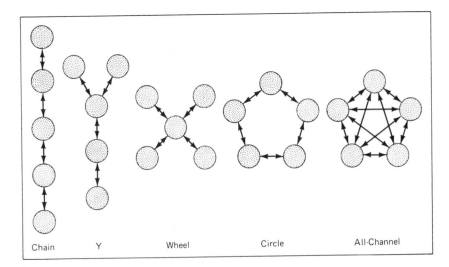

| Chain | Y | Wheel | Circle | All-Channel |

Figure 4-1 Common Communication Networks (H. Cohen, "Changing Small Group Communication Networks," *ASQ* 6 [March 1992], p. 448. Reprinted by permission.)

sergeant, who in turn answers to the lieutenant, who reports to the captain, who is responsible to the chief of police.

If we turn the Y network upside down, we can see two subordinates reporting to a supervisor, with two levels of hierarchy still above the supervisor. This is, in effect, a four-level hierarchy.

If we look at the wheel diagram in Figure 4-1 as if we were standing above the network, it becomes obvious that the wheel represents a police supervisor with four officers. However, there is no interaction between the subordinates. All communications are channeled through the supervisor.

The circle network allows members to interact with adjoining members, but no further. It represents a three-level hierarchy in which there is vertical communication between superiors and subordinates and lateral communication only at the lowest level.

Finally, the all-channel network allows each subject to communicate freely with the other four. It is the least structured. While it is like the circle in some respects, the all-channel network has no central position. However, there are no restrictions; all members are equal. This network is best illustrated by a task force, where no one member either formally or informally assumes a dominant or take-charge position.

Which Is Most Effective?

Which network is most effective totally depends on your purpose. No single network will be best for all situations. If speed is critical, the wheel and all-channel networks are preferred. The chain, Y, and wheel score high on accuracy. The structure of the wheel facilitates the emergence of a leader. The circle and all-channel networks are best if the goal is to have high employee satisfaction. Again, what are your intentions as a police supervisor in transmitting a particular message? This determines which network you should employ.

FLIP SIDE OF "INFORMATION AGE"

The phrase "information age" has come to denote the explosion in information technology and its impact upon society. The industrial age manufactured things, whereas the information age generates information.

We now rely on several sophisticated electronic media to carry our communications. In addition to the more common media (the telephone or a public address system), we have closed-circuit television, voice-activated computers, xerographic reproduction, and a host of other electronic devices that we can use in conjunction with speech or paper to create more effective communication. Electronic mail (E-mail) and FAX machines are two recent and rapidly growing technologies. The cellular car phone will further expand our communications capacity. The "car FAX" will also.

Electronic capabilities, especially via digitalization, have expanded so rapidly that new technologies with new capabilities appear even before society has adjusted to the impact of present technology. Many of us still struggling to master a multiprogrammable VCR are being offered Prodigy and other television information services. Disseminating information has become a major factor in the economy. Roughly 1,000 specialized periodicals hit the mail every year, progressively examining narrower subjects. Publishers print 1,000 new book titles each day, and the sum of printed information doubles every eight years. Less than ten years ago, IBM introduced the desktop personal computer. Within three years, 10 million personal computers sat on office desks across the country. Now, more than 40 million operate in homes and offices. Currently, nearly 50 percent of the U.S. work force helps create, process, or transmit information, and 40 percent of all business investments go into information technology.

To handle the tidal wave of information generated via faster transmission systems, miniaturization has become evermore popular. One 5¼-inch compact disk can now store an entire 250,000-page encyclopedia and still have room left over. Other technologies promise to harness ever greater tasks and place them at the disposal of the user.

Even though these technological advances originally sought to control information and bring order to the office, in many instances they have done just the opposite. The electronic office promised to reduce paper work and lessen work loads, but it has, in fact, generated more information that must still be printed and—even more challenging—*be assimilated.* Since computers entered office systems, *paper use has increased sixfold and work weeks have lengthened.* From 1973 to 1987, leisure time shrank from 26.2 hours per week to 16.6, according to a Roper Organization study in *Psychology Today* magazine, and the number of hours spent at the office rose to 47 from 41. The 1990s are revealing the same trend—more work and less play.

The harder people work, the less time they have, and that creates anxiety. It also encourages the creation of new instruments that further the anxiety. During 1988, businesses purchased more than one-half of the 1.6 million FAX machines currently in use—and added another 1.2 million in 1989.

Given the opportunity, many people would leave the electronic environment altogether. A recent survey asked respondents what activities they would pursue if given an extra four hours a day. Their responses ignored the new technology and showed a strong desire to sever contact with the electronic flow:

- 33 percent—read
- 31 percent—fix things around the house
- 27 percent—pursue hobbies
- 26 percent—socialize

(The total exceeds 100 percent because respondents could select more than one answer.)

Information alone does not answer bigger questions. From a social viewpoint, information has not brought individuals any closer to understanding the deeper, significant questions of life and morality. From that perspective, learning from information becomes merely functional, not enlightening. Additionally, while technology such as E-mail and FAX machines have enhanced the movement of information, they in turn are impeding communication. There is no substitute for face-to-face communications. We see "FAX potatoes" emerging. They'll FAX you a message rather than walk a few feet to communicate with you in person. We're getting tons of information with only a few pounds.

Robert Fulghum's popular book, "*All I Really Need to Know I Learned in Kindergarten*," cuts through the information glut to reconnect with some cultural fundamentals. The lessons of kindergarten — *interpersonal and psychological development — remain significant*, Fulghum insists, whereas later lessons — skills for acquiring, digesting, and using information — seem transient. For those overcome by the rising tide of facts and figures, seeking more personal and long-lasting communications may offer a stabilizing response to the information overload.

BARRIERS TO EFFECTIVE COMMUNICATION

Today, communication itself is the problem. We have become the world's first overcommunicated society.

—Al Ries and Jack Trout

Unfortunately, positioned in between you, the sender, and the receiver are a number of barriers or distorters that create confusing or misinterpreted messages. The more salient are:

- *Filtering.* This involves either the sender or receiver intentionally manipulating information.
- *Selective perception.* The receiver, in the communication process, selectively sees and hears based on his or her needs, motivations, experience, background, and other personal characteristics. The receiver also projects his or her interests and expectations into communications in decoding them.
- *Emotions.* How the receiver feels at the time of receipt of a communication message influences how he or she interprets it.
- *Words.* Words mean different things to different people. Age, education, and cultural background are three of the more obvious variables that influence the language people use and the definitions they give to words. Senders tend to assume that the words and terms they use mean the same to the receiver as they do to them. This, of course, is often incorrect and thus creates communication difficulties.
- *Information overload.* Technology makes it possible for police supervisors to have, at their fingertips, a wealth of up-to-date information on those activities for which they are responsible or that they need to know about. Supervisors are forced to ignore or give only a cursory review of many

messages. The result is that some messages are overlooked or misinterpreted.

- *Nonverbal signs.* When nonverbal cues are inconsistent with the oral message, the receiver becomes confused and the clarity of the message suffers. The lieutenant who tells you that he sincerely wants to hear about your problem and then proceeds to read his mail while you talk is sending conflicting signals.
- *Time pressures.* Supervisors frequently function under time pressures. These pressures can create communication problems when, to expedite matters, formal channels are short-circuited, leaving some people in the dark, and when messages that are transmitted are incomplete or ambiguous to the receiver.

REMOVING THE BARRIERS

In times of complexity, information is a rather cheap and available commodity. There are many providers, from internal government to private data houses. Insight, implication, applications skill in communication are not readily available. When someone asks for information, more often than not what he or she really wants is insight or solution.

—Arnold Brown and Edith Weiner
Super Managing: How to Harness Change for Personal and Organizational Success
(New York: McGraw-Hill Book Company, 1984), p. 26

The importance of maintaining effective communications was never more vital than it is today. Every aspect of human endeavor within a police organization depends in some way on communication. Although it is a vital part of every police supervisor's job, communication remains a highly personal art. Human beings have been communicating with each other by gestures and signs since the origin of the species, by spoken words for perhaps half a million years, and by some form of writing for more than four thousand years. We should be experts at it by now! The major problem today is not that we are not experts at communication, but that the demands now being placed on human communication threaten to exceed its capacity. Since communications is a human activity, even though machines may be used to assist people in interacting, we emphasize a fundamental principle: The effectiveness of communication tends to be directly proportional to the degree to which both the sender and the receiver regard and treat each other as "human" in the sociocultural context of the event. The following techniques or basics for effective communication should be evaluated and implemented with this principle in mind.

A tremendous number of techniques have been developed whereby supervisors may remove or bypass the blockage at each point in the communication process. The major techniques may be broadly classified in terms of the blockage they remedy. There are five areas where blockage might occur in a communication system: (1) senders, those who initiate a message; (2) message, the vehicle for transmitting information; (3) symbol, the content and format of the information; (4) channel, the means for interchanging messages; and (5) receivers, those who receive a message. The major techniques for overcoming the blockages follow:

Overcoming Sender Blockage

The sender of a message should:

- Create special positions or units whose function is to disseminate information inside or outside the organizations.
- Use formal and informal reporting systems.
- Use the grapevine.
- Solicit feedback.
- Simplify language.
- Use appropriate nonverbal cues.

Reducing Message Blockage

The content of a message can be clarified by:

- Using more than one medium (e.g., written and verbal).
- Regulating the timing to avoid periods of information overloads.
- Repeating the message at a certain time interval.
- Developing format standards for the reports.
- Summarizing long or complex messages.

Decreasing Symbol Blockage

The symbols we transmit, or words, are more apt to accurately depart the sender and access the receiver if:

- All are trained in the use of special terms and acronyms (DOA, FTO, 211, TA, etc.).
- Visual aids, graphs, charts, and so on, are used.
- One is alert for emotionally charged symbols and nonverbal cues.

Coping with Channel Blockage

Communications channels can be cleared by the following practices:

- Carefully routing messages into the most proper channel (e.g., face-to-face conversation).
- Developing openness and human trust.
- Using more than one channel.
- Being concise.

- If the channel you use bypasses someone who should be informed, making certain that she or he is made aware of that particular message. No surprises!

Combating Receiver Blockage

The receiver should endeavor to:

- Opt for more than a single message.
- Ask for definition on all symbols that are ambiguous or are subject to more than a single translation.
- Know thyself. What are your predilections and biases?
- Seek the advice of others when interpreting the contents of a message.
- Listen actively.
- Watch for nonverbal cues.

Point

The use of such techniques is, by itself, no guarantee of better communication. Any one of them, in helping to cope with one source of blockage, may create still another kind. If many of them together resulted in much more communication, the result could be a serious increase in the information overload. The appropriate use of well-known techniques and the invention of new ones are rooted in the broader reasoning of police supervisors who have acquired an interest in the communication process and the ability to communicate. The supervisor with an interest in communication is one who, instead of taking communication for granted, is always aware of the possibility of blockage at any point. Perhaps of greatest importance is that the police supervisors understand the communication system in their organization.

Counterpoint

Given our knowledge that information can be a significant source of power in a police department, it should not come as a surprise to find that supervisors do not always seek to achieve maximum clarity in their communication. There are very few police supervisors who will publicly come out against better communication; however, many resist initiatives to improve communications because it works against their personal interests and those of their unit. Keeping communications fuzzy cuts down on questions, permits faster decision making, minimizes objections, reduces opposition, makes it easier to deny one's earlier statements, preserves freedom to change one's mind, helps to preserve mystique and hide insecurities, allows one to say several things at the same time, permits one to say "no" diplomatically, helps to avoid confrontation and anxiety, and provides other similar benefits that work to the advantage of the supervisor.

Ironically, clear communications tie supervisors' hands and limit their flexibility in responding to contingencies. Therefore, it should be expected to find practicing supervisors using communication barriers as a technique for gaining and maintaining power.

CONCLUSION: A CHALLENGE

A wise man's heart guides his mouth, and his lips promote instruction.

—Proverbs 13:13

As a supervisor, you are a gatekeeper. It is through you that information is channeled to the top of the department. Too often the greatest mistake made by supervisors is thinking that information is independent of the manner in which it is communicated. It is not; nor should it be. The voluminous report may speak well of effort but speak not at all of insight, implication, or value added. The summary page may be cleverly composed but may lose all the richness and depth of understanding embodied in preliminary material.

Review the nature of the information that leaves your desk by deed, voice, or written word. Is it just information? Or are you genuinely and personally excited by the intriguing nature of what is contained in your document or presentation? Have you truly considered your audience and what would motivate it to act on your information? Is there enough in what you have to say that is new? Have you made pronouncements of change in a threatening manner, or have you skillfully assured the recipient that opportunity is to be had from seemingly threatening new circumstances? Have you thought through the internal political consequences of the information you are transmitting, even to the extent of having done some preliminary work in building a broad-based constituency in support of your information or suggested actions? And, most important, do you undermine yourself by appearing to believe that you are smarter than those to whom you are delivering the information and therefore oversimplify or excessively repeat the contents of your presentation? Finally, have you taken advantage of opportunities made available to you to bring others along in the acquisition and acceptance of information about change?

KEY POINTS

- Supervising is basically a communication process.
- Communications is the sending and understanding of a message.
- Communications is influenced by our perceptions and experiences, makes demands on us, is related to but different than information, and is best when not "one-way."
- Communication channels are of two types: formal and informal.
- We transmit messages three ways: orally, in writing, and via nonverbal cues.
- In an organization, messages can travel laterally, upward, and downward.

- Empathic listening is based on first understanding another person and then making one's self understood.
- Written messages can be categorized as reports, memoranda, inquiries, queries, proposals, and decisions.
- There are five communications networks. Each has its own unique purpose and limitations.
- An information glut is hampering communications.
- There are seven barriers to effective communications, ranging from filtering to time pressures.
- Steps can be taken to reduce the adverse influence of each barrier.
- Your effectiveness as a supervisor and communicator is directly tied to your motivations to be effective.

DISCUSSION

1. What is the key link between the supervisor serving as a leader and acting as a decision maker?
2. What information do we usually find moving in a formal channel as compared to the informal channels?
3. Of the three main methods for communicating, which is best?
4. In which direction is it most difficult (up, down, horizontally) for a supervisor to communicate? Why?
5. Of the five communications networks, which is best? Why?
6. What have you or your organization done to improve the human communications process?
7. When have you either performed or observed empathic listening? What did the listener actually do?

STRUCTURED EXPERIENCES

1. Exercise: Mutual Understanding

Purpose. The intent of this exercise is to enhance mutual understanding, appreciation, and cooperation among team members.

Instructions. Each participant is to take a piece of posterboard and one or more felt-tip pens. Divide the posterboard into eight areas. Use symbols, pictures, or words to depict each area as follows:

Area 1. My immediate major job challenge is . . .

Area 2. Professionally, I am looking forward to . . .

Area 3. In the past six months I have assisted another department/team member by . . .

Area 4. In the past six months I have received assistance from another department/team member in the way of . . .

Area 5. In the past twelve months my major accomplishment was . . .

Area 6. In the past twelve months my major failure was . . .

Area 7. Presently, or soon, I will need team support in . . .

Area 8. I wish to thank (*team member*) for . . .

You have twenty minutes to complete your chart. Then each person will stand and make a three-minute presentation explaining each area.

2. Exercise: Group Communications

At the recent police management staff meeting (the management team is comprised of captains, lieutenants, and sergeants), the chief announced with detectable pride that the department had received a grant award (one year) of $450,000 from the Brookings Institution. The only stipulation attached to the grant is that the funds must be expended on a "career-oriented employee morale development program." Any monies not used will be returned to Brookings. The program will be closely monitored in terms of successful and nonsuccessful components. In addition, an external evaluator will be employed to fully assess the overall value of the entire program. The chief stressed that the program is destined to receive nationwide attention and may well be selected as an "exemplary project." Furthermore, the city council and city manager have given their full and unanimous approbation to the program.

The chief has instructed the management staff to generate a tentative program for his review and concurrence. The staff has approximately one hour to formulate a proposal. The following list gives estimated costs for various employee-oriented improvements that might enhance morale—if implemented. *The list is open-ended and can be augmented as deemed appropriate.* (Ball-park figures are acceptable when assessing an option not cited. However, the agency has about 120 sworn personnel, which should be considered when computing an estimated expenditure of funds.) The chief's parting comment was most pointedly, "What can be done to increase morale within this department of ours? I have a lot of faith in your judgment, gentlemen!"

Possible List	Estimated Cost
Full medical/dental reimbursement	$ 45,000
Academic pay incentive	78,000
Four/forty (ten plan) work week	110,000
Three more days of holidays	55,000
Three more days of vacation	55,000
Management/supervision merit pay incentive	97,000
Improved retirement (age fifty)	149,000
Prepaid life insurance	31,000
In-service training programs	27,000
	(Continued)

Possible List	Estimated Cost
Senior officer plan (police agent)	42,000
Educational reimbursement	24,000
New patrol/detective radio cars	157,000
Physical fitness training room	93,000
Departmental psychologist	34,000
Employee recreational program	16,000
Assign city cars to all police captains	9,000
Clothing allowance for all uniformed staff	9,000
Physical fitness pay incentive	8,500
Shooting pay incentive	7,500
One and one-half paid overtime	103,000
Fully paid retirement	97,000
Paid sabbatical (every eight years) of three months	73,000
Other	?

At this time the group is to negotiate a proposed program for elevating the morale of the officers on the department. Use as much of the total grant dollar figure as is possible. Assume that your discussion and recommendations are being tape recorded.

3. Exercise: Empathetic Listening

1. Identify a situation in which you should use the skill and attitude of empathy.

_____

_____

_____

2. What benefit might occur from your use of empathy in this situation?

_____

_____

_____

3. What may happen if you don't use empathy?

_____

_____

_____

4. Would it be helpful to inform the other person of your intention to try to be a better listener and to ask for his or her support as you try out this approach? Why or why not?

_____

_____

_____

RESPONSIBILITY FIVE

Time Management: Focusing on Values, Ethics, Leadership, and Communications

Time\tim\n[Me,fr]: the measured or measurable period during which an action, process, or condition exists or continues.

Once you have a clear vision of your priorities (values and ethics); an understanding of the individual requirements for being a leader; and a means to effectively convey the foregoing to others, then you organize and execute around them.

Have you ever heard or used the expression, "I'll save some time by taking this approach?" Or, "I really lost a lot of time by doing it that way?" Time is not ours to bank or spend. It is a precisionally measured period of seconds, minutes, and hours that eventually become a day and, with a great deal of time, we arrive at a millennium (e.g., the year 2000).

On May 6, 1954, Roger Bannister achieved a major breakthrough in time — he ran a 3:59:6 mile. Now, many track athletes have run a sub–four-minute mile. Will the year 2000 see a sub–three-and-a-half-minute mile, or a sub–two-minute-mile marathon? The athletes that eventually will succeed in doing so will not be managing time, they'll be managing themselves.

Once you've finished this chapter, you'll be managing your time by managing yourself. This responsibility will, if you truly intend to manage your time, require much more thought and effort than the mere number of pages would suggest. If done properly, this responsibility will require twice the investment of time as compared with the other fourteen responsibilities. You'll discover that much of what you will do depends on the accomplishment of the four prior responsibilities. If you have those well in mind, you'll find the necessary steps for fulfilling Responsibility Five to be richly rewarding and even fun. Moreover, you'll be incrementally closer to what we earlier assumed you sought to become—an effective police supervisor.

A COUPLE OF QUESTIONS FOR YOU

On a sheet of paper write down a short answer to the following questions. (Later on you'll find that your responses are important—be certain to write your answers.)

First, what one thing could you do consistently (i.e., you're not doing it now) that would make a significant change in your personal life?

Second, what one thing in your career life would cause similar results?

OUR MISSION

We gain control of time and events by understanding how they relate to our mission. Responsibility Five is the exercise of our independent will for becoming a more effective supervisor, which automatically means a more effective person. We do not lead a compartmentalized life. The various roles that we play out in life definitely overlap and influence one another. If you spot a wise time manager at work, you'll probably discover that this individual also prudently manages time as a father or mother, family member, sports participant, hobby enthusiast, and so on. Conversely, the worker who is managed by time, misses deadline dates, is late to work, or unprepared to do the tasks is probably the same way in attempting to fulfill other life roles.

Hence, our approach to time management *must* involve the total you. Dealing with your role of supervisor exclusively would be meaningless, or at best a long list of "to-do's," many of which would never get done. Obviously we'll concentrate on making your time at work more productive. At the same time, remember when we use the term *mission* we mean your comprehensive mission in life—the total you.

PEOPLE, PEOPLE, PEOPLE

A nationally recognized business leader wrote, "My firm basically is comprised of manufacturing, service and people. In order of importance they are: people, people, people."

Ken Blanchard has produced a business around the concept of a "one-minute manager." His logo is a one-minute readout from the face of a modern digital watch. The logo is intended to remind us to take a minute out of each day to look into the faces of the people we supervise and to realize that *they* are our most important asset. Our proposition is that clearly much more than one minute should be devoted to this interaction.

If you accept the preceding premise that people are a police agency's greatest asset, then supervisors must understand how to bind them together in a culture wherein they feel truly motivated to achieve high goals. Face-to-face communication, ongoing training and development, creative incentive programs, and job security all display the sort of sensitivity that nurtures strong departmental cultures. Every strong culture derives from management's sensitivity. Without it police employees feel unmotivated, underused, and even exploited. Building the kind of work culture and work team you want obviously takes time. Quality time. Priority time. In the next few pages we'll show you how to do it.

TIME DIMENSION

One complexity is ever present in every supervisory job: every decision, every action demands due consideration of the time dimension. Supervisors have to assess both today and tomorrow—the present and the future. Little Orphan Annie sang in the musical of the 1980s, "Tomorrow, tomorrow, tomorrow is just a day away." The astute supervisor understands and reacts to the tacit message conveyed in this lyric.

The challenge of harmonizing today and tomorrow exists in all areas and especially with people. The time dimension is inherent in supervision because supervision is concerned with decisions for *action*. The time dimension influences decisions for *progress* (e.g., crime reduction, crime prevention). Finally, the supervisor's time dimension entails the *future*. One international airline's motto is "Being prepared in everything." The successful police supervisor is in constant preparation for the incoming future—the next event, the next decision, the next risk, all the while knowing that they'll be different. Again, time for action, time for progress, and a time for tomorrow—you've got to get a grip on this threefold time dimension.

TIME AND PRODUCTIVITY

Most of us want to feel productive. Those who do, do not want to waste their time. After all, time is our most perishable resource. There is nothing less productive than idle time of capital equipment (patrol cars) or wasted time of highly paid and able police employees. Equally unproductive—even counterproductive—may be jamming more work effort into time than it will comfortably hold. For instance, the attempt to provide full patrol coverage by repeatedly paying overtime to officers that are daily becoming more fatigued and less quality conscious. The most productive—or least productive—time is that of the supervisor himself. Yet it is usually the least known, least analyzed, and least managed factor of delivering police services.

Time and productivity are causally linked. You have to pay attention to both factors. However, *solid time management is the forerunner of highly productive supervisors.*

OVERLOADS

Many years ago you would hear police supervisors complain, "I don't get enough information to do my job." The 1950s started to flip such statements to where today we hear, "Good grief, there's just too much information. I don't have the *time* to process it!"

There has never been more media—new television networks and channels, video and film, record numbers of new magazines, newsletters, journals, and newspapers—dedicated to delivering you the changing news of the day. Compounding this is the computer—desktop, laptop, in-car terminals, and even wrist-top. You don't have to look for a telephone today—they're in airplanes, trains, automobiles, and frequently seen on a person's hip. We have "E-mail" and "voice mail." Then there is the omnipresent FAX. Finally, we have the advanced photocopying machines—"Let's make a copy for everybody!"

What are you absorbing? Do you have the time to process the multitude of incoming messages, much less add yours to the information glut? Incidentally, have you noticed that the so-called paperless society actually has more paper than before? And, while you're receiving and sending more information, much faster, much of it doesn't make sense, or you haven't the time to make sense out of it.

Without a structure, a frame of reference, the vast amount of data that comes your way each day will probably whiz right by you.

Probably in reaction to the overloads of his day, Lao Tzu wrote nearly 4,000 years ago to the leaders of China:

Endless drama in a group clouds consciousness. Too much noise overloads the senses. Continual input obscures genuine insight. Do not substitute sensationalism for learning.

Allow regular time for silent reflection. Turn inward and digest what has happened. Let the senses rest and grow still.

Teach people to let go of their superficial mental chatter and obsessions. Teach people to pay attention to the whole body's reaction to a situation.

When group members have time to reflect, they can see more clearly what is essential in themselves and others.

It takes time for reflection. Overloads attempt to block such time allocation. The supervisor must assign it a high priority. If not, any endeavor to manage one's time is doomed to fail. Mark McCormack (sports consultant) puts it this way—"You must take some time to take control of your time."

IF IT'S WORTH DOING, IT'S WORTH DOING POORLY

Take a moment and re-read the title of this section. This comment was made by a very successful person. Think about it. Before reading further attempt to develop some type of a rationale for refuting or confirming, "If it's worth doing, it's worth doing poorly."

Let us now add—*to make the best use of your time, you have to make a habit of using it flat out.* Conversely, do you not agree with the proposition that working hard is not necessarily the same as working smart? One more thought —is working hard and working fast synonymous?

Many of us prefer fast decisions to slowness and wrong ones to none at all. Throughout his writings Tom Peters challenges us to "move, move, move." The preceding heading essentially means that if something is vitally important, make a decision quickly. It may cause less than perfect results (even poor results), but the fact remains someone is taking on the problem. It's the quick and timely response, with the underlying knowledge that you're doing the best you can. Now the big *but—slow decisions are usually better than fast ones.* It has been demonstrated again and again that shared or participative decision making produces significantly better results. Further, shared decision making typically builds in a commitment on the part of those involved to implement it.

Fast or slow—which should it be? No doubt both approaches impact on your truly unreplaceable commodity—time. We believe the answer to this puzzle is both—sometimes a fast, sometimes a slow application of time. Both have their place in police organizations. An emergency situation (e.g., robbery in progress) obviously requires fast decisions, a fast timeframe. Many supervisors fall prey to all decisions being made fast, when in most cases there is ample time to involve those in the decisions that are going to affect them. Getting one or two really good ideas normally requires at first, getting a lot of ideas. Later we'll consider "empowerment." Fast decisions impede empowerment.

We're not against fast decisions. At times they're needed. What we are arguing for is flexibility. Sometimes fast, sometimes slow—it all depends on the situation.

FOUR GENERATIONS OF TIME MANAGEMENT

According to Steve Covey (management consultant), there are four generations of time management. Each one builds on the other. The first three conform to the axiom: *organize and execute around priorities.* The first generation is characterized by notes and checklists. It essentially recognizes the varying demands made on our time. The second generation is epitomized by calendars and appointment books. Here we see an endeavor to schedule ahead. The third generation portrays the more prevalent form of time management. It takes the above two and adds the dimension of prioritization. It focuses on values toward which time and energy are allocated. (The higher the priority of a value—the more time spent.) It is planning with a purpose. The emerging fourth generation recognizes that "time management" is misconstrued! The challenge is not to manage time, after all, time by its very nature manages itself. Rather than concentrating on *activities* and *time*, fourth generation emphasizes preserving and enhancing *relationships* and on getting results through *teamwork*.

Time-Management Matrix

The matrix that follows categorizes activities or things as fast or slow, and critical or noncritical. Fast activities press us to respond now. Critical matters have to do with results, the fulfillment of our job duties. Let's examine Table 5-1.

Category I is both fast and critical. All of us operate on occasion in this area. Regretfully, some become habitual crises persons. Push, push, faster, faster. These people are frequently experienced as task driven and aggressive. Unfortunately, they beat themselves up while tackling the crises (e.g., stress, burnout, overloads, always putting out fires). When exhausted they often retreat to Category IV, with little attention paid to Category II. There are others who expend a lot of time in Category III, believing that they're in Category I. They are confronting crises all right, only the issues are relatively unimportant in terms of their mission. In fact, they are likely responding to the values and expectations of others. *Those of us who spend most of our time in Categories III and IV basically lead irresponsible lives.* Effective supervisors stay out of Categories III and IV because, urgent or not, they aren't critical.

Category II is the crux of managing ourselves. It deals with things that do not require a fast response, but are critical such as building trust; enhancing

TABLE 5-1 Fourth Time Management Matrix

Fast	Slow
I	II
Activities	Activities
Crises (shots fired)	Prevention of conflicts
Pressing problems (computers down)	Relationship building
Deadline-driven projects (staff reports)	Recognition of new opportunities
	Planning, recreation
	Team building
III	IV
Activities	Activities
Interruptions, some calls (open door)	Trivia, busy work
Some mail, some reports (in-basket)	Some mail
Some meetings (roll call)	Some phone calls
Proximate, pressing matters (evaluation)	Time wasters
Popular activities (code 7)	Pleasant activities

candid communications; long-range planning; physical exercise; preparation; and renewal. These are high leverage, capacity-expansion activities.

Stop—now take a look at the two answers you wrote down earlier. What category do they fit in? They probably relate to Category II. But, because they do not require a ready-aim-fire response, we neglect them. Your effectiveness will measurably grow if you focus on them. They will make a tremendous, positive difference in your professional and personal lives.

Tom Peters describes a Category II activity that he discovered at Hewlett-Packard—managing by wandering around (MBWA). In this case we'd propose that the police supervisor is "SBWA." We've seen some engage in SBWA and were astonished at the favorable results—everything from new ideas through increased job satisfaction to improved understanding and trust.

Just Say No

The only place to get time for Category II in the beginning is from Categories III and IV. You can't ignore the urgent and important activities of Category I, although it will shrink in size as you spend more time with prevention and preparation in Category II. But the initial time for Category II has to come out of III and IV. You have to be proactive to work on Category II because Categories I and III suck you in. To say "yes" to critical Category II priorities, you have to learn to say "no" to other activities, sometimes apparently urgent things. If we expect kids to "just say no to drugs," we as adults are equally capable of just saying no to the time wasters.

Time Wasters

Please turn to Structured Exercise 1 at the end of this chapter and complete it before reading further.

Now compare your list with those that are most commonly cited (in rank order).

1. Telephone interruptions
2. Drop-in visitors
3. Meetings (scheduled and unscheduled)
4. Crisis
5. Lack of objectives
6. Cluttered desk and personal disorganization
7. Ineffective delegation of responsibilities, and too much involvement in routines and details
8. Too much work attempted at once and unrealistic time estimates
9. Lack of or unclear communications or instructions
10. Inadequate, inaccurate, or delayed information
11. Indecision and procrastination
12. Confused responsibility and authority

13. Inability to say *no*

14. Tasks left unfinished

15. Lack of self-discipline

We are convinced that the last point (lack of self-discipline) is the principle villain and essentially allows the other fourteen wasters to surface and bug us.

ON BECOMING A CATEGORY II POLICE SUPERVISOR

The objective of a Category II supervisor is to manage our lives effectively — from a center of sound principles, from a knowledge of our overall (career and personal) mission, with a focus on the "critical" as well as the "fast," and within the framework of maintaining a balance between increasing our actual production and increasing our capability for producing.

Category II organizing requires producing

- Individual mission statement
- Identification of roles
- Selection of your goals
- Weekly scheduling
- Taking action and being flexible

Your Mission Statement

When you read your agency's mission statement, or one from another police department, it is probably interesting reading and does not appear to require a formidable set of tasks.

Hold it! What you're reading is in reality a *values statement*. Moreover, if the people that represent the statement believe in it and act accordingly, you'll quickly understand where they intend to go. (Frequently the statement will convey *how* they intend to get there.)

The Sheriff of the Los Angeles County Sheriff's Department created a task force to design a new mission statement. After several months of arduous thinking and interaction with all units of the department, the following mission statement (Figure 5-1) was mailed to every employee in the department with a covering letter from the sheriff. (Incidentally, it took a while because there are more than 10,000 employees.) As you peruse the statement, take your highlighter or writing instrument and point out the values that are included. Essentially, when you see members of their department doing what is stated, they're conforming and should be commended. Conversely, if you see personnel doing the opposite then they should be corrected. While everyone may not be in conformance, they all know what is expected of them and what they stand for. And thus the stage is set for pursuing organizational excellence!

Now it's your turn. Don't worry; your completion of the work in Respon-

OUR MISSION

The quality of neighborhood life, its safety and welfare comes from the commitment of each of its citizens. The **Los Angeles County Sheriff's Department** takes pride in its role as a citizen of the community; partners with its members in the delivery of quality law enforcement services. We dedicate our full-time efforts to the duties incumbent upon every community member. As we act, we are universal citizens deriving our authority from those we serve. We accept our law enforcement mission to serve our communities with the enduring belief that in so doing, we serve ourselves. As professionals, we view our responsibilities as a covenant of public trust, ever mindful that we must keep our promises. As we succeed, our effectiveness will be measured by the absence of crime and fear in our neighborhoods and by the level of community respect for our efforts. In accomplishing this all important mission, we are guided by the following principles:

To recognize that the primary purpose of our organization is not only the skillful **enforcement** of the law, but the delivery of **humanitarian services** which promote community peace.

To understand that we must maintain a level of professional **competence** that ensures our safety and that of the public without compromising the constitutional guarantees of any person.

To base our decisions and actions on **ethical** as well as practical perspectives and to accept **responsibility** for the consequences.

To foster a collaborative relationship with the public in determining the best course in achieving **community order.**

To strive for **innovation**, yet remain **prudent** in sustaining our fiscal health through wise use of resources.

To never tire of our **duty**, never shrink from the difficult tasks and never lose sight of our own humanity.

Figure 5-1 Mission Statement (Reprinted with permission of the Los Angeles County Sheriff's Department.)

sibility One will facilitate your efforts here. If you choose not to do what is required next, then you've also chosen not to be a fourth-generation time manager.

First of all, return to Responsibility One and write down on a separate sheet of paper the top six or seven values that you identified at that point. Using those values, create a one-page mission statement for yourself. (It is likely this will take three or four drafts before you are pleased with it.) (We have numerous copies of police mission statements. If you would like copies, at no expense, telephone 714-498-7085.)

We'll try to help you by conceiving a hypothetical: Philip Clark, Police Sergeant, age twenty-seven, is married with two children. Clark's core values were, in rank order (1) integrity; (2) spouse; (3) children; (4) parents; (5) police work; (6) house; (7) financial security; and (8) physical and mental health. Here is what he might have written.

MISSION STATEMENT
PHILLIP D. CLARK
AGE TWENTY-SEVEN

My mission in life is to demonstrate integrity consistently in myself and with others as follows:

- I will love and care for my wife, being certain that she is receiving top priority time.
- I will serve as an example of responsible citizenship for my children. They will be daily recipients of my love and help.
- (and so forth)

All right, once you've finished your mission statement you're ready to move to identifying your various roles in life.

Your Roles

The first step is to record your main roles. Write down what immediately comes to mind. You have a role as an individual. You may want to list one or more roles as a family member—a husband or wife, mother or father, son or daughter, a member of the extended family of grandparents, aunts, uncles and cousins. You certainly want to list a few roles in your police job, indicating different areas in which you wish to invest time and energy on a regular basis. You may have roles in church or community affairs. (Your mission statement will coach you on what they are.)

You don't need to worry about defining the roles in a way that you will live with forever—just preview the week and write down the areas you see yourself spending time in during the next seven days. For example, our Sergeant Clark might list the following seven roles:

1. Husband
2. Father
3. Son and brother
4. Police sergeant—human relations
5. Police sergeant—production
6. Self-growth—mental and physical
7. Investor

Note how Clark's values, mission statement, and roles are integrated, systematic, and indeed logically compelling. Complete this step for yourself now, and then proceed to the next.

Your Goals

It's late Sunday afternoon and Sergeant Clark has set aside thirty minutes for managing himself during the ensuing week. Clark lists the following:

Role	Goals
Husband	Discuss vacation plans; review life insurance; schedule a dinner and movie; ask about her job.
Father	Discuss school work; play one group game; play one individual game; develop a new sport.
Son and brother	Phone parents; send photographs of family; write sister.
Police sergeant– human relations	Complete performance evaluations; counsel Officer Mead; meet with each officer for coffee (fifteen minutes each).
Police sergeant— production	Analyze called-for services; prepare a problem-oriented approach to a major need; assess assigned equipment.
Self-growth—mental and physical	Read assigned text; book chapters; read *Time* and fifty pages in fictional book; fifty minutes of exercise five times; read national newspaper daily.
Investor	Paint interior of small bathroom (first coat); read *Money* magazine, assess CDs.

You're probably wondering how in the world Clark is going to accomplish all of the preceding goals. At this point it is straightforward, and all he has to do is *schedule*. It is now your turn to specify your goals for the next week. Stop here and do so.

Your Schedule

Now you can look at the week ahead with your goals in mind and schedule time to achieve them. For example, if your goal is to telephone your parents you may want to set aside a fifteen-minute block of time on Sunday to do it. Sunday is often the ideal time to plan your weekly organizing.

If you set a goal to become physically fit through exercise, you may want to set aside an hour three or four days during the week, or possibly every day during the week, to accomplish that goal. There are some goals that you may only be able to accomplish during work hours or some that you can only do on Saturday when your children are home. Do you now see some of the advantages of organizing the week instead of the day? Having identified roles and set goals, you can translate each goal to a specific day of the week, either as a priority item or, even better, as a specific appointment.

Let's return to our Sergeant Clark to illustrate what must be done at this juncture. To begin with he has to: (1) divide up the goals on a per-day basis and (2) at the same time assign them a priority. We'll cover Monday and Tuesday as examples of what you'll soon be doing.

	MONDAY	TUESDAY
Priorities	Complete performance evaluations	Meet with officers
	Meet with officers	Assess equipment
	Analyze called/service	Council Mead
	Read assigned text	Read assigned text
	Exercise fifty minutes	Exercise fifty minutes
	School work	College class
Time	**Activity**	**Activity**
0500–0600	Awaken 0530	Awaken 0530
0600–0700	Jog	Drive to work
		Audio tape
0700–0800	Drive to work	Lift weights
	Audio tape on current affairs	
0800–0900	Briefings/roll call	Briefings/roll call
0900–1000	Meeting with officers	Meeting with officers
1000–1100	Performance evaluations	Meeting with officers
1100–1200	Performance evaluations	Review reports
1200–1300	Lunch/read text	Lunch/read text
1300–1400	Analyze called/services	Assess equipment
1400–1500	Field supervision	Council Mead
1500–1600	Field supervision	Field supervision
1600–1700	Report review	Report review
1700–1800	Drive home	Drive to college/dinner
1800–1900	Dinner	College course
1900–2000	Review school work	College course
2000–2100	Games with children	College course
2100–2200	Alone time with wife	Drive home/wife

It's time for us to integrate another step with the preceding ones. Turn to Structured Exercise 3 and fill in the blanks. (Remember to prioritize your goals before scheduling the specific activities.) For future time-management planning you're welcome to copy and use the form or design one of your own. Obviously, the timeframes will vary according to night- or early morning-shift work. One more reminder, keep the Category II activities prominent in your goal setting, prioritizing, and scheduling.

Action and Being Flexible

With Category II weekly organizing, daily action becomes more of a response to daily adaptations, of prioritizing activities and adjusting to emergent circumstances, relationships, and experiences in a systematic way. As mentioned earlier, you can analyze each incoming day and fine tune your schedule as appropriate. (Your after-work-shift travel home or elsewhere is often a convenient time to review the immediate past and confirm your schedule for tomorrow.) You're now organizing and executing around your goals and priorities. While you actually cannot manage time, you certainly can manage yourself—if you want to.

Figure 5–2 shows five steps, in summary.

Step 5
Action and Flexibility

Step 4
Plan Your Week

Step 3
Identify Your Goals

Step 2
Identify Your Key Roles

Step 1
Develop a Personal Mission Statement

Figure 5-2 Fourth Generation: Five Steps to Effective Management of Priorities

KEY POINTS

Fourth-generation management is devoted to ensuring us that as we manage ourselves, we more effectively supervise others. It is a constant reminder that *people are always more important than things.* It has been successful because it

- Is *value laden*; it encompasses our driving forces
- Is *conscience focused*; it helps you make the correct choices about what comes first, second, and so on
- *Defines your individual mission* including values and goals that are prioritized
- Is an *alignment of various life roles* and scheduling time accordingly
- *Provides an expanded framework for organizing* by scheduling weekly activities

DISCUSSION

- If working as a group, divide into subgroups of five to six people and review your responses to Structured Exercise 1, which follows. Subsequently, share with one another the contents. Attempt to identify one or two common time wasters.
- Earlier you were asked to write down the answers to two questions that we had posed. (See "A Couple of Questions for You.") First share the responses to question one, and then do the same with the second question. What are some interesting similarities? What are some unusual considerations?
- Review the existing overloads that individuals in the group are experiencing both at work and on a personal basis. What are some of the tactics for handling or avoiding overloads?
- What decisions should receive a "fast response?" Conversely, what decisions can and should take more time?
- Reevaluate the Category II activities that we listed earlier. Expand on our list by adding activities. Next, identify one or more examples of each activity.
- Share with one another your individual successes in developing and using a fourth-generation time-management form.

STRUCTURED EXPERIENCES

STRUCTURED EXERCISE 1
SOURCES OF WASTED TIME AT WORK

The major contributors to wasting my time at work are as follows:

1. _____

2. _____

3. _____

4. _____

5. _____

6. _____

7. _____

8. _____

9. _____

10. _____

STRUCTURED EXERCISE 2
JOB-TIME ANALYSIS FORM

The following Job-Time Analysis Form is provided to help you assess the specific areas of time management in which you need improvement. List the individual tasks you perform on the job, and complete each column for each task.

Job task	What percentage of my time does it consume?	What is its priority (high, medium, or low)?	Do I like or dislike performing it?	Can I delegate it?	Is it discretionary or nondiscretionary?

After completing the Job-Time Analysis Form, review it for accuracy. Showing the analysis to colleagues at work and learning their opinion might be helpful in this respect. After ensuring the accuracy of the completed analysis, answer each of the following questions:

1. What unnecessary tasks am I performing?
2. On which tasks am I spending too much time?
3. On which tasks am I spending too little time?
4. What tasks am I performing that could be performed better by others?
5. What specific changes do I plan to make in the way I manage my time?

STRUCTURED EXERCISE 3

MANAGING PRIORITIES AND SCHEDULING

The WEEKLY WORKSHEET	Week of:	Sunday	Monday	Tuesday	Wednesday	Thursday	Friday	Saturday
Roles	Goals	Weekly Priorities	Today's Priorities		Today's Priorities			

Appointments/Commitments

Sunday	Monday	Tuesday	Wednesday	Thursday	Friday	Saturday
8	8	8	8	8	8	8
9	9	9	9	9	9	9
10	10	10	10	10	10	10
11	11	11	11	11	11	11
12	12	12	12	12	12	12
1	1	1	1	1	1	1
2	2	2	2	2	2	2
3	3	3	3	3	3	3
4	4	4	4	4	4	4
5	5	5	5	5	5	5
6	6	6	6	6	6	6
7	7	7	7	7	7	7
8	8	8	8	8	8	8
Evening	Evening	Evening	Evening	Evening	Evening	Evening

Part Two

KNOW YOUR STAFF

RESPONSIBILITIES

- *Motivation*

- *Goal Setting*

- *Performance Evaluation*

- *Employee-Oriented Supervision: Empowerment and Participation*

- *Employee-Oriented Supervision: Conflict Resolution*

- *Stress Management*

RESPONSIBILITY SIX

Motivation: Inspiration and Perspiration

Winners make it happen; losers allow it to happen.

Dennis Waitley

In understanding, predicting, and controlling individual behavior, there is probably no concept more important than motivation. A cursory look at any police agency quickly suggests that some personnel work harder than others. An individual with outstanding abilities may consistently be outperformed by someone with obviously inferior talents. Why do officers exert different levels of effort in different activities? Why do some employees appear to be "highly motivated," while others are not? These are questions we shall attempt to answer in this chapter. But before we proceed, let us address the fundamental issue: *If you want others to be motivated, it must start with you.*

ROLE OF THE POLICE SUPERVISOR

Employee motivation is clearly one of the most important roles for police supervisors. There are numerous reasons for this.

Police organizations have three *behavioral requirements* of the people who work in them.[1] First, people must be attracted to join the police department and remain with it. Second, police personnel must dependably perform the tasks they were hired for. Third, employees must surpass routine tasks and engage in some form of creative, spontaneous, and innovative behavior at

[1]Daniel Katz and Robert L. Kahn, *The Social Psychology of Organizations*, 2nd ed. (New York: Wiley, 1975), pp. 165–177.

work. These three behavioral requirements deal squarely with the issue of motivation. Motivational techniques must be used by the police supervisor not only to encourage police employees to join and remain with an agency, but also to perform in a dependable fashion and to think and take advantage of unique opportunities.

With respect to the ever-tightening constraints that are placed on police departments by unions, courts, and legislative bodies, agencies must find ways to improve their efficiency and effectiveness in the community. Much of the organizational slack that was tolerated in the past has diminished, requiring that all resources, especially human resources, be utilized to their maximum.

Increased attention is being devoted to motivating police employees to become resources, a sort of talent bank, from which departments can draw in the future. Examples of these efforts are seen in the increase in management development programs, work force planning, and job redesign. The supervisor is in a key position to support this effort.

From the individual's standpoint, motivation is a key to a productive and satisfying life. Work consumes a sizable portion of our waking hours. If this time is to be meaningful and contribute toward the development of a healthy personality, the individual must be willing to devote effort toward task accomplishment. Alternatively, the employer expects in return a satisfying job. *Effective* supervision plays a central role in determining an employee's job satisfaction.

WHAT IS MOTIVATION?

Motivation is the willingness to do something and is conditioned by an action's ability to satisfy some need for the individual. A *need*, in our terminology, means some internal state that makes certain outcomes appear attractive.

Motivated employees are in a state of tension. To relieve this tension, they engage in activity. The greater the tension, the more activity will be needed to bring about relief. Therefore, when we see police personnel working hard at some activity, we can conclude that they are driven by a desire to achieve some goal that they perceive as having value to them.

Figure 6-1 graphically displays the motivational process. Our description of the process is built on the assumption that our values will determine if a need(s) is satisfied or not. When unsatisfied, a need activates the process. Basically, we find it in our *self-interest* to satisfy our needs. How simple to state, but how complex in operation.

From the great volume of theories and research on human motivation, we will briefly cover only two schools of thought. Space does not permit otherwise. The two schools can be typed as (1) needs and (2) process. Our focus will be on how supervisors can motivate their police personnel and what their endeavors to do so mean to individual officer job satisfaction.

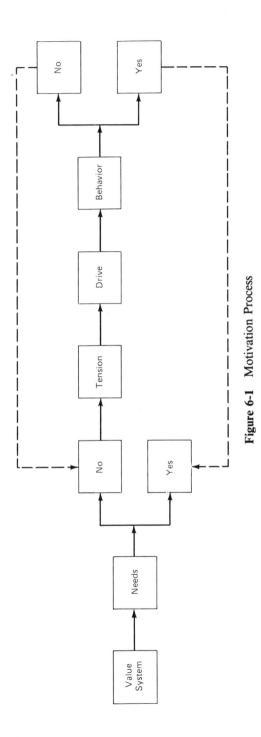

Figure 6-1 Motivation Process

SCHOOL OF MOTIVATIONAL THOUGHT BASED ON NEEDS

> *It's an old saw that we get two kinds of wages from our job—the pay in our paycheck and the pay that isn't in our paycheck.*

Four major theories center on our needs.

1. Maslow's hierarchy of needs

2. ERG theory

3. Achievement, power, and affiliation

4. Herzberg's motivation–hygiene theory

Maslow's Hierarchy of Needs

The most widely accepted need classification scheme was proposed by Abraham Maslow over a quarter of a century ago.[2] His list of five needs is conveniently short, yet covers most of the dimensions that psychologists have found to be important.

1. *Self-actualization.* The drive to become what one is capable of becoming; includes growth, achieving one's potential, and self-fulfillment.

2. *Esteem.* Includes internal esteem factors, such as self-respect, autonomy, and achievement, and external esteem factors, such as status, recognition, and attention.

3. *Belongingness.* Includes affection, belonging, acceptance, and friendship.

4. *Safety.* Includes security and protection from physical and emotional harm.

5. *Physiological.* Includes hunger, thirst, shelter, sex, and other bodily needs.

Maslow separated the five needs into higher and lower levels. Physiological and safety needs were described as lower-order needs, and love, esteem, and self-actualization as higher-order needs. As each of these needs becomes substantially satisfied, the next need becomes dominant. In essence, the individual moves up the hierarchy. From the standpoint of motivation, the theory would say that, although no need is ever fully gratified, a substantially satisfied need no longer motivates.

Maslow's need theory has received wide recognition, particularly among practicing managers. This can be attributed to the theory's intuitive logic and ease of understanding. Unfortunately, however, research does not generally validate the theory. A super theory, but alas no hard data to support it.

---

[2]Abraham Maslow, *Motivation and Personality* (New York: Harper and Row, 1954).

ERG Theory

Clayton Alderfer argues that there are three groups of core needs—existence, relatedness, and growth—hence the label ERG theory.[3] The existence group is concerned with providing our basic material existence requirements. They include the items that Maslow considered as physiological and safety needs. The second group of needs are those of relatedness: the desire we have for maintaining important interpersonal relationships. These social and status desires require interaction with others if they are to be satisfied and coincide with Maslow's belongingness need and the external component of Maslow's esteem classification. Finally, Alderfer isolates growth needs: an intrinsic desire for personal development. These include the intrinsic component from Maslow's esteem category and the characteristics included under self-actualization.

The ERG theory wisely did not assume that a certain group of needs, for example, the existence needs, must be substantially satisfied before another set can emerge. Variables such as education, family background, and cultural environment can alter the importance or driving force that a group of needs holds for a particular individual. For example, one's need for esteem may overshadow needs that would promote safety.

Achievement, Power, and Affiliation Needs

David McClelland proposes that we have three central needs.[4]

1. *Need for achievement.* The drive to excel, to achieve in relation to a set of standards, to strive to succeed.

2. *Need for power.* The need to make others behave in a way that they would not have behaved otherwise.

3. *Need for affiliation.* The desire for friendly and close interpersonal relationships.

Researchers and practitioners have given greatest attention to the achievement need. Given that this need drives people to act on the basis of an internally induced stimulus rather than relying on externally imposed motivators, there are several implications for police supervisors. First, since achievement can be taught and has been positively related to higher work performance, supervisors can consider having police officers undergo achievement training to stimulate this need. Second, an understanding of the concepts behind this need and the characteristics that individuals high in achievement seek in their jobs can assist police supervisors in explaining and predicting employee behavior.

---

[3]For further details, see Clayton P. Alderfer, *Existence, Relatedness, and Growth* (New York: Free Press, 1972).

[4]David C. McClelland, *The Achieving Society* (New York: Van Nostrand Reinhold, 1961).

Herzberg's Motivation — Hygiene Theory

Frederick Herzberg's research[5] led him to conclude that

1. There is a set of extrinsic job conditions that, when not present, result in dissatisfaction among employees. However, the presence of these conditions does not necessarily motivate employees. These conditions are the *dissatisfiers*, or hygiene factors, because they are needed to maintain at least a no-dissatisfaction level, and they are related to the context of the job. Potential dissatisfiers include
   - Job security
   - Salary
   - Working conditions
   - Status
   - Company policies
   - Quality of technical supervision
   - Quality of interpersonal relations among peers, supervisors, and subordinates
   - Fringe benefits

2. A set of intrinsic job conditions exists that helps to build levels of motivation, which can result in good job performance. If these conditions are not present, they do not result in dissatisfaction. This set of aspects is related to the content of the job and is called *satisfiers*. Satisfiers include
   - Achievement
   - Recognition
   - Work itself
   - Responsibility
   - Advancement
   - Personal growth and development

The opposite of satisfaction is not dissatisfaction, as was traditionally believed. Removing dissatisfying characteristics from a job does not necessarily make the job satisfying. Hygiene factors in the workplace provide the necessary foundation for the motivator factors to function, because they bring motivation to a "zero point" by preventing negative behavior. By themselves, hygiene factors do not motivate individuals to better performance. The motivators, or satisfiers, are higher-level needs. These are the job-content factors that motivate people to perform. According to Herzberg, only such aspects as a challenging job, recognition for doing a good job, and opportunities for advancement, personal growth, and development will function to provide a situation for

---

[5]For further information on this theory, see Frederick Herzberg, B. Mausner, and B. Synderman, *The Motivation to Work* (New York: Wiley, 1959).

motivated behavior. Clearly, the police supervisor is in a position to affect these critical needs.

What Did I Learn about Need Theories?

In summary, we found that

1. Considerable attention has been given to our needs and how they can motivate us.
2. There are points of agreement and disagreement over which of our needs are the most central to us. Clearly, we possess many needs.
3. We differ from one another due to our needs, and the police supervisor should be alert to those differences. His or her success depends on it.
4. The police supervisor is in a key position to meet or block our needs.

SCHOOL OF MOTIVATIONAL THOUGHT BASED ON PROCESS

> *If human beings were not endowed with freedom of the will and the power of free choice, to be exercised in the pursuit of the ultimate good that they are morally obligated to seek, they would not have, by nature, a right to liberty of action.*
>
> —Mortimer J. Adler
> *Six Great Ideas* (New York: MacMillan, 1981), p. 12

The process theories covered here are equity, goal setting, reinforcement, and expectancy. Each of these theories has its own emphasis. For instance, *equity theory* is specifically concerned with whether individuals perceive that rewards are being allocated fairly. *Goal-setting* theory looks at the specificity and difficulty of goals as a primary explanation of effort. *Reinforcement theory* emphasizes the pattern in which rewards are administered. *Expectancy theory* focuses on an individual's perception of the relationship of rewards to performance and the value that the individual assigns to the rewards.

Equity Theory

Equity theory states that, if one perceives a discrepancy between the amount of rewards received and one's efforts, one is motivated to reduce efforts; furthermore, the greater the discrepancy, the more one is motivated to reduce it. Discrepancy refers to the perceived difference that may exist between two or more people.

Adams has been associated with the initial development and testing of the theory.[6] He defined a discrepancy, or inequity, as existing whenever a person

---

[6]J. S. Adams, "Toward an Understanding of Inequity," *Journal of Abnormal and Social Psychology*, 31 (November 1963), pp. 422–436.

perceives that the ratio of his or her job outcomes to job inputs is unequal in comparison to a reference person's job outcomes to job inputs. The reference person may be someone in an individual's group, in another group, or outside the organization. In equity theory, *inputs* are aspects such as efforts, skills, education, and task performance that one brings to or puts into a job. *Outcomes* are those rewards that result from task accomplishment, such as pay, promotion, recognition, achievement, and status.

The equity theory provides at least three guidelines for police supervisors to consider.

1. The emphasis on equitable rewards for police employees is worth notice. When individuals believe that they are not being rewarded in an equitable fashion, certain morale and productivity problems may arise.

2. The decision concerning equity (or inequity) is not made solely on a personal basis, but involves comparison with other workers, both within and outside the police organization.

3. One's reaction to inequity can take many different forms. Motivated behavior to reduce an inequity can include changes in inputs and in outcomes, with the level or direction depending on whether the inequity was perceived to be underpayment or overpayment.

Goal Setting

For centuries it was commonly thought that goals motivate people. Finally, in the 1960s research evidence confirmed this belief. We can now with confidence say that *specific* goals increase performance and that difficult goals, when accepted, result in higher performance than easy goals.[7] If factors like ability and acceptance of the goals are held constant, we can also state that the more difficult the goals, the higher the level of performance. However, it's logical to assume that easier goals are more likely to be accepted. But once an employee accepts a hard task, he or she will likely exert a high level of effort until it is achieved, lowered, or abandoned.

If police employees have the opportunity to participate in the setting of their own goals, will they try harder? Usually. But a major advantage of participation may be in increasing acceptance of the goal itself as a desirable one to work toward. Resistance is greater when goals are difficult. If police officers participate in goal setting, they are more likely to accept even a difficult goal than if they are arbitrarily assigned it by their supervisor. The reason is that we are more committed to choices in which we have a part.

[7]Gary P. Latham and Gary A. Yukl, "A Review of Research on the Application of Goal Setting in Organizations," *Academy of Management Journal*, 17 (December 1975), pp. 824–845.

Reinforcement Theory

Reinforcement theory is broadly based on learning theory and the works of Skinner.[8] The foundation of this approach is based on three fundamental factors.

1. It is believed that we are basically passive, and that we merely mediate the relationship between the forces acting on us and our output. Behavioral explanations that assume that we actively initiate behavior on our own are rejected.

2. Reinforcement theorists reject the explanation that behavior is based on needs, drives, or goals, because they consider such aspects to be unobservable and hard to measure.

3. Reinforcement theorists state that a relatively permanent change in our behavior results from reinforced behavior or experience. (Stated differently, by proper reinforcement, the likelihood that desired behaviors will be exhibited can be increased, and the likelihood that undesired behaviors will be exhibited can be reduced, or both.)

If we look further, we find that the most important lesson from Skinner is the role of positive reinforcement, of rewards for a job well done. Skinner and others take special note of the asymmetry between positive and negative reinforcement (essentially the threat of sanctions). In short, negative reinforcement will produce behavioral change, but often in strange, unpredictable, and undesirable ways. Positive reinforcement causes behavioral change, too, but usually in the intended direction.

Why spend time on this? It seems to us that central to the whole notion of supervising is the superior–subordinate relationship and the corollary that orders will be issued and followed. The threat of punishment is the principal implied power that underlies it all. To the extent that this underlying notion prevails, we are not paying attention to people's dominant need to be winners. Moreover, repeated negative reinforcement is usually a dumb tactic. It doesn't work very well. It usually results in frenetic, unguided activity. Furthermore, punishment doesn't necessarily suppress the desire to "do bad." Positive reinforcement, on the other hand, not only shapes behavior but also teaches and in the process enhances our own self-image. Additionally, it encourages good things in a program or process instead of ripping them out.

In regard to reinforcing behavior, we would recommend the following guidelines:

[8]See B. F. Skinner, *Contingencies of Reinforcement* (Englewood Cliffs, N.J.: Prentice Hall, 1969); and *Beyond Freedom and Dignity* (New York: Knopf, 1971).

- Do not give the same type of reward to everyone.

- Failure to respond to behavior has reinforcing consequences: supervisors are bound to shape the behavior of the staff by the way in which they utilize the rewards at their disposal. Therefore, supervisors must be careful that they examine the consequences on performance of their nonactions as well as their actions.

- Tell an officer what behavior will be reinforced.

- Tell an officer what he or she is doing wrong.

- Punish in private, praise in public.

- Make the consequences equal to the behavior.

Expectancy Theory

Expectancy theory argues that the strength of a tendency to act in a certain way depends on the strength of an expectation that the act will be followed by a given outcome and on the attractiveness of that outcome to the individual. It includes, therefore, three variables.[9]

1. *Attractiveness.* The importance that the individual places on the potential outcome or reward that can be achieved on the job. This considers the unsatisfied needs of the individual.

2/3. *Performance–reward linkage.* The degree to which the individual believes that performing at a particular level will lead to the attainment of a desired outcome.

Figure 6-2 presents a graphic overview of the expectancy theory. It is best understood by studying from your right to left. First, what *perceived* outcomes does police work offer the employee? Outcomes may be positive: pay, security, companionship, trust, fringe benefits, a chance to use talents or skills, congenial relationships. On the other hand, employees may view the outcomes as negative: fatigue, boredom, frustration, anxiety, harsh supervision, threat of dismissal. Importantly, reality is not relevant here; the critical issue is what the individual employee *perceives* the outcome to be, regardless of whether or not her or his perceptions are accurate.

Second, how attractive do police officers consider these outcomes? Are they valued positively, negatively, or neutrally? The type and degree of value determines the person's *drive*. This obviously is an issue internal to the individual and considers her or his personal values, personality, and needs. The officer who finds a particular outcome attractive, that is, positively valued, would prefer attaining it to not attaining it. Still others may be neutral.

Third, what kind of actual performance must the employee produce to achieve these outcomes? The outcomes are not likely to have any effect on the

[9]Victor Vroom, *Work and Motivation* (New York: Wiley, 1964).

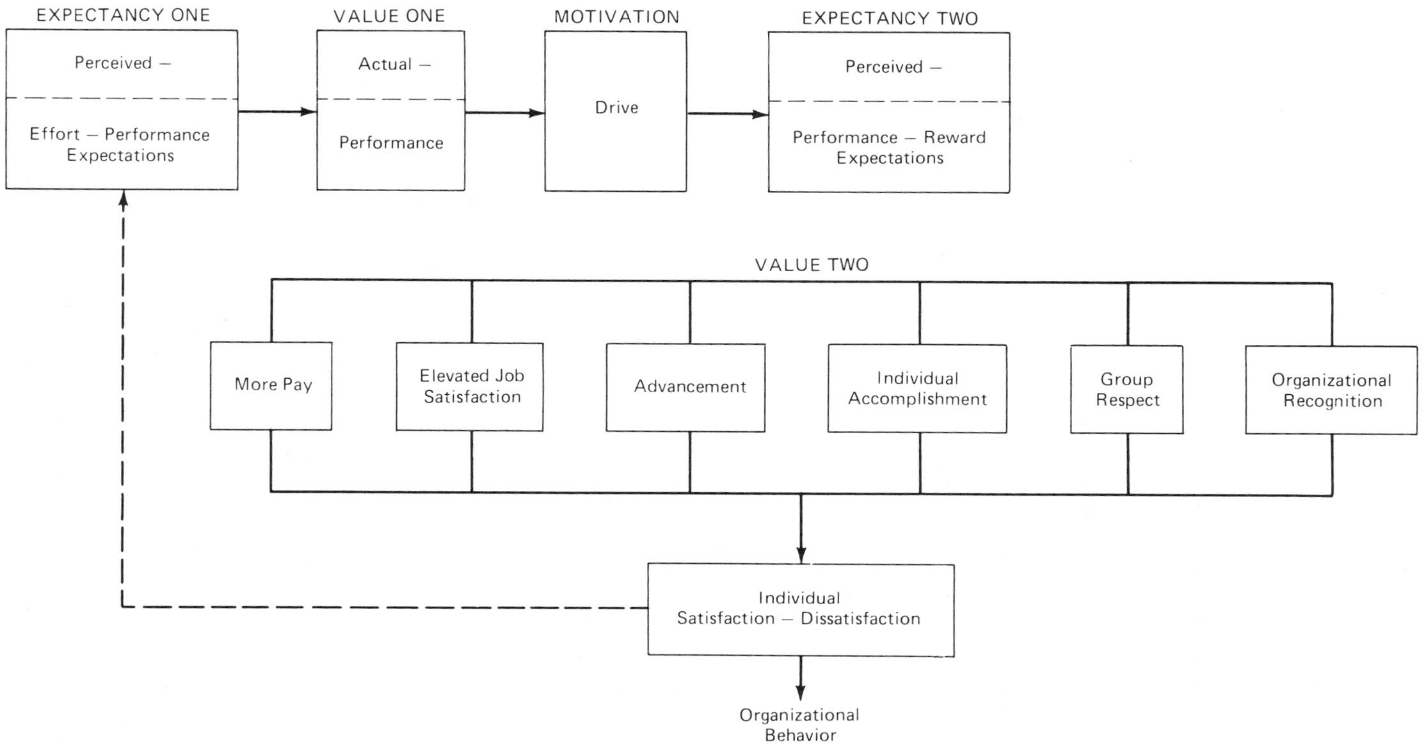

Figure 6-2 Expectancy Theory of Motivation

officer's performance unless they know what they must do to achieve them. For example, what is "doing well" in terms of performance appraisal? What are the criteria the officer's performance will be judged on?

Fourth, how does the officer *perceive the required effort* needed for successful performance?

What Did I Learn about Process Theories?

To recap, we saw that:

1. We are judgmental and comparative in nature (equity).
2. Goals propel us in one direction as opposed to others (goal setting).
3. Rewards and sanctions can promote and discourage engaging in certain forms of behavior (reinforcement).
4. A perceived reward determines the amount of drive and effort we will expand (expectancy).

In summary, we are creatures of our environment, very sensitive and responsive to external rewards and punishment. We are also strongly driven from within, self-motivated.

MOTIVATION, WORK PERFORMANCE, AND JOB SATISFACTION

> *People who produce good results feel good about themselves.*
>
> —Kenneth Blanchard and Robert Lorber
> *Putting the One Minute Manager to Work*
> (New York: William Morrow and Co., 1984), p. 18

Producing good results, in this case police work, is obviously important for the supervisor. And feeling good about oneself depends to a considerable degree on one's job satisfaction. Being satisfied with our job does not automatically mean that we will produce good work. Have we not witnessed a person who is very happy with his job mainly because he is allowed to do nothing; or, conversely, a person who works very hard in order that time will pass quickly because she despises her job. The key linkage between results and satisfaction is the supervisor. The *effective* police supervisor will provide a work climate that (1) enhances job satisfaction and (2) encourages goal setting and results.

Our value system is expressed in our needs and choices. Together these needs and choices comprise a self-directing motivation that determines to a major extent our level of job satisfaction. The other major determinant is the working environment. With this degree of human complexity, we can appreciate the numerous unanswered questions about motivation and job satisfaction.

MORALE

The basic fact with which one is impressed upon reviewing research findings concerning morale is that job satisfaction is an individual feeling while morale is a group phenomenon. To put it another way, job satisfaction is the degree of liking that we have for our work role. Morale is the degree of liking that our group has for its particular work assignment. Before leaving this subject, it should be understood that positive attitudes toward the job are conceptually equivalent to job satisfaction and negative attitudes to job dissatisfaction. Findings from recent studies indicate that job satisfaction and job dissatisfaction are located at two different points on a continuum. Between these two points is a very important third point of neutrality (neither pleased nor unhappy). An individual's position on a job satisfaction continuum (or a group's position on a morale continuum) is determined primarily by the amount of value fulfillment provided by the work role.

JOB SATISFACTION: CAUSES AND CONSEQUENCES

Let's first examine the causes or factors influencing job satisfaction. Then we will look at the consequences or outcomes of satisfaction with one's job.

Causes

The causes of job satisfaction can be grouped into four categories, representing four levels in a police agency: (1) organization-wide factors, those variables widely available or applied to most employees; (2) immediate work-environment factors, those variables that make up the work unit; (3) job-content factors, or the actual job activities; and (4) personal factors, those characteristics that differentiate one person from another. Causes of police employee satisfaction can be found in all four levels, as shown in Figure 6-3.

Organization-wide factors
    Pay system
    Promotional opportunities
    Departmental policies and procedures
    Organization structure

Immediate work-environment factors
    Supervisory style
    Participation in decision making
    Work-group size
    Co-worker relations
    Working conditions

Job-content factors
    Job scope
    Role clarity and conflict

Personal factors
    Age
    Tenure
    Personality

Figure 6-3 Primary Cases Influencing Overall Job Satisfaction

Organization. In respect to *organizational structure*, higher job satisfaction coincides with a higher position in the department and increased decentralization in decision-making correlates with increased satisfaction.

Environment. It has been repeatedly shown that a more participatory *supervisory style* is apt to create enhanced satisfaction.

Content. *Job scope* refers to those attributes that characterize a job, like the amount of variety, autonomy, responsibility, and feedback provided. For a few employees, however, such as those who have low needs for achievement, providing a challenging job may lead not to satisfaction but to increased anxiety and frustration because of either an unwillingness or an inability to respond to the challenge. *Role ambiguity* and *role conflict* have both been found to lead to increased stress and reduced job satisfaction for many people. Basically, we feel more secure and prefer situations in which we know what is expected of us and where we have clear tasks.

Personal. *Age* and *tenure* are associated with favorable job attitudes. One explanation might be that as we get older and acquire seniority we typically move into more responsible (and perhaps challenging) positions. While our personality has some relationship to our job satisfaction (the needs for achievement and self-esteem are examples), the primary causes of job satisfaction reside in the workplace.

Consequences

Job satisfaction plays a strong influence on officer:

- Absenteeism
- Turnover
- Performance
- Grievances
- Physical and mental health
- Accidents
- Learning
- Organizational effectiveness

IN SEARCH OF JOB SATISFACTION: SOME SUGGESTIONS

It is important to acknowledge the kind of work we do because we are what we do, and what we do shapes society.

—John Naisbett
Megatrends (New York: Warner Books, Inc., 1982), p. 33

We've examined a number of theories in Responsibility Six, many of which have reasonably strong application. If you're a police supervisor, responsible for motivating your officers, how do you apply these theories? There is no simple, all-encompassing set of guidelines. The following suggestions, however, draw the essence out of what we know about motivating employees in organizations.

Winning Environment

In 1982 Peters and Waterman released their research findings on what makes organizations successful. Their celebrated best-selling book entitled *In Search of Excellence* disclosed how 100 business firms became and remain highly competitive. The majority of the findings have direct and beneficial use in police departments. One dealt with a particular philosophy. They discovered that the excellent companies have a deeply ingrained philosophy that says, in effect, "respect the individual," "make people winners," "let them stand out," "treat people as adults." More significant, both for society and these companies, these institutions create environments in which people can blossom, develop self-esteem, and otherwise be excited participants in the business and society as a whole. Clearly, this thinking and *practice* tend to motivate employees to become winners.

Intrinsic Rewards

People work primarily for money—and what money can buy. The trouble is that today, give or take a few cents, most police agencies pay about the same wages for the same kind of work. To make a job with your department more attractive to an individual than a job with another agency, you've got to look far beyond the paycheck. Remember the famous salesman Elmer Wheeler who sells the sizzle, not the steak? Selling jobs to employees is a lot like that. You must show them how their job as a police officer with a particular agency brings them prestige among their friends, skill that represents security for them, and a feeling of accomplishment.

Monetary Rewards

Don't forget money. The allocation of performance-based wage increases and other pay incentives is important in determining employee motivation. Perhaps the best case for "money as a motivator" is a recent review of eighty studies evaluating motivational practices and their influences on employee productivity.[10] Goal setting alone produced, on average, a 16 percent increase in productivity; efforts to redesign jobs to make them more interesting and challenging yielded 8 to 16 percent increases; employee participation in deci-

---

[10]Edwin A. Locke and others, "The Relative Effectiveness of Four Methods of Motivating Employee Performance," in K. D. Duncan, M. M. Gruneberg, and D. Wallis (eds.), *Changes in Working Life* (New York: Wiley, 1980), pp. 363–383.

sion making produced a median increase of less than 1 percent; while monetary incentives led to an average increase of 30 percent.

Allow for Individual Differences

Almost every motivation theory recognizes that employees are not homogeneous. People have different needs. They also differ in terms of attitudes, personalities, and human capacities. A "winning" environment will not only permit but encourage us to respect one another's unique individuality.

Matchmaking

Motivational benefits accrue from carefully matching people to jobs. For example, don't put a high achiever into a job that is inconsistent with his or her needs. Achievers will do best where the job provides opportunities to participate in goal setting and where there is autonomy and feedback. Remember that not every police officer will be motivated by assignments with increased autonomy, variety, and responsibility.

Goal Setting

Supervisors should ensure that officers have firm and specific goals, as well as feedback on how well they are doing in pursuit of those goals. For those with high achievement needs, typically a minority in any organization, the existence of external goals is of less importance because these people are already internally motivated.

- *Usually* the officer should participate in setting the goals.
- *Always* be certain that the goals are *perceived* as attainable.
- *Consistently* use an appraisal process by which performance and goal attainment will be reliably evaluated.

Rewards

Supervisors should seek to

- Use their knowledge of the officer to individualize rewards over which they have control. Scheduling and assignments are two examples.
- Link the reward to performance. Consistent with maximizing the impact of the reward contingency, supervisors should look for ways to increase the visibility of rewards.
- Ensure that rewards or outcomes are perceived by police employees as equating with the effort and results they produce.
- Say thank you—yes, *thank you.*
- Actively *listen* to others—on occasion emphatically listen to others.
- *Smile!*

The latter three rewards may seem rather dull or impotent. They're not for most of us. *People who thank us for our efforts, listen to us when we voice a need or an opinion, and smile at us tend to motivate us.* They are simple rewards—but they tend to motivate. If you disagree with us, we'd ask whether you have ever worked for a supervisor who never or rarely said thanks, ignored you when you spoke, and seldom smiled. Did this person seem motivated? Did he or she motivate you?

INSPIRATION AND PERSPIRATION

Responsibility One showed that our value system served, among others, as a motivating force. Our work ethic may include such values as integrity, loyalty, accountability, caring, and more. Or, is our work ethic one of lying, greed, irresponsibility, and not caring? Are you inspired to set an example, create a positive work culture, get results? Are you willing to exert yourself, perspire if necessary to get your job done as a supervisor?

If you're not inspired, if you're not burning energy as a supervisor—how in the world can you expect it from others? *Motivation starts with you.*

We hear a lot about "burnout," and at times see it in ourselves and others. We would be the first to acknowledge that constant inspiration, 100 percent perspiration, is unrealistic. Nevertheless, with the proper mix of commitment, technical skills, positive attitude, and a willingness to try, you'll evidence motivation—you'll motivate others. For one, I want to be the lead mule. Will Rogers put it this way, "Only the lead mule gets a change of scenery."

As far as burnout is concerned, *we'd rather burn out than rust out."* Inspiration and perspiration—high octane motivational fuel for top performance.

KEY POINTS

- Motivation starts with you.
- The police supervisor is in a vital position to motivate others.
- One school of motivational thought centers on our needs.
- Another school of motivational thought concentrates on the human process.
- Basically, both our fundamental needs and human processes drive and guide us.
- Job satisfaction does not guarantee good performance.
- The link between job satisfaction and good performance is the police supervisor.
- Individual job satisfaction, when calculated for a work group, indicates its morale.

- The causes of job satisfaction stem from the organization, work environment, job content, and person.
- The efforts that a supervisor can make to increase job satisfaction involve work climate, intrinsic and monetary rewards, tolerance for uniqueness, matchmaking, goal setting, and use of rewards.

DISCUSSION

1. What are the distinguishing features of the needs theories?
2. Similarly, what are the unique aspects of the process theories?
3. What are the important differences between the two schools of motivational thinking? Are there any points of agreement?
4. How does one's motivation and job satisfaction relate to one another?
5. Attempt to expand the list of causes of job satisfaction.
6. Also, endeavor to increase the list of consequences of poor job satisfaction.
7. Re-read the section on "Inspiration and Perspiration." Do you agree with it or not? Why do you agree or disagree?

STRUCTURED EXPERIENCES

This section contains two exercises on motivation and job satisfaction. The first deals with your perception of relative job factors. The second will assist you in assessing your current degree of job satisfaction.

1. Exercise: Motivation Factors in the Job

The purpose of this exercise is to

1. Examine the application of motivation theories to job factors.
2. Understand the relationship between motivation and differences in individuals.

How to set up the exercise

Set up groups of four to eight for the forty-five to sixty-minute exercise. The groups should be separated from each other and asked to converse only with members of their own group.

Instructions for the exercise

The following instrument presents a list of twelve factors that relate to most jobs in police organizations. Two specific job levels are identified: (1) middle-level managers and (2) first-line police officers.

1. Individually, group members should rank in order the twelve factors on the basis of their influences on motivation from 1 (most influential) to 12 (least influential for motivation). No ties. The individual group members should provide two rank orders: (a) as they believe middle-level managers

would respond to these factors, and (b) as they believe nonsupervisory police officers would respond to these factors.

2. As a group, repeat the instructions presented in step 1.
3. The group ranking should be displayed and a spokesperson should discuss the rationale for the group decision and how much variation existed in individual ranks.

Factors	Line Officers	Supervisors
1. *Recognition*. Receiving recognition from peers, supervisor, or subordinates for your good work performances.		
2. *Sense of achievement*. The feelings associated with successful completion of a job, finding solutions to different problems, or seeing the results of one's work.		
3. *Advancement*. The opportunity for advancement or promotion based on one's ability.		
4. *Status*. Being accorded various position-based aspects, such as your own nicely appointed office, selected parking place, or other prestige elements.		
5. *Pay*. A wage that not only covers normal living expenses but provides additional funds for certain luxury items.		
6. *Supervision*. Working for a supervisor who is both competent in doing his or her job and looks out for the welfare of subordinates.		
7. *Job itself*. Having a job that is interesting, challenging, and provides for substantial variety and autonomy.		
8. *Job security*. Feeling good about your security within the department.		
9. *Co-workers*. Working with co-workers who are friendly and helpful.		
10. *Personal development*. Given the opportunity in your job to develop and refine new skills and abilities.		
11. *Fringe benefits*. A substantial fringe benefit package covering such aspects as personal protection.		
12. *Working conditions*. Safe and attractive conditions for doing your work.		

2. Exercise: Job Satisfaction Questionnaire

1. How satisfied are you with the sort of work you are doing?

1	2	3	4	5

    Very dissatisfied   Very satisfied

2. What value do you think the community puts in your service?

1	2	3	4	5

    None   Very great

3. In your daily work, how free are you to make decisions and act on them?

1	2	3	4	5

    Not at all   Very free

4. How much recognition does your supervisor show for a job well done?

1	2	3	4	5

    None   Great deal

5. How satisfied are you with the type of leadership you have been getting from your supervisor?

1	2	3	4	5

    Very dissatisfied   Very satisfied

6. To what extent do you get to participate in the supervisory decisions that affect your job?

1	2	3	4	5

    None   Great deal

7. How closely do you feel you are observed by your supervisor?

1	2	3	4	5

    About right   Too closely

8. Are you satisfied with the department as it now stands?

1	2	3	4	5

    Very dissatisfied   Very satisfied

9. How satisfied are you with your prestige within the city government?

1	2	3	4	5

    Very dissatisfied   Very satisfied

10. How satisfied are you with your possibilities of being promoted to a better position?

1	2	3	4	5

    Very dissatisfied   Very satisfied

11. How satisfied are you with your present salary?

1	2	3	4	5

    Very dissatisfied   Very satisfied

12. How satisfied are you with your status in the community?

1	2	3	4	5

    Very dissatisfied   Very satisfied

13. Would you advise a friend to join this department?

1	2	3	4	5

    No   Yes

14. Do you receive a feeling of accomplishment from the work you are doing?

| | 1 | 2 | 3 | 4 | 5 |

Very dissatisfied   Very satisfied

15. Rate the amount of pressure you feel in meeting the work demands of your job.

| | 1 | 2 | 3 | 4 | 5 |

Very dissatisfied   Very satisfied

The higher the total score, the greater is your job satisfaction. A general rule of thumb is:

55+	Very high
50–54	High
45–49	Above average
40–45	Average
35–39	Below average
34–	Take this job and shove it

RESPONSIBILITY SEVEN

Goal Setting: Supervising by Objectives

I know of no more encouraging fact than the unquestionable ability of man to elevate his life by conscious endeavor.

Henry David Thoreau

Our beginning should be with an end in mind. In other words, before we start our journey, we should have a destination or goal set for ourselves. Please re-read the preceding quote—the key word for us is "conscious." Are you conscious of where you are now with your life and *where* and *why* it is headed?

By keeping the end clearly in mind (your consciousness), you can make certain that whatever you do on any particular day does not stray from the goal you have set as supremely important, and that each day of your life contributes in a logical way to the vision you have of your life as a whole.

Organizations share the same urgent need for beginning with an end in mind. The "end" is typically referred to as a "mission statement." And, within the mission statement, you'll find the "ends" or goals of the organization—in our case, a *police organization*. Police organizations should have a clear understanding of their goals. It means that they are *conscious* of where they're going so that they better comprehend where they are now and so that their efforts are always pointed in the right direction.

A while ago, we conducted a three-day team-building workshop for a large, full-service sheriff's department. The sheriff is a tall, rugged, red-headed, affable guy. At that time, he'd been the sheriff of the 1,800-person organization for twelve years. The workshop was comprised of an undersheriff, four assistant sheriffs, a coroner, and fifteen captains. The second day started with a discussion of a pending shift in the allocation of sworn personnel. Within a few minutes, the fifteen captains were adamantly defending their assigned turfs. The sheriff sensed this and asked, "Hey, what are our goals?" No one said a word. We saw his face start to match the color of his hair. In a louder voice he stated, "I guess there's no reason to ask you: What are our priorities?" Now there was silence—perhaps 60 seconds, which seemed like an hour.

Finally, one brave captain ventured out with, "Sheriff, in my opinion, our number one priority and goal is corrections. After all, about one-half of our personnel are assigned to it." In a second the sheriff's obvious anger switched to puzzlement. He dropped his head and then looked up and scanned the group. He proceeded to surprise us by saying, "I apologize. I thought you knew. It's my mistake for not telling you, and then retelling you. Our goals, in order of their priority are (1) drug abuse enforcement; (2) contract cities; (3) corrections; (4) county patrol areas; and (5) the coroner's office. Now, don't forget them." We're confident no one has—we certainly haven't.

It is very easy to get in an "activity trap," in the busy-ness of police work, to work harder and harder at producing results only to discover that they're unnecessary. A police organization without goals can be highly efficient and very ineffective. *The police organization that lives without goals will spend its future in the present.*

ROLE OF THE POLICE SUPERVISOR

The crux of this book bears repeating here—the primary responsibility of a police supervisor is to get results through people. The first step is to set the requisite goals for doing so. Second, the supervisor must generate plans that propel him or her in the direction of *goal fulfillment*. Finally, the police supervisor must construct a method for combining *goals* and *plans* to attain them. Finally, we conclude with an argument for the use of MBO.

The effective police supervisor will set goals, plan for their execution, and apply MBO to connect goals with plans and ultimately performance. Hence, the police supervisor is a goal setter, planner, and monitor.

GOAL SETTING

Trenell began to explain: "Once he has told me what needs to be done or we have agreed on what needs to be done, then each goal is recorded on no more than a single page. The One Minute Manager feels that a goal, and its performance standard, should take no more than 250 words to express. He insists that anyone be able to read it within a minute. He keeps a copy and I keep a copy so everything is clear and so we can both periodically check the progress."

—Kenneth Blanchard and Spencer Johnson
The One Minute Manager (New York: William Morrow and Co., Inc., 1982), p. 37

A goal is something we desire, we hope for in the future. An *objective* is a goal, only it is more finite and time certain. For example, a police supervisor may set a goal of developing his or her assigned personnel to the maximum of their innate strengths. An objective that would support fulfillment of this goal could be: all personnel within my purview will have attended an officer survival course within the next six months. Note that the goal is more broad in scope, while an objective is specific, with an assigned time frame.

Multiplicity of Goals

At first glance, it might appear that organizations have a singular objective: for police departments to apprehend criminals. But closer analysis demonstrates that all organizations have multiple objectives. Police agencies also seek to increase public safety and provide general government services. No one measure can effectively evaluate whether an organization is performing successfully. Emphasis on one goal, such as crime, ignores other goals that must also be achieved if long-term safety is to be achieved. Additionally, the use of a single objective almost certainly will result in undesirable practices, since supervisors will ignore important parts of their job in order to look good on the single measure.

Real versus Stated Goals

Stated goals are official statements of what an organization says and what it wants various publics to believe are its objectives. But stated objectives, which can be pulled from the organization's charter, annual report, public relations announcements, or from public statements made by a police chief, are often conflicting and excessively influenced by what society believes police organizations *should* do.

The conflict in stated goals exists because organizations respond to a vast array of constituencies. Unfortunately, these constituencies frequently evaluate the organization by different criteria. As a result, police management is forced to say different things to different audiences.

Given the diverse constituencies to which police management is required to respond, it would be a surprise to find a department with a set of objectives stated to everyone that actually describes what the organization seeks to achieve.

There is visible evidence to support, for example, the idea that police managers give much attention to their social responsibilities in the decisions they make and the actions they take. The overall goals that top management states can be the actual or real, or fiction. If you want to know what a police department's *real objectives* are, closely observe what members of the organization actually do. It is behavior that counts.

If we are to develop comprehensive and consistent plans, it is important to differentiate between stated and real objectives. An understanding of the latter's existence can assist in explaining what otherwise may seem like management inconsistencies.

What Business Are We Really In?

An old story tells of three stonecutters who were asked what they were doing. The first replied, "I am making a living." The second kept on hammering while he said, "I am doing the best job of stonecutting in the entire country." The third one looked up with a visionary gleam in his eyes and said, "I am building a cathedral."

—Peter F. Drucker
Management (New York: Harper and Row, 1974), p. 57

The third man is, of course, the true supervisor. The first man knows what he wants to get out of the work and manages to do so. He is likely to give a "fair day's work for a fair day's pay." But he is not a supervisor and will never be one. The second man is a problem. Workmanship is essential; in fact, an organization demoralizes if it does not demand of its members the highest workmanship they are capable of. But there is always a danger that the true workman, the true police professional, will believe that he is accomplishing something when in effect he is just polishing stones or collecting footnotes. Workmanship must be encouraged in the police enterprise. But it must always be related to the needs of the whole.

The effective police supervisor will quickly and easily be able to assert the real goals of the department. Hence he or she understands existing values and possesses a clear vision of the incoming future.

FROM GOAL SETTING TO PLANNING

The whole of life should be spent thinking about how to find the right course of action to follow. Thought and forethought give counsel both on living and achieving success.

—Baltsar Gracian, S.J.C.

In a police enterprise, supervisors are not automatically directed toward a common goal. On the contrary, organization, by its very nature, contains four powerful factors of misdirection: (1) the specialized work of most supervisors, (2) the hierarchical structure of management, (3) the differences in vision and work and the resultant insulation of various levels of supervision and management, and (4) the compensation structure of the management group. To overcome these obstacles requires more than good intentions, sermons, and exhortations. It requires policy and structure. It requires that planning be purposefully organized and be made the living law of the entire supervisory cadre.

Planning Defined

Planning is the process of implementing objectives. It is concerned, then, with means (how it is to be done), as well as with ends (what is to be done). Planning can be further defined in terms of whether it is informal or formal. All police supervisors engage in planning, but it may be only the informal variety. Nothing is written down, and there is little or no sharing of objectives with others in the organization.

When we use the term *planning*, we are implying formal planning. There exist specific objectives. These objectives are typically committed to writing and available to organization members. They cover a period of months or years. Finally, specific action programs exist for the achievement of these objectives; that is, supervision and management have clearly defined the path that they want to take from getting where they are to where they want to be.

Why Planning?

Why should police supervisors engage in planning? Because it gives direction, reduces the impact of change, minimizes waste and redundancy, sets the standards to facilitate control, and increases performance.

First, planning establishes coordinated effort. It gives directions to supervisors and officers alike. When everyone knows where the agency is going and what they are expected to contribute toward achieving the objectives, there should be increased coordination, cooperation, and teamwork. A lack of planning can foster "zigzagging" and thus prevent a department from efficiently moving toward its objectives. Second, planning is a way to reduce uncertainty through anticipated change. It also clarifies the consequences of the actions supervision might take in response to change. Planning forces supervisors to look ahead, anticipate changes, consider the impact of these changes, and develop appropriate responses.

Third, planning can also reduce overlapping and wasteful activities. Coordination before the fact is likely to uncover waste and redundancy. Additionally, when means and ends are clear, inefficiencies become more obvious. Fourth, planning reinforces the objectives or standards that are to be used to facilitate control. If we are unsure of what we are trying to achieve, how can we determine if we have achieved it? In planning, we implement the objectives. In the controlling function, we compare actual performance against the objectives, identify any significant deviations, and take the necessary corrective action. Without planning, there can be no control.

Finally, there is considerable evidence that supervisors and organizations that plan outperform those that do not. Although the evidence is strong, do not assume that all efforts require planning. After all, planning can be time consuming and costly. The key question is, Does the planning effort appear to be justified in view of the expected gains or outcomes?

Types of Planning

The most popular way to describe plans is by their breadth. Plans that are organization-wide, that establish the organization's overall objectives, and that seek to position the police organization in terms of its environment are called *strategic* plans. Plans that specify the details on how the overall objectives are to be achieved are called *operational* plans.

Strategic plans. Strategic planning typically encompasses a long-term time frame (three to five years or more), has an open-ended perspective, and attempts to predict emerging "driving forces." This form of planning is just now being introduced into police organizations. Since this process is usually executed by top management, we will provide a benchmark reference for those of you who want to learn more about this vital method: George A. Steiner, *Strategic Planning: What Every Manager MUST Know* (New York: Free Press, 1979).

Operational plans. There are two categories of operational plans, *single use* and *standing*. The first is nonrecurring, such as multiagency police planning for the 1984 Olympic Games. In other words, any plan that identifies how the organization's primary objectives are to be achieved, is developed for a specific purpose, and dissolves after this purpose is accomplished is a single-use plan.

The two main single-use plans are *programs* and *budgets*. A program is a complex of miniplans for achieving an objective. Administrators in a police agency develop a program to respond to the acts of a terrorist or other unexpected disaster. The plan is designed for the particular requirements of the occurrence. Once the victims have been helped, the plan is assessed, updated, and stored for future application.

The most familiar single-use plan is the numerical budget. Police management typically prepares budgets for revenues, expenses, and capital expenditure needs such as personnel and equipment. It's not unusual, though, for budgets to be used for improving time, space, and human resource utilization.

Police supervisors are not planning for future decisions. Rather, they are planning for the future impact of those decisions that they currently make. Decisions made today become a commitment to some future action or expenditure.

FROM PLANNING TO MBO

Management by objectives (MBO) is essentially a threefold process that

1. Sets a course of desired direction—the objective
2. Motivates the person to proceed in that direction—the result
3. Ensures self-control via feedback—the managing/supervising

MBO necessitates participatively set goals that are tangible, verifiable, and measurable. Rather than using goals to control, MBO seeks to use them to motivate. The remainder of this section concentrates on the development and use of MBO in police organizations. The practice of MBO by police supervisors has enormous positive payoffs for the overall organization. In the material that follows, *mentally translate the M in MBO into that all-important S for supervisor.*

What Is MBO?

Management by objectives is not new. The concept dates back over thirty years. Its appeal undoubtedly lies in its emphasis on converting overall organizational objectives into specific objectives for organizational units and individual members. MBO operationalizes the concept of objectives by devising a process by which objectives cascade down through the organization. As depicted in Figure 7-1, the organization's overall goals are translated into specific objectives for each succeeding level (i.e., division, bureau) in the police department. This linking ensures that the objectives for each unit are compatible with and supportive of the unit just above it. At the individual level, MBO provides specific personal performance objectives. All police personnel, therefore, have an identified specific contribution to make to their unit's performance. If all the individuals achieve their objectives, then their unit's objectives will be attained and the organization's basic goals are pursued:

- Crime control
- Crime prevention
- Order maintenance
- Human services

Goals and Objectives

For our purposes, a *goal* is comprised of one or more objectives. An *objective* is a more precise statement of what an organization or individual seeks to accomplish. Also, it typically has a shorter time frame, ranging from a few months to a

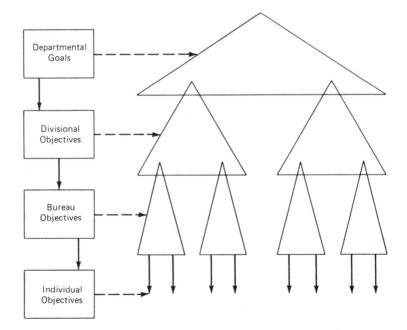

Figure 7-1 From Goals into Objectives

few years. The following quotation is probably best defined as a goal. The concrete steps specified as necessary to accomplish the goal are objectives.

Need for Local Objectives and Priorities

While the scope and objectives of the exercise of the government's police power are properly determined in the first instance by state and local legislative bodies within the limits fixed by the Constitution and by court decisions, it should be recognized there is considerable latitude remaining with local government to develop an overall direction for police services. Within these limits, each local jurisdiction should decide upon objectives and priorities. Decisions regarding police resources, police personnel needs, police organization, and relations with other government agencies should then be made in a way which will best achieve the objectives and priorities of the particular locality.[1]

Once the goals and the more specific objectives have been decided, we find ourselves in a position to manage—in this case supervise—by them. While the literature on MBO is extensive and covers both public and private organizations, the term still remains subject to varying definitions. Peter Drucker first coined the term in 1954 and describes MBO as a mutual understanding between the manager and his or her subordinates of what their contribution will be for the organization over a given period of time. It thus establishes parameters of *self-control* and *common direction*.[2] Moreover, it establishes parameters that target the individual and the agency, both in the direction of accomplishing the much to be desired goals.

Dynamics of MBO

MBO is not a simple or undemanding chore. It requires a major commitment and effort. For workers seldom automatically cooperate, and even more rarely do they cooperate in the pursuit of a common goal. Regretfully, there are many distorting influences. First, the top or middle managers can create dysfunctional situations by egoism or ingrained biases. Also, by merely filtering information up, down, and laterally within the hierarchy, one finds excessive differences in interpretations of the subject matter at hand. Finally, status differentials—whether they be rank, pay, or position based—cause errant decisions on what to do, when, and where.

Specific Objectives

Are we not at a point where one should ask, "What are the objectives of the police supervisor?" Each manager, from the chief down to the supervisor,

---

[1]Advisory Committee on the Police Function, *The Urban Police Function* (Washington, D.C.: American Bar Association, 1973), p. 4.

[2]Peter F. Drucker, *Management: Tasks, Responsibilities, Practices* (New York: Harper & Row, 1973), p. 438.

needs clearly spelled out objectives. Otherwise, confusion can be guaranteed. These objectives should specify what performance a supervisoral unit is supposed to achieve. They should indicate what contribution the supervisor and his or her unit are expected to make to help other units attain their objectives. Finally, they should detail what contribution the supervisor can expect from other units toward the attainment of his or her own objectives. Right from the start, in other words, emphasis should be on *teamwork* and *team* results. These objectives should always derive from the goals of the police agency.

The objectives of every supervisor should spell out his or her contribution to the attainment of agency goals in all areas of the police service. Obviously, not every supervisor has a direct contribution to make in every area. To obtain balanced efforts, the objectives of all police supervisors on all levels and in all areas should also be keyed to both short- and long-range considerations. And, of course, all objectives should always contain both the tangible police objectives and such "intangible" objectives as supervisory development, worker performance and attitude, and public responsibility. *Anything else is short-sighted and inappropriate.*

Who Sets Objectives?

Another critical consideration about MBO deals with the question of how the supervisor's objectives ought to be set and by whom. Most basically, the supervisor's objectives should be established by the supervisor in light of (1) his or her expected contribution to the agency, (2) the expectation of his or her subordinates, and (3) the expectation of his or her manager. The supervisor's manager has, as the supervisor should have, the ultimate purview for approval or rejection.

To accomplish all three, a sizable amount of information exchange must occur. Thus, managing supervisors, or supervising police employees, requires special efforts not only to establish common direction but to eliminate misdirection. Mutual understanding can never be attained by "communications down," can never be created by talking. It can result only from "communications down, up, and across." It requires both the superior's willingness to listen and a tool especially designed to make the employee not only heard but understood.

Measuring Performance

To be able to control his or her own performance, a police supervisor needs to know more than what the objectives are. The supervisor must be able to measure his or her performance and results against the expressed objectives. It should be an axiomatic practice to supply supervisors with clear and universal measurements in all areas of activity. These measurements need not be rigidly quantitative; nor need they be precise. But they have to be *clear, simple,* and *rational.* They have to be germane and direct attention and efforts to where they should go. They have to be reliable—at least to the point where their margin of error is acknowledged and understood. Supervisory control is best manifested by directives explicit in a MBO program that concentrates on one's performance, which is constantly measured in relation to the expressed objectives.

Each police supervisor should have the information she or he needs to measure her or his own performance and that of subordinates and should receive it soon enough to make any changes necessary for the desired results. And this information should go to the supervisor as well as her or his manager. It should also be reported to the police employee. More and accurate information can result in a blessing or a curse, depending on how it is used. For the new capability to produce, measuring information will make possible effective self-control; and if so used, it will lead to a tremendous improvement in the effectiveness and performance of supervision. But if this new capability is abused to impose rigid or excessive control on supervision from above, the new technology will cause incalculable harm by demoralizing supervisors and police officers, which in turn tends to reduce their effectiveness.

Your Assumptions

MBO forces the supervisor and the police officer to exert self-discipline in light of meeting the stated objectives. Indeed, it may well lead to demanding too much rather than too little. This has been the main criticism leveled against the concept. Yet it remains that MBO is linked to one's ability to accept self-discipline. A supervisor must assume that the vast majority of subordinates are capable of doing so. If not, then MBO will fail. A supervisor who starts out with the assumption that people are weak, irresponsible and lazy will get weakness, irresponsibility, and laziness. He or she corrupts. A supervisor who assumes strength, responsibility, and desire to contribute may experience a few disappointments. But the supervisor's first task is to make effective the strengths of people, and this can be done if he or she starts out with the assumption that people—and especially supervisors and professional police officers—want to achieve. Above all, the police supervisor must make this assumption with regard to the young educated people of today who will be tomorrow's police officers. They may not know what they mean when they demand to be allowed to "make a contribution." But their demand is the right demand. And they are right also that supervision, as it has been practiced so far in most police agencies, does not act on the assumption that the young educated people want to make a contribution. Police supervisors need to be subjected—and to subject themselves—to the discipline and the demands of MBO.

A Philosophy

The police organization is in need of a philosophy of management and supervision that will give full scope to individual strength and responsibility, as well as common direction to vision and effort; establish teamwork; and harmonize the desires of the individual with the goals of the agency. MBO substitutes for control from outside the stricter, more exacting, and more effective control from inside. It motivates the supervisor and subordinates to action, not because somebody tells them to do something or talks them into doing it, but because the objective task demands it. They act, not because somebody wants them to, but because they decide that they have to. Finally, this philosophy must permeate the entire hierarchy of the agency. It must apply to every manager, every supervisor, and every employee, whatever the level or assignment.

SUPERVISING BY OBJECTIVES

Policy making for the police is complicated by the fact that, at least in large cities, the police department is an organization with at least two objectives, one of which produces conflict and the other of which cannot be obtained.

—James Q. Wilson
Varieties of Police Behavior (New York: Basic Books, Inc., 1968), p. 135

The decision to set objectives on the part of a police agency automatically presents a major challenge to its entire decision-making process. MBO first requires a series of decisions on what objectives ought to be pursued. Second, an infinite number of decisions are needed to accomplish them. Odiorne's book provides testimony to this thinking in its title, *Management Decisions by Objectives*.[3] He states that three steps of objectives should be rank ordered according to the level of difficulty in their achievement. In order of ascendancy, they are

1. Regular or routine: measured by exceptions from standards objectives
2. Problem solving: measured by solutions and time established as objectives
3. Innovative goals: measured by productive changes sought and achieved in time

Regardless of the type of objective, a singular and common process can be used to set them. Again, the complexity, the challenge, the certainty, and the time frame will vary based on the type of objective involved. The objective-setting process consists of seven interrelated steps.

1. Identification of the problem
2. Definition of the problem in specific, operational terms
3. Development of alternative strategies to deal with the problem
4. Selection of the appropriate alternative
5. Implementation
6. Evaluation
7. Feedback

---

[3]George S. Odiorne, *Management Decisions by Objectives* (Englewood Cliffs, N.J.: Prentice Hall, 1969), see Chapter 7.

Identification of the Problem

At first glance this might appear to be an oversimplification, but experience has shown that this step is often the most difficult part of the entire process. For example, let us assume that a sergeant in a medium-sized police department has the responsibility for supervising a team of fourteen police officers. In addition to this overall responsibility, he is responsible for the division's in-service training program and supply requisitioning. He is actively pursuing his own formal education and will soon be awarded his associate of arts degree from the local college. The chief of police is interested in converting the traditional patrol patterns and assignments to a team-policing program. The agency has never experienced such an ambitious undertaking and, in fact, is understrength by approximately four personnel. Because the department uses a formal hierarchy, the sergeant's immediate supervisor is a lieutenant (of which the agency has four). The chief has selected the sergeant to research, develop, and present to him a position paper exploring the team-policing concept for their agency.

In reviewing this example and placing yourself in our sergeant's shoes, what would you say is the real problem—the one to which meaningful objectives must ultimately be addressed? Is it time, personnel, converting the attitudes of the department to accept the change, or training, or is it a combination of all these? If you selected the last alternative, then our description of the difficulty of adequately defining the problem is becoming clear.

Various techniques can assist the supervisor in this step. These include reflective thinking, analyzing available data, generating new data about the problem, brainstorming, paper slip techniques, personal observation, or asking someone internal or external to the agency who may have had more experience with such problems. The critical part, however, remains thinking clearly about the problem and then writing it down in the most specific terms possible. This might require several attempts, and the supervisor is encouraged to keep at the task until he or she is satisfied that what he or she has written is an accurate statement about the problem—and that it is the *real* problem.

Specific Statement

This step of the process is somewhat similar to the identification step; however, it is separated due to its importance. In addition to the advice and cautions offered previously, the supervisor should reflect on the "objective statement" he or she has developed about the problem. It is often productive to use colleagues and a work group as a sounding board to modify, correct, or reinforce the objective statement and to assure himself or herself that what has been written is in fact a specific problem statement amenable to solution and measurement.

Alternative Strategies

In this step of the process, the supervisor is to develop as *many* alternatives as possible to solve the problem. In the first phase of the exercise, the supervisor should not disregard any possible alternative. The same techniques as indicated before can be utilized to do this—ranging from individual thinking to group thinking. After all the possible alternatives have been identified, the supervisor can then proceed to reduce the list to the handful that hold the most promise. Factors that affect the decision to leave an alternative on the list or remove it are almost limitless. A few of the more outstanding include

- Time
- Money
- Personnel
- Political ramifications
- Tradition and custom
- Attitudes
- Skill of the participants

The skill and expertise of the individual and the size of the problem also influence the choice of techniques used to evaluate each alternative. These range from a simple weighing system to complex mathematical formulas and system techniques.

Selection of an Alternative

This step is what the supervisor has been aiming toward from the start of the process. After following the preceding steps, the supervisor is finally ready to select the paramount one and implement it. One caution deserves to be reinforced here; that is, the best alternative is not always the most feasible one. The supervisor should be aware of this and should not become disillusioned when the "number one" alternative cannot be implemented. This is caused by a variety of reasons ranging from money to politics.

Implementation

Following the selection step, we are ready for implementation. In preparing to implement the selected alternative, the supervisor should have thought through the alternative to the point where he or she knows which individuals are going to be impacted, how they will be affected, and where the alternative will be exercised. In effect, the supervisor has a "battle plan" for following through with the selected alternative. This also proves useful in the last two steps, evaluation and feedback.

Evaluation

There is a growing awareness in the police community of the worth of evaluation. The benefit accrues from such things as being able to explain and justify action taken, fend off criticism of the approach to the problem that was taken, demonstrate the cost-effectiveness of the objective, and reinforce the value of introducing new techniques and methodologies into the police profession. Here, again, a host of techniques can help the supervisor evaluate the program. These range from simple statistical review to esoteric schemes developed by the aerospace industry to evaluate space flights. The selection of the correct technique depends on such factors as the size of the program, number of people involved, cost, geographical area involved, and number of interrelated components in the program.

Feedback

Finally, in the context of this process we are using the term *feedback* to mean communicating the results of our objective-setting process back to those above *and* below us in the hierarchy. Whether or not the results are favorable or unfavorable, it is imperative that we communicate the results back into our system. This is done for the following reasons:

- It keeps people informed of results.
- It leads to refined objectives, one building on the results of the last.
- It continues the process of constantly refining our ability to affect problems in our work group.
- It builds a data base on which to build future objectives and decisions.

In reviewing the theme of this section, the *objective-setting process is critical in the supervisor's role of problem solving*, the following series of questions should be asked of each objective:

- Is the objective a guide to action?
- Is it explicit enough to suggest certain types of action (alternatives)?
- Does it suggest tools to measure and control effectiveness?
- Is it challenging?
- Does it show cognizance of internal and external constraints?

OBSTACLES TO MBO

Much like the "I've got good news and bad news for you, which do you want first?" jokes, I have discussed but one side of MBO—the good news. Now for some bad news. MBO is not without obstacles. As expressed thus far, the advantages are that police managers and supervisors are encouraged to think seriously about their objectives and to try to get them into meaningful and also measurable terms; also, it encourages forecasting, planning, and dialogues between all administrative levels. The disadvantages are that the system is basically foreign to those systems that have developed in both industry and government; most planners fail to see MBO as a system; government sees successful applications of MBO in the private sector as an obstacle; and there is insufficient commitment to MBO among those at executive levels. More specifically, common obstacles include dilution of efforts, crisis management, employer–employee goal divergence, organizational structure, cost inflation, and macro-personal problems. In addition, limitations to MBO particular to police agencies include organizational structure and basic goals, processes, and economic rewards largely set by statute.

We can conclude our discussion of MBO by suggesting three contingency variables that may determine whether it succeeds or fails: organization culture, top management commitment, and organizational type. It's very likely that those instances when MBO has not succeeded can be explained by an unsupportive culture, lack of top management commitment, or organizational constraints that undermine MBO ideology.

KEY POINTS

- The supervisor is responsible for (1) setting goals, (2) creating plans for their accomplishment, and (3) linking goals and plans via MBO.
- A goal is a desired future. An objective is one form of a goal, only it includes a more specific and time limited dimension.
- Police organizations have multiple goals and objectives.
- Real goals and stated goals may differ from one another.
- Planning is a process for implementing goals and objectives.
- Police supervisors who plan their work typically outperform others who do not.
- In MBO, the objectives must be specific, set in collaboration with the employee, and used to measure performance.
- MBO is comprised of seven sequential steps: (1) identify the problem(s), (2) create a specific statement, (3) develop alternative strategies, (4) select a strategy, (5) design an implementation plan, (6) evaluate the results, and (7) provide feedback to the police employee.
- The three main obstacles to MBO are (1) a resistive working culture, (2) lack of top management backing, and (3) departmental constraints.

DISCUSSION

1. Is the phrase "to protect and serve" a goal or an objective? Why?
2. Convert the statement, "We had best reduce our burglary rate," into an objective.
3. In your opinion, what are the *real goals* of a police agency?
4. Besides the budget, can you identify one or more plans in your agency? (Or, if not your department, then someone else's.)
5. "Rather than using goals to control, MBO seeks to use them to motivate." Explain this assumption.

6. Earlier we covered the *assumptions* and *philosophy* we hold about people as workers. What are your assumptions and philosophy about police employees? Is there any need to make adjustments so as to increase your effectiveness as a supervisor?

STRUCTURED EXPERIENCES

1. Case Study: "That's Not Fair . . ."

As a newly promoted police sergeant, you recently attended a mandatory and state-certified two-week "Supervisors' Course." You were an enthusiastic and active learner, graduating number three in a class of eighty-two sergeants. Not everything you heard during the course seemed potentially useful on the job. Nonetheless, you vowed to apply the ideas that appeared plausible, the foremost being MBO.

Presently you are one of three field sergeants assigned to the uniform patrol evening watch (1600–2400). Your span of control and responsibility includes seven patrol officers. All are deployed in single-person patrol cars. Their experience ranges from one to fourteen years, with an average of five years. One is a white female, and one is a black male. The others are white males. Three of the seven you know well, having worked with them in the past. Your police experience includes two years as a cadet, three years in patrol, and one year as a detective. During that period of time you acquired a bachelor's degree in Criminal Justice with a grade point average of 3.96.

You consider yourself to be fair, practical, goal oriented, intelligent, and approachable. Among your weaknesses, you include impatience, stubbornness, and a lack of affability. In knowing your weaknesses, you constantly guard against them.

After one month of supervising your officers, you asked for feedback on your style and tactics. The comments were generally favorable (e.g., "I have no problems with you," "You're O.K. so far," "I'm glad you're our boss").

For one week you lectured your officers on the merits of MBO and alerted them to the eventual use of it in your work unit. Simultaneously, you secured the tentative approval of your superior, Lieutenant Lance, for its implementation. He commented, "O.K. it's your crew. But don't make any waves."

You carefully set a number of objectives for the entire group as well as each individual officer. The objectives are, in your opinion, clear, precise, practical, and attainable. The objectives for the work group are:

1. Reduce residential burglaries by 5 percent within six months
2. Increase the number of traffic citations (nonparking) by 3 percent in three months
3. Reduce citizen complaints from two per month to one per month within three months
4. Improve the service response time from an average of 4.6 minutes per call to 4.0 minutes per call.

Your first MBO conference is scheduled today with Officer Mike D. Nadler. The officer uses the D as his middle initial to denote "*Dynamo*," a hard-working street cop with eleven years experience in patrol. His performance ratings have rarely been "outstanding"; however, he has always been rated above average. He is highly dependable, prone to light-hearted sarcasm, and has completed fifteen units of college courses.

After the usual social amenities, you hand Mike a written copy of the MBO agreement. Besides the group's objectives, you listed for him (1) to seek an assignment in another function within one year in order to broaden his experience, (2) to bring his ratings up to the "outstanding" category within six months, and (3) to enter college and complete a minimum of three units per semester starting with the next semester.

Mike appeared to like what he was reading in that his facial expression gradually developed into a relaxed smile. He finished his reading, handed the form back to you, and candidly remarked, "Very amusing, Sergeant. But unless you order me to do so, I'm not signing this form. Why should I? It could be used against me. After all, I work hard. I'm proud to be a patrol officer; why should I become a detective? Also, I have three young kids and all my spare time is devoted to them. I'll be damned if I'll commit any of it to a college course. Are you ordering me to sign the form or not, Sergeant?"

1. How should you respond to Officer Nadler?
2. Define the problem.
3. How can you correct this situation?
4. What will be your future approach to MBO, if any?

2. Exercise: Goal Setting

This exercise is intended to build your skill as a supervisor in the use of MBO. Based on the agency for which you work, select one of the following subjects, or generate one of your own. Write a goal (objective) statement related to the subject using no more than 250 words. Be certain that the goal statement complies with the guidelines expressed earlier in this chapter (e.g., clear, specific, attainable, etc.). A few subjects of concern might be:

- Residential burglary rate
- Commercial burglary rate
- Commercial robbery rate
- Officer-involved traffic accidents
- Citizen complaints
- Response times
- Care and maintenance of equipment
- In-service training

If in a group setting, then divide into teams of five to seven individuals. Each person reads aloud his or her goal statement. Then collaborate to refine the statement into a highly practical objective worthy of implementation in a police department. This process should be repeated at least once or twice. Practice ensures your successful use of this powerful supervisor's tool.

3. Exercise: Goal Substitution

This is a simple but powerful exercise to help you understand the significance of goal substitution.

- Imagine learning that you have to retire in one year. List three things you'd like to accomplish during this last year.
- Assume eleven months have passed, and you have one month left. Again, list three things you would like to do.
- Make a new list assuming you have one week left and another assuming that you have only forty-eight hours left.
- Examine what you've written. If your list includes activities you're not currently pursuing, what's stopping you from pursuing them now? *Get on track!*

(*Note:* This exercise can be easily modified to focus on your personal life. Merely assume that you have one year to live. List three things you'd want to do within the year and so on to forty-eight hours.)

RESPONSIBILITY EIGHT

Performance Evaluation: Feedback—The Making of Winners

If the minimum wasn't good enough—then it wouldn't be the minimum.

Lieutenant Maynard

In Responsibility Two we told you about Lieutenant Maynard. You may recall that he alone was destroying the intent of a very important training program. Finally, fed up and angry, the chief confronted Maynard in private at the end of the day. He said, "Maynard, since you've been with this department, you've done nothing but the minimum!" His reply appears above. . . . No wonder police chiefs and supervisors get gray hair.

Ever since that event, I have wondered if Maynard had been subjected to performance evaluations. I've also wondered if he was, subsequent to the confrontation, subjected to performance evaluations. Could his behavior be the fault of a nonexistent or unreliable performance appraisal system?

GETTING QUALITY RESULTS THROUGH PEOPLE

Police supervisors accomplish things by working through other people. They need and depend on police personnel to achieve their unit goals. It's important, therefore, for supervisors to get their employees to behave in ways that police management considers desirable. But how do supervisors ensure that police employees are performing as they are supposed to?

Basically, the police supervisor uses two methods. The first occurs on a day-to-day basis: supervisors oversee employees' work and make corrections as they occur. The supervisor who spots a police officer taking an unnecessary risk when operating his or her radio car will point out the correct way and tell the employee to do it this way in the future.

The second method is a formal process whereby supervisors assess the work of their employees through systematic performance evaluations. An employee's recent performance is appraised. Based on that appraisal, sanctions follow. If performance is positive, the employee's behavior is typically reinforced with a reward, such as a new assignment. If performance is below standard, supervisors seek to correct it or, depending on the nature of the deviation, may discipline the employee. Both performance-evaluation methods (informal daily and formal periodic) are best supported by an MBO program.

ROLE OF THE POLICE SUPERVISOR

Take a Minute:
Look at Your Goals
Look at Your Performance
See If Your Behavior Matches Your Goals

—Kenneth Blanchard and Spencer Johnson
The One Minute Manager (New York: William Morrow and Co., Inc., 1982), p. 97

The test of a police organization is the spirit of performance, and it is the very cornerstone of a supervisor's role to develop this spirit. To manifest this spirit, you must not fall prey to mere exhortations, lofty sermons, or well-meaning intentions. *It must be practices.* Specifically, there are four required practices:

1. The focus of the police agency must be on *performance.* The first requirement of the spirit of organization is high performance standards, for the group as well as for each officer. The department must establish a habit of achievement. However, performance does not mean "success every time." Performance is rather a "batting average." It will, indeed it must, have room for mistakes and even for failures. What performance has no room for is complacency and low standards.

2. The focus of a successful police agency must be on *opportunities* rather than on problems.

3. The decisions that affect people, their placement, pay, promotion, demotion, and severance, must express the values of the organization. They are the true controls of an organization. (See Responsibility One on values.)

4. In its people decisions, supervision must demonstrate that it realizes that *integrity* is one absolute requirement of an effective supervisor. It is the one quality that you have to bring with you and cannot be expected to acquire later.

Hence, your role as a police supervisor requires you to think and act in such a fashion that you

• Emphasize performance

- Create opportunities
- Promote values
- Evidence integrity

PERFORMANCE EVALUATION DEFINED

Most simply, performance evaluation is a complex process with two key purposes: behavioral motivation and control. Also, you are destined to learn that, to a large extent your success as a supervisor is directly related to your ability to appraise the performance of your assigned personnel.

Performance evaluation (or performance appraisal or rating) can be defined as both a process and a method by which a police agency obtains feedback on and provides guidelines for the effectiveness of its personnel—feedback, in the sense that past work effort is evaluated, and guidelines, to the extent that performance objectives are specified for the immediate future. Traditionally, the evaluation process and methods were designed with feedback as an end in mind; having guidelines as part of the evaluation system is more recent. An evaluation system that uses both feedback *and* guidelines is commonly referred to as MBO.

In general, the process and method serve an auditing and control function by generating information upon which many departmental decisions are made. In practice, performance evaluation is very difficult for several reasons.

First, it must serve many purposes, from evaluating the success of selection decisions, to assessing the effectiveness of a leader, to evaluating training efforts, to determining the quantity and quality of individual work effort. Second, the assessment of performance itself is a difficult measurement task because so many factors influence performance, including environmental, organizational, and individual factors. Finally, a great number of ethical and emotionally charged issues arise when performance is evaluated. The results of the process can have profound influences on the jobs, careers, attitudes, personal self-concepts, and general sense of well-being of police employees.

COMPLEX PROCESS

Imagine for a moment that you are a supervisor in command of a criminal investigations unit. Because of the retirement of one of your detectives, it has become necessary to select a new investigator from the ranks of the patrol operation or administrative services. You review the performance evaluation forms of police personnel with two or more years of service with the agency. A patrol officer and a training officer have received outstanding ratings over the past three years. However, the training officer is three percentage points higher than the patrol officer. As a result, you decide to request that the chief of police transfer the training officer to your division. When you announce your decision, the patrol officer asks to confer with you.

The patrol officer makes five points. (1) The officer questions the ade-

quacy of the performance evaluation form used to make six-month performance reviews, arguing that how well one scores on the form depends upon who
is doing the evaluation and that the form does not rate the truly proper aspects
of the job. (2) The officer charges that those in patrol are rated more strictly
than are those in administrative assignments. (3) The officer indicates that it
appeared you made your decision based on a single trait: that of the training
officer's friendly disposition. (4) The officer argues that the ratings reflect past
performance without in any way predicting one's success as a detective. (5) The
officer asserts that his last performance appraisal was mainly drawn from the
three weeks prior to the actual rating, and that most of his fine accomplishments during the entire six months were ignored.

This situation raises a number of prominent issues, all of which cause or
can cause major problems for police management. Performance evaluation is
linked to personnel decisions that determine assignments, salary adjustments,
promotions, training, affirmative action, discipline, and the overall individual.
This chapter addresses these issues in the way of offering practical advice and
proven recommendations that are intended to eradicate the "damned if we do"
possibilities in assessing an employee's performance.

VARIETY OF PURPOSES

Personnel decisions can be made without performance evaluation systems.
They can be made by drawing random numbers, by choosing whomever you
like best, by choosing the person you owe a favor to, or by choosing someone
who wears the best-smelling aftershave lotion or perfume, and so on. Clearly,
an effective organization requires a proficient process and method for assessing
the past performances and the future potentials of their most valuable asset:
human resources.

Performance evaluation plays an important role in control because it
serves as an audit, which facilitates control and motivation. Performance evaluation, then, is an auditing procedure that generates the information necessary
to control and direct the process of an organization. The review procedure
would usually start at the first level of operations, with each employee's performance being reviewed by immediate supervisors in each division. Entire
departmental performance would be reviewed at the next level of analysis.
Finally, the city manager, city council or sheriff would evaluate the overall
performance of the entire agency.

Control and motivation can take many forms, all involving supervisory
decisions. One way of controlling and motivating performance is through
selection, job placement, and promotion. The kind of person who is selected for
employment and the type of assignment in which he or she is placed will have a
direct influence on level of job performance. Another set of decisions that is
intended to control performance involves job and organizational design. Performance results may be used to suggest ways of redistributing tasks and
responsibilities in the police organization. In addition, when management
wants to tie rewards and performance together, performance evaluation is a

critical basis for making differential reward decisions. Furthermore, any decisions that a police agency makes with regard to improving performance through training and other forms of organizational change and development must be based on appraisals of skill deficiencies made during performance evaluations. Decisions on individual performance objectives (MBO) serve to direct the individual police employee *and* the police organization toward desired ends or goals. As a consequence, one can see that performance evaluation serves at least the following purposes:

1. Promotion, separation, and transfer decisions
2. Feedback for each employee regarding how the organization views his or her performance
3. Evaluations of relative contributions made by individuals and entire departments in achieving higher-level organizational goals
4. Reward decisions, including merit increases, promotions, and other rewards
5. Criteria for evaluating the effectiveness of selection and placement decisions, including the relevance of the information used in those decisions
6. Ascertaining and diagnosing training and developmental needs for individual employees and entire divisions within the organization
7. Criteria for evaluating the success of training and development decisions
8. Information upon which work-scheduling plans, budgeting, and human-resources planning can be based
9. Specification of new performance objectives (MBO) for the ensuing time period

Performance Evaluation Must Be Job Related

All the problems to which police supervisors and employees point when performance is reviewed can be summarized by two terms: *reliability* and *validity*. Both terms are qualities of the entire evaluation process and refer to the adequacy of the information that is generated and employed in subsequent decisions about employees.

Reliability. The first demand that must be made of a performance appraisal procedure is that it be reliable. Reliability actually refers to two major characteristics of the method by which performance information is collected: consistency and stability. *Consistency* demands that two alternative ways of gathering the same data should substantially agree in their results. For example, when two items are used on the same rating form to measure the same aspect of job performance, the supervisor's responses to them should agree with each other when evaluating the same subordinate. Similarly, two interviewers who evaluate the same employee should substantially agree in their findings. *Stability* demands that the same measuring device give the same results several times in a row if the characteristic it is supposed to be assessing has not changed. Thus, if the way in which a patrol officer treats citizens has not changed between Monday and Tuesday, we would expect a rating form to yield the same information about this aspect of performance on both days.

In actual practice, a variety of situational and personal factors can lead to either form of unreliability—inconsistency and instability—when police employees are evaluated. The most common error sources are illustrated in Figure 8-1.

One must recognize that *no specific appraisal forms or methods are universally reliable across police functions and across police agencies.* Indeed, the burden of reliable assessment rests on those who are going to *use* performance appraisal. A form or a technique that is reliable in one police organization may very well be totally inadequate in a different one.

Validity. Although reliability is a necessary precondition for validity or relevance, it does not alone ensure that a measure will actually be valid. For a method of appraisal to be relevant, three considerations must be taken into account: performance dimensions, the level of abstraction, and time. The single most important problem in designing an appraisal system is to take all three fully into account.

1. *Performance dimensions.* The validity problem, with respect to performance dimensions, is to adequately determine the different aspects of work

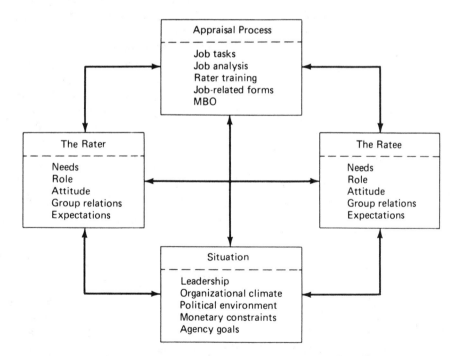

Figure 8-1 Performance Appraisal Process (Paul Whisenand, *The Effective Police Manager,* © 1981, p. 200. Reprinted by permission of Prentice Hall, Inc., Englewood Cliffs, N.J.)

behavior and performance to be evaluated. Very rarely is there a job that is unidimensional: For example, the job of a patrol officer must at least include the accuracy of social judgments, quality of direct citizen assistance, management of paraprofessionals, and interaction with peers. One of the first major steps in performance appraisal research in an organization is to empirically determine how many dimensions of performance must be assessed in order to validly appraise an employee's job performance—that is, job analysis.

Performance measures that do not define and assess all relevant dimensions of the job will be deficient and therefore not completely valid. However, measures that include dimensions that are not properly part of the job will be seen as invalid.

2. *Level of abstraction.* In addition to static performance dimensions, the validity of a performance measure depends on using the proper level of organizational analysis. We have pointed out that there are many models of organizational effectiveness, many of which differ in the level at which they conceptualize effectiveness (organizational, group, or individual). In practice, an evaluation system must incorporate and deal with all three levels of analysis. This problem is indicated in Figure 8-2, which also illustrates three possible levels of analysis or abstraction in performance appraisal.

3. *Time.* Time is the third critical dimension influencing the validity of performance appraisal; it operates in two major ways as an influence. First, immediate, intermediate, and ultimate criteria have a short-run and a long-run orientation. Specific and immediate criteria (such as job behaviors) are appropriately measured in the short run, at the time the work is being done. Less immediate outcomes (such as group task performance) and organizational outcomes (such as crime prevention and efficiency) may require months and perhaps years to become apparent. Assessing various criteria at too early or too late a time may seriously limit the validity of performance appraisal. Moreover, not collecting facts over a protracted period of time can cause considerable distortions in any performance review. Human nature unfortunately emphasizes the most recent past in recollections. Thus, one's being "good" or "bad" in the past month is likely to strongly bias the appraisal. (One way to offset this effect is to employ the "significant incident" technique; more will be said about this technique later.)

Job Analysis Leads to Reliability and Validity

The prime means for a police agency to ensure the job relatedness (reliability and validity) of a performance evaluation system is *job analysis*. A *job* is a relatively homogeneous cluster of work tasks carried out to achieve some essential and enduring purpose in an organization; *job analysis* consists of defining the job and discovering what the job calls for in employee behaviors. Job analysis, then, is a procedure for gathering the judgment of people who are

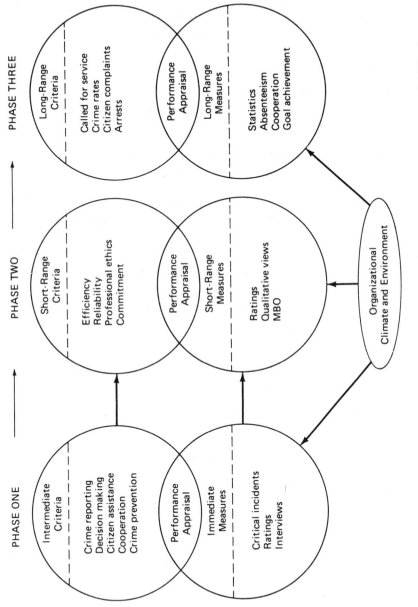

Figure 8-2 Performance Appraisal: Criteria and Measures (Paul Whisenand, *The Effective Police Manager*, © 1981, p. 203. Reprinted by permission of Prentice Hall, Inc., Englewood Cliffs, N.J.)

knowledgeable about the organization, the positions within it, and the specific content of a job. Furthermore, the *content* of the job is defined to be specific work activities or tasks. In effect, job analysis is a broad term describing an entire series of judgments that are made in the design of an organization. Figure 8-3 illustrates the purposes served in job analysis.

Three Methods of Performance Evaluation

Performance appraisal may serve many purposes; because of this, there can be no general method that is appropriate for all purposes. The problem for police supervisors is to determine what kind of performance-appraisal method is adequate, given the purpose to be served.

Specifically, the problem for you is to select a performance-appraisal method that is appropriate given the following considerations:

1. Specific *organizational and environmental properties*, such as technology, the design of the agency, the firm's industry, and other factors indicated in Figure 8-4

2. Unique *individual characteristics* that influence police performance including specific skills and abilities and motivation levels

3. The mix of specific *work behaviors* that are appropriate, given departmental and individual officer considerations

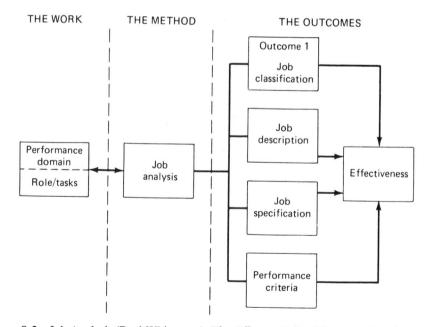

Figure 8-3 Job Analysis (Paul Whisenand, *The Effective Police Manager*, © 1981, p. 205. Reprinted by permission of Prentice Hall, Inc., Englewood Cliffs, N.J.)

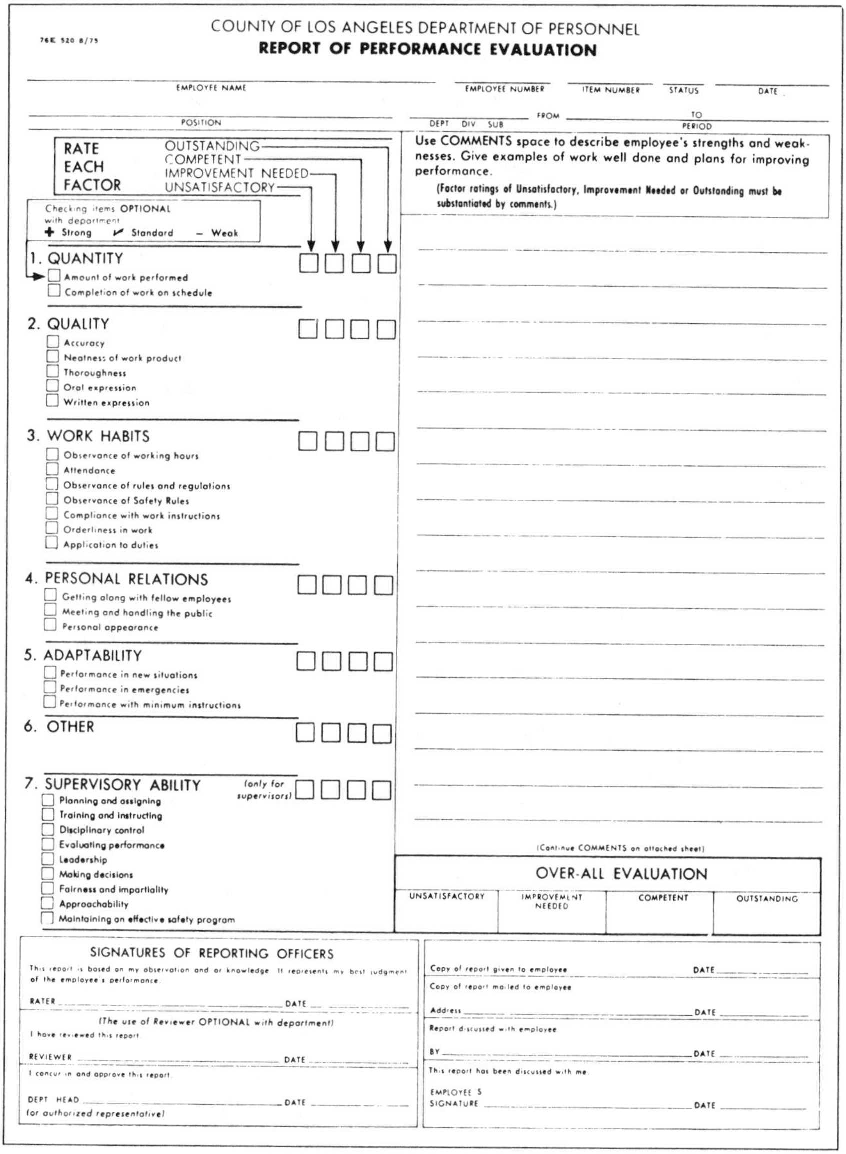
76E 520 8/75

COUNTY OF LOS ANGELES DEPARTMENT OF PERSONNEL

REPORT OF PERFORMANCE EVALUATION

EMPLOYEE NAME | EMPLOYEE NUMBER | ITEM NUMBER | STATUS | DATE

POSITION | DEPT DIV SUB | FROM | TO | PERIOD

RATE EACH FACTOR: OUTSTANDING / COMPETENT / IMPROVEMENT NEEDED / UNSATISFACTORY

Checking items OPTIONAL with department
+ Strong ✓ Standard – Weak

Use COMMENTS space to describe employee's strengths and weaknesses. Give examples of work well done and plans for improving performance.
(Factor ratings of Unsatisfactory, Improvement Needed or Outstanding must be substantiated by comments.)

1. QUANTITY
- ☐ Amount of work performed
- ☐ Completion of work on schedule

2. QUALITY
- ☐ Accuracy
- ☐ Neatness of work product
- ☐ Thoroughness
- ☐ Oral expression
- ☐ Written expression

3. WORK HABITS
- ☐ Observance of working hours
- ☐ Attendance
- ☐ Observance of rules and regulations
- ☐ Observance of Safety Rules
- ☐ Compliance with work instructions
- ☐ Orderliness in work
- ☐ Application to duties

4. PERSONAL RELATIONS
- ☐ Getting along with fellow employees
- ☐ Meeting and handling the public
- ☐ Personal appearance

5. ADAPTABILITY
- ☐ Performance in new situations
- ☐ Performance in emergencies
- ☐ Performance with minimum instructions

6. OTHER

7. SUPERVISORY ABILITY (only for supervisors)
- ☐ Planning and assigning
- ☐ Training and instructing
- ☐ Disciplinary control
- ☐ Evaluating performance
- ☐ Leadership
- ☐ Making decisions
- ☐ Fairness and impartiality
- ☐ Approachability
- ☐ Maintaining an effective safety program

(Continue COMMENTS on attached sheet)

OVER-ALL EVALUATION

UNSATISFACTORY	IMPROVEMENT NEEDED	COMPETENT	OUTSTANDING

SIGNATURES OF REPORTING OFFICERS

This report is based on my observation and or knowledge. It represents my best judgment of the employee's performance.

RATER ________ DATE ________

(The use of Reviewer OPTIONAL with department)

I have reviewed this report.

REVIEWER ________ DATE ________

I concur in and approve this report.

DEPT HEAD ________ DATE ________
(or authorized representative)

Copy of report given to employee ________ DATE ________

Copy of report mailed to employee

Address ________ DATE ________

Report discussed with employee

BY ________ DATE ________

This report has been discussed with me.

EMPLOYEE'S SIGNATURE ________ DATE ________

Figure 8-4 Deputy Evaluation Form of the Los Angeles County Sheriff's Department

4. The mix of *relevant performance dimension*, given a consideration of the agency and personnel involved
5. The specific set of *goals* to be achieved at divisional and departmental levels

We will now examine three methods or forms for assessing an officer's performance: the traditional method and two advanced methods.

Traditional method: the global rating scale.   The most frequently used forms of appraisal today by police agencies are still based on traditional methods, and usually take one of two basic forms: rating or ranking. Both kinds of appraisal methods are based on traditional, descriptive forms of job analysis: Observers make a very brief study of the job, focusing on several major task dimensions; they note these in broad, descriptive language and use these dimensions as a basis for designing ad hoc rating scales or ranking forms. The police sergeant applies this form once or twice a year to rate or rank his or her subordinates.

Figure 8-4 displays a traditional form. Forms or scales of this sort are known as *global rating scales* (GRS), because they define the qualities to be assessed and levels of such qualities in broad, global terms. As such, they are extremely vulnerable to a variety of errors that reduce their reliability and validity. The most common errors of GRS can be summarized as follows: halo errors, strictness errors, leniency errors, and central-tendency errors.

Halo errors occur when an evaluator incorrectly treats two or more dimensions of performance as if they were identical or highly correlated. For example, the evaluator making this error might believe that, if a police employee's work performance deserves a high rating on quality, it should also merit a high rating on cooperation. The result is that employees show no variation in ratings across dimensions; they are rated consistently high, medium, or low on all performance dimensions.

Strictness errors occur when an evaluator rates all employees as very poor performers. Ratings given by this type of evaluator tend to cluster closely towards the low end of the rating scale.

Leniency errors are the opposite of strictness errors; with leniency errors the evaluator mistakenly gives all employees uniformly high ratings. Ratings given by this type of evaluator cluster together at the high end of the scale.

Central-tendency errors are similar to leniency and strictness errors, except that in this case the ratings made by the evaluator cluster artificially at the middle of the scale.

The traditional method of appraising a police employee is full of validity and reliability holes. It is clearly wise to avoid the use of a GRS.

Advanced method: the performance domain rating scale.   Some police agencies have recognized the urgent need for making their evaluation method more relevant to the operating task environment of a police officer. To this end, they have often succeeded in designing highly valid and reliable rating scales. These scales are produced in conjunction with the performance domain; that is, what the officer should be doing in his or her work assignment is what is appraised. This can be referred to as a *performance domain rating scale* (PDRS). A PDRS is job related and thus does not fall prey to the inadequacies of a GRS. Figure 8-5 presents a PDRS that (with necessary modifications) may

(*text continued on page 178*)

City of Arvada

POLICE DEPARTMENT
OPERATIONS BUREAU POLICE OFFICER

EVALUATION OF PERFORMANCE

Employee Name: *   Employment Date: *

Position: *   Div./Dept.:   Patrol/Public Safety

Appraisal Period from: *   Time in Position: *

Appraised By: *   Title: *

PART I. EVALUATION OF PAST YEAR'S PERFORMANCE:

A. Accomplishment of Objectives

During the past year, what were results of the employee's work? The purpose is to compare the objectives agreed upon in the previous evaluation with actual performance.

OBJECTIVES	COMMENTS ON ACCOMPLISHMENTS
*	

Figure 8-5   Police Department Evaluation of Performance (Courtesy Arvada Police Department, Arvada, Colorado.)

PART II. PERFORMANCE STANDARDS

Evaluators are to review each and every item of performance under each of the Standards. The degree to which an employee is <u>capable</u> of engaging in a specific item may vary with the shift or assignment.

When evaluating the employee, the evaluator is to check off the appropriate rating for each element of an evaluation category. Each rating is given a value as follows:

Unsatisfactory	= 1
Below Expectations	= 2
Meets Expectations	= 3
Exceeds Expectations	= 4
Distinguished Performance	= 5

After completing the evaluation of each element of a category (i.e., Customer Service - Community Problem Solving), the evaluator is to total the rating scores in that category and multiply by the <u>Weight</u> for that category. This provides a score for that category. At the conclusion of the evaluation, all category scores are totalled to yield a final evaluation <u>total</u> which is divided by the possible total score of 935 to give the percentage score which can be used (as can the point score) to determine the overall performance rating of the employee.

The supervisor must be able to articulate, in detail, the justification for a specific performance category (element) score. "Description of Performance Guidelines" as found in the <u>Supervisor's Guide to Performance Evaluations</u> is to be used when assigning one of the 5 performance levels to a given Standard of performance. A narrative explanation <u>must</u> accompany any score which is either a "Distinguished" or below the "Meets Expectations" level. This narrative must detail the reasons for the score and, in the case of "Below Expectations" and "Unsatisfactory", there must be a plan explaining what is necessary to improve performance to a "Meets Expectations" level. These comments are to be done by listing the letter (a, b, c, etc.) of the corresponding element in the "Comments" section of the page, followed by the brief explanation.

When a general category (i.e., Customer Service) contains a series of "4" (Exceeds Expectatons) ratings, the evaluator must justify that rating, but may provide that justification in the "Comments" area with detailing each sub-section (i.e., a, b, f, i).

Figure 8-5   (Continued)

1. CUSTOMER SERVICE/COMMUNITY PROBLEM SOLVING - WEIGHT 3	1	2	3	4	5
a. Responsive to service requests	*				
b. Displays helpful, cooperative attitude					
c. Sensitive to citizen needs					
d. Participates in community programs including Neighborhood Watch Meetings, D.A.R.E. classes/graduations, community meetings					
e. Actively identifies and recognizes the origins of community problems, evaluates issues and develops possible solutions to problems					
f. Awareness of and use of community/citizen/city government resources					
g. Appropriate use of citizen contacts					
h. Achieves a positive community image					
i. Effective initiation of and follow-up on Police Service Requests					
TOTAL (Element Score)					

Weight 3 x Total of All Element Scores ____*____ = Performance Standard Score ___*___

COMMENTS:

*

2. TEAMWORK/INTERPERSONAL ACTIONS - WEIGHT 2	1	2	3	4	5
a. Takes steps to eliminate bias in the department when observed	*				
b. Cooperates with others in establishing reasonable objectives and achieving desired results					
c. Displays behavior which builds trust and mutual respect and cooperation among fellow workers					
d. Has a positive approach when participating in routine activities, assignments, and problem solving					
e. Avoids unnecessary confrontation and adequately resolves conflicts when necessary					
f. Shares information with other members of the organization					
g. Respectful when interacting with co-workers and supervisors					
h. Actively seeks the opportunity to assist peers with their work performance					
i. Displays an awareness of shift/department workload and makes himself/herself available to assist fellow workers					
j. Makes comments and takes action to constructively enhance a team environment					
TOTAL (Element Score)					

Weight 2 x Total of All Element Scores ____*____ = Performance Standard Score ___*___

COMMENTS:

*

Figure 8-5 (Continued)

3. COMMUNICATIONS - WEIGHT 3	1	2	3	4	5
a. Radio transmissions are clear, concise and follow procedures	*				
b. Expresses thoughts in writing and orally in a clear, concise, and well organized manner					
c. Displays good penmanship, grammar, and spelling in written reports					
d. Courtroom testimony is clear, accurate, and prepared					
e. Demonstrates ability and willingness to listen					
f. Understands and properly carries out instructions and orders					
g. Able to give and receive constructive feedback					
h. Ability to adjust communicative style for differing groups and situations					
i. Follows chain of command					
j. Comments, suggestions, and criticisms are presented in a constructive manner					
k. Written reports are grammatically correct and clearly understandable					
TOTAL (Element Score)					

Weight 3 x Total of All Element Scores ____*____ = Performance Standard Score ___*___

COMMENTS:

*

4. INITIATIVE - WEIGHT 3	1	2	3	4	5
a. Accepts direct responsibility for District/assignment	*				
b. Shows initiative in everyday work activity - identifies and addresses community problems - initiates PSR's based upon knowledge of problems					
c. Ability to adapt to change					
d. Strives to improve the work product					
e. Serves as a role model for peers					
f. Ability to work constructively with a minimum of supervision					
g. Volunteers to direct or manage tough assignments					
h. Demonstrates ability to organize and coordinate various activities/operations					
i. Generates ideas and approaches to improve Police Department/City performance and the operation of the organization					
j. Maintains activity and productivity levels consistent with shift averages and expectations of supervisors and the community					
k. Looks for, and engages in, non-assigned productive activities which try to fulfill the community's needs.					
l. Looks for opportunities to conduct follow-up investigation on own initiative					
TOTAL (Element Score)					

Weight 3 x Total of All Element Scores ____*____ = Performance Standard Score ___*___

COMMENTS:

*

Figure 8-5 (Continued)

5. PROFESSIONAL JUDGEMENT - WEIGHT 3	1	2	3	4	5
a. Demonstrated awareness of impacts of decisions	*				
b. Ability and willingness to make sound decisions based on available information without the assistance of supervisors					
c. Willing to take acceptable risks, but not recklessly					
d. Accepts responsibility for decisions and the subsequent results					
e. Proper use of police discretion					
f. Sensitive to needs of community or individuals					
g. Alert to surroundings and able to understand and react quickly and appropriately					
h. Has full understanding and application of the laws, rules and procedures governing the use of force, pursuit policy, search and seizure, arrest, and domestic violence					
i. Exercises proper degree of assertiveness when needed					
TOTAL (Element Score)					

Weight 3 x Total of All Element Scores ____*____ = Performance Standard Score ___*___

COMMENTS:

*

6. WORK PERFORMANCE/QUALITY - WEIGHT 3	1	2	3	4	5
a. Keeps current with legal changes and changes in Rules and Procedures Manual	*				
b. Proper recognition, collection and preservation of evidence					
c. Demonstrated understanding and application of State/Federal Laws, Municipal Ordinances, Departmental Rules and Procedures, Rules of Criminal Procedure, legal decisions, and directives					
d. Knowledge of and proper use of equipment and investigative techniques: Radar, Intoxilyzer, camera equipment, crime scene equipment (fingerprinting), computers, Nystagmus, firearms, to include follow-up activities when appropriate					
e. Assignments/investigative reports are properly carried out and completed in a timely manner					
f. Knowledge of police patrol districts					
g. Continuous adherence to the RPM and other procedural guidelines					
h. Work product is consistently completed in a professional, thorough manner					
i. Documentation is an accurate reflection of a thorough investigation to include the elements of the crime, proper classification, correct report formatting, complete witness information, MO, and suspect information					
TOTAL (Element Score)					

Weight 3 x Total of All Element Scores ____*____ = Performance Standard Score ___*___

COMMENTS:

*

Figure 8-5 (Continued)

7. PERSONAL APPEARANCE, GENERAL SAFETY PRACTICES AND PRIDE IN WORKING ENVIRONMENT - WEIGHT 1	1	2	3	4	5
a. Cares for uniform, equipment, police facility, vehicle, and weapons as required	*				
b. Cognizant of personal health and keeps physically fit					
c. Maintains positive image in appearance and demeanor at all times among peers and members of the public					
d. Exercises proper field survival practices					
e. Operates motor vehicles in a safe and prudent manner - obeys traffic laws					
TOTAL (Element Score)					

Weight 1 x Total of All Element Scores ____*____ = Performance Standard Score ___*___

COMMENTS:

*

8. PROFESSIONAL AND ORGANIZATIONAL COMMITMENT - WEIGHT 2	1	2	3	4	5
a. Is a positive role model for others to emulate	*				
b. Demonstrates loyalty and commitment to department and profession					
c. Continually strives to improve the image of the Arvada Police Department in the eyes of the public	*				
d. Demonstrates pride in the performance of others as well as self					
e. Demonstrates understanding of and commitment to Accreditation Standards					
f. Takes overt steps to overcome and combat bias in the community					
TOTAL (Element Score)					

Weight 2 x Total of All Element Scores ____*____ = Performance Standard Score ___*___

COMMENTS:

*

Figure 8-5 (Continued)

PART III. Overall Rating

1. Customer Service/Community Problem Solving   _____

2. Teamwork/Interpersonal Actions   _____

3. Communications   _____

4. Initiative   _____

5. Professional Judgement   _____

6. Work Performance/Quality   _____

7. Personal Appearance, General Safety Practices, and Pride in Work
    Environment   _____

8. Professional and Organizational Commitment   _____

                         TOTAL POINT SCORE   _____

   Total __Point Score__   = __*__ %
          935 Points

                 OVERALL RATING SCORE = ___*___

	Below	Meets	Exceeds	Distinguished
Unsatisfactory [__]	Expectations [__]	Expectations [__]	Expectations [__]	Performance [__]
(20-34)	(35-54)	(55-71)	(72-91)	(92-100)

Relative to this employee's overall work record during this evaluation period, I recommend:
(Include status and salary recommendations within the parameters listed in the "City of Arvada
Supervisor's Guide to Performance Evaluations")

   *

PART IV. EMPLOYEE ASSESSMENT

Based upon current performance, what are the <u>current</u> employee strengths and development
needs?

A. Employee Strengths:

   *

B. Development Needs:

   *

Figure 8-5   (Continued)

C. Enter other comments relevant to the employee's performance.

•

PART V. ESTABLISHMENT OF OBJECTIVES FROM *   TO *

This section establishes the objectives to be accomplished during the next evaluation period. Objectives should be as specific as possible, including where appropriate, completion date. The supervisor's objectives for the employee <u>and</u> the employee's objectives for her/himself are to be included.

OBJECTIVES	PLANS TO MEET THE OBJECTIVE	PROPOSED COMPLETION DATE
•		

Figure 8-5   (Continued)

PART VI.

Comments:

_____   _____   _____
Supervisor's Signature   Title   Date

Comments:

_____   _____   _____
Lieutenant's Signature   Title   Date

Comments:

_____   _____   _____
Bureau Commander's Signature   Title   Date

Comments:

_____   _____   _____
Chief of Police's Signature   Title   Date

Comments:

_____   _____   _____
Admin. Ass't. Signature   Title   Date

Comments:

_____   _____   _____
Personnel Signature   Title   Date

Figure 8-5 (Continued)

PART VII.

Any comments which the employee would like to make, or modifications of performance evaluation by the Supervisor due to the discussion of this evaluation, should be noted here.

My Supervisor reviewed and discussed the contents of the Performance Evaluation with me. My signature below does not indicate whether I agree or disagree with this evaluation.

_____   _____
Employee's Signature   Date

Employee Comments Reviewed By:

_____   _____   _____   _____   _____
Supv. Init.   Div.Hd. (Lt.)   Bur.Cmdr.   C.O.P.   Admin.
                               Init.   Init.   Init.   Asst. Init.

_____
Personnel
Init.

Figure 8-5 (Continued)

Police Officer Performance

935 Possible Points

	Percentage Spread	Point Spread	Salary Adj.-*Scale
Distinguished	97-100	906-935	10%
	92-96	860-905	9%
Exceeds	87-91	813-859	8.5%
	82-86	766-812	8%
	77-81	720-765	7.5%
	72-76	673-719	7%
Meets	67-71	626-672	6%
	60-66	561-625	5%
	55-59	514-560	4%
Below	50-54	467-513	2%
	40-49	374-466	0
	35-39	327-373	-2%
Unsatisfactory	30-34	280-326	-3%
	25-29	233-279	-4%
	20-24	187-232	-5%

*Non-top step employees - Increases are only possible up to the maximum top step.

Figure 8-5   (Continued)

improve the effectiveness of your overall rating system. (Keep in mind that this particular PDRS does *not* apply to other performance domains, such as non-sworn, supervisory, and so on.) Depending on the unique characteristics of each agency, three to six PDRSs may be required to ensure and maintain job-related personnel evaluations. One final comment: A key feature of a PDRS that is often overlooked is that it elicits narrative comments. Without written comments, the PDRS starts to show some signs of the deficiencies of the GRS, expressed earlier. Although it is obviously not a panacea, a PDRS is certainly a far superior method for employee evaluation than is a GRS.

Of the many available examples of a PDRS, we chose to include here the Arvada Police Department's (Colorado). On behalf of Chief Ahlstrom, Commander Scott wrote a letter of explanation as follows. (His letter is one of the reasons that we decided to present their PDRS.)

In order for you to better understand these evaluations, I would like to provide you with some background information on the process used to arrive at the content and format of these evaluations. Since time immemorial, supervisors and officers within the department have complained about a variety of concerns with the previous evaluation formats. Supervisors expressed the desire to have a check-off type of evaluation form. At the same time, officers and supervisors were concerned with the fact that a generic evaluation for a given rank did not address the specifics found within particular job assignments; i.e., the difference between detective, patrol officer, traffic officer, narcotics officer, etc.

In the interim, the City Personnel Department and the City Manager's Office came down with a mandate that the various city departments would develop evaluations which would have weighted values for various performance categories and would also be utilized, based upon overall score, to determine salary increases or decreases. When the original mandate came down from the City Manager and Personnel Department, performance categories were examined for content and revised to a greater or lesser degree to more accurately reflect the expectations of various assignments within the department. Nevertheless, the final forms were still somewhat generic and really did not address the specific expectations of particular assignments.

. . . I began the revision process for the performance evaluations within the Operations Bureau. I took the previous evaluation format which, in essence, consisted of a series of performance categories which were then explained by a paragraph of narrative detail. These performance categories were then broken down by myself into particular elements within a category with a point rating of 1 to 5 for the level of performance for each of those particular elements within a category. The category was then weighted based upon input from supervisors and the personnel to be evaluated. This weight value was then multiplied times the raw score to give an overall score for that performance category. At the end of the evaluation, the supervisors are to tabulate all of the calculated scores (raw score times weight value) to calculate a final raw score. This raw score is then divided by the total possible points for that particular evaluation to determine a percentage score, which is then used to determine the overall quality of performance and which can then be correlated with the City's breakdowns for salary increase or decrease.

I have instructed each of the elements and units within the Operations Bureau to critically evaluate and review the performance evaluation for each of their units. They are then authorized as a unit to revise the performance evaluation . . . based upon what they perceive as those elements which specifically address the performance and expectations in their particular unit. For example, the undercover officers, while they are still police officers, have very specific performance criteria that are much different than the detectives (police officers) and street officers (police officers). In this way, each unit can develop a customized evaluation for the members of that unit. They are free to add, delete, and revise the elements within the performance criteria for that unit, based upon their specific expectations and job duties. This will allow for the customization of evaluation forms for specific ranks and assignments within the Operations Bureau. This allows the evaluation process to be dynamic and changeable through the years as programs and priorities change with time. In the end, the total possible points will vary, depending upon the degree of customization for that particular form, but the percentage utilized by personnel for determination of salary increase or decrease will still be available by dividing the total possible points into the performance points totaled at the end of the form.

While this all may seem fairly complex and confusing, it is being done in a systematic manner in an attempt to reduce the amount of confusion felt by the supervisors and employees. I would like to call your attention to page 2 of each of the performance evaluations, making special note of the areas which state that documentation must be provided to varying degrees depending upon the evaluation score for each of the elements within an evaluation category. This is to insure that supervisors are, in fact, able to justify the scores given to their personnel and be able to provide feedback, and in the case of the low expectations performance, a program for improvement, to both the employee being evaluated and the individuals reviewing all performance evaluations.

Advanced method: the behaviorally anchored rating scale. In recent years, a series of techniques has been developed that show promise of overcoming the problems of reliability and validity. These are called *behaviorally anchored rating scales* (BARS) of job performance, because they focus on detailed evaluation of specific acts or behaviors, rather than on global aspects of performance. By design, they treat job performance as multidimensional, and use actual instances of behavior to illustrate effective and ineffective performance on these dimensions.

Figure 8-6 depicts a BARS that is designed to assess the performance of a police officer. Similarly to the PDRS, it should significantly increase the validity and reliability of your personnel system.

A BARS incorporates all the important benchmarks of an effectiveness measure. For example, it (1) is derived from experienced observers' reports of actual behavioral episodes regarded as illustrative of actions that are instrumental to continued organizational functioning, (2) samples behavior over the long term, as opposed to short-range judgments or impressions, (3) specifies with precision the myriad information-processing activities that constitute the multiple facets of effective police behavior, (4) implies many possible configu-

CRIME PREVENTION

Job Category A

Knowledge of effective crime prevention, such as silent alarms, security fences, lighting and random patrol; educating citizens to aid in deterring criminal activity or in aiding apprehension of suspects; maintaining security in keeping relevant information from potential criminals; being aware of trends in criminal activity; keeping an eye on potential or known criminals in the area.

The officer went to every late night gas station in his/her area to alert the attendants about a group of hold-up people who had been hitting gas stations. He/she left a description of the people, a phone number to call and detailed instructions on what to do if the persons were spotted. Because of his/her actions the hold-up people were apprehended.

— 9

When eight burglaries had occurred in a small area, the officer told a citizen that he/she would tell them how to help if they wished. The citizen organized a coffee party where the officer's tips on what to do led to the arrest of six young people.

— 8

— 7

An officer, after checking apartment house parking lots for car prowlers, would make a note of any apartment that didn't have good lighting and then tell the caretaker during the day.

— 6

The officer advised a bar owner who had been burglarized to wire a bell to the back door so a bartender who lived above the bar could tell when there was a break-in.

— 5

— 4

After there had been a rash of burglaries, the officer began spending more time patrolling the area they occurred in.

— 3

While on his/her night beat, an officer observed a business with one of the windows open. Finding no evidence of a break-in, he/she failed to report the open window to the owner the next day.

— 2

A burglar who was being transported to jail asked how the officer had known he/she had broken in. The officer then explained all about silent alarms--how they worked, how to spot them, etc.--educating him/her for his/her next job.

— 1

While on patrol an officer takes his/her coffee and lunch breaks at the same time and same place every night. He/she also patrols his/her beat in the same pattern every night.

Figure 8-6 Patrol Officer Evaluation Form (Excerpted from Marvin D. Dunnette and Stephan J. Motorvido, *Police Selection and Career Assessment* [Washington, D.C.: U.S. Government Printing Office, 1976]. Reprinted with permission.)

rations or patterns of effective officer behavior, rather than just one presumed best mode, (5) forces attention on what the employee does on the job, thereby guarding against defining his or her level of success in terms of other causal agents, and (6) takes account of an employee's membership in several organizational units, and of his or her potential impact on their continued functioning.

There are other patrol officer job categories such as "The Use of Physical Force." Space does not allow us to include them. Clearly, they are worth your time to review. Additionally, this document contains BARS for a number of other police positions (e.g., investigator) and ranks (e.g., sergeant).

Recommendations for the Design and
Implementation of a Personnel Evaluation System

It is time to coalesce our thinking and to travel from a method to a single system of evaluation — in this case, the job of performance evaluation. Remember the common precept of this entire book: that there is no *one* best way to do anything, organizationally speaking. However, there are *better* ways of doing things. The system to be described here seeks to proffer a *better* (not perfect) way to assess police personnel.

Job analysis: what is to be evaluated?   The first step to be taken in building a reliable and valid evaluation process is to conduct a comprehensive, in-depth job analysis. A prior section dealt with this subject. The point to be made here is that job analysis is a start, and a must for successful performance evaluation. Without it, the remainder of the recommended steps are likely to fail.

A method: PDRS or BARS?   As a step, we would recommend that one of the two advanced methods (PDRS or BARS) be adopted for implementation. Now that a method of rating has been identified, we will proceed to a discussion of who will do the rating.

The raters.   There are five possible sources of performance appraisal: (1) supervisors, (2) peers, (3) the appraisee himself or herself, (4) subordinates of the person to be appraised, and (5) people outside the immediate organization, such as citizens. Who the best person is to make the appraisal depends on the purpose of the appraisal and the level of the criteria being evaluated (immediate behavior versus intermediate and ultimate outcomes). Most performance appraisals are made by an officer's immediate superior. This is particularly true when the major purpose of the appraisal is for evaluation rather than for employee development. To overcome problems of stress and perceived threat, a few police agencies have tried to introduce evaluation by peers and self-evaluation, pointing out that these two methods work best under conditions of high interpersonal trust, highly specialized skills, high visibility among peers, and when development rather than evaluation is the major purpose to be served by the appraisal.

Since the primary goal in this instance is to assess an officer's performance, the immediate supervisor should have the fundamental responsibility for conducting the appraisal; however, a couple of significant alterations should be made.

First, it is recommended that multiple raters be used in completing the form: for example, the current supervisor, most recent past supervisor, and a supervisor who is on the same work shift. The present supervisor would be responsible for coordinating efforts and conducting the one-on-one interview with the officer. There are many advantages to the use of more than one rater, such as enhanced objectivity, improved clarity, more information, greater acceptance on the part of the ratee, and others. The only disadvantage that has been voiced deals with the amount of time that is consumed. The response to this concern resides in a question, "Where is the largest percentage of the agency's budgeted dollars allocated?" The majority responding would answer that it is to personnel (80 percent to 90 percent). Thus, is it not sensible to expend considerable time and effort in assessing their effectiveness?

The second feature involves self-appraisal, which will be covered in the MBO section that appears later.

Trained raters, rating the raters, and a rating manual. We have frequently asked police supervisors and managers if they are required to assess the performance of their subordinates' work activities, and the majority say yes. However, when we ask the same group of people if they received any training on rating, the most common answer is no! As a result, it is strongly recommended that *those responsible for rating should be trained as raters.*

We have also perceived that, although rating is acknowledged to be a highly fundamental and critical task of a police supervisor, in many cases the raters are *not* rated on their own willingness or ability to rate. In other words, a paramount dimension is being missed in terms of assessing a supervisor or manager's performance, which would be analogous to expecting patrol officers to behave with proper attitudes toward the public, but not rating them on their citizen contacts. *Raters should be evaluated on their rating skills.*

All performance-evaluation systems need a guide or a manual. Without a set of common definitions (such as the meaning of "community and human relations"), instructions, and procedures, the entire process is apt to suffer severe problems of ambiguity and integrity. A pertinent rating manual should address the obligations and concerns of the police agency, the police rater, and those to be assessed. *A manual is a must.*

Significant (critical) incidents: a data base. We are prone to have a better recall of the immediate past, which is human nature. Thus, when rating, a rater normally has a clearer remembrance of those events that occurred over the preceding few weeks than of those that occurred months ago. Indeed, by being "officer perfect" shortly before evaluation, one can probably receive a fairly high evaluation. Regrettably, though, if one's performance had been good for eleven months but during the last four weeks one's luck turned (such as getting citizen complaints, damaging the radio car, or arguing with one's supervisor over the vacation schedule), then the rating would probably be poor.

This phenomenon cannot be totally eliminated, but fortunately it can be guarded against through the use of the significant (critical) incident technique (SIT).[1] The SIT involves the recording of what can be termed significant or highly important behavior on the part of a police officer, which can be of either a positive or negative nature. Over the course of the evaluation period, the rater documents the significant behavior of his or her ratees (typically, two to three

---

[1]The critical-incident technique (CIT) was first introduced in a business setting as a single method for evaluating a person's performance. We see it as a most helpful technique in a performance-evaluation system. We prefer to substitute the term "significant" for "critical" to avoid the negative connotations of the latter term.

are generated per week). At the time of rating, the supervisor should utilize this data base for purposes of completing the rating form and the interpersonal interview. Also, the SIT is most useful in executing the activity that follows next.

Counseling: event and time triggered. Police employee–supervisor counseling is a clear-cut must. It can be event counseling, time-triggered counseling, or preferably both. In event counseling, as favorable conduct is observed it should be positively reinforced (such as "Good job, officer. Let's discuss it for a few minutes"); and as misconduct is witnessed, it should be corrected ("Hey, officer, you really fouled up! Let's discuss it for a few minutes"). Most of us want to know when we are doing right or wrong—not once every six to twelve months, but at that moment in time, so that we can continue or abandon a particular behavior. Such events are best made a part of an SIT. Time-triggered counseling will be covered in the subsequent section.

Management by objectives. You should recall from Responsibility Seven that MBO is the setting of performance objectives, tracking progress (or lack of progress), and evaluating results. While you as a supervisor should initiate the MBO process, it is best structured as a two-way channel. As a type of a contract, both parties ought to be included in drafting and approving the agreement. Because an MBO statement acts as both a basis for *past and future performance rating*, it should encompass the thinking of both the rater and the ratee. All police supervisors should separately produce a *tentative* MBO contract for employees. Concurrently, employees should be requested to independently generate their own contracts. Once both contracts have been finished, the two should confer and negotiate a final form.

Both event and time-triggered counseling (feedback) are necessary. Monitoring an employee's performance assists in determining when which type should be applied. Time-triggered feedback is especially relevant for MBO in that set time periods or milestones should be reviewed according to schedule on a one-to-one basis (supervisor–subordinate). This is where SITs and counseling merge to act as a reinforcer or corrective motivator for getting the needed performance. See again Figure 8-5 which has MBO built-in.

In evaluating performance, it is essential that a variety of proven techniques be forged into a reliable and valid *system*. The police supervisor should develop and apply a system that at minimum includes

- Job analysis
- BARS/PDRS
- Multiple raters
- Trained raters
- Raters that are rated
- A rating manual
- Significant incident technique
- MBO

This system is not a panacea, but it *is* the least-imperfect set of methods for *effectively* appraising an employee's performance.

Organizational effectiveness is derived from individual effectiveness; individual effectiveness is heavily dependent on an accurate and valid personnel evaluation process. Also, a well-designed evaluation process is only as effective as the boss who is responsible for administering it.

KEY POINTS

- The police supervisor has two interrelated performance-appraisal methods: informal daily and formal periodic.
- The most reliable test of a police department is its spirit of performance.
- The two key reasons for assessing a person's performance are behavioral: control and motivation.
- Performance evaluation serves a large number of purposes, ranging from decisions about promotions through dealing with MBO contracts.
- For a performance evaluation system to be reliable *and* valid, it must be job related.
- Job-related performance appraisal systems are based on a *job analysis.*
- Basically, there are three performance-evaluation methods: (1) global rating scales, (2) performance domain rating scale, and (3) behaviorally anchored rating scale.
- An internally and externally sound performance rating system must include (1) a job analysis, (2) more than one rater, (3) trained raters, (4) raters who are rated for their rating skills, (5) a rating manual and the recording of significant incidents, (6) MBO, and *of course* (7) a job-related rating form.

DISCUSSION

1. One of four ways to develop a "spirit of performance" is via *establishing a habit of achievement.* How does a supervisor create such a habit?
2. Return to the section entitled, "A Complex Process." Imagine for a moment that you are the supervisor of the patrol officer who did not receive the desired assignment. After hearing his fine points, what are your (1) thoughts and (2) verbal reactions?
3. What do *reliability* and *validity* mean? How do they differ? And what is the best tool for ensuring that they exist in a rating process?
4. Review the three rating scales presented earlier. Which would you, as a supervisor, prefer to use and why?
5. It is underscored that the raters must be trained to ensure the integrity of a performance-appraisal process. What are some of the ways to train police supervisors as raters?

STRUCTURED EXPERIENCES

1. Case Study: They're All Outstanding?

As a new police supervisor, you take your job most seriously, especially performance rating. During your recent two-week Supervisor's Training Course, eight hours (10 percent) was devoted to the do's and don'ts of rating.

Your agency uses a global rating scale (see Figure 8-4), which it applies once a year in the month of March. Your lieutenant instructed you and the other field sergeant to administer the scales. He went on to add, "In the next few months a number of critical personnel decisions will be made. Your ratings are likely to determine the outcome of some of these spending decisions."

You have a fairly good feel for the police personnel in your unit as compared to the other sergeant's. If anything, your group is a slight cut above the other crew. Nonetheless, you recognize that your staff is not perfect. The results of your first rating are (1) two "improvement needed," (2) four "competent," and (3) one "outstanding." All seven officers read, discussed with you, and signed the form. No problem!

Three days later it was revealed that your colleague sergeant rated all seven of his personnel "outstanding." Rumors and complaints quickly surfaced among your team of officers.

The lieutenant has asked to see you and the other sergeant about this situation. What is on your mind? What are you planning to say? What is your position(s) on this matter? How might it be resolved?

2. Performance Appraisal: Practice Session

The goals of this exercise are to (1) give participants an opportunity to create agenda for performance appraisals; (2) allow participants to experience the roles of supervisor, subordinate, and observer in a performance appraisal; and (3) provide participants with an opportunity to give and receive feedback on performance-appraisal techniques.

Any number of triads can engage in this exercise. The time required is approximately one hour.

The materials needed are

- One copy of the Performance Appraisal Supervisor's Role Sheet for every participant
- One copy of the Performance Appraisal Subordinate's Role Sheet for every participant
- One copy of the Performance Appraisal Observer's Role Sheet for every participant
- Blank paper and a pencil for each participant
- A portable writing surface for each participant
- A newsprint flip chart and a felt-tipped marker
- Masking tape for posting newsprint

The participants are assembled into triads. One member of each triad is given a copy of the supervisor's role sheet; another member is given a copy of the subordinate's role sheet; and the third member is given a copy of the observer's role sheet.

The facilitator asks the participants who have the supervisor's role sheets to interview the person playing the role of subordinate according to the instructions on their role sheets. The observer takes notes about the nature of the subordinate's job. The facilitator then interrupts the interviews and asks each supervisor and subordinate to create and prioritize agenda for the performance appraisal as instructed on the role sheets. The observers take notes on the agreed-on agenda.

The facilitator instructs the triads to begin the performance-appraisal process. At the end of ten minutes, the facilitator stops the appraisal. The facilitator next instructs each supervisor and his or her subordinate to continue the conversation just long enough to summarize what they have already discussed. The subordinate is instructed to make notes that could be used later to write a summary. Each observer is instructed to give feedback to the other two members of the triad and to allow them to ask for clarification and suggestions at the end of the feedback.

Each subordinate is given a copy of the supervisor's role sheet; each observer is given a copy of the subordinate's role sheet; and each supervisor is given a copy of the observer's role sheet. The facilitator announces that each participant will play the role that corresponds to the new sheet. Subsequently, the preceding steps are repeated.

The total group is reassembled, and the facilitator leads a discussion on the following questions:

1. How did you feel when you played the role of supervisor? Subordinate? Observer?
2. What did you like/dislike about each role?
3. Which role was most helpful to you in understanding the performance-appraisal process? How?
4. In what ways were the agenda helpful? In what ways were they a hindrance?
5. In what ways were the summaries helpful?
6. What types of statements or topics caused problems during the appraisal? How?
7. What topics, phrases, statements, or behaviors enhanced the process? How?
8. What discoveries have you made about the performance-appraisal process?
9. How can this experience benefit you and your organization in the future?

Performance Appraisal Supervisor's Role Sheet. You will play the role of the supervisor during a performance appraisal. Before the appraisal process begins, you will interview the person who is playing the role of your subordinate to find out what type of organization he or she works for, what kind of work he or she does, and other details that would help you appraise the subordinate's performance.

The facilitator will interrupt your interview and ask you and your subordinate to create agenda for the performance appraisal. You will write down topics that you want to discuss while your subordinate is writing down topics that he or she wants to discuss. When you finish, you and your subordinate will exchange agenda and discuss them, and come to an agreement about which items will remain on the final agenda.

Because time is limited for this activity, you will not be able to cover every agendum. Therefore, you and your subordinate will prioritize the items on the final agenda.

Some items that you may want to include on the agenda are listed subsequently.

1. Things that the subordinate has done well
2. Things that the subordinate needs to improve
3. Progress on previously set goals
4. Goals toward which the subordinate might work
5. Things that the supervisor does that help or hinder the subordinate's work

After you have completed the agenda, the facilitator will tell you to begin the performance appraisal.

When giving feedback to your subordinate, cite specific behavior. For example, say, "Your weekly reports were late twice last month," or "Your errors dropped from six in January to only two in February," not "Your work is always lagging behind," or "Your accuracy seems to be improving."

Resist the temptation to sandwich negative criticism in between compliments. For example, do not say, "Your investigative work is excellent, you make too many mistakes on the crime reports, and I think you are a very good organizer." Instead, remind the subordinate that you had to return six crime reports for corrections last week, and that one of his or her goals should be to proofread typed material carefully before giving it to you. Make sure the subordinate understands your complaint before proceeding further.

The facilitator will interrupt the performance appraisal and instruct you and your subordinate to summarize jointly what you discussed during the appraisal. Your subordinate will be instructed to take notes. (In a real situation, the subordinate is sometimes asked to write a summary of the appraisal and to present it the following day to the supervisor for discussion.)

Performance Appraisal Subordinate's Role Sheet. You will play the role of the subordinate during a performance appraisal. Before the appraisal process begins, you will be interviewed by the person who is playing the role of your supervisor. Expect that person to ask you about where you work, what kind of work you do, and other details that would help in giving a performance appraisal.

The facilitator will interrupt the interview and ask you and your supervisor to create agenda for the performance appraisal. While your supervisor is writing down topics that he or she wants to discuss with you, you should also write down topics that you want discussed. When you finish you will exchange agenda with your supervisor and will discuss them and come to an agreement about which items will remain on the final agenda.

Because time is limited for this activity, you will not be able to cover every agendum. Therefore, you and your supervisor will prioritize the items on the final agenda.

Some items you may want to include on your agenda are listed subsequently.

1. Things that I do well
2. Things that I need to improve
3. Progress on previously set goals
4. Goals for the future

After you have completed the agenda, wait for the facilitator to tell you to begin the performance appraisal.

If your supervisor asks you for feedback on his or her performance, cite specific behavior. For example, say, "You missed a meeting we scheduled for last Thursday," not "You're never around," or say "The note you wrote me about my crime statistics report inspired me to try to finish on time every month," not "You are always giving me encouragement."

The performance appraisal will be interrupted by the facilitator, who will instruct you and your supervisor to summarize jointly what you discussed. At this point, you will be asked to make notes so that you would be able to write a summary later. (In a real situation, the subordinate is sometimes required to write a summary of the performance appraisal and to present it to the supervisor the following day for discussion.)

Performance Appraisal Observer's Role Sheet. You will play the role of the observer during a performance appraisal. When real performance appraisals are conducted, the supervisor's supervisor sometimes observes the process and gives feedback to the person performing the appraisal. Your task will be to give feedback to *both* parties.

Before the performance appraisal, the person playing the role of supervisor will interview the person playing the role of subordinate to obtain information about the person's job. The supervisor and subordinate will also plan the agenda.

During the interview, agenda setting, and performance appraisal, take notes but do not interrupt or join the conversation. The other two members of your triad will probably become so involved in their conversation that they will not even be aware of your presence.

You should not give feedback on the performance appraisal until the facilitator instructs you to do so. When you have finished giving feedback, you should allow the other members of your triad to ask you for clarification and suggestions.

If you play another role after being an observer, try to benefit from the feedback you gave the other members of your triad.

The following items provide a checklist that may be helpful as you observe the supervisor and subordinate:

1. The supervisor and subordinate created the agenda jointly.
2. The supervisor and subordinate followed the agenda they created.
3. The supervisor was in control of the process.
4. The supervisor used concrete examples to describe performance.
5. The subordinate reacted to the supervisor's feedback nondefensively.
6. The supervisor and subordinate set goals jointly.
7. The supervisor solicited feedback about his or her performance.
8. The subordinate used concrete examples to describe the supervisor's performance.
9. The supervisor reacted to the subordinate's feedback nondefensively.
10. The supervisor and subordinate shared the discussion.
11. The supervisor and subordinate summarized the discussion jointly.
12. The subordinate took notes on the summary.

RESPONSIBILITY NINE

Employee-Oriented Supervision: I. Empowerment and Participation

I ordered dinner from the waitress, waited about ten minutes and it arrived totally screwed up. She immediately snatched up my meal and quickly disappeared. Within five minutes I spotted her jogging out of the kitchen with my new meal. I appreciated her smile and hustle on behalf of my empty stomach. I commented, "I'm impressed!" and then inquired, "Why did you push the panic button for me?" With all candor, she looked at me and said, "Because I'm 100 percent responsible!"

Skagway, Alaska
June 29, 1991

Somewhere, someone convinced the waitress that she, she alone, is 100 percent responsible for making it happen—making it right. Unfortunately, many police organizations have not discovered the formula for making their personnel 100 percent responsible. If they have, then they're not applying it. Indeed, we frequently encounter the opposite: "I'm not responsible for this mess, but everyone else is, especially my boss." (What we have here is a clear case of nonempowerment.)

If you want the members of your shift, work team, or whatever to begin to think and act "100 percent responsible," then three things must occur.

- You've got to be 100 percent in favor of empowering your officers.
- You have to delegate.
- You must allow (not compel) them to participate in decisions that affect them.

EM-POWER-MENT

Many of us approach some of our most vital ideas and emotions as if they were finite—limited. For example, there is only so much beauty to go around. Fairness can be counted up to 100 percent. Love is like a pie, there are only so many pieces to serve. The same can be thought of in terms of loyalty, trust, integrity, and power. All of these concepts are unlimited in mind and deed.

Some would agree, as we do, that the more you give away, the more you're likely to possess. Rogers and Hammerstein wrote in lyric, "A bell is not a bell until it is rung, a song is not a song until it is sung, and love is not love until you give it away." Similarly, *power is not power until you give it away.*

You should recall that we defined power earlier as the capacity to perform an activity. It stands to reason that the police supervisor who opts to give a share of his power to others automatically expands his sphere of influence. Basically, he has empowered others. He is, in turn, in a much better position to accomplish his assigned tasks.

By now you may see the link between empowerment and delegation. *Delegation means sharing power, sharing power leads to empowerment, and empowerment means that employees experience ownership of their job.* In essence, they are given the opportunity to become 100 percent responsible.

Next we'll cover delegation in detail and then later on its partner in empowering others—participation. Remember the following simple but proven formula:

$$\text{Delegation} + \text{Participation} = \text{Empowerment}$$

DELEGATION

Delegation of responsibility has been a central topic in supervisory and management texts through the ages. But today's demands on police employees to initiate far-reaching actions and think creatively propels the subject toward the top of the list.

Delegation frees up the police organization to work faster and with less traditional hierarchy (e.g., strict adherence to chain of command, rules and regulations for everything, established routines, etc.). Much more delegation is required now than ever before in meeting the challenges of police work.

Yes, But

A very bright trainer once commented, "When you delegate you are always delegating one thing for certain—uncertainty!" In other words, will the person who now possesses the responsibility come through? Will the empowered individual perform the task, and, if so, will it be done correctly?

The media is quick to expose police corruption. It makes exciting news. In many instances the newspaper article will implicitly point out that someone or a group of officers failed to execute their duties correctly or faithfully. The officers may have been delegated certain responsibilities and either accidentally or willfully violated the trust placed in them.

Is it any wonder why many police supervisors are fearful of delegating? After all, when something goes sideways, they're accountable. They must answer for their decision to delegate. At the same time, how would police work ever get done if delegation did not occur? The "yes, but" syndrome is often voiced like this, "Yes, but if I delegate this task it may not get done, or at least done to my satisfaction." This leads us to not really "letting go."

Really Letting Go

The plain fact is that nine out of ten police supervisors are not delegating enough. They think they are. They hand over tasks and pass out assignments routinely. But rarely does the officer really become empowered with true ownership—and its parallel, the sense of being 100 percent responsible.

What goes wrong? First of all, there is a distinction between "letting go" and "really letting go." However, does really letting go mean chaos, confusion, and substandard performance? Perhaps but not necessarily so. Steps can be taken to avoid the pitfalls of delegation, all the while assuring that its advantages are secured for the police agency. Before we review these steps it's important that we consider the benefits of delegation.

Who Benefits

First of all many police organizations would cease to function, or at minimum be highly dysfunctional, if delegation did not occur. After all, the chief or the sheriff cannot effectively administer the department and conduct criminal investigations. Watch commanders cannot *effectively* supervise their crew if they're responding to police radio calls. The key word here is "effectively." Yes, they can engage in police work if they choose to do so. Unfortunately, there are some police managers and supervisors that just can't let go, let alone really let go.

A police officer or deputy sheriff is expected to produce a service—get desired results. With each role we play in life (spouse, parent, friend, etc.) are attached production expectations (see Responsibility Five). But when we are expected to work with and through people and systems to produce results, we become a supervisor or manager. Many of our other life roles involve working with and through people such as family and friends.

We can (assuming no loss of efficiency) generate one hour of effort and produce one unit of results or police services.

A supervisor, conversely, can invest one hour of energy and create ten or fifty or a hundred units of services through effective delegation. Police supervision, after all, is shifting the fulcrum over to achieve 1:10 or 1:50 or 1:100. *Effective supervision is effective delegation.*

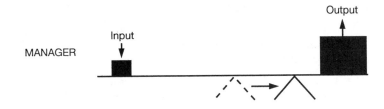

There are four parties that benefit from appropriate delegation. First, there is the community—you and me. Empowered police employees are typically more skillful and dedicated. Hence we get better, less costly services. We in turn are more likely to respect and support our police department.

Second, the organization itself harvests the wealth of brain power that exists within its sworn and civilian ranks. Everyone takes on the mantel of "I'm 100 percent responsible!" Everyone sets their sights on *excellence*.

Third, you benefit as a supervisor because you're

- Building *commitment* for getting the job done
- Increasing *mutual trust* between yourself and your officers
- Enhancing the officers' *job skills and knowledge*
- Encouraging a feeling of *ownership* and
- Leveraging *your power to provide quality police services* (most important)

Fourth, your staff benefits by becoming more

- *Committed* to their work
- *Trusting* and *trust worthy*
- *Professional*
- *Competent*
- *Self-confident*
- *Capable of producing top-notch police work* (most important)

Obviously everyone stands to benefit from really letting go. Again, far too many of us are unwilling to take the risk, and resort to the "yes, but" tactic. The "yes, but" game that some of us play today cannot be tolerated any longer. Empowerment is the game, and being 100 percent responsible is the price you pay to play it.

Setting the Context

Eight forces must be at work when you delegate. Without them you're taking a big risk. With them in place and functioning you are apt to achieve superb performance.

- Those being delegated to must be *well trained* in doing their job.

- The training must be ongoing, reliable, and pertinent.
- You should project *high standards*, which you live and demand of everyone uniformly—including yourself.
- You should understand the *values and needs* of each employee.
- From the preceding, establish and maintain a conduit for *open and candid communications*.
- Known anticipations should exist for those who fulfill their duties —*rewards*.
- Known anticipations should exist for those who do not fulfill their duties—*reprimands*.
- Create *feedback* systems. The new employee should receive feedback more often because he or she is earning your trust. The established officer should receive feedback less frequently because he or she has gained your faith.

When delegating, therefore, you must set a context that imposes training, standards, values and needs, communications, rewards, reprimands, and feedback. With such a context operating for you, you'll reap the benefits of being a delegator—you'll like it, and so will those who work for you.

Ownership-Lonership

Have you heard about the mushroom theory of delegation? You put the police employees into a dark, damp closet and feed them fertilizer. We doubt many supervisors would subscribe to such a theory let alone practice it.

Let us assume that you: (1) understand the virtues; (2) are not a "yes, but" supervisor; (3) are really willing to let go; and (4) have developed the proper context for successful delegation. The next consideration centers on just what should you delegate. Will the responsibility result in empowering ownership or mere lonership? Will the responsiblity produce meaningful individual growth or monotonous routine? Such a matrix looks like the one on page 195:

Remember, we accomplish all that we do through delegation—either to time or to other people. If we delegate to time, we manifest *efficiency*. If we delegate to other people, we generate *effectiveness. Delegating to others is the single most powerful high-leverage activity there is.*

There are two polar types of delegation—ownership and lonership. Both contain opportunities for growth as well as humdrum, non–learning experiences.

Lonership delegation. Lonership delegation occurs when I give you something to do and then very closely direct it. It may also be referred to as "oversupervision." Although I may consider myself as having delegated something to you, you'll likely not think of it as delegation. In fact, you're more apt to look on it as unnecessary meddling. You're apt to feel like a "gofer."

Gofer delegation is a form of lonership wherein you go for this, go for that. You're not encouraged to think of the task as being a part of *your job*. Indeed,

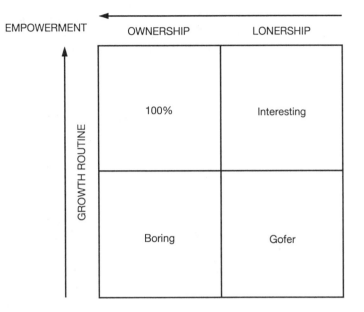

you're probably not encouraged to think at all. Some police supervisors suffer from this practice. In most instances, they're afraid that if they do not direct your each and every moment the work won't be done right. How much does gofer delegation really accomplish? How many people is it possible to supervise when you oversupervise? The answers are, respectively: "not much" and "very few." Gofer delegation is a turn-off for police employees. Ask them—they'll tell you it is. Some may open up and respond with, "Why don't you just do the job yourself? I'm merely an errand boy."

Lonership delegation can be interesting—even with oversupervision. Let us say you're being trained to work in a new assignment such as vice operations. It's different and requires additional police skills and knowledge. The sergeant loans you some responsibility and then carefully monitors how you perform. He trains you along the path to becoming a proficient vice officer. Each day he loans you more responsibility. Eventually you'll reach a point of being able to assume responsibility for the assigned tasks.

When an officer is ready for 100 percent responsibility and ownership, then it is up to the supervisor to really let go. If the supervisor fails eventually to transfer the lonership into ownership, then regression to a gofer situation will occur. In essence, the training and growth phase devolves into one of over-supervision. Skill development is substituted with ill will.

Ownership. Ownership delegation concentrates on results instead of methods. It affords police personnel with a choice of method but, more important, makes them 100 percent responsible for results. Admittedly it takes more time in the beginning. But it's time wisely invested. Ownership delegation moves the production fulcrum way over, thereby *increasing your empowerment leverage*. This holds for both *growth* and *routine* activities.

In addition to the eight forces that should be operational before you delegate (see earlier), ownership delegation involves

- Clear, up-front mutual understanding
- Commitment regarding expectations in five areas

Desired Results.   Generate a mutual understanding of what needs to be accomplished, focusing on *what*, not how, and *results* not methods. Spend time. Visualize the needed outcome. Have the officer describe for you how the results will look and when they will be achieved.

Guidelines.   Carefully identify the boundaries within which the person must function. These should be as few and inflexible as possible. If you know of any land mines, be certain to reveal them. In other words, instruct them in what *not* to do but do not tell them what *to* do. Keep the responsibility for their performance with them — *to do whatever is essential but within the guidelines*.

Resources.   Identify the various resources that the person can elicit to obtain the preferred outcomes.

Accountability.   Establish minimum standards that will be applied in evaluating the work effort and when it will occur.

Consequences.   Indicate what will happen, both positive and negative, as an outcome of the evaluation. This involves rewards and reprimands.

Ownership delegation on occasion may include some highly routine processes. Writing crime reports after a while can become monotonous. Routine work is unavoidable. It happens to all of us. We can choose to insert some change at times. Write the report differently, drive a new route to work, whatever. The saving grace is that at least it's our routine and not someone else's. We own it and can even change it within the guidelines.

Ownership delegation means no nagging on your part. Within the guidelines and standards *you* set, the other person becomes the boss.

Delegation and Trust

Trust brings out the very best in us. But it takes time and persistence, which includes constant training and consistent encouragement for people to enhance their competencies. Ownership delegation changes the nature of a supervisor–police employee relationship. The police officer, civilian dispatcher, or criminal investigator becomes his or her own boss, governed by a conscience that lives commitment to agreed-on, desired outcomes. It also frees creative forces for conduct that is in harmony with the mission of the department.

With mature employees you provide more challenging expectations, fewer guidelines, less frequent accountability, and less measurable criteria. With the immature employee (we define maturity as emotional wisdom) it is the exact opposite — fewer challenging expectations and so on.

Ownership delegation is perhaps the best indicator of effective supervision because it is so fundamental to both professional and personal growth.

How Do I Know?

Are you really letting go? Here is a checklist of questions that will help you know if you are or not.

- Have you transmitted the overarching vision with clarity? Does the officer, through demonstrated behavior, clearly "buy in"?
- Is the person aware of the level of performance standards?
- Do you trust the person and have you conveyed it?
- Are you known for butting in at the last minute to handle a problem that someone is experiencing with their assignment?
- Do you hold your tongue on asking questions about someone's work efforts?
- Have you avoided excessive reporting?
- When the officer stops by, do you avoid giving direct orders or implying that such and such may be a better approach?

Common Chord

We would be sorely remiss if we failed to mention Napoleon, Moshe Dayan, and coaches Vince Lombardi and Bear Bryant. They furnish us with a final and highly valuable message about delegation. All four were tough task masters. In word and deed they expected the ultimate from their personnel/players—and got it. Beneath their incessant drive, however, was abiding love and respect for their people. And the people knew it!

Most treatments of delegation focus exclusively on letting go, with a bit on formal feedback for keeping track. Few discussions of delegation emphasize the place of faith, belief, vision, caring, intensity, and the psychological contract that the effective police supervisor sets up with his or her staff. Small things enhance delegation. Even smaller things destroy it.

Confidence and *caring* are twin pillars of successful delegation. Without them everything expressed thus far on the subject of delegation is senseless.

PARTICIPATION

We have seen on the desks of a couple of police supervisors the epigram, "When I want your opinion, I'll give it to you." Unfortunately, we discovered that they weren't kidding. A few years ago a police chief told us, "I'm a great believer in participative management. I'm going to manage, and you'd damn well better participate." How do you feel about working for such a person? Are you working for that person right now? (Are you that type of a supervisor?) What's delegation like in your organization? How about empowerment?

Misconceptions about Participation

Allowing others to have an opportunity to express their ideas, needs, and hopes about an issue or pending decision that affects them is what we mean by participation.

We've heard some police supervisors voice irritation with, and resistance to, participation as follows, "We're not running a democratic vote here. I'll make the decision, and they're expected to get with it." In part we agree. A police organization cannot be effective if the majority rules. Can you imagine a police sergeant, during roll call briefing, asking his officers to vote on whether they want to patrol or stay in the station? The sergeant is being paid to make such decisions.

Our proposition is rather simple but extraordinarily compelling—when a decision is going to affect others, let them have a chance to express their ideas. Do you wonder why people reject an idea, general order, new policy? Often it is because they had no input—"No one asked me!"

Letting others participate in decisions that may affect them does not surrender your authority or responsibility for the ultimate decision. It's yours; you got it when you decided to become a supervisor. You can give it away, but no one can take it away from you. Through the participation of others you listen, you learn, and then you're likely to make a much more reliable decision.

Why, And Why Not, Allow Others to Participate?

Let us rephrase the preceding heading—why, and why not, *encourage* others to participate in decisions that (will or might) affect their ability to do their job? Here are some reasons that you will want to review.

The best means for getting a good idea is to generate a lot of ideas.

- It builds others' faith that you really care about their welfare and workfare.
- Others' inclusion in a decision-making process usually increases their commitment to its eventual implementation.
- Increased commitment often causes increased productivity.
- A sense of *teamwork* is fostered.
- Teamwork leads to *synergy* wherein the mental energy of a few people multiplies into what hundreds are capable of contributing.

Let's now examine some reasons not to encourage your staff to get involved in the decision process.

- Participation takes time—you have to listen to others (eight, nine, or more people).
- You may experience a sense of frustration or insecurity when confronted with ideas that refute yours.
- You may be convinced on the correctness of their approach—the easy route—and thus opt for group consensus.

• Some may accuse you of manipulation, being conned. "The sergeant asked me for my opinion. He then proceeded to do the exact opposite of what I suggested." (This can be corrected by simply providing feedback on the reasons for your decision. It may be so candid as, "My guts told me so.")

The preceding list of reasons for and against participation is a starter list. Please add to it as you deem appropriate. Albeit, if you've decided to empower yourself and those who work for you, then participation is *in*.

We'll now review one of the primary tactics for building participation— quality circles. In this case, think of it as "quality service." The emphasis is therefore placed on what participation is really all about—*better police services*.

QUALITY CIRCLES

Quality circles are only the latest in a long line of tools that can either be very helpful, or can simply serve as a smoke-screen while management continues to get away with not doing its job of real people involvement.

—Thomas J. Peters and Robert H. Waterman
In Search of Excellence (New York: Harper & Row Publishers, 1982), p. 241

In the past twenty years, the field of supervision has evolved from the vast amount of theories and techniques produced in the behavioral sciences and aimed at increasing organizational productivity and/or individual effectiveness. The latest addition to this field, and one that is enjoying a great deal of success, is the concept of quality circles (QCs). Although the QC certainly is not a panacea for supervisory decisions, the results thus far indicate that, if installed properly and nurtured carefully, this approach has high potential for dealing with issues of productivity and officer involvement.

Background and Definition

First implemented in Japan in 1962, quality circles are an *outcome of American thinking*, the result of quality-control technology introduced to Japan by Deming and Juran and behavioral science inputs from Herzberg, McGregor, and Maslow. In effect, quality circles are the latest refinement of organization development technology that has been developed and practiced in the United States since the early 1960s (again, back to the basics).

A *quality circle* is a group of three to ten people from the same work area that voluntarily meets on a regular basis usually for one hour once a week, to identify, analyze, and solve problems in that work area. The quality circle is useful in any organization in which effectiveness can be measured and there is an authentic concern for increased productivity and human potential.

A quality-circle program has two major objectives: (1) to improve the quality of supervision within the police organization and (2) to use the creative problem-solving skills of the police personnel. Although increased service productivity and cost reductions usually are two of the results, these are the *measures* of a successful program and *not* its objectives. Some other benefits derived from an effective QC program are improved communication, improved attendance, increases in performance and productivity, better teamwork, and enhanced technical knowledge.

Key Components

Although the QC focuses on the police officer, everyone in the department is to some degree actively or passively affected. In a QC program, seven components encompass the entire staff of a police agency.

1. *Steering committee.* The steering committee is comprised of police personnel who represent various functional areas in the agency, usually mid- and upper-level managers, and it may include the police chief and union leaders from within the department. The responsibilities of the steering committee are to establish the QC program: set policies, philosophy, procedures, and objectives; provide guidance and support; demonstrate management's committment by setting high priorities on circle recommendations; meet and work closely with the facilitator; monitor effectiveness (usually quarterly); and provide needed resources. The steering committee usually meets weekly during the organization phase of the program and may meet bimonthly once the program is established.

2. *Facilitator.* The facilitator is the key to the success of the program. When there are more than six circles operating, the facilitator may fill a full-time position. The facilitator is responsible for training the circle leaders and members; meeting with each circle leader prior to the circle meeting to review the plans; forming the necessary links between the circle program and the rest of the police organization; locating specialists to assist the circles with particular problems; maintaining records; coordinating circle activities; working with and being a member of the steering committee; assisting leaders and members with problems; and attending and monitoring circle meetings. A facilitator *must* be an active listener.

3. *Circle leader.* Usually the circle leader is the first-line supervisor of the officers who make up the circle. The responsibilities of the QC leader are to run the circle meetings; assist the facilitator in training the members in problem-solving techniques; meet with the facilitator prior to each meeting to review that meeting's agenda; act as liaison to other departments and support personnel; know and understand QC tools and techniques; plan circle activities; and be an active member of the circle. As a circle leader, you *must* use a participative approach during the circle meeting. You have only one vote and, generally, will use it only in order to break a tie.

4. *Circle member.* The circle member is a police officer or civilian worker who volunteers to participate in a quality circle. No one is required to

participate and no one is barred. The responsibilities of the circle member include being trained in problem-solving techniques; attending and participating in all meetings; and identifying, analyzing, and implementing solutions to problems in the work area.

5. *Top management.* Top management's support will either make or break the quality-circle program. The chief's responsibilities include making the final decisions concerning the QC program and the recommendations of the individual circles; actively supporting the program; attending meetings at the invitation of the circles; and *providing role models* for participative management.

6. *Middle management.* Although middle management plays no active role in the program, its support is vital to the success of the program. Middle management's responsibilities include not scheduling activities that conflict with QC meetings; openly supporting circle activities; implementing circle recommendations or explaining why they are not to be implemented; including circle activities in reports to top police management; and meeting periodically with circle leaders.

7. *Noncircle police worker.* Because participation in a QC is voluntary, there are always some personnel that prefer not to be involved in the program. The noncircle worker continues on the job when the circle(s) for his or her department meet(s).

Building QCs

If they are to be effective, QCs must be planned thoroughly before being introduced into a police organization. Typically, an agency will start with four to six circles and add one or two more circles at a time. A *minimum* of six months of planning and preparation is required from the time a decision is made to initiate a QC program until the first circles are operative. The process cannot be rushed. A typical start-up process will proceed through twelve steps.

1. *Deciding to proceed.* The decision to begin a QC program is made by the chief of the department with whomever he or she chooses to include in the process.

2. *Getting some advice.* Although it is not essential, using an external consultant has advantages. A qualified consulting firm can explain the program to the chief, train the facilitator and the supervisors, and help the department to avoid pitfalls during the implementation of the program.

3. *Introducing QCs to the police management team.* Once the decision is made to proceed, it is essential that all police supervisors in the department be informed and be given an opportunity to voice their support or resistance. It is also wise to include union leaders as soon as possible in the process.

4. *Establishing a data base.* Although not essential, it frequently is wise to obtain various measures of police service productivity in key areas of the

agency before starting the program. Although increased service and increased efficiency are not the objectives of the program, they are two of the usual benefits and obtaining a data base in the beginning is a good way to monitor the cost efficiency of the program.

5. *Selecting the QC police steering committee.* Because the steering committee is to provide the necessary support, especially during the early stages of the program, every functional area in the police organization, including the association union, should be represented.

6. *Selecting the facilitator.* The facilitator is the most important individual in terms of the success or failure of the program. The facilitator (usually chosen by the steering committee) can come from anywhere within the police department, but knowledge of the agency and its technical basis is a solid advantage. Some of the qualities essential in the facilitator are enthusiasm for the position; an ability to relate well to the workers; the respect of police management and easy access to the chief; a willingness to work hard (and at odd hours if circle meetings are to occur during second or third shifts); and the capacity to train others in good communication skills.

7. *Informing all police employees of the plan.* Police employees can be informed of the plan to start the program in a number of ways. The only requirement is that the approach be well thought out and well executed. One approach is to call a meeting of all police employees and make a formal presentation.

8. *Selecting circle police supervisors.* When all police supervisors understand the nature of the program, the best approach is to ask for volunteers. Because a program usually begins with only four to six circles, there usually are more than enough volunteers. Circle leaders should have enthusiasm for the program, should work well with people, should not be involved in any serious union issues, and should be able to obtain measurable results from their units.

9. *Forming circles.* Once the units and the circle supervisors have been identified, police employees from those units are asked to volunteer. In most cases there will be more volunteers than the circle can absorb.

10. *Training the facilitator.* Generally, a forty-hour program is required to train the facilitator. The first phase deals with the cognitive, problem-solving techniques that will be used in the circles: problem identification, data gathering, problem analysis, and presentation techniques. The second phase focuses on process (consultative) skills, such as participative leadership, communication, team building, conflict management, and training people how to train.

11. *Training the circle police supervisors.* Generally, circle police supervisors undergo a twenty-hour training program. They are trained in the same problem-solving methods as is the facilitator and also in participative leadership skills.

12. *Training the circle members.* The first eight weeks of the circle's life are dedicated in the training of its police officer members. After a thorough

introduction to quality circles, the officers receive eight hours of training in problem-solving techniques and presentation skills. Although the facilitator and you, the supervisor, may be trained by an outside consultant, the officers are trained by the supervisor with the facilitator's assistance.

Circle Workshop

When all training has been completed, the circle picks a name for itself and then begins to meet for one hour, once a week, to deal with problems relating to the work area. The typical one-hour, weekly meeting includes opening remarks by the leader, a brief reading of minutes of the last meeting, the introduction of new topics, "next steps" on existing projects, work assignments (for circle projects) for the next week, and the closing.

Certain guidelines are always in effect and are agreed to by all members; for example, (1) criticize ideas, not people; (2) the only stupid question is the one not asked; (3) everyone in the group is responsible for the group's progress and process; and (4) be open to the ideas of others.

The types of issues that the circle will address are work quality, cost reduction, officer safety, work methods, technology and equipment, interorganizational communications, and process and procedures. A quality circle does not deal with issues such as wages and salaries, hours of work, personalities, new product design, hiring, firing, and disciplinary decisions.

Causes of QC Failure

Merely installing the technology correctly does not guarantee success in a QC program. The following is a partial list of the factors that can cause a program to fail.

1. *Management impatience.* Demanding immediate results, expanding the program too quickly, cutting down on training time or start-up time, demanding that certain issues be considered by the circles, or unrealistic expectations.
2. *Lack of police supervisory support.* Not making all needed information available to the circles; postponing circle meetings for any reason; not educating police supervisors in the process; denying or forcing participation in the program; not publicizing the program internally or establishing arbitrary criteria, deadlines, or cost-savings demands.
3. *Inadequate implementation and planning.* Not using a facilitator or poor choice of facilitator; little support from the steering committee; little or no training; not following a formal pattern; not including union representatives; not planning for turnover of members or little police management involvement; inadequate assessment of organizational readiness for the program; or poor coordination among the facilitator, the steering committee, and your boss (chief or sheriff).

Benefits of Police QCs

1. *It is the only approach that is initiated by police management but run solely by the police officers.* Although participative principles are underlying and essential elements of a quality circle program, it actually has evolved into what could be called a "partnertive" approach. Police management does not participate in a QC program after it is installed and running; they merely provide support when needed. This is quite different from participative management, in which the goal is to include the worker in relevant management considerations.

2. *It allows the installation of participative values in segments of the police department, abruptly changing the structure or value system of the agency.* The most important element in the survival and growth of a QC program is management's philosophy concerning career development and quality of work life. There is no room for lip service.

3. *The most beneficial payoffs occur externally to the program.* Although the circle meets under a strict set of participative rules, the circle leader (you, the supervisor) is bound by them only during the circle meeting, one hour per week. The rest of the time, each leader is free to lead in his or her usual style.

4. *It provides a constant, established base for ongoing police training and officer development.* The circle provides a rich resource of training criteria; officers learn to identify objectives, to analyze and solve problems, and to explore resources, along with numerous other work-related skills. The QC provides an established setting into which training can be introduced. Training can be more readily accepted and absorbed when the officer can see how the information can help in dealing with and overcoming police problems. Facilitators and sergeants can apply additional process training not only to their circles but also to their day to day jobs.

GETTING THE QUALITY OUT OF QUALITY CIRCLES

To function effectively, the members of a QC must develop certain behaviors that allow them to complete the problem-solving procedure. These behaviors include not only participating collaboratively in QC efforts, but also *listening carefully* to fellow members and *withholding judgment* about various ideas and suggestions until it is time to select a final solution.

The problem-solving procedure that calls for the use of these behaviors includes the following steps.

1. *Identifying problems.* To identify work-related police problems, the members use a technique called brainstorming in which they take turns contributing problems that might make worthwhile projects. When used effectively, brainstorming works in the following way:

    • As ideas are contributed, they are listed on newsprint or a chalk board.
    • Each member offers only one idea per turn. If a member does not have a

contribution to make on any particular turn, he or she simply says "pass."

- *No opinions about ideas, either positive or negative, may be stated.* The withholding of judgment at this point is important so that creativity is not stifled.
- The process continues until all contributions have been exhausted.

2. *Selecting a problem.* A circle works on solving only one problem at a time. The officers discuss all problems identified in step 1 and then choose one. The process used to arrive at this choice is governed by the following principles:

- No voting, bargaining, or lobbying is permitted.
- Each officer must be offered an opportunity to express his or her opinion and the reasons for holding this opinion.
- No member may say that the opinions of another member are "wrong."
- All members must care about the problem that is finally chosen; they must be willing to commit themselves to its resolution.
- The members must be able to do something about the chosen problem. Problems that the quality circle cannot possibly solve either on its own or with help provided by police management constitute inappropriate projects.

3. *Analyzing the problem.* After a problem has been selected, it must be defined in writing in precise, detailed terms. Defining includes specifying why the situation or condition is a problem; where and when the problem exists; and the impact of the problem on productivity, morale, and so forth. Another task to be completed is determining the causes of the problem that may necessitate obtaining data from others.

4. *Generating and evaluating possible solutions.* During this setup the members think as creatively as possible to come up with a wide range of alternative solutions. Brainstorming is the technique that is generally used for this process. Subsequently, the benefits, costs, and possible ramifications of each alternative are considered.

5. *Selecting a solution.* After each alternative has been analyzed, the members choose the one that seems most appropriate.

6. *Implementing the solution.* A detailed plan to guide the implementation is essential. When developing this plan, the members outline what should be done, when the work should begin, and who should do it. They consider potential problems and ways to deal with these problems. Finally, they develop a plan for evaluating the solution by determining what they will accept as evidence that the solution has worked, how they will collect this evidence, who will collect it, and when it will be collected.

In the following spaces, list the work-related problems that are currently plaguing your immediate work group. Think of a problem as a situation or condition for which you can identify a difference between how things are and how you would like them to be. Be as specific as possible in stating each problem.

1. _____
   _____
   _____
2. _____
   _____
   _____
3. _____
   _____
   _____

SUPERVISING EFFECTIVE POLICE WORK GROUPS

A team in an ordinary frame of mind will do only ordinary things. In the proper emotional stage, a team will do extraordinary things. To reach this stage a team must have a motive that has an extraordinary appeal to them.

—Knute Rockne

There are several ways police supervisors can encourage police groups to be more effective.

Awareness

Police supervisors should make themselves more aware of the nature of groups and the functions groups perform for police officers. By understanding why individuals join groups, for example, supervisors should be able to better understand the motivational implications of group dynamics. Is high group cohesiveness in a particular police group a result of high commitment to the police department and its goals, or is it a result of alienation from the department?

Use

Police supervisors should use or develop group norms to the extent that they become a force for high organizational performance. The potency of group norms has been clearly established. It has also been shown that police agency policies can increase the likelihood that norms will work to the benefit of the department.

Conformity and Independence

Groups often place significant pressures on officers to conform. Conformity can represent a mixed blessing. On one hand, there are many work situations where police supervisors typically want officers to conform to standard operating procedures. Conversely, employees must be sufficiently free to take advantage of what they believe to be unique or important opportunities on behalf of the police department. If pressures for conformity are overwhelming, then the officers' innovativeness may be lost. Hence, the department suffers an unfortunate reduction in needed creativeness.

Teamwork

Teamwork alone does not guarantee group effectiveness. Supervisors must show their police personnel how and why they will benefit from working together to produce results. Rewarding group results, as opposed to individual police officer effort, is one way. As the slogan states, "A good crew is happiness." Or, in other words, "A good team is effectiveness."

Participation

Police supervisors should accept the fact that there are (1) many positive reasons for them to encourage officers to share in decisions that affect them, and (2) participation does not necessarily erode the supervisor's control; indeed, it can expand it. Regretfully, many police supervisors profess to use a participative style, but fail to do so in practice. What about *your* supervisory style?

Decision Making

We know that police work groups, as well as individual officers, make decisions. Groups offer certain pluses: more complete information and knowledge, increased acceptance of a solution, and greater legitimacy. On the other hand, groups are time consuming, create pressures to conform, and cloud responsibility. It is up to you, the police supervisor, whether group decisions are a helpful or harmful practice within your particular police agency.

TEAMWORK = PARTICIPATIVE SUPERVISION

Unless the group of people you supervise believes that what you want them to do is to their advantage as well as to yours, you'll have little success as a police supervisor. The solution lies in permitting the group to set their goals along with your concurrence and in showing them that these goals are attained through group action—teamwork.

You may feel that to permit a group of police officers to get into the decision-making act will subvert your authority. It needn't be. First, make it clear that you have a responsibility for retaining a veto power over a group decision (but don't exercise it unless absolutely necessary). Second, provide rules for their participation beforehand, and make these guidelines clear. Last, supply enough information for the group so that they can see situations as you do. It's when people don't have enough of the facts that they question authority. And, in mentioning authority, remember it is *bottom-up*!

Why Is Participation So Effective?

Perhaps you've heard about the benefits of employee participation. Most of what you've heard is accurate. In today's employer–employee relations, few practices have been so successful in developing consensus and the attainment of common goals as the development of participation by the police supervisor.

- Participation is an amazingly simple way to inspire police employees. And its simplicity lies in the definition of the word: "To share in common with others."
- *Sharing*, then, is the secret. You must share knowledge and information with others to gain their cooperation. You must share your own experience so that officers will gain from it. You must share the decision-making process itself so that personnel can do some things the way they'd like to. And you must share credit for achievement.

Participation or sharing may not come easy for you. However, once you've learned how to share, participation is self-perpetuating. Supervision becomes easier when police employees begin to share responsibility with you. No longer do you alone have to watch for every problem. An employee won't wait for you to say what to do in an emergency. You'll find the officers using their own initiative to keep crime down. So sharing pays off as employees share your decisions and their work accomplishments with you.

Three Rules

There are three fundamental rules to abide by. First, recognize that without group support your chance of achievement is slim. Second, your best chance for winning group support is by allowing the forces within the group to formulate a decision with minimum interference from you. But you must not stand by while your "team" strikes off in the wrong direction. You can offer sound coaching by providing facts that might be overlooked and by asking the group to weigh pros and cons of various options. Third, be honest with yourself. Are you using participation to motivate or manipulate? If it is the former—congratulations. If it is the latter, eventually the officers will discover that they are being conned. When this happens, kiss both your supervisory power and leadership goodbye.

KEY POINTS

- Delegation plus participation leads to *empowerment* of personnel.
- There are four parties that benefit from proper delegation: the community; the department; the supervisor; and the staff.
- If we delegate to *time* we create efficiency. If we delegate to other *people* we produce effectiveness.
- Confidence and caring are time pillars of successful delegation.

- Letting others participate in decisions that are going to affect them *does not* surrender a supervisor's authority or responsibility for the final decision.
- QC services are intended to increase both organizational and individual effectiveness.
- QC services are a tool for identifying and solving problems.
- Teamwork is participative supervision.
- People must believe that what you're asking them to do is to their advantage.

DISCUSSION

1. What is meant by "really letting go" when one delegates? What are the advantages in doing so? Are there any risks involved?
2. There are eight forces that must be functioning when you delegate (see "Setting the Context"). Rank order the eight forces in terms of their importance.
3. How can a supervisor engage in ownership delegation as compared with lonership?
4. What are the reasons for others to participate in decisions that are going to affect them? What are the reasons not to?
5. Select a common problem and subject it to the QC method of problem solving.
6. What is the key or secret of participation? Why is it effective?

STRUCTURED EXPERIENCES

1. Alpha II Suggested Regulations Sheet

The following group exercises will assist you and your associates to identify the key variables in group dynamics, decision making, consensus, and conflict resolution. Enjoy your journey to Alpha II.

Background

Scientists have discovered that the second planet orbiting Alpha Centauri is almost an exact duplicate of earth, except there are no intelligent life forms. A colonization party, including you and your group, has been formed to settle on Alpha II. The five hundred members of the colonization party come from many different regions and cultures with many differing customs and mores.

Instructions

Your group has been asked to recommend a list of the five most important rules from the following list to govern social conduct and relationships both on the space journey and on Alpha II. You need not concern yourself with questions of enforcement; assume that all rules can be enforced.

Rules Recommended by the International Social Control Commission (can be revised)

1. The social control process shall be governed by a three-member body representing the police, courts, and corrections.
2. There will be no plea bargaining in the court system.
3. The Bill of Rights will apply in total on Alpha II.
4. There will be no death penalty.
5. The police will not carry guns.
6. No juvenile, regardless of the offense, will be incarcerated in an institution.
7. The social-control mechanism (police, courts, and corrections) will be at the national level of government.
8. All social-control personnel will not be under civil service but serve at the pleasure of the community.
9. No harmful or addictive drugs will be permitted in Alpha II.
10. There shall be no public displays of sexual behavior, but sexually explicit literature will be available privately as desired.
11. No individual shall be discriminated against or be guilty of any sexual act because of his or her sexual preferences.
12. All police officers will possess a bachelor's degree.

2. Delegation

Make a list of responsibilities you could delegate, and the police personnel you could delegate to or train to be responsible in these areas. Determine what is needed to start the process of delegation or training.

_____

_____

_____

_____

_____

_____

_____

3. Empowerment: Involvement, Independence, and Innovation

Instructions

Twenty-seven statements follow. They are statements about your job environment. If you feel the statement is *true* or *mostly true* of your job environment, mark it *T*. Conversely, if you believe the statement is *false* or *mostly false*, mark it *F*.

1. The work is really challenging.
2. Few employees have any important responsibilities.
3. Doing things in a different way is valued.
4. There's not much group spirit.
5. There is a fresh, novel atmosphere about the place.
6. Employees have a great deal of freedom to do as they like.
7. New and different ideas are always being tried out.
8. A lot of people seem to be just putting in time.
9. This place would be one of the first to try out a new idea.
10. Employees are encouraged to make their own decisions.
11. People seem to take pride in the organization.
12. People can use their own initiative to do things.

13. People put quite a lot of effort into what they do.
14. Variety and change are not particularly important.
15. The same methods have been used for quite a long time.
16. Supervisors encourage employees to rely on themselves when a problem arises.
17. Few people ever volunteer.
18. Employees generally do not try to be unique and different.
19. It is quite a lively place.
20. Employees are encouraged to learn things even if they are not directly related to the job.
21. It's hard to get people to do their work.
22. New approaches to things are rarely tried.
23. The work is usually very interesting.
24. Things tend to stay just about the same.
25. Supervisors meet with employees regularly to discuss their future work goals.
26. Things always seem to be changing.
27. Employees function fairly independently of supervisors.

Scoring

This awareness is comprised of three dimensions: involvement, independence, and innovation (I^3). We believe that a high I^3 score for you means high empowerment. The lower the I^3 score, the greater the likelihood that you're not experiencing much if any empowerment at work.

Give yourself one point if you've marked the following statements as follows: $1 = T$; $4 = F$; $8 = F$; $13 = T$; $17 = F$; $19 = T$; $21 = F$; and $23 = T$. Your score for *involvement* is _____.

Give yourself one point if you've marked the following statements as follows: $2 = F$; $6 = T$; $10 = T$; $12 = T$; $16 = T$; $18 = F$; $20 = T$; $25 = T$; and $27 = T$. Your score for *independence* is _____.

Following the same pattern: $3 = T$; $5 = T$; $7 = T$; $9 = T$; $14 = F$; $15 = F$; $22 = F$; $24 = F$; and $26 = T$. Your score for *innovation* is _____.

If your scores were 0 to 3, that particular dimension is very low; 4 to 5 is below average; 6 is average; 7 is above average; 8 is well above average; and 9 is very high.

Obviously we're hoping that you are looking at scores from 6 on up. An understanding of your job environment can help you deal with both the positive and negative aspects of your work. This information may help you in improving the various aspects of empowerment.

RESPONSIBILITY TEN

Employee-Oriented Supervision: II. Conflict Resolution

RESOLVING OUR CONFLICTS THE INUPIAT ESKIMO WAY: THE SONG DUEL

An Inupiat Eskimo, when felt wronged by another person, would challenge that individual to an exchange of belittling songs. The entire tribe would gather to witness the duel. The disputing parties would take turns singing songs which via wit and derision described the wrongdoing or perversity of the other person. The tribe would respond with laughter to each song and the duel would continue until one person withdrew in shame. The issue was expected to be resolved and closed with the ending of the song duel.

We heard one supervisor comment with chagrin, "Being a sergeant could be relatively easy, if it weren't for those miserable _____s that I have to supervise." Supervision is a people process. A select few people will command more of your thinking and attention than others. People problems can occur on an individual basis (malingering) or on a group basis (the whole crew is malingering). People problems—singular or plural—are a major job responsibility for you.

KEEP IN MIND . . .

Most police officers are honest, hard working, and helpful human beings. They project a *positive mental attitude* (PMA) and will make your job as a supervisor a rewarding one. Similarly, the majority of police work groups possess one or

213

two individuals who are seemingly dedicated to making you miserable. As their supervisor, however, you can master their fate.

Problem police employees come in a variety of symptomatic packages. Basically, they can be categorized as either honest (mistakes of the mind) or dishonest (mistakes of the heart). Oddly, the honest problem employee, for example, the "whining, sniveling, malcontent" (WSM) is frequently more difficult to handle. The dishonest officer is detected, apprehended, discharged, and probably prosecuted. The WSM requires considerably different treatment.

As a supervisor, you are destined to expend a large portion of your energy on the handling of problem employees. They will tax your patience, at times push your anger control, and test your ability to develop a creative response. Alternatively, you must not lose sight and contact with the PMAs, the productive and team-spirited employees. Concentrate on, reinforce, and reward the productive officer. The strength of your work team is centered here. Nobody said supervising was easy. If it was easy, everyone would be doing it.

ROLE OF THE POLICE SUPERVISOR

All that a man achieves and all that he fails to achieve is the direct result of his own thoughts.

—James Allen
As a Man Thinketh (New York: Grosset and Dunlap, 1983), p. 49

Supervision is nothing more than motivating other people. First, however, you must be motivated. If you're not a "turned-on" supervisor, the likelihood of your "constructing an environment in which they motivate themselves" is very low. Remember, the first person to motivate is yourself.

The second ingredient for building a motivating environment is listening. Yes, listen. If you're not listening (ears, eyes, and intuition), then you'll not know who is responding to the opportunity to participate together as a team. Vince Lombardi, the legendary football coach, once commented, "Most people call it team spirit. When the players are imbued with that special feeling, you know you've got yourself a winning team."[1]

For a variety of reasons, there are at times a few employees who either cannot or will not make a team commitment. Through either professional or personal difficulties, or both, they march to a different drummer. Your role as a police supervisor, very simply stated, although not easily fulfilled is: All problem employees have a different drummer, one that is causing him or her to conflict with the pace and direction of the work unit. This drummer should be discovered and brought into line.

The remainder of this chapter examines conflict as potentially both a positive and negative human force.

---

[1]As quoted by Lee Iacocca, *Iacocca: An Autobiography* (New York: Bantam Books, 1984), pp. 56–57.

CONFLICT: THE INTERNAL CONSEQUENCES

> *Having thought about your interests, you should go into a meeting not only with one or more specific options that would meet your legitimate interests but also with an open mind. An open mind is not an empty one.*

—Roger Fisher and William Ury
Getting to Yes (Boston: Houghton Mifflin, 1981), p. 55

Human conflict is to be expected; indeed a certain amount of internal conflict can be considered healthy. An analogy would be the necessity for tension on the mainspring of a watch. At the same time, however, too much tension will cause it to break. In an organizational setting, too much conflict is counterproductive to goal attainment. The police supervisor is in a unique position to control the degree of conflict in an agency.

When we use the term conflict, we are referring to perceived incompatible differences resulting in some form of interference or opposition. Whether the differences are real or not is irrelevant. If people perceive the differences exist, then a conflict state exists. Additionally, our definition covers a range that includes the extremes, from subtle, indirect, and highly controlled forms of differences to overt acts, such as physical altercations, job terminations, and criminal acts.

Competition is different from conflict. Conflict is directed against another party, whereas competition is aimed at obtaining a goal without interference from another party. Of course, competition can lead to conflict. If three police supervisors in a patrol watch are competing for the number one performance rating, the scarceness created by availability of only one top position can result in conflict.

This section covers conflict of an internal situation. The next chapter deals with conflict as an external phenomenon.

Conflict: A Plus or a Minus?

The response to the question of conflict being either a plus or a minus in a work group is, "It all depends."

Some conflicts support the goals of the organization: these are functional conflicts of a constructive form. Additionally, there are conflicts that hinder an organization in achieving its goals; these are dysfunctional conflicts and are destructive forms.

Of course, it is one thing to argue that conflict can be valuable, but how do you tell if a conflict is functional or dysfunctional? Unfortunately, the demarcation is neither clear nor precise. No one level of conflict can be adopted as acceptable or unacceptable under all conditions. The type and level of conflict that create healthy and positive involvement toward one department's goals may, in another department or in the same department at another time, be highly dysfunctional. Functionality or dysfunctionality, therefore, is a judgment call on your part. Hence, it remains for you to make intelligent judgments concerning whether conflict levels in your unit are appropriate, too high, or too low.

Value of Conflict

If harnessed and channeled, conflict can produce the following results for you and your team officers:

- Major stimulant for change
- Fosters creativity and innovation
- Clarifies issues and goals
- Encourages individuality
- Enhances communication
- Increases energy within a unit
- Promotes cohesiveness
- Psychologically healthy

Return for a moment and reread what we wrote about the "drummer." If you have autocrative leanings, you probably thought "Yes, let's all get into step." Conversely, if your supervisor emphasizes a democratic approach, you likely questioned the notion of a so-called drummer. It is vital that you, as a supervisor, not only tolerate but respect an officer's individuality and preferences as long as they do not detract from getting police work done in a professional and legally accepted manner. If you as a supervisor push for uniformity and ignore individual strengths and styles, you are promoting the negative aspects of conflict.

Because conflict has positive attributes, you can, as appropriate, stimulate it. QCs are probably the best vehicle for developing ideas, risk taking, openness, and competition.

Sources of Conflict

Conflict can emanate from one of four sources: (1) existing conditions (especially novel ones), (2) our attitudes, (3) our thoughts, (4) our behavior. Typically, all four combine to produce the conflict.

Fortunately most conflicts are of minor importance. Few police officers are likely to be psychologically crippled by trying to decide between two patrol routes. Few of us encounter daily conflicts that we cannot respond to in a routine or "programmed" manner. The police officer, however, generally experiences the unusual. He or she is more often than not faced with highly diverse nonprogrammable choices. Briefly stated, the police officer typically deals with novelty rather than familiar and precedented problems. Today there is a hidden conflict in our lives between the pressures of acceleration and those of novelty. One forces us to make faster decisions while the other compels us to make the hardest, most time-consuming type of decisions.

Conflict Resolution

Fundamentally, there are seven tactical routes for resolving conflict. They can be applied singularly or in various mixes. Be certain to accurately comprehend the source of a conflict before you use a particular tactic. If the tactic you select does not fit the situation, you will regretfully exacerbate the problem at hand.

Superordinate goals. Common goals that two or more conflicting parties each desire and that cannot be reached without the cooperation of those involved are called *superordinate* goals. These goals must be highly valued, unattainable without the help of all parties involved in the conflict, and commonly sought. Evidence supports the fact that, when used cumulatively, superordinate goals develop long-term "peacemaking" potential, thereby reinforcing dependency and developing collaboration.

Expansion of resources. Police officers are usually competitive by nature and seek opportunities to advance professionally. Some agencies have responded to this need by creating corporal senior officer or field training officer positions. Others have established sergeant one and two positions, lieutenant one and two positions, and so on. This technique is extremely successful because it leaves the competitive parties satisfied. However, its use is obviously restricted by the nature of its inherent limitation; that is, resources rarely exist in such quantities so that they can be easily expanded.

Avoidance. One method of dealing with conflict is simply to avoid it. Avoidance does not offer a permanent way of resolving conflict, but it is an extremely popular short-term solution. In our day-to-day relations, each of us frequently withdraws from the arena of confrontation or suppresses a particular conflict. The method has obvious limitations, but it has nonetheless been described as "society's chief instrument for handling conflict."

Smoothing. Smoothing can be described as the process of playing down differences that exist between individuals or groups while emphasizing common interests. Differences are suppressed in smoothing and similarities are accentuated. When we recognize that *all* conflict situations have common points of interest or agreement, we see smoothing represents a way in which one minimizes differences.

Compromise. Compromise techniques make up a major portion of resolution methods. Included here are external or third-party interventions, plus internal compromise between conflicting parties through both total-group and representative negotiation and voting. What differentiates compromise from the other techniques is that in a compromise solution each party must give up something of value. While there is no clear winner, there is also no clear loser. In our democratic society and in many police agencies, compromise is the classic method by which conflicts can be resolved.

Forcing. In police organizations, probably the most frequently used method for formally resolving opposing interactions is the use of forcing or formal authority. Members of the police departments, with rare exception, recognize and accept the authority of their superiors, and even though they may not be in agreement with their decisions, they will almost always abide by them. Thus, forcing is highly successful in achieving short-term reduced conflict levels. As a supervisor, constantly remember that its major weakness is the same as that of avoidance, smoothing, and compromise; that is, the cause of the conflict is not treated, but only its effects.

Reorganize. If a conflict's source is the police organization's structure, it seems only reasonable to look again at structure for the solution. You might, for instance, transfer or exchange members between departments, create coordinating or buffer positions, develop an appeals system, realign department boundaries, or change individual responsibilities.

PROBLEM EMPLOYEES: WORKER RELATIONS

Problem employees are the chronic absentee, the rule breaker, the boss hater, the psychosomatic, the malingerer, the person who's lost his confidence, the heavy drinker, the alcoholic, the WSM, and, yes, even the workaholic. Problem police employees are expensive to have on the payroll. They are characterized by excessive tardiness and absences. You are apt to find that they are difficult to supervise. They have a tendency to upset the morale of the work group. Consequently, you should worry about (1) hiring a problem employee in the first place, (2) handling him or her on the job so that he or she reaches maximum productivity with the least disruption of the team's overall performance, and (3) determining whether a problem employee has become so seriously maladjusted that he or she needs professional attention.

This section focuses on the police employee that is causing internal problems. The following section centers on the police employee who is generating external problems for the department. Obviously, both categories overlap and there is not any clear demarcation—except when an officer commits a crime. That is really a worst-case problem employee.

Recognizing Problem Employees

Many problem employees fall into these categories: They are perpetually dissatisfied, given to baseless worries, tire easily, are suspicious, are sure that superiors withhold promotions, that their associates gossip maliciously about them. Some are characterized by drinking sprees, are insubordinate, or have ungovernable tempers.

Among themselves, problem employees differ widely, just as more normal people do. But within the framework of their symptoms, they are surprisingly alike in their reactions.

The behavior of a psychotic or neurotic employee can become your concern. Both terms sound pretty ominous. But only the police officer with a psychosis is seriously ill. The most common type of psychosis is schizophrenia, or "split personality." A schizophrenic lives partly in a world of his imagination. Especially when the world seems threatening to him, he withdraws. He may be able to adjust to life, even have a successful career. But when he loses his grip, his problem is beyond the scope of a supervisor.

Conversely, most of us are neurotic to a degree. People who have exaggerated fears, who feel the need to prove themselves, or who are irritable, hostile, opinionated, timid, or aggressive (which somewhere along the line describes most of us) have the seeds of neurosis in them. It's when this condition becomes exaggerated that a neurotic employee becomes a problem to associates and to the supervisor.

A couple of samples of neurotic employees: The officer who boasts about his drinking and sexual prowess. The supervisor who gets pleasure from reprimanding a police employee in front of others. The detective who visits a medical doctor every other day with some minor ailment. The dispatcher who meticulously arranges his or her workplace in the same manner every day, who can't begin his or her job unless everything is exactly as he or she wants it.

Recognizing Problem Supervisors and Managers

During the 1984 Olympics, a police officer planted a bomb in the wheel of a bus scheduled to transport some of the participating athletes. He was apprehended, discharged, and prosecuted. When asked why he committed this act, he replied, "My sergeant was driving me nuts, and I had hoped the situation would get me transferred."

Yes, there are supervisors and police managers who preach too much, who are rigid in their interpretation of policy, who enjoy assigning employees to jobs they particularly dislike, or who continually hold some sort of threat, veiled or otherwise, over their employees' heads.

Then, too, you and your boss especially are beset with more than ordinary obstacles at work. And not only do they have their own phobias to contend with, they must listen to and try to assuage those of their employees. Is it any wonder that a supervisor or police manager becomes a problem employee?

Helping the Problem Employee

The psychotic or highly neurotic employee requires professional assistance. Many police departments have either full-time or on-call psychiatrists and clinical psychologists. With your superior's approval, you should refer these unfortunate people to such specialists.

You can help the problem police employee toward better adjustment only after you have reassured the officer that you are trying to help him or her keep his or her job—not looking for an excuse to get rid of him or her. No approach does more harm with a person of this nature than the "better get yourself straightened out or you will lose your job" attitude on a supervisor's part. You have to believe, and make them believe, that your intentions are good, that you want to help them. Then you must give the officer every opportunity to help himself or herself. This approach is called counseling, and there are fifteen rules for you to follow.

1. Listen patiently to what the employee has to say before making any comment of your own. This act on your part may be sufficient to resolve the difficulties.
2. Refrain from criticizing or offering hasty advice on the employee's problem.
3. Never argue with a police employee while you are in the process of counseling.
4. Give your undivided attention to the employee.
5. Look beyond the mere words of what the employee says; listen to see if the officer's trying to tell you something deeper than what appears on the surface.
6. Recognize what you are counseling an employee for. And don't look for immediate results. Never mix up the counseling interview with some other action you may want to take, such as discipline.
7. Find a reasonably quiet place where you're sure you won't be interrupted and won't be overheard. Try to put the employee at ease. Don't jump into a cross-examination.
8. Depending on the nature of the situation, multiple sessions may be necessary. They should last from fifteen to thirty minutes per session.
9. If after two counseling sessions you are not making progress, you should consult with your manager concerning referral to a professional therapist.
10. Get conditioned to the fact that it is your job and you can't run away from it.
11. Look at your task as a fact-finding one, just as in handling grievances.
12. Control your own emotions and opinions while dealing with the employee.
13. Be absolutely sold on the value of listening rather than preaching.
14. Recognize your own limits in handling these situations. You're not a clinical psychologist. You're a person responsible for getting results out of your assigned officers.
15. If all else fails, then you still have your prerogative to use discipline.

Make no mistake: Handling a police employee who has become a problem isn't easy. Sometimes it can become downright unpleasant. But the sooner you face up to this key supervisory responsibility, the sooner the problems get solved.

PROBLEM EMPLOYEES: CITIZEN RELATIONS

In order to strengthen administrative review and control, responsibility should formally be delegated to the police for developing comprehensive administra-

*tive policies and rules governing the duties and responsibilities of police of-
ficers together with procedures and sanctions for ensuring that these duties and
responsibilities are met.*

—American Bar Association, *The Urban Police Function*
(Washington, D.C.: American Bar Association, 1973), p. 163

One of the main reasons for your job is to strengthen agency review and
control of police conduct. Plainly, it is impossible to construct an effective
system of accountability (see Figure 10-1) without a strong and functional
mechanism for maintaining behavioral control over police personnel. While
the exclusionary rule, criminal and civil actions against police officers, and
other external remedies serve as important constraints, you must accept primary responsibility for controlling the vast discretionary power of police
officers.

Unfortunately, some police supervisors have not yet accepted this challenge, and this is the basic reason why there has been constant pressure for
civilian review boards, ombudsmen, and other such external review agencies.

Your agency may be efficient and large enough to afford an "internal
investigations" or "professional responsibilities" unit. Nevertheless, the creation of an internal investigation unit *does not* relieve you of the need to
maintain discipline. On the contrary, it strengthens it by providing assistance to
supervisors *on request*, in the investigation of alleged misconduct of their team
members.

Drawing the Lines

While the community may disagree with or be vague about what constitutes
police misconduct, the police cannot. Granted, without community consensus
on this subject the problem is a highly perplexing one for our police. Nonetheless, wrongdoing must be *defined* and *policies* must be set by the agency. Lines
must be clearly drawn. Essentially these lines should encompass three forms of
misconduct: (1) legalistic, (2) professional, and (3) moralistic. The first involves
criminal considerations; the second may or may not be criminal in nature but
does entail professional considerations; and the third may or may not include
professional canons, but does embody personal ethics. Each form of errant
behavior is examined further in the following paragraphs. It will be noted that
there is a descending degree of clarity or precision with each type of wrongdoing. Conversely, there is an ascending degree of managerial ambiguity on
police and procedural violations.

Legalistic misconduct. This type of misconduct is also commonly
referred to as "corruption." Police corruption is an extremely complex and
demoralizing crime problem, and it is not new to our generation of police
personnel. Police corruption includes (1) the misuse of police authority for the
police employee's personal gain, (2) activity of the police employee that com-
promises, or has the potential to compromise, his or her ability to enforce the
law or provide other police service impartially, (3) the protection of illicit

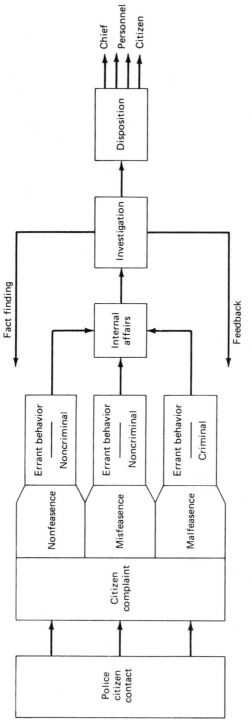

Figure 10-1 Internal Discipline: A System of Accountability (Paul Whisenand and Fred Ferguson, *The Managing of Police Organizations, 2nd ed.,* © 1978, p. 349. Reprinted by permission of Prentice Hall, Inc., Englewood Cliffs, N.J.)

activities from police enforcement, whether or not the police employee receives something of value in return, and (4) the police employee's involvement in promoting the business of one person while discouraging that of another person. Police corruption means, therefore, acts involving the misuse of authority by a police officer in a manner designed to produce *personal gain for the officer or for others*. And this is illegal!

Professional misconduct. This form of misconduct can range from physical to verbal abuse of a citizen. On the one hand, a criminal or civil violation may have occurred, while, on the other, agency standards of professional conduct may be at issue. The possibilities for wrongdoing in this instance can fall within two rubrics: the law and professional conduct "unbecoming an officer." The distinction, again, between this type of wrongdoing and corruption is that no personal gain for the officer or others is involved. The key question is: What conduct is permissible? Hence there is a need for established policies, procedures, rules, and sanctions that explicitly encompass the conduct of police employees.

Moralistic misconduct. If an officer thinks certain citizens are deserving of aggressive police practices, the likelihood of his behaving aggressively is enhanced, perhaps to the point of overreaction or even physical abuse. Or if the officer thinks certain citizens are deserving of no police attention, the likelihood of his or her behaving passively is increased, perhaps to the extent of no reaction, and thus the possibility of corruption occurs. Space does not allow adequate coverage of this subject. Nonetheless, it is at the very crux of other forms of misconduct.

Citizen Complaints

Frequently you will be the first to hear a citizen's complaint. "I want to see your supervisor" is a pervasive request on the part of a citizen who feels he or she has been mistreated. A complaint starts with its *receipt*, then proceeds to an *investigation*, and concludes with *adjudication*. More specifically, the three phases are as follows:[2]

PHASE 1: COMPLAINT RECEIPT

1. A viable complaint reception provides you with a useful tool for officer performance evaluation.
2. It is imperative that all complaints (letters, telephone, in person) be investigated.
3. A form should be designed and used for complaint processing (see Figure 10-2).

(*text continued on page 228*)

[2]This section is excerpted from the National Advisory Commission on Criminal Justice Standards and Goals, *Police* (Washington, D.C.: U.S. Government Printing Office, 1973), p. 483.

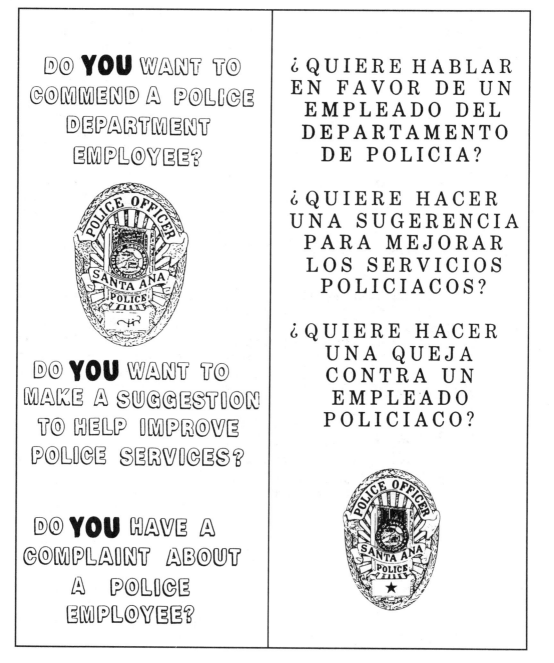

Figure 10-2 Example of a Complaint Procedure [partial version of spanish language is displayed] (Courtesy Orange County Sheriff's Department, Santa Ana, Calif.)

The police officer in every community is an unmistakable symbol not only of the law, but of the entire community. Because of this they are the obvious target for grievances against any short-comings of our governmental system. The police officer can solve the complex problems of a community only when working in concert with an entire community.

The mission of the Santa Ana Police Department is to ensure the safety and security of all the people in our City, by providing responsive and professional police service with compassion and concern. Our mission is accomplished within the moral and legal standards of our community through a partnership of the community and members of our department.

Therefore, it is the policy of the Santa Ana Police Department to accept, register and thoroughly investigate all complaints of the alleged misconduct on the part of the police officers and non-sworn personnel which emanate from within the department and from the community.

PAUL M. WALTERS
CHIEF OF POLICE

-1-

● **WHAT IF I WANT TO COMMEND AN OFFICER?**
Just fill out this form and return it to the Santa Ana Polce Department.

● **WHAT IF I WANT TO MAKE A SUGGESTION?**
If you would like to make a suggestion that you think would improve police services in Santa Ana, fill out this form and return it to the Santa Ana Police Department.

● **WHAT IF I WANT TO MAKE A COMPLAINT?**
Fill out this form and return it to the Santa Ana Police Department.

DOES THAT MEAN THE POLICE DEPARTMENT WANTS COMPLAINTS?
Of course not. A complaint may mean that someone hasn't done a good enough job. But, we do want to know when our service needs to be improved or corrected.

BUT WILL YOU LISTEN TO MY COMPLAINT?
Certainly. We want to find out what went wrong, if anything, so that we can see to it that it doesn't happen again.

BUT WHO WILL INVESTIGATE MY COMPLAINT?
Either a special investigator from the Internal Investigations Section or the officer's supervisor would investigate a complaint against an officer.

-2-

Figure 10-2 (Continued)

WELL THEN, WHO SHOULD I GO TO FIRST?
You should take a complaint about an officer to his supervisor. If he is not there, ask for the on-duty Watch Commander.

BUT I WANT TO TAKE THIS ALL THE WAY TO THE TOP. I WANT THE CHIEF OF POLICE TO KNOW.
And he will. The Chief of Police gets copies of ALL complaints against officers. Each of the officer's superiors is notified as well.

DO I HAVE TO COMPLAIN IN PERSON?
No. We prefer to talk to you in person; but we will accept a complaint by telephone or letter if necessary. It won't make any difference in the attention we give it.

I'M UNDER 18; DO I HAVE THE RIGHT TO COMPLAIN?
Yes; just bring one of your parents, guardians or a responsible adult in with you.

WHAT ABOUT THE LIE DETECTOR?
In certain cases, where we can't find the truth any other way, you may be asked to take a polygraph examination. The same is true for our officers.

WHAT WILL HAPPEN TO THE OFFICER?
That will depend on what he did. If his actions were criminal, he will be dealt with like any other citizen. If they were improper, but not criminal, he will be disciplined by the Chief of Police. If the facts of the investigation support the conclusion that the officer's actions were legal and proper he/she will be exonerated. Should the facts indicate your complaint is false, the complaint will be unfounded. You will, in any event, **always** receive the results results of our investigation.

WHAT IF I'M NOT SATISFIED WITH THE RESULTS OF THIS INVESTIGATION?
We sincerely hope that would never happen. If it did, you could go to the Santa Ana Human Relations Commission for assistance. You could also contact your representative on the City Council; or, in some cases, the Orange County District Attorney or Grand Jury.

Our goal at the Santa Ana Police Department is that you will never need to use the information contained in this folder to register a complaint. We don't want to fail in our continuing efforts to give **YOU** the best possible police service.

-3-

-4-

CS. 876

Figure 10-2 (Continued)

```
          (Ms.)
          (Miss)
          (Mrs.)
MY NAME IS (Mr.)_____
                  (first)         (middle)              (last)


I LIVE AT_____
                                     AM        AM
MY HOME PHONE IS_____ OR BETWEEN ___ PM AND ___ PM I CAN BE REACHED

AT WORK, PHONE _____ EXT. _____ . MY AGE IS _____ YEARS.

___  I WANT TO COMMEND
                                (BADGE(S)
___  I WANT TO SUGGEST THAT     (OFFICER(S) _____

___  I WANT TO COMPLAIN ABOUT       ON (date) _____

AT (location) _____
                        AM   HE
AT ABOUT (time) _____ PM, THEY _____

      _____

      _____

      _____
                  (Attach as many sheets as necessary)


I DECLARE THAT THE INFORMATION CONTAINED IN THIS FORM IS TRUE.

DATE _____

                              _____
                              (Signature)


      POLICE USE ONLY         _____
      _____     (Signature of parent/guardian)
      Accepted By:_____ (if you are under 18 years of age)

      Date:_____Time:_____
```

Figure 10-2   (Continued)

4. The complaining citizen should be given a completed copy of the form as a receipt.
5. Results of the investigation should be submitted to the complaining party.
6. If the citizen complaint is found to be intentionally malicious, then the officer has legal redress available.

PHASE 2: INVESTIGATION

1. All supervisors assigned should be given specific training in investigating internal discipline complaints and should be provided with written investigative procedures.
2. Every police agency should establish formal procedures for investigating internal misconduct allegations.
3. Every supervisor should conduct internal investigations in a manner that best reveals the facts while preserving the dignity of all persons and maintaining the confidential nature of the investigation.
4. Every police agency should provide at the time of employment and, again, prior to the specific investigation all its employees with a written statement of their duties and rights when they are the subject of an internal discipline investigation.
5. Every police chief should have legal authority during an internal discipline investigation to relieve police employees from their duties when it is in the interests of the public and the police agency.
6. All internal discipline investigations should be concluded 30 days from the date the complaint is made unless an extension is granted by the chief executive of the agency.

The role of the supervisor during phase 3 is normally in an advisory role to the police manager. More than anyone else, the immediate supervisor should be able to evaluate the overall conduct and performance level of his or her staff and, if a penalty is indicated, to determine how severe it should be. Or, conversely, the supervisor may argue that (1) the officer should be exonerated, (2) unfounded (the act did not occur), or (3) not sustained (insufficient facts to make a determination). If the charge against the officer is sustained, then the supervisor can recommend one of the following penalties:[3]

- Oral reprimand
- Written reprimand
- Remedial training
- Loss of time or of annual leave in lieu of suspension
- Suspension up to thirty days (but no longer)
- Removal from service

[3]Ibid., p. 492.

PHASE 3: ADJUDICATION

1. A complaint disposition should be classified as sustained, not sustained, exonerated, unfounded, or misconduct not based on the original complaint.
2. Adjudication and, if warranted, disciplinary action should be based partially on recommendations of the involved employee's immediate supervisor.
3. An administrative fact-finding trial board should be available to all police agencies to assist in the adjudication phase. It should be activated when necessary in the interests of the police agency, the public, or the accused employee, and should be available at the direction of the police chief or upon the request of any employee who is being penalized in any manner that exceeds verbal or written reprimand. It should be advisory to the chief.
4. The accused employee should be entitled to representation and logistical support equal to that afforded the person representing the agency in a trial board proceeding.
5. Police employees should be allowed to appeal a chief's decision. The police agency should not provide the resources or funds for appeal.
6. The chief should establish written policy on the retention of internal discipline complaint investigation reports. Only the reports of sustained and, if appealed, upheld investigations should become a part of the accused employee's personnel folder. All disciplinary investigations should be kept confidential.
7. Administrative adjudication of internal discipline complaints involving a violation of law should neither depend on nor curtail criminal prosecution. Regardless of the administrative adjudication, every police agency should refer all complaints that involve violations of law to the prosecuting agency for the decision to prosecute criminally. Police employees should not be treated differently from other members of the community in cases involving violations of the law.

PREVENTING THE PROBLEM EMPLOYEE

Leadership is the lifting of a man's vision to higher sights, the raising of a man's performance to a higher standard, the building of a man's personality beyond its normal limitations. Nothing better prepares the ground for such leadership than a spirit of management that confirms in the day-to-day practices of the organization strict principles of conduct and responsibility, high standards of performance, and respect for the individual and his work.

—Peter F. Drucker
Management (New York: Harper and Row, 1974), p. 5

As a supervisor, you hold a responsibility for producing the type of leadership that Drucker writes about. Quickly reread his admonition to you.

Now recognize and keep this in focus as you supervise others: Some problem employees simply do not want to change their negative attitudes and malcontent behavior. And, in spite of your efforts, they won't. That's the bad news. However, with time many will cast off their negative shell. That's the good news!

All the preceding chapters are focused on helping you in "problem employee prevention." Furthermore, if it should occur, how to correct a person's counterproductive attitude and behavior was discussed. Your difficult workers are likely to be few in number. Nonetheless, you'll find yourself expending considerable energy and thought in bringing them back on board the team.

MOST OFTEN . . .

Most often you are likely to experience reasonably cooperative individuals forming into perfectly difficult groups. These groups come in all sizes and possess a wide range of values and purposes. Sometimes the values and purposes are confusing, even covert in nature: for example, the leader of a neighborhood watch program that patiently seeks burglary prevention, but in reality is attempting to build a political base to eventually run for a city council seat. At times the values and purposes conflict with existing departmental policies and professional ethics. A case in point here are police associations and unions; for example, they may tell their members "reduce your productivity," while you are telling them not to. (Paradoxically, you may be a union member.)

NEGOTIATIONS: GETTING TO YES

The height of human wisdom is to bring our tempers down to our circumstances, and to make a calm within, under the weight of the greatest storm without.

—Daniel Defoe

If you will commit yourself to the supervisor's role and hope to approach its fulfillment, then the following is equally logical and practical in respect to coping with difficult groups of people. First, think of yourself as a change agent, better still—a negotiator. Second, act like one.

Whether a work group or a group of citizens, they will on occasion pose for you, as a supervisor, problems, issues, conflicts, obstacles, and confrontations. It is up to you, and perhaps some others, to perform the following:

Dysfunctional	Supervisor Negotiates	Functional
Problems	into	Potentialities
Issues	into	Initiatives
Conflicts	into	Challenges
Obstacles	into	Opportunities
Confrontations	into	Cooperation

Being an adept negotiator is important to your success as a supervisor because (1) you are destined to experience conflicting situations and groups, and (2) you are in a front-line position to convert potentially negative conflict into positive problem solving.

GENERAL APPROACH FOR NEGOTIATING DIFFERENCES

Negotiation is a basic means of getting what you want from others. It is back-and-forth communication designed to reach an agreement when you and the other side have some interests that are shared and others that are opposed.[4] More and more occasions require negotiation; conflict is a growth industry. Everyone wants to participate in decisions that affect them; fewer and fewer people will accept decisions dictated by someone else. People differ, and they use negotiation to handle their differences.

Conflict resolution techniques may be applied at any of several pressure points. Their effectiveness and appropriateness depend on the nature of the conflict and on the supervisor's style of supervision. The major challenge, however, is not the elimination of conflict and ambiguity from organizational life; it is the containment of these conditions at levels and in forms that are at least humane, tolerable, and low in cost and which at best might be positive in contribution to individual and organization.

Because of the wide range of problems to be solved by the supervisor, the *process* of resolving conflicts rather than particular issues will be emphasized. Once the process has been mastered, actual problem solving should become all the easier. From this point on we will refer to the supervisor when seeking to resolve conflict as a third-party *intervener*. The strategy, in turn, can be called *process intervention*. More often than not, when intervening the supervisor will find that to solve the problem, she or he must develop the following: direct structural changes into the organization, new criteria of selection and placement, tolerance and coping abilities of individuals, and a stronger interpersonal bond among organizational members.

Intervention: Where, When, and How?

Where, when, and how to intervene in a dispute, if at all, are the most fundamental choices to be made by the supervisor. Even before these decisions must come the realization that she or he cannot wait for others to request that intervention in a dispute. Moreover, the supervisor must not become a silent observer of "people" problems. The police supervisor—that is, the effective supervisor—has to be alert for organizational arguments and, once they are detected, must rapidly attempt to resolve them. The supervisor must, in a single work, *intervene*! Once the police supervisor has decided to intervene, follow-up decisions must be made:

---

[4]This section is taken from Paul M. Whisenand and Fred Fergusen, *Managing Police Organizations*, 2nd ed. (Englewood Cliffs, N.J.: Prentice Hall, 1981), pp. 410–413.

- Should the place of conflict resolution be entirely neutral to all parties (the disputants and the supervisor), or should it be geared to assist one or the other? For example, if the supervisor decides to hold the meeting in his or her office, the location would tend to reflect that aura. But if the supervisor chooses to resolve the participants' problems at a social meeting, personal power would be manifested.
- Should the place of conflict resolution be formal or informal? To illustrate, if the supervisor insists on job titles being used during group interaction, then considerable formality occurs. But if the situation permits the use of first names, informality will result. (It is just as easy, and much more effective, to state, "Joe, you're wrong!" as compared to "Officer Cline, the department is hereby and herein reprimanding you for inappropriate activities.")
- Should the time period within which the conflict resolution be short or long? By this we mean, "You two have a problem—please think it through and, when decided, report back to me" or "You two are constantly arguing—resolve your difficulties before the day is over!"
- Should the supervisor include himself or herself and/or others in the argumentative dialogue, or is it best limited to the disputants? This is to say, "It's just the two of you—closet yourselves and please come forth with a reasonable solution to your problems."

Based on the preceding decisions, certain additional activities on the part of the police supervisor become necessary:

- Refereeing the discussion (often heated) between employees
- Recommending a format that should be followed during the dialogue
- Providing clarification of information important to one another
- Assisting in the discussion by offering feedback
- Seeking to identify the issues that caused the conflict
- Suggesting a means of communication that would promote discussion
- Indicating the problems in interpersonal communications
- Constant counseling relative to the primary goals and standards of the department as they impact on the conflict

The aim of "creative" conflict resolution is integration that allows both parties to achieve their objectives. The basic goal is a win-win approach rather than a win-lose approach. However, the latter is much more common in our competitive society, and it does indeed take creative conflict management to find integrative solutions. A confrontation mode might or might not facilitate achieving integrative results. It can mean getting all the cards on the table, expressing goodwill in empathizing with alternative viewpoints, and actively seeking solutions that satisfy both (or all) protagonists. Obviously not easily done, but certainly possible.

Intervention: Supervisory Attributes

Certain attributes of the supervisor and of his or her relations with the disputants influence the supervisor's ability to perform the functions and implement the interventions described previously. The following attributes are required of the third party (supervisor): establishing professional expertise, exerting power, and manifesting neutrality and candor.

Professional expertise. The supervisory attributes that give the principals confidence in entering an open confrontation and facilitate confrontation processes include (1) diagnostic skill, (2) behavioral skills in breaking impasses and interrupting repetitive interchange, (3) attitudes of acceptance, and (4) a personal capacity to provide emotional support and reassurance to all involved.

Personal power. The real or perceived power of the supervisor and her or his general knowledge of the principals, issues, and background factors are important attributes. At least moderate knowledge of the principals, issues, and historical factors usually is an advantage. It not only enhances the supervisor's credibility with the principals but also increases the likelihood that her or his intervention will be on target. Also, the prior knowledge reduces the amount of time that the principals spend talking to the supervisor rather than each other (this admittedly is not always an advantage). One factor arguing against a supervisor's being highly knowledgeable about the issues and persons involved is that it is harder for the principals to believe she or he does not have her or his own opinions, about either the issues or the persons' views, which disqualify her or him as a disinterested party.

Neutrality. Naturally, differences in the supervisor's relationships to the two principals can influence effectiveness. Three different types of supervisory justice and balance are critical: Is the supervisor neutral with respect to outcome? Is the supervisor attitudinally equally distant from the parties in a personal sense? Does the supervisor eliminate rules for handling differences that would inadvertently create an advantage for one and a disadvantage for the other?

Self-reality. "To thine own self be true" is the crux of the message contained herein. It is *not* important that the supervisor's personal style or the way she or he comes across to others be taken into account to more fully understand her or his power. Moreover, it *is* critical for the general theory and practice of conflict resolution to know that such personal attributes and styles do condition the role and the behavior of the person. Those involved in the process have to believe that the supervisor is attempting to impartially and accurately "redress the balance" between the differing parties.

Interventions: Conflict "Prevention"

Since conflict is inherent in organizations, what can the police supervisor do in the face of the inevitable? If the supervisor is wise, he or she will be alert to the demands imposed on his or her subordinates and offer them the support of his or her authority and position and his knowledge and experience in resolving conflict. The supervisor must also review conflicting demands frequently, for they will not remain static over time. As the organization and its members adjust to changes in technology, personnel practices, and the types of people joining the organization, the expectations of those who impose demands will change as well. Therefore, detection of group and interpersonal conflict requires periodic analysis and definition of position content.

Frequent consultation with subordinates, open communication between organizational levels, joint problem-solving meetings, and management by objectives are all means to detect the existence of role conflict. Once the nature of recurring conflicts is understood, it is possible to collect information useful in resolving them.

SEVEN STEPS YOU CAN TAKE FOR GETTING TO YES

Candor, when properly used, is one of the most powerful, effective—and underused—negotiating techniques I know of.

—Mark H. McCormack
What They Don't Teach at Harvard Business School
(New York: Bantam Books, 1984), p. 16

Whether in police work, personal business transactions, or your own family, we reach most decisions through negotiation. Even if we go to court, we almost always negotiate a settlement before trial. Although negotiation takes place every day, it is not easy to do successfully. Our natural approaches for negotiation often leave us and others dissatisfied, fatigued, or withdrawn—and frequently all three.

We find ourselves in a "Catch 22." We envision two ways to negotiate, easy or tough. The easy negotiator wants to avoid personal conflict and so makes concessions readily in order to reach agreement. This person wants an amicable resolution; yet he or she often ends up exploited and feeling bitter. The tough negotiator perceives any situation as a highly competitive contest of wills in which the side that takes the more extreme positions and perseveres *wins*. Such people need to win; yet they often end up creating an equally tough response, which exhausts them and their resources and harms their relationship with the other side. Other typical negotiating strategies fall between tough and easy, but *each includes an attempted trade-off between getting what you want and getting along with people.*

A Better Way

There is a third and better way for you as a supervisor to negotiate. It is neither tough nor easy, but oddly *both*! It can be referred to as *principled negotiations.*[5]

[5]Much of the methodology described in this section is excerpted from Roger Fisher and William Ury, *Getting to Yes: Negotiating Agreement Without Giving In* (Boston: Houghton Mifflin, 1976).

This approach strives to decide the issues on their merit rather than who wins. It urges that you look for mutual gains wherever possible and that, where your interests conflict, you should agree that the result be based on fair standards independent of your will and that of your adversary. The method of principled negotiations is tough on the merits, easy on the people. It employs no tricks and no posturing.

Principled negotiation shows you and your opponent how to obtain what you are entitled to and still be civil. It enables you to be equitable while protecting both of you against being taken advantage of. What follows is an all-purpose strategy. Unlike almost all other conflict-resolution strategies, if your adversaries learn this one, it does not become more difficult to use; it becomes easier. If they read this chapter, all the better for the two of you.

First: Don't Bargain Over Positions

When we bargain over our positions, we tend to lock ourselves into those positions. The more we clarify our position and defend it against attack, the more committed we become to it. As more attention is paid to positions, less attention is devoted to meeting our underlying concerns. Agreement becomes less likely. Any agreement reached may reflect a mechanical balance of the difference between final positions, rather than a solution carefully forged to meet our legitimate interests.

1. Arguing over positions creates, at best, unsatisfactory agreements.
2. Arguing over positions is inefficient because the conflicting parties usually start at an extreme position and stubbornly hold to it, while at times making small concessions. This is highly time consuming and thus inefficient.
3. Arguing over positions endangers an ongoing relationship because each side tries to *force* the other to change its position.
4. When there are many parties involved, all of the above is compounded because coalitions are formed.

Second: Being Nice Is Not the Answer

Many people understand the high costs of hard positional bargaining, particularly on the parties and their relationship. They hope to avoid them by following a more pleasant style of negotiation. Instead of seeing the other side as adversaries, they prefer to see them as "friends." Rather than emphasizing a goal of victory, they emphasize the necessity of reaching agreement. In a soft negotiation game the standard moves are to make offers and concessions, to trust the other side, to be totally affable, and to yield as necessary to avoid confrontation. However, any negotiation focused on the relationship runs the risk of producing a weak agreement. More seriously, pursuing a soft and friendly form of positional bargaining makes you vulnerable to someone who plays a hard game of positional bargaining. In positional bargaining, a hard game dominates a soft one. The remedy for playing hardball is *not* pitching marshmallows.

The answer to the question of whether to use soft positional bargaining or hard is "neither." Change the game! The new game proposed to you is referred to as principled negotiation or negotiation on the merits. It consists of four basic points. Each point deals with a basic element of negotiation and suggests what you should do about it.

1. People: Separate the people from the conflict.
2. Interests: Concentrate on interests, not positions.
3. Options: Generate a variety of options before deciding what to do.
4. Criteria: Insist that the solution be based on some objective standard.

Each point is examined further in the sections that follow.

Third: Separate the People from the Conflict

This point acknowledges that you and I are creatures of strong emotions who often have radically different perceptions and have difficulty communicating clearly. Emotions typically become entangled with the objective merits of the problem. Taking positions just makes this worse because people's egos become identified with their positions. Hence, before working on the substantive problem, the "people problem" should be disentangled from it and dealt with separately. We should see ourselves as working side by side, attacking the problem, not each other. Hence the first proposition: Separate the people from the conflict.

Four: Concentrate on Interests, Not Positions

The second point is designed to overcome the drawback of concentrating on people's stated positions when the object of a negotiation is to satisfy their underlying interests. A negotiating position often obscures what you really want in a conflicting set of situations. Compromising between positions is not likely to produce an agreement that will effectively take care of the human needs that led people to adopt these positions. The second basic element of the method is to *concentrate on interests, not positions.*

Five: Generate a Number of Options

The third point responds to the difficulty of designing optimal solutions while under pressure. Trying to decide in the presence of an adversary narrows your vision. Having a lot at stake inhibits creativity. So does searching for the right answers. Keep in mind that, usually, there is more than a single right solution or answer to the conflict.

Set aside a designated time within which to think up a wide range of possible solutions that advance shared interests and creatively reconcile differing interest. Hence, the third basic point: Before trying to reach agreement, invent numerous options for mutual gain.

Six: Adopt Objective Criteria

Where interests are directly opposed, an officer may be able to obtain a favorable result simply by being stubborn. That method tends to reward intransigence and produce arbitrary results. However, as a sergeant you can counter such an officer by insisting that his or her single say-so is not enough and that the agreement must reflect some fair standard independent of the naked will of either side. This does not mean insisting that the terms be based on the standard you select, but only that some fair standard such as custom, expert opinion, prior decisions, or law determine the outcome.

By discussing a fair criteria rather than what the parties are willing or unwilling to do, neither party need give in to the other; both can defer to a fair solution. Hence the fourth basic point: Adopt objective criteria.

Seven: Take Three More Steps

The four basic propositions of principled negotiations are relevant from the time you begin to think about negotiating a solution to a conflict until the time either an agreement is reached or you decide to stop the effort. That period can be divided into three steps: analysis, planning, and discussion.

1. *Analysis.* During the analysis step you are simply trying to diagnose the situation—to gather information, organize it, and think about it. You will want to consider the people problems of biased perceptions, hostile emotions, and unclear communication, as well as to identify your interests and those of the other side. You will want to note options already on the table and identify any criteria already suggested as a basis for agreement. (Because police personnel are trained investigators, this step could be a natural one.)
2. *Planning.* During the planning step you deal with the same four elements a second time, both generating ideas and deciding what to do. How do you propose to handle the people problems? Of your interests, which are most important? And what are some realistic departmental objectives? You will want to generate additional options and additional criteria for deciding among them.
3. *Discussion.* Again during the discussion step, when the parties communicate back and forth looking toward agreement, the same four elements are the best subjects to discuss. Differences in perception, feelings of frustration and anger, and confusion in communication can be acknowledged and addressed. Each side should come to comprehend the interests of the other. Both can then jointly generate options that are mutually beneficial and seek agreement on objective standards for resolving opposed interests.

Remember that "anger" is only one letter away from "danger."

SUMMARY

In contrast to positional bargaining, the principled negotiation method of emphasizing basic interests, mutually satisfying options, and fair standards normally produces a wise agreement. The method permits you to reach a solid consensus on a joint decision efficiently without all the emotional costs of digging in to positions only to have to dig yourself out of them. And removing people from the problem allows you to deal directly with the other negotiator as a human being, thus making possible a fair agreement.

KEY POINTS

- Human conflict is a natural, and therefore a normal, phenomenon.
- It is up to the supervisor to convert dysfunctional conflict into productive energy.
- The first person to motivate is—yourself!
- Conflicts emanate from (1) existing conditions; (2) our attitudes; (3) our thoughts; and (4) our behavior.
- The creation of an internal investigations unit does *not* relieve the supervisor of his disciplinary duties.
- Citizen complaints start with the receipt of the complaint. Next comes an investigation, and finally an adjudication.
- As a conflict resolver, the supervisor usually negotiates between opposing factions.
- When intervening in a conflict, a supervisor should rely on his or her professional expertise, personal power, neutrality, and self-reality.
- In negotiating ("getting to yes"), do not bargain over positions or believe that being nice will resolve the conflict.
- Furthermore, in negotiating separate the people from the conflict; concentrate on interests, not positions; generate a number of options; adopt objective criteria; and analyze, plan, and discuss the proposed solution to the conflict.

DISCUSSION

1. Have you witnessed conflict being a plus for an organization? If so, describe how it occurred and what the results were.
2. If you have not done so, develop a QC and practice its precepts on either actual or hypothetical problems.
3. How have you dealt with a problem employee (co-worker, boss, subordinate) of late? Were you successful or not? Why?
4. Conflict can be a positive force. Why? Give examples.
5. Of the four supervisory attributes needed for successful intervention (pro-

fessional expertise, etc.), which is the most and least important for success?

6. Why not bargain over positions? Any examples?

7. Develop an actual or hypothetical conflict. Now apply the key steps in principled negotiations to it. Critique the results.

STRUCTURED EXPERIENCES

Case Studies

You will evaluate six different situations, each of which includes conflict. Apply the *principled negotiations method* described earlier in this chapter.

You are a member of the advisement task force to the chief of police. The chief has asked the task force to give recommendations concerning four administrative problems. Your task force is to discuss each problem and come to an agreement on the most appropriate solution to each. You are to make the recommendations as specific as possible. Suggest specific content of discussions. You cannot say, "His supervisor should have a talk with him." Try to anticipate all possible consequences of your recommendations when they are implemented and suggest responses to each.

Assume that your discussion is being tape recorded and your recommendations will be transcribed and submitted. You will not have to submit a report in writing, but be sure everything that should be in a report is discussed. Task force members should show their concurrence with the group's decision by voting on every problem. The chief wants your recommendations in *one hour*.

Problem 1

You are currently enrolled as a public administration major at the local university. After having acquired your bachelor of science degree in Criminal Justice last year, you desired to continue your education. As a result, you entered the School of Public Administration as a part-time student at the graduate level. Your graduation plans call for the awarding of a master of science degree in Public Administration within three years. Upon walking into your first class on campus, you were pleased to see four co-workers from your agency in the class. The remainder of the graduate seminar is comprised of seventeen full and part-time students representing a broad spectrum of public-service interests.

Professor Esoteric, a new member of the faculty, spent the first class session reviewing his philosophy on the administrative ethic. Near the end of the class he asked each student to discuss his personal and professional background. When one of your co-workers mentioned that he worked for a police department, Esoteric interrupted and commented, "Dammit, isn't it possible to do anything in today's world without surveillance by the Gestapo?"

During the next four weeks at each three-hour class session, Dr. Esoteric made brief, but caustic, remarks about the American police. Casual conversation has revealed that there are currently eight hundred majors in the graduate program. Of the eight hundred, fifty-six represent local law-enforcement agencies.

At the last class meeting, Dr. Esoteric returned to you a graded written examination. He gave you a letter grade of D without any further written comment. After class you learned from your co-workers that they had also received D's. The four of you approached Professor Esoteric and inquired as to the reason for the failing grades. His reply was, "Don't threaten me! I am prepared to immediately go to your City Council and inform them that I am being harassed."

Your chief of police has a master of science degree in Business Administration and encourages members of your department to attend college courses. The university that you are attending is the only one within seventy-five miles of your agency. Furthermore, there is an academic pay incentive program of 5 percent for a master of science degree. When comparing your grade-point average to your co-workers, it was found that the mean average was 3.54. Also, you have discovered that the sister of the dean of public administration is a member of your city council. You have submitted a written report to the chief who, in turn, asked the Task Force to make a recommendation(s).

Problem 2

Officer Errant had been repeatedly warned about his misconduct over the four years he had been on the department. While most of the criticisms were verbal and proffered by his immediate supervisor, some did appear in writing and were now a part of his personnel folder. In the main, Officer Errant had garnered five citizen complaints for abusive language, two court actions (not guilty) for use of excessive force during an arrest, ten instances of tardiness to roll call, four instances of grossly erroneous crime reports, and two minor situations involving insubordination to command officers.

Yesterday his sergeant was called to the scene of a civil disturbance. Errant had requested assistance at the location and Sergeant Rectitude responded. Upon his arrival he observed that Errant had two subjects in custody, handcuffed, and standing by the patrol car. Rectitude asked what was happening, and Errant replied, "These two assholes kept arguing so I decided to book their hips." It was discovered that they were husband and wife, and the dispute was minor. Rectitude took immediate action and essentially apologized for the mistake. Errant, in turn, called Rectitude a "Spineless kiss-ass."

The situation was reported, in writing, to the chief. The chief summoned both Rectitude and Errant to his office. After having heard from both of the involved parties, Chief Unequivocal stated that, in his judgment, Errant should be penalized for insubordination. With that Errant blurted out, "You out-of-touch jerk! You can go to hell." The chief loudly retorted, "I'm not going to hell; on the contrary I'm staying around long enough to see you fired!" The meeting then ended.

The following day Chief Unequivocal received a registered special delivery letter from Errant's attorney. Basically it stated that Errant (1) had been unjustly threatened, (2) his fundamental rights had been violated, and (3) he would seek legal redress if the chief decided to sanction Errant. What should the chief do?

Problem 3

It has come to the attention of the chief that an increasing number of police officers are holding a second full- or part-time job over and above their department employment. Second jobs are particularly common among field officers who are working a four-day forty-hour week. While there is a great debate among the police managers and supervisors about the actual effect on job performance of the second job, all are agreed that they do not like the general idea because they feel officers do not have the proper enthusiasm for their police jobs. Additionally, there have been at least two instances in which the outside employment represented a potential conflict-of-interest situation. The department has just announced a policy under which police employees must secure prior approval of any outside employment. The police union that represents the department's officers immediately issued a statement that challenged the legality of the policy, charging that it infringes on the civil rights and constitutional guarantees of its members. The only law regarding outside job employment prohibits a person from having two government jobs at the same time. How should this matter be handled?

Problem 4

Ten workers, all over fifty years of age, from the department's Communications and Data Processing Unit have submitted a letter of complaint to the chief about the status of the older workers in their unit. As they explain it, the nature of the communications and data-processing systems operation is such that college-trained younger people are constantly being brought into the unit to work on a part-time basis. These youngsters, in their view, are more interested in short-term benefits and working procedures than are the older workers. When initially receiving the complaint, the chief told them that considerable savings is achieved by the employment of the younger workers. The older employees have hinted they may seek redress through the Fair Employment Practices Commission. What should the chief say and do at this point?

Problem 5

The captain in command of Uniform Field Operations Bureau (patrol and traffic) has complained bitterly to the chief on two occasions that the department's Special Operations Bureau (SOB) has significantly reduced the quality of police–citizen relationships. He has asserted that the personnel in his unit are making every effort to provide just and effective law enforcement. The captain finds that the SOB, however, disrupts the development of a mutually supportive police–community relation by their heavy-handed tactics. When questioned, the lieutenant in charge of the SOB indicated that his special enforcement staff was clearly successful in reducing major felonies. Furthermore, he implied that perhaps the captain was getting "soft" and could best be assigned elsewhere. The chief is convinced that both individuals are dedicated and professional individuals. Also, both have highly commendable performance records with the department. How should the chief resolve this situation?

Problem 6

Sixty percent of the detectives in the investigations unit filed a grievance regarding their performance evaluations. The percentage of grievances has been going steadily upward. The chief is beginning to think that the reason for this occurrence is that a grieving employee almost always gets some portion of his rating raised. Increasingly it appears that the feeling among the detectives seems to be "why not" or "if the other guy does it, I had better also." How should the immediate situation be handled? What should be done in the long run?

Exercise: Conflict-Management Climate Index

Your Name _____
Organizational Unit Assessed _____

Instructions: The purpose of this index is to permit you to assess your organization with regard to its conflict-management climate. On each of the following rating scales, indicate how you see your organization as it actually is right now, not how you think it should be or how you believe others would see it. Circle the number that indicates your sense of where the organization is on each dimension of the Conflict-Management Climate Index.

1. Balance of Power

1	2	3	4	5	6

Power is massed either at the top or at the bottom of the organization.	Power is distributed evenly and appropriately throughout the organization.

2. Expression of Feelings

1	2	3	4	5	6

Expressing strong feelings is costly and not accepted.	Expressing strong feelings is valued and easy to do.

3. Conflict-Management Procedures

1	2	3	4	5	6

There are no clear conflict-resolution procedures that many people use.	Everyone knows about, and many people use, a conflict-resolution procedure.

4. Attitudes toward Open Disagreement

1	2	3	4	5	6

People here do not openly disagree very much. "Going along to get along" is the motto.	People feel free to disagree openly on important issues without fear of consequences.

5. Use of Third Parties

1	2	3	4	5	6

No one here uses third parties to help resolve conflicts.

Third parties are used frequently to help resolve conflicts.

6. Power of Third Parties

1	2	3	4	5	6

Third parties are usually superiors in the organization.

Third parties are always people of equal or lower rank.

7. Neutrality of Third Parties

1	2	3	4	5	6

Third parties are never neutral, but serve as advocates for a certain outcome.

Third parties are always neutral as to substantive issues and conflict-resolution methods used.

8. Your Leader's Conflict-Resolution Style

1	2	3	4	5	6

The leader does not deal openly with conflict but works behind the scenes to resolve it.

The leader confronts conflicts directly and works openly with those involved to resolve them.

9. How Your Leader Receives Negative Feedback

1	2	3	4	5	6

The leader is defensive and/or closed and seeks vengeance on those who criticize him or her.

The leader receives criticism easily and even seeks it as an opportunity to grow and learn.

10. Follow-Up

1	2	3	4	5	6

Agreements always fall through the cracks; the same problems must be solved again and again.

Accountability is built into every conflict-resolution agreement.

11. Feedback Procedures

1	2	3	4	5	6

No effort is made to solicit and understand reactions to decisions.

Feedback channels for soliciting reactions to all major decisions are known and used.

12. Communication Skills

1	2	3	4	5	6

Few, if any, people possess basic communication skills or at least do not practice them.

Everyone in the organization possesses and uses good communication skills.

13. Track Record

1	2	3	4	5	6

Very few, if any, successful conflict-resolution experiences have occurred in the recent past.

Many stories are available of successful conflict-resolution experiences in the recent past.

Conflict-Management Climate Index Scoring and Interpretation Sheet

Instructions: To arrive at your overall Conflict-Management Climate Index, total the ratings that you assigned to the thirteen separate scales. The highest possible score is 78 and the lowest is 13. Then compare your score with the following conflict-resolution-readiness index range.

Index range	Indication
60–78	Ready to work on conflict with little or no work on climate.
31–59	Possible with some commitment to work on climate.
13–30	Very risky without unanimous commitment to work on climate issues.

Assess your overall score. If in a group setting, compare your bottom-line results to others in your group. Attempt to explain your lowest and highest scores per item. Use case examples when possible.

RESPONSIBILITY ELEVEN

Stress: A Choice for Wellness

Life is ours to be spent.

D. H. Lawrence

It seems that everyone ten years old and older has an opinion or theory about stress. How do the following odds affect you?

> The chance of your home being burglarized is 30 percent higher if your family's total annual income is less than $25,000 than if it is $50,000 or more.
>
> The chance of dying from adverse reactions to prescription drugs is greater than the chance of dying in a highway accident—125,000 deaths per year versus 50,000.
>
> The chance of an airplane crashing and someone being killed is 1.6 in 10 million. You are six times more likely to be killed from simply falling down than while traveling in an airplane.
>
> The chance of completing four years of college is 19 percent.

Did any one or more of the preceding statistics push your stress button? Was it a positive reaction or a negative one? We're going to make a case here for stress to be accepted as normal—a normal and natural adjustment to change. We'll be emphasizing a *choice* for wellness. In mentioning "stressors" and "choices," let us consider Victor Frankl.

Frankl was a psychiatrist and a Jew. He was imprisoned in the death camps of Nazi Germany, where he directly experienced the living hell of the Holocaust. Except for his sister, his entire family died. He suffered torture and the daily uncertainty of being sent to the gas ovens. (At this point, we're disclosing the ultimate in *distress*.)

One day, naked and alone in a small room, he became aware that his Nazi captors *could not take away his freedom or power to choose, within himself, how all of the threats, punishment, and injustices were going to affect him.*

Through his disciplined mind, and applying mainly his memory and imagination, he exercised his freedom of choice until he actually had more freedom than his captors. He survived the death camps, and wrote and lectured about his experiences for many years thereafter.

Why this story? Everyday we have many choices facing us. One choice is for using stress or incoming demands for change as a positive force for wellness.

STRESS: THE DEMAND FOR CHANGE

All of us have been, are now, and will continue to be stressed. Some of us can control stress, which is the nonspecific response to a demand for change, better than others. Some people can anticipate it in some situations, while it surprises others. How one copes with stress—and there are certainly a number of things to cause stress that are associated with police supervision—determines how one behaves, thinks, and feels. Too much stress is clearly not good and, ironically, too little stress is not healthy. Unless stress is harnessed and converted into a "steady state," over time, stress will make one ill—perhaps very ill.

Stress, the demand for change, can either arrive from an external source or may be generated from within. The main thing to do is to recognize that everyone is destined to be stressed. First, it is critical that one be aware of being stressed. There are scientifically documented signs and events that can disclose when one is being stressed and to what extent or degree. Second, there are proven techniques not only for coping with *distress* (the injurious type), but, more importantly, converting it into *eustress* (the favorable type). Relaxation exercises are one example of a method for controlling stress. We have a choice, to either cope with and thus master stress or to allow it to wear and tear us.

ROLE OF THE POLICE SUPERVISOR

The role of the police supervisor is to understand and effectively deal with the individual and organizational implications of stress in police work.

Individual Implications

There seems to be a "stress fad" or syndrome in police organizations today. Granted, police work is a stressful occupation. But so are many others. We can assure you that the business supervisor, fire captain, supervising nurse, construction supervisor, and so on, experience stress in their daily activities. What counts is that the supervisor (1) know when stress has become too much or too little, and (2) maintain a stress reduction or wellness program. This applies to both the supervisor and his or her assigned personnel.

Police supervision is largely a constant process of adaptation to the "spice of life" that is change. The prescription for health and happiness is (1) to successfully adapt to everchanging circumstances, and (2) to remember that the penalties for failure to adjust to change are illness (physical and mental) and unhappiness. Interestingly, the very same stressful event or level of stress that may make a person ill can be a motivating experience for someone else. It is through the *general adaptation syndrome* (GAS) that the various internal organs, especially the endocrine glands and the nervous system, help one (1) to adapt to the constant changes that occur in and around one and (2) to navigate a reasonably steady course toward whatever one considers a meaningful purpose.

As a police supervisor, then, you should understand that:

- Stress in daily life is natural, pervasive, unavoidable, and thus to be expected.
- Depending on how one copes with stressful events, the experience of stress can be positive (healthy and happy) or negative (sick and unhappy).
- Since people differ in a variety of ways, each person's means and success in coping with stressful incidents will vary.
- There is a mental–physiological mechanism, known as the general adaptation syndrome, that assists one to adjust to demands for change.
- By definition, stress is the nonspecific response of the body to any demand for change. The demand can be from within, or from one's surrounding environment.
- Police supervisors are subjected to megachanges. As a result, they typically experience high levels of stress.
- The supervisor is in a key position to help others cope with stressful events.

Organizational Implications

A major concern for the police manager and supervisor is the effects of stress on job performance. The stress–performance relationship resembles an inverted bell-shaped curve, as shown in Figure 11-1. At low stress levels, individuals maintain their current level of performance. Under these conditions, individuals are not activated, do not experience any stress-related physical strain, and probably see no reason to change their performance level. If not supervised well, a person could become bored, lazy, and a poor performer.

On the other hand, under conditions of moderate stress, studies indicate that people are activated sufficiently to motivate them to increase performance. Stress, in modest amounts, acts as a stimulus for the individual, as when a police supervisor has a tough problem to solve. The toughness of the problem often pushes supervisors to their performance limits. Similarly, mild stress can also be responsible for creative activities in police personnel as they try to solve challenging (stressful) problems.

Finally, under conditions of excessive stress, individual performance

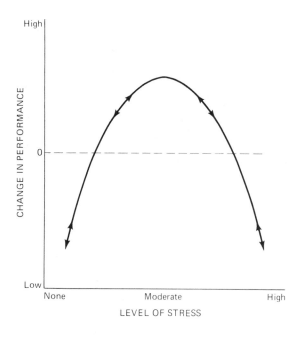

Figure 11-1 Relationship between Stress and Job Performance

drops markedly. Here the severity of the stress consumes attention and energies, and individuals focus considerable effort on attempting to reduce the stress. Little energy is left to devote to job performance, with obvious results. Some refer to this as *burnout.*

Here it is important for the supervisor to recognize that

• Stress has a significant relationship to job performance.
• Very low or very high stress levels can be counterproductive.
• Moderate amounts of stress can be a positive influence in a work setting.

STRESS AS A DEMAND FOR CHANGE

Stress is essentially reflected in the rate of all the wear and tear caused by life. Although stress cannot be avoided, a great deal has been learned about how to keep its damaging side effect, which is distress, to a minimum. For instance, it is just beginning to be seen that many common diseases are largely due to errors in the adaptive response to stress of humans, rather than being due to direct damage by germs, poisons, or life experience. In this sense, many nervous and emotional disturbances, high blood pressure, gastric and duodenal ulcers, and certain types of sexual, allergic, and cardiovascular disorders appear to be essentially *diseases of adaptation.*

Medical Findings

Research on stress was limited because there were no objective, measurable indexes to assess it, until it was found some fifty years ago that stress causes certain changes in the structure and chemical composition of the body, which can be accurately studied. Some of these changes are merely signs of *damage*; others are indications of the body's *adaptive reactions* (its mechanism of defense against stress). The totality of these changes, the GAS, develops in three stages: (1) the alarm reaction, (2) the stage of resistance, and (3) the stage of exhaustion.

The *nervous system* and the *endocrine* (or hormonal) *system* play particularly important parts in maintaining resistance to stress. They assist in keeping the structure and function of the body steady, despite exposure to stressor agents (e.g., tension, wounds, infections, and poisons). This steady state is defined as *homeostasis*.

In summary, the response to stress involves a threefold mechanism, consisting of (1) the direct effect of the stressor on the body, (2) internal responses that stimulate tissue defense or help to destroy damaging substances, and (3) internal response that cause tissue surrender by inhibiting unnecessary or excessive defense. Resistance and adaptation depend on a proper balance of these three factors. Specific steps to protect yourself and your personnel are covered later in the section on "wellness." But, for now, realize that most standard medical textbooks attribute anywhere from 50 to 80 percent of all disease to psychosomatic or stress-related origins. And stress-related psychological and physiological disorders have become the major social and health problem in the last decade. Stress-induced disorders have long since replaced epidemics of infectious disease as the major medical problem of the postindustrial nations.

Turbulent Changes, Supervising, and Stress

Stress that is handled properly can be an invigorating force in relationships, at work, and in self-development, providing one knows how to control its negative effects.

—Sidney Lecker, M.D.
The Natural Ways to Stress Control (New York: Grosset and Dunlap, 1978), p. 6

The promise of the future for any person in a police supervisor role is a life of increased change and thus increased stress. The accelerating rate of change is a reality. Toffler's *Future Shock* and Naisbett's *Megatrends* are present and operating in our lives. Brown and Weiner inform us that planning for change, not just for the sake of change but for survival, is more than a new discipline— it's a whole new philosophy.[1] If we are to better control situations of stress, we

---

[1] Arnold Brown and Edith Weiner, *Supermanaging* (New York: McGraw-Hill, 1984), pp. 1–36.

must place more emphasis on the better control of self and the police work we must do to enhance our professional growth and development.

Selye[2] writes:

> Many scientific studies were performed to establish the stressor effects of executive responsibilities in middle and top management, relative to that of subordinate employees in various occupations. Undoubtedly, executive responsibilities, if taken very seriously, produce severe distress with somatic and psychic manifestations often conducive to actual disease. However, here, as in all considerations of stress manifestations, conditioning factors must be taken into account, for whatever a person's position in the hierarchy of command, the stressor effect of his decision-making depends mainly upon the way he reacts to it.

SOURCES AND FORMS OF STRESS: THE STRESSORS

The police supervisor will experience stress from one of three sources: personal, environmental, and organizational/social. The first source is within the individual; the latter two are external. Most often they present their demands for change in combination with one another. Let us explore the sources in more detail and then focus our attention on the four types of stress they produce for all employees in a police organization.

Three Sources of Stress

Personal. A review of all the possible personal or inner stressors would be impossible here. They can range from sexual disorders, through grief due to the loss of a loved one, to a fear of flying. We will center on those that are directly or potentially job related. Roughly, they can be assigned to one of two categories: our emotions and our power base.

Emotions. The majority of us have received absolutely no training in how to deal with our own emotions. At best, we have probably been given some advice on what to do during emotional periods, for example, being told that "there is nothing to fear but fear itself" when we are feeling frightened. Such advice is rarely ever truly helpful in overcoming the effects of the emotion. There are five very potent emotions that you should be able to recognize and deal with: depression, anxiety, guilt, failure, and disapproval. More will be said about these five emotions later when we discuss stress-reduction methods.

Responsibility One covered this subject. You may recall that a value is an enduring belief that a particular course of action (means or goal) is to be preferred over an alternate one and that values cause us to *behave* in certain

[2]Hans Selye, *The Stress of Life*, 2nd ed. (New York: McGraw-Hill, 1976), p. 15. Chapter 5 is primarily based on Selye's research and writings on stress—and appropriately so. Selye "discovered" stress in 1936. Often referred to as "Dr. Stress," Selye has been a member of the University of Montreal faculty for over thirty years and in 1978 founded the International Institute of Stress in Montreal. He continued to add to the growing body of knowledge on stress until nearly eighty years of age.

ways, to *want* to behave in certain ways, to *think* in certain ways, and to *feel* in certain ways. Obviously, they are extremely important to us. Hence, "we are what we value." Values can induce stress when there is a conflict between one's own needs and the need for one's own values, and the alarm called anxiety may go off. Many people do not know how to use this alarm and either fear or idealize it, instead of understanding that it is simply a signal that is calling attention to some process. When one sets one's values too high or exacting, one then becomes vulnerable to feelings of failure and guilt, and if one fails to identify or consider one's values, one opens oneself to depression.

Power. The position of supervisor involves both the *right* to supervise and the *opportunity* to lead others. The right to supervise is centered in the position of police supervisor, while the opportunity to provide leadership is centered in one's personal ability to do so. Since supervision and power are closely allied, they both involve stress and responsibility. Police supervisors who feel the pangs of stress are usually responding to the use of supervisor power (by them or others) to cause change. For some, the term "power" suggests a negative action. Let us think of it in a positive view:

The more mechanical and complicated our world is, the more we need the simplicity of power to guide us and protect us. It's the one gift that allows us to remain human in an inhuman world—for "the love of power is the love of ourselves."

—William Hazlett
Los Angeles Times, May 6, 1979, Part II, p. 5

Environmental. The environmental stressors can be labeled as either technological, economic, or political. Frequently, an environmental stressor can be assigned to all three. For example, the computer is causing numerous and profound technological changes for the police manager (interactive terminals in the office). Economically, they require capital outlay and maintenance. And politically, they imply power. Pollution in the work setting can be stressful (noise, air, filth, etc.). Insufficient work space often elevates tension. We could continue, but we believe you know what they are because you're probably experiencing some of them right now.

Organizational/Social. In this instance we will catalogue the stressors as too much, too little, uncertain conditions, and problem personalities. Although posed in a job sense, many demands for change will occur via the family and other nondepartmental relationships.

Too Much. There are two types of input overload or hyperstress: quantitative and qualitative. *Quantitative input overload* is a result of simple demands, but too many of them for the time allotted—for example, too many phone calls to make, memos to read, or meetings to run in the time allowed. Increases in blood pressure, pulse rate, and cholesterol are associated with quantitative input overload. *Qualitative input overload* is a result of complexity and of limited time. There are not as many jobs, but the time allotted to do these jobs is less than is needed to do them up to standard.

Too Little.   Low levels of mental and physical activity can cause hypostress; that is, hypostress is caused by quantitative and qualitative input underloads. Naturally, certain forms of hypostress (such as recreation and self-reflection) are eustressful (desirable); but if a protracted period of nothingness is experienced, one may be confronted with hypostress, which is distressful (undesirable). Similar to hyperstress, hypostress can be either good or bad, depending on how one adjusts to its demands.

Uncertain Conditions.   A police supervisor is responsible for making decisions (often high-risk ones) under above-average conditions of uncertainty. Herbert A. Simon alluded to this situation when he described programmable decisions in comparison with nonprogrammable decisions. (The supervisor frequently experiences an arena of nonroutine, nonprogrammable, high-risk decision making.)

Clearly, the bureaucratic, decision-making, operational turf of a police supervisor is filled with ambiguity and confusion, which may be stress inducing.

Problem Personalities.   Certain types of personalities commonly act as stressors. We realize that a police supervisor often simply cannot stay clear of these types of personalities; indeed, his or her agency may be plagued with more than its fair share of them, and the supervisor may find them in his or her primary social groups. However, whenever feasible, you should minimize your exposure to them. Who are these problem personalities? (Some introspection may be helpful here, in that you ought to ask yourself if you are one of those defined.)

- *Type A behavior.* Aggressive, competition for the joy of competing, in a hurry, impatient, tense, concentration on self-interest.
- *The worrier.* Rehearsing disaster scenarios, dependent, fatalist, frequent pain.
- *The guilt-tripper.* Overdose of conscience, rear-view-mirror thinking, cynical, contrite at all costs, humble to a fault.
- *The perfectionist.* Can be done better, faster, cheaper; drugged in optimism; ignores success and focuses on failure.
- *The winner.* Addicted to winning, number one at all costs; nothing for fun, all for victory; creates competitive situations; belittles the loser.
- *WSM.* The Whining, Sniveling, Malcontent; every organization has a few. The WSM actively seeks opportunities to carp, complain, and voice displeasure. Conversely, the WSMs are never available to correct any of the reasons for their constant woes.

Four Types of Stress

Figure 11-2 depicts the four major dimensions that comprise stress or change:

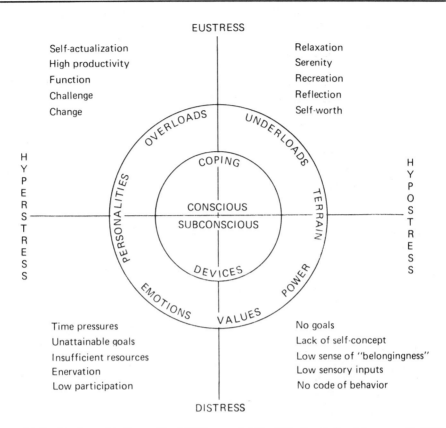

Figure 11-2 Coping with Stress (Paul Whisenand, *The Effective Police Manager*, © 1981, p. 280. Reprinted by permission of Prentice-Hall, Inc., Englewood Cliffs, N.J.)

1. *Hyperstress.* Overloaded with change
2. *Hypostress.* Underloaded with change
3. *Eustress.* Favorable or positive changes
4. *Distress.* Unfavorable or negative changes

The main sources of stress (see again Figure 11-1) are implicit in each section of Figure 11-2.

Our coping mechanisms are divided into two basic categories: the subconscious and the conscious. Space does not permit adequate treatment of the subconscious mechanisms, but, essentially, the subconscious coping techniques are developed through our formative years and we have learned to rely on one or more much like a reflexive action. The conscious coping techniques are those that one can test and use to reduce stress and perhaps even to convert distress into eustress.

DETECTING ONE'S STRESS LEVEL

General Signs of Stress

Our mind and body report stress in many ways. For example, when stressed we may experience the following discomforting feelings:

- Dry throat
- Nervous tic
- Stomach disorders
- Pounding of the heart
- Elevated blood pressure
- Inability to concentrate
- Muscle spasm
- Insomnia
- Sweating
- Migraine headaches

Unfortunately, many of these symptoms are either ignored or fail to alert our senses. We may be experiencing excessive stress, not coping well if at all, and thus exposing ourselves to any number of diseases.

Clearly, it is important for the police supervisor to develop a perceptual capability for accurately detecting signs and symptoms of distress within himself or herself and others.

Specific Signs of Stress

We now offer you an opportunity to assess your own and others' existing stress level. The four questionnaires should be self-administered (1) once a year, (2) at the time of frequent and/or major changes in your life, or (3) when you notice certain telltale signs of mounting tension or uneasiness in you or members of your department. The scales probe for hyperstress (eustress and distress). Hypostress cannot be effectively dealt with in the pages allotted for this subject. (The majority of police supervisors rarely experience this form of stress.) The data presented following these instruments include scores with which to compare your scores.

Listed in Table 11-1 are many organizational events that have been found to stimulate stress reactions in employees. The numerical value of each event reflects the degree of disruption it causes in the average person's life. Generally, the higher the score, the greater the probability of a significant health change in the near future. (*Note:* Because individuals vary in their tolerance for stress, the total score should be taken as a rough guide only.)

For each of the events listed in Table 11-1 that you have experienced during the *past twelve months*, place its Value in the My Score column. If you have experienced an event more than once within the past twelve months, you

TABLE 11-1 Episodic, Work-Related Stress Evaluation

Event (Last 12 Months)	Value	My Score
1. Being transferred against my will to a new assignment	81	_____
2. Being assigned a less important job	79	_____
3. Experiencing a decrease in status	68	_____
4. Being disciplined/reprimanded by my boss	67	_____
5. Having my request to transfer to a better job rejected	65	_____
6. Sustaining an abrupt and major change in the nature of my work	60	_____
7. Learning of the cancellation of an important project I was involved in	60	_____
8. Encountering major and/or frequent changes in policies or procedures	59	_____
9. Being promoted/advanced at a slower rate than planned	58	_____
10. Voluntarily transferred to a new position or assignment (not a promotion)	52	_____
11. My forthcoming retirement	47	_____
12. Experiencing a major reorganization in my unit	46	_____
13. Experiencing a sudden reduction in the number of positive strokes for my work accomplishments	46	_____
14. Encountering a major change (increase or decrease) in the technology affecting my job (computers, techniques)	46	_____
15. Giving a major briefing (not roll call) or formal presentation	46	_____
16. Encountering a significant deterioration in environmental conditions such as lighting, noise, temperature, space, and filth	45	_____
17. Acquiring a new boss	45	_____
18. Sustaining an immediate, significant *decrease* in the pace of my work	43	_____
19. Sustaining an immediate, significant *increase* in the pace of my work	43	_____
20. Undergoing a major physical relocation of my workplace	31	_____
21. Acquiring an increase in status	30	_____
22. Being compelled to work more hours per week than usual	29	_____
23. Experiencing the transfer, resignation, termination, or retirement of a close co-worker	24	_____
24. Being promoted or advanced at a faster rate than I expected	24	_____
25. Acquiring new subordinates	23	_____
26. Receiving a major change in my work schedule	23	_____
27. Acquiring new co-workers (peers)	21	_____
28. Experiencing an increase in the number of positive strokes for my accomplishments	20	_____
29. Encountering a significant improvement in environmental conditions such as lighting, noise, temperature, and space	17	_____
30. Undergoing a minor physical relocation of my workplace	5	_____
Total episodic, work-related stress score		_____

may record its value *twice.* Then add all the numbers in the My Score column to obtain your total episodic, work-related stress score.

Listed in Table 11-2 are many nonwork events in life that have been found to produce stress for us. The scale value of each event reflects the degree of disruption it causes in the average persons' life. Generally, the higher the score, the greater is the probability of a significant health change in the near future. The severity of health change also tends to increase with higher scores. (Again, since individuals vary in their tolerance for stress, the total episodic, nonwork-related stress score should be taken as a rough guide only.)

Stressful day-to-day conditions, such as those listed in Table 11-3, often exist at work. Indicate the relative frequency with which you experience each of the following sources of stress by assigning the correct number.

FREQUENCY SCALE

1. Never
2. Infrequently
3. Occasionally
4. Frequently
5. Always

Listed in Table 11-4 are several potentially stressful conditions of life at home and in our society generally. Indicate how stressful each is for you personally by selecting a number from the severity scale.

SEVERITY SCALE

1. Not stressful
2. Somewhat stressful
3. Moderately stressful
4. Very stressful
5. Extremely stressful

To summarize, stress both on and off the job causes disruptions, triggers a chain reaction, and requires a certain amount of personal adjustment. The more often we trigger the stress response with either kind of change event, the more likely it is that we will become ill. Although specific kinds of stress usually cannot be linked to specific diseases, with excessive stress our latent tendencies to become ill or psychologically distressed are more likely to become manifest.

Long-term stress, even after we become accustomed to it, causes pressures that induce illness, lowers our feelings of satisfaction, and inhibits growth and work effectiveness. When many *episodes* involving work-related change occur

TABLE 11-2 Episodic, Nonwork-Related Stress Evaluation

Event	Value	My Score
Death of spouse	100	————
Divorce	73	————
Marital separation	65	————
Jail term	63	————
Death of close family member	63	————
Personal injury or illness	53	————
Marriage	50	————
Fired from work	47	————
Marital reconciliation	45	————
Retirement	45	————
Change in family member's health	44	————
Pregnancy	40	————
Sex difficulties	39	————
Addition to family	39	————
Business readjustment	39	————
Change in financial status	38	————
Death of close friend	37	————
Change to different line of work	36	————
Change in number of marital arguments	35	————
Mortgage or loan over $10,000	31	————
Foreclosure of mortgage or loan	30	————
Change in work responsibilities	29	————
Son or daughter leaving home	29	————
Trouble with in-laws	29	————
Outstanding personal achievement	28	————
Spouse begins or stops work	26	————
Starting or finishing school	26	————
Change in living conditions	25	————
Revision of personal habits	24	————
Trouble with boss	23	————
Change in work hours or conditions	20	————
Change in residence	20	————
Change in schools	20	————
Change in recreational habits	19	————
Change in church activities	19	————
Change in social activities	18	————
Mortgage or loan under $10,000	17	————
Change in sleeping habits	16	————
Change in number of family gatherings	15	————
Change in eating habits	15	————
Vacation	13	————
Christmas season	12	————
Minor violation of the law	11	————

Total episodic, nonwork-related stress score ————

TABLE 11-3 Long-Term Work-Related Stress Evaluation

Frequency		Condition
_____	1.	I am uncertain about what is expected of me.
_____	2.	My peers appear unclear about what my role is.
_____	3.	I have differences of opinion with my superiors.
_____	4.	The demands of others for my time are in conflict.
_____	5.	I lack confidence in top management.
_____	6.	My boss expects me to interrupt my assigned work for new priorities.
_____	7.	Conflict exists between my unit and others it must work with.
_____	8.	I get feedback only when my work is unsatisfactory.
_____	9.	Decisions or changes that affect me are made without my knowledge or involvement.
_____	10.	I am expected to endorse the decisions of management without being informed of their rationale.
_____	11.	I must attend meetings to get my work done.
_____	12.	I am cautious about what I say in meetings.
_____	13.	I have too much to do and too little time in which to do it.
_____	14.	I do not have enough work to do.
_____	15.	I feel overqualified for the job I have.
_____	16.	I feel underqualified for the job I have.
_____	17.	The personnel I supervise are trained in a field that is different from mine.
_____	18.	I must go to other units (bureaus) to get my job done.
_____	19.	I have unsettled conflicts with my peers.
_____	20.	I get no personal support from my peers.
_____	21.	I spend my time "fighting fires" rather than working according to a plan.
_____	22.	I do not have the right amount of interaction (too much or too little) with others (bosses, peers, staff).
_____	23.	I do not receive the right amount of supervision (too much or too little).
_____	24.	I do not have the opportunity to use my knowledge and skills.
_____	25.	I do not receive meaningful work assignments.
_____	Total	

List below any ongoing sources of stress you experience at work that are not included in the evaluation form.

_____

_____

_____

_____

TABLE 11-4 Long-Term Nonwork-Related Stress Evaluation

Severity		Condition
_____	1.	Noise (traffic, airplanes, neighbors, etc.)
_____	2.	Pollution (air, water, toxic waste, etc.)
_____	3.	Personal standard of living and ability to make ends meet financially
_____	4.	Crime and vandalism in immediate neighborhood
_____	5.	Law and order in society
_____	6.	Personal, long-term ill health
_____	7.	Long-term ill health of family member or close friend
_____	8.	Racial tensions
_____	9.	Regular drug or alcohol abuse of family member or close friend
_____	10.	Concern over future of my own career
_____	11.	Concern over values or behaviors of family members
_____	12.	Political situation in this country
_____	13.	Possibility of war
_____	14.	Concern over financing my own retirement, my children's education, and so on
_____	15.	Economic situation in this country
_____	16.	Changing morals in our society (regarding family life, sexuality, and so on)
_____	Total	

List here any ongoing nonwork-related sources of stress you experience that are not included in the evaluation form.

_____

_____

_____

_____

in an organization in which people are already working in long-term, highly stressful conditions, the occurrence of sick leave and the seriousness of illness, accidents, and inattention to work can increase rapidly.

- The four evaluation sheets have been included to help determine sources of stress.
- Is there any pattern to the four set of results?
- Is one type or source of stress more prevalent than the others?
- Discussing scores with a friend or police colleague should provide additional insights.

Reliable Data

The four scales that you've completed vary in their reliability. But we are not implying that they are unreliable. On the contrary, many have discovered that they accurately forecast degrees of our human wellness (or lack of same). How they vary is in accordance with the individual longevity of their scientific validation. The first scale, in particular, is exceptionally well known and accepted; it has over 30 years of hard data to demonstrate its potency to detect distress.

The first step in any stress-management or wellness program is to secure reliable data. The bottom-line scores are *indicants* (not guarantees) of health or, conversely, ill health. From our professional perspective and human experience, the following scores or higher should cause you reflective concern:

- Episodic, work-related   300 points
- Episodic, nonwork-related   150 points
- Long term, work-related   64 points
- Long term, nonwork-related   33 points

Our observations plus scientific validation of the four scales give us cause to alert you to their predictiveness. If we self-administered the scales (and we do annually), and discovered our scores on one (and especially more) of the scales to be above those cited above (ours have been so on a few occasions), then we would immediately check for signs of distress and simultaneously implement a program of wellness (we've done this too).

If practical, compare the scores you've posted with other people who have completed the scales. Focus on common and dissimilar results and particular stressors. Also, share your thoughts and feelings about the levels and types of stress you are now experiencing. Afterward, proceed to the next section, which describes some of the methods for coping with distress.

CONVERTING STRESS INTO WELLNESS

Now that we have learned about the sources, effects, and our own stress levels, we can consider stress management and our desire for wellness. Keep in mind that *a healthy police supervisor is in much better shape to be an effective one.* Obviously, this holds true for all employees of the police agency.

Step 1: Affixing Responsibility

Twenty-four centuries ago in Greece, Hippocrates, the Father of Medicine, told his disciples that disease is not only suffering (*pathos*), but also work (*ponos*); that is, disease is the fight of the body to restore itself to normal. This is an important point, and one that, although being constantly reinforced during the intervening centuries, is not yet generally acknowledged even today. Disease is not a mere surrender to attack; it is also a fight for health. *Unless there is fight, there is no disease.* Or, to state this another way, our health is our *responsibility.* And we must work at it!

Step 2: Reliable Data

While medical science continues to develop new means to keep us alive, we nullify such efforts by refusing to slow down, relax, and consume less. Our American way of life is killing people at an early age. The United States is sixteenth among countries in the world for male longevity and eighth for female longevity. (The greatest life expectancy in the industrialized world is in Sweden.) It appears that it is our life-style, as well as fear of old age, that is killing us off before we reach our longevity potential. An undisciplined, random, fast-paced existence is dangerous to our wellness. It is essential that we know our varying levels of change. The two sections on general and specific stress signs afford us the opportunity to reliably measure our life change units. In knowing ourself we can, if we choose, know our stress. And, in knowing our stress factors, we are in a position to take accurate and positive action. In other words, by assuming the responsibility for your health, you automatically create the need for *reliable data* about it.

Step 3: An Action Plan for Wellness

It seems that everyone has a particular stress-reduction program that he or she wants others to use. What works for one person, may not work for the other. Jogging, for example, may be helpful stress therapy for one public employee, while another may find it harmful to one's knees. Hence, a stress management and wellness program must be *customed designed* to meet the specific requirements of the individual.

Our review of the literature on wellness and the successful adaptation to the accelerating thrust of change leads us to propose six fundamental coping strategies. The astute police supervisor will select components from one or more of these strategies and *act on them*. Briefly, here are the coping strategies to maintain our wellness and defeat the harmful consequences of distress and burnout.

Supportive relationships

- Build supportive structures in one's home, which will include sacred times, family rituals, and protected settings for recuperation. Build supportive structures within oneself, which are associated with one's own attitude toward discomfort, work, personnel needs, and the like.
- "No person is an island": This statement has proved to be an axiom in terms of mental health and coping with stressors. Each person *needs* people, especially helpful people, who will give support when one is depressed, anxious, unhappy, angry, or simply distressed. Whom do you turn to at midnight when you are experiencing a strong sense of impending failure?
- Such thinking as "Oh, I can handle that myself" or "Dealing with this problem alone will make me stronger" is not only erroneous, it can be dangerous to the point of possible injury to oneself.

- In establishing a supportive relationship, one should remember two things: (1) a supportive relationship requires cultivation; if it is unattended; it may dissolve; and (2) be certain that the relationship is reciprocal, that is, that there is both giving and taking.
- Finally, it takes *positive strokes* to develop emotionally healthy persons with a sense of O.K.ness. Without supportive relationships the latter would be impossible.

Mental discipline

- *Step 1.* Learning to reduce the complexity and the number of tasks that confront you will help to reduce stress. You will cope more effectively when problems are handled one by one, on a priority system and in manageable installments. As we have seen displayed on car bumpers and office walls, "One day at a time."
- *Step 2.* Learning to reduce the time pressures on yourself will help to reduce stress. Nature has been good enough to give us a natural reflex for reducing time pressures when faced by overwhelming stress, but many of us fight nature's automatic mental stress-control mechanism. The old adage, "Who's going to know the difference in 100 years?" seems proper here.
- *Step 3.* Mind-focusing exercises are very helpful ways of reducing mental stress. Various meditative methods have been developed and promoted to help people unload tensions by focusing their minds on neutral thoughts, such as a mantra, a number, or deep breathing (a deep-breathing exercise concludes this chapter). In effect, meditation allows you to put down your mental burdens several times a day, to rest your mind for twenty minutes, and then to pick up your burdens once again with more mental energy. It has been found that people who practice mind-focusing or meditation respond better to stress, and they seem to recover much more rapidly from the effects of stress than do nonmeditators.

A Safe and Happy Place. All of us need a comfort zone, which causes one to feel good, to feel secure, and indeed, allows one to feel one's feelings. A "safe and happy place" (SHP) should be one of your own choosing, but you must find one if you have not already done so. Your SHP may be a particular room, a camper van, a fishing stream, an athletic club, a mountain trail, a book—anything, anyplace. Moments to undergo self-renewal, relaxation, introspection, and serenity can and frequently occur there.

Otherness

- *Step 1.* Develop the skills to read the signs of distress, anger, and depression in yourself and others.
- *Step 2.* Develop skills to listen. Most police supervisors who are concerned about doing or solving something forget how powerful and helpful it is just to be a concerned and active listener.

- *Step 3.* Tend to the people issues that are associated with changes. Remember that change is the cause of stress, so there needs to be more than just preparation for the change. There must also be aftercare, which concerns such things as listening and understanding the processes that unfold in individuals and groups after significant changes. This is not working harder, but smarter.
- *Step 4.* Put issues into words. Words are structures in themselves. Sometimes they need to be written down, particularly when one is working to build supportive structures for oneself or one's family. Problems that are terribly difficult to manage and that hang over one's head for weeks or even for years may surprisingly dissolve once they have been cast into words.

The three R's

- *Step 1. Reading* for fun and enjoyment.
- *Step 2. Relaxation* as a voluntary control of stress.
- *Step 3. Recreation* as a release and as a revitalization.

Altruistic egoism

- Hans Selye coined the expression and advanced the practice of "altruistic egoism," which basically is *looking out for oneself*, but in an altogether different frame of reference than one might initially suspect.[3] Selye went on to reveal that this self-ism is to be developed in and around being necessary to others. Eliciting the support and goodwill of others is a key ingredient in the practice of altruistic egoism.
- "Earn thy neighbor's love." This motto, unlike love on command, is compatible with our natural structure and, although it is based on altruistic egoism, it could hardly be attacked as unethical. Who would blame anyone who wants to assure his or her own homeostasis and happiness by accumulating the treasure of other people's benevolence? Yet this makes the person virtually unassailable, for nobody wants to attack and destroy those upon whom he or she depends. People are social beings. Avoid remaining alone in the midst of the overcrowded society that surrounds you. Trust people, despite their apparent untrustworthiness, or you will have no friends, no support. If you have earned your neighbor's love, you will never be alone.

THE GOOD NEWS

The query, "As a police supervisor, do I need to live with unusually high levels of stress?" or the assertion that "My work environment generates unavoidable

---

[3]Selye, *The Stress of Life*, pp. 452, 453.

distress" can be responded to with an unequivocal answer—no! Fortunately, each person has a considerable freedom of choice. Included within this infinite set of choices is one that deals with stress. Plainly put, do you, as a police supervisor, want behavioral patterns that possibly lessen your ability to cope with stress? Similarly, do you, as a police supervisor, want others to mismanage their life unit changes? Again, the obvious answer is no! Supervising police employees requires the effective managing of one's stress. This chapter has been designed to assist you to deal better with the pervasive phenomenon of stress—more specifically, the *stress of management*.

KEY POINTS

- Stress is a demand for change.
- Stress is a natural phenomenon.
- When stress is mismanaged, it can be harmful.
- There are three sources of stress: (1) personal, (2) environmental, and (3) organizational/social.
- There are four types of stress: (1) hyperstress, (2) hypostress, (3) eustress, and (4) distress.
- Due to the very nature of the job, a police supervisor is assured of experiencing all four types of stress—especially hyperstress.
- Distress can seriously reduce the effectiveness of a police supervisor.
- The police supervisor should be alert for the general and specific symptoms of distress.
- The supervisor should maintain a program of wellness by (1) recognizing that he or she is responsible for his or her health, (2) collecting reliable data on one's stress level, and (3) designing and using a custom-designed plan for wellness.

DISCUSSION

1. An earlier section dealt with the reality of "turbulent changes." As a group, identify the five major changes affecting you or your work group.
2. Of the four stressors listed as organizational/social, which one seems to dominate in your organization?
3. At the end of the Episodic, Work-related Stress Evaluation Scale, you were asked to cite three events you personally felt to be the most stressful. Discuss them as a group. Be alert for similarities and uniqueness.
4. Drawing from the six strategies for wellness, custom design a stress-management action plan for yourself.

STRUCTURED EXPERIENCES

1. A Relaxed State

The way to reduce physical stress is relatively simple. The principle underlying physical stress control is that it is impossible for anyone to exist in two contradictory states simultaneously. You cannot be short and tall at the same time. You cannot be pregnant and not pregnant concurrently. Vigor and fatigue cannot coexist. Similarly, it is impossible to be stressed and physically relaxed at the same time. If you know how to find a state of physical relaxation and how to sustain it, you will be better able to prevent the occurrence of physical stress overload, and you will be able to control excessive tension once it has occurred.

A stress-control formula is useful here. You need to learn how to focus on physically relaxed states, how to rehearse physical relaxation responses until they can be achieved quickly and with ease, and then learn when and how to implement the physical relaxation response at a time preceding or during a stressful event.

Focusing on a physically relaxed state is achieved by three means:

First, use diaphragmatic breathing in slow, four-second "in" and four-second "out" excursions to assist the relaxation process. Lie down on a flat surface, facing up, and place your hand on your stomach. When you breathe in, your stomach should slowly rise, because the diaphragm, acting like a piston, moves out of the chest cavity to suck air into your lungs. At the same time, the diaphragm descends into the abdominal cavity, pushing your intestines down and forward—the cause of your rising stomach. Exhale slowly, and your stomach falls. Your rib cage should be quite still. It is only needed during extreme exertion. Breathing to a count of four on each inhalation and exhalation is a restful breathing pattern.

Second, you must learn to relax your muscles and blood vessels. When your blood vessels are relaxed, your hands feel warm. When the blood vessels in your body are tense, your hands feel cold and clammy. You can increase the warmth of your hands by focusing on the sensations in your hand as its rests on the arm of the chair beside you. You can feel the texture of the arm of the chair upon which your hand rests. Whatever the room temperature may be, your hands can feel the sensations of airy coolness as well as of warmth. If you wish to intensify the warmth, simply keep "warmth" in a relaxed focus in your mind. Imagine lying on a sunny beach with the sun beating down on your hand. Imagine your body filling up with warmth from the toes on up.

To relax your muscles, you can take the hand that is gently resting on the arm of the chair beside you and tense all your fingers without pressing them into the chair. Your hand will feel like it is hovering just above the arm of the chair. Tense muscles make your limbs feel light. Now relax your arm, wrist, and fingers. The limb will feel heavy as it slouches on the arm on the chair.

Third, starting from the top of your head and proceeding through every muscle and joint in your body down to your toes, contract each muscle to feel the sensation of tension—the lightness—and then feel the weight and heaviness associated with muscular relaxation.

You must now learn to rehearse warming your hands, relaxing your muscles and joints, and breathing slowly with your diaphragm. Take about twenty minutes to do so. Do not watch the clock—just guess at a time span of roughly twenty minutes, and rehearse the relaxation of your breathing, blood vessels, and muscles.

While relaxing your body, you may wish to simultaneously relax your mind by using a mind-focusing exercise. When I practice relaxation, I breathe in cycles of three breaths repeating in my mind

Breath 1. Give up caring
Breath 2. Heavy and warm
Breath 3. Breathe and relax

As distractions enter my consciousness, I do not let them trouble me, even if they temporarily throw me off my pattern. I simply resume my slow, three-breath cycle of

Breath 1. Give up caring
Breath 2. Heavy and warm
Breath 3. Breathe and relax

When you have rehearsed these relaxation exercises for a period of several days, you can then begin to implement them in your daily life.

2. "I Love to Laugh . . ."

Ed Wynn sang, "I love to laugh. It gets worse every year" in the venerable motion picture *Mary Poppins.* We can recall his laughter, sparking it ourselves. The more fun he had, the happier he became and so did we. Fun and laughter are de-stressors. There is a law—an axiom—*if you learn to laugh at yourself, you'll never run out of material.*

Norman Cousins, the former editor of *Saturday Review of Literature,* was informed by a battery of medical doctors in the 1970s that he would die within six months of a rare and untreatable disease. He tells the story of being informed and then immediately checking out of the hospital. He registered at a deluxe hotel, rented a VCR and a very humorous movie. Mr. Cousins proceeded to laugh himself well. (He also consumed 3,000 units of vitamin C a day.) After three months, the doctors reexamined him, and the terminal disease had evaporated.

There are psychobiological explanations for this miracle. The bottom line is—fun and humor are healthy for us. (By the way, Mr. Cousins laughed his way to nearly eighty years of age.)

Let us see if we can start you on a humor kick. The animals and insects in the jungle divided their ranks into two football teams. The large jungle animals were on one team, and the smaller jungle animals and insects were on the second. At half-time, the large animals were ahead 28–0. The large animals received the kick-off to start the second half. On the first play, the large animals were sacked for a six-yard loss. When the players unpiled, at the bottom was a tiny centipede. The large animals sent the elephant off-tackle on the next play. Again, a loss of four yards. At the bottom of the heap was the centipede. In desperation, on third down, they ran the cheetah around end. Bang! Down he went for a seven-yard loss. Who's at the bottom of the pile—the centipede. The coach of the small animals and insects called time-out and had his team come to the sidelines. He looked at the centipede and asked, "Where in the hell were you during the first half when we needed you?" The centipede frowned and said, "Coach, I was taping my ankles."

We laughed at this cute story—it made us feel better—relaxed and nonstressed.

3. Jello

There are some tabloids that report on events such as "Mother Gives Birth to Eighty-Year-Old Twins." You'll find them at newsstands and markets. Recently, one of us spotted a front-page headline, "The Ultimate Secret to Stress Reduction." For $0.50 how could I go wrong? Here is what I learned.

A fellow in Canton, Ohio, buys an enormous amount of jello. When distressed, he puts it into his bathtub, gets in, and lays there until it congeals. He assured me, the reader, that it works. His worries were removed, no more troubles, aches and pains gone.

Well, I didn't try it. It made for amusing reading, though. Do you know, it probably helped him. The reason for this scenario is simply: What works for one person may not work for another.

Now, here is what I learned. Wellness programs must be custom designed. What works for me may not help you. Nonetheless, you must identify and apply those highways that avoid the barriers of distress and provide the carriers of success. At this point, construct your own unique wellness program. Good luck!

Part Three

PUTTING OURSELVES TO WORK

RESPONSIBILITIES

- *Teamwork*

- *Community-Oriented Policing*

- *Problem-Oriented Policing*

- *Total Quality Services*

RESPONSIBILITY TWELVE

Teamwork

Interdependence is a higher value than dependence.

Steven Covey

One of a baby's earliest words in "mine." We enter the world totally dependent on others for our very survival. Most of us are encouraged as we grow up to be independent—to be self-sufficient, to be competitive. We place a high value on being independent. But, Steve Covey argues that being *interdependent* is a higher value than being dependent.

As we grow and mature, we become increasingly aware that all of nature is interdependent, that there is an ecological system that governs nature including society and the organizations within it. We further discover that human life also is interdependent.

Let us look at maturity as a continuum.

- Dependence is seeing the world in terms of *you*—you take care of me; you help me; you're responsible for me.
- Independence is seeing the world in respect to *I*—I can do it; I am responsible; I can choose.
- Interdependence is the model of *we*—we can do it; we can cooperate; we are responsible.

Dependent people need others to get what they want. Independent people can get what they want by their own effort. Interdependent people combine their efforts—form a team—to achieve their goals.

It is the successful supervisor who realizes the need for the best thinking, a coordinated effort, mutual support to be truly effective. Independent supervisors who do not have the maturity to think and act interdependently may be good individual producers, but *they won't be good leaders or team players.*

A PARADIGM

The Greek word paradigm basically means an explanation, or a model, or a map. Responsibility Twelve is a paradigm. It is our map of *the way we see things now.* We see, for example, police organizations that lack teamwork (interdependence). We see police employees who prize and nurture their independence.

It is also our map of *the way things should be.* We see police organizations that evidence teamwork. We see police personnel who continuously work at teamwork.

The trick is to bridge these two maps in such a way that you can pass from the existing over to the desired vision. Our paradigm for less independence and more teamwork consists of *perceptions* and *training.* Together they serve as the "trick" for bridging from one map (reality) to the other (hoped for).

Perception

Any discussion of perception begins with the realization that the way we see the outside world need not be the same as the world really is. We tend to see the world the way we want to perceive it. In other words, we do not see reality, but rather we interpret what we see and call it reality. Apparently, perception is like beauty in that it lies "in the eye of the beholder."

In attempting to explain and predict behavior, reality is secondary to what is perceived. People's responses are based on their perceptions. It would be nice if they perceived reality clearly, but there are a number of influences within us and at work that create distortions and may result in reduced levels of performance and satisfaction.

Certain behaviors that are desirable for police employees to exhibit—being to work on time, following directions, obeying rules, doing a good job—are, for the most part, learned before we ever seek gainful employment. The fact that some people are chronically late for work, while the majority are prompt, suggests that some individuals have learned different work habits. Because most of the things police officers do on their job have been learned, if we want to explain and predict this behavior, we need a fundamental understanding of the concepts and processes of learning. An understanding of how people learn will also prove beneficial when we find employees behaving in ways that we consider undesirable. Why? Because change requires unlearning or extinguishing the old behaviors and relearning new behaviors. The police supervisor plays a central and daily role in the learning process. As such, the supervisor can be looked upon as a "change agent."

ROLE OF THE POLICE SUPERVISOR

Police employees are constantly being subjected to stimuli, or cues, from their environment, all of which compete for their attention. In the workplace, these stimuli include such things as supervisors' instructions, co-workers' comments, citizens complaining about a police contact, people walking by, and posted signs and notices. Given the very large number of these stimuli, individuals are faced with the problem of how to make sense out of so many variables, how to organize and interpret the more relevant stimuli, and how to respond to them. The process by which this is done is *perception.*

Supervisors face a variety of barriers to accurate perception of others in the work situation. These barriers may be directed at the police supervisor or held by the supervisor. Perceptual processes play an important role in the decisions managers make concerning employee selection, placement, and promotion. Most people have subtle biases that affect their decisions. In view of the significance of supervisory decisions, both for the individuals involved and for the police organization, it is important to understand as clearly as possible how these biases are formed and how they affect our attitudes and behavior.

The point is that by recognizing the existence of perceptual problems supervisors can take measures to remedy situations. First, however, they must be convinced of the importance of the problem. If this can be accomplished, several avenues of approach are open to them. These approaches are the subject of future chapters.

Because learning takes place on the job as well as prior to it, police supervisors will be concerned with how they can teach employees to behave in ways that most benefit the department. When we attempt to mold individuals by guiding their learning in graduated steps, we are shaping behavior.

Consider the situation in which a police officer's behavior is significantly different from that sought by the chief of police. If the supervisor only reinforced the individual when he or she showed desirable responses, there might be very little reinforcement taking place. In such a case, shaping offers a logical approach toward achieving the desired behavior.

We shape behavior by systematically reinforcing each successive step that moves the individual closer to the desired response. If an officer who has been chronically ten minutes late for work comes in on time, we can reinforce this improvement. Reinforcement would increase as responses more closely approximate the desired behavior.

WHAT IS PERCEPTION?

All that a person achieves and all that a person fails to achieve is the direct result of his own thoughts.

—James Allen
As A Man Thinketh (New York: Grosset and Dunlap, 1983), p. 12

Perception is a process by which we organize and interpret our sensory impressions in order to give meaning to our environment. What one perceives can be substantially different from objective reality. It need not be, but there is often disagreement. For example, it is possible that all police employees in a department may view it as a great place to work—favorable working conditions, interesting job assignments, good pay, an understanding and responsible management—but, as most of us know, it is very unusual to find such consistencies. All of us have given instructions and thought that they were clear. Later we found that the listener misperceived the intent of our message. Perceived reality as compared to *reality* is frequently a problem for the police supervisor. A supervisor may have the finest of intentions, but if perceived as wrongful or in error by the officers, they will react accordingly. A supervisor may take elaborate steps to be accurately understood, only to discover that the messages were misinterpreted. The sections that follow explain how this happens and what it portends for the police supervisor if not dealt with effectively.

HOW PERCEPTION WORKS AT WORK

> *Everyone is a potential winner. Some people are disguised as losers; don't let their appearances fool you.*
>
> —Kenneth Blanchard and Spencer Johnson,
> *The One Minute Manager* (New York: William Morrow and Company, 1982), p. 53

Thus far, we have focused on an examination of basic perceptual processes: how we see objects or attend to various stimuli. We are now ready to examine a special case of the perceptual process: social perception as it relates to police work. Social perception consists of those processes by which we perceive our co-workers. There are three basic categories of influence in the way we perceive our co-workers: (1) the characteristics of the person being perceived, (2) the characteristics of the particular situation, and (3) the characteristics of the perceiver. When taken together, these three major influences are the dimensions of the work environment in which we view other police employees. As such, it is important for police supervisors to understand the way in which these sets of influences interact if perceptual accuracy is to be improved at work (see Figure 12-1).

Characteristics of the Person Perceived

The way in which police employees are perceived in social situations is greatly influenced by their characteristics. That is, our dress, talk, and gestures determine how others see us. There are four primary characteristics that we bring to work with us every day:

1. *Physical appearance.* Our appearance can either agree with or refute what we *ought* to look like. For example, a police supervisor who is grossly

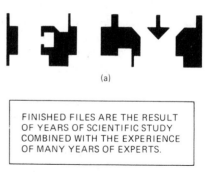

Figure 12-1 Cognitive Complexity: Can you see the word in the upper figure? How many F's are there in the sentence? Are you sure?

overweight, unshaven, and sloppily dressed is apt to be perceived as a poor leader.

2. *Verbal communication.* What we say and how we say it influences the perceptions that others have of us. The tone of our voice, accent, and choice of words tell others about us.

3. *Body language.* Our posture, gestures, and facial expressions play a major factor in how we are perceived.

4. *Ascribed attributes.* Our status, educational background, and reputation precede us and, as a result, will strongly influence how others see us.

Characteristics of the Situation

The second major influence on how we perceive others is the situation in which the perceptual process occurs:

1. *Social context.* The work setting influences our perceptions of our job and co-workers. For example, when members of a group or committee are congenial, they tend to be more accurate in assessing the work motives and goals of their colleagues.

2. *Organizational role.* Where you work in a department influences your perceptions. If you're the chief of police, the budget is a perceived key issue. If assigned to traffic enforcement, then vehicle code violators are viewed as the major problem.

3. *Location of event.* How we interpret events is also influenced by the location of the event. Behaviors that may be appropriate at the police facility locker room (teasing about a dirty uniform) would be seen as inappropriate at the front lobby counter.

Characteristics of the Perceiver

The third major influence on social perception is the perceiver. Several characteristics unique to our personalities can affect how we see others:

1. *Self-concept.* Our self-concept represents a major influence on how we perceive others. First, when we understand ourselves (i.e., can accurately describe our own personal characteristics), we are better able to perceive others accurately. Second, when we accept ourselves (i.e., have a positive self-image), we are more likely to see favorable characteristics in others. Conversely, less secure people often find faults in others. Third, our own personal characteristics influence the characteristics we are likely to see in others. From a supervisory standpoint, these findings emphasize the importance for police supervisors to understand themselves.

2. *Cognitive structure.* The more complex our cognitive structure (i.e., our ability to differentiate between objects and people using multiple criteria), the more accurate is our perception of others. Figure 12-2 dramatizes this need for cognitive complexity. People who tend to make more complex assessments of others also tend to be more positive in their appraisals; hence, the importance of selecting supervisors who exhibit high degrees of cognitive complexity. These individuals should form more accurate perceptions of the strengths and weaknesses of the police officers and thus be able to capitalize on their strengths while ignoring or working to overcome their weaknesses.

3. *Particular needs.* Similar to the earlier discussion of personal factors that influence perceptions (immediate needs and wants), our particular needs or desires play an important role in social perception because we have a tendency to see what we *want* to see.

4. *Previous exposure.* Our previous experiences with others often influence the way in which we view their current behavior. When a police employee

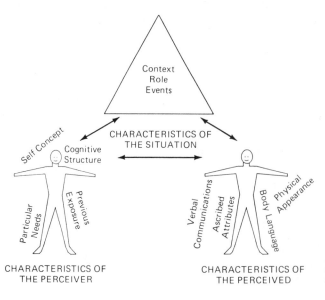

CHARACTERISTICS OF
THE PERCEIVER

CHARACTERISTICS OF
THE PERCEIVED

Figure 12-2 Key Influences of Perception at Work

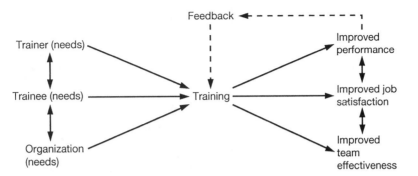

Figure 12-3 Training Process. (Paul Whisenand, *Police Supervision: Theory and Practice*, © 1976, p. 284. Reprinted by permission of Prentice-Hall, Inc., Englewood Cliffs, N.J.)

has consistently received poor performance evaluations, a marked improvement in performance may go unnoticed because the police supervisor continues to think of the individual as a poor performer. Similarly, employees who begin their career with several successes develop a reputation as fast-track individuals and may continue to rise in the department long after their performance has leveled off or even declined. The supervisor should guard against this natural tendency.

Figure 12-3 graphically summarizes this section.

PERCEPTUAL SHORTCUTS

Frequently, we use a number of shortcuts when we judge others. Perceiving and interpreting what others do is burdensome. As a result, we develop techniques for making the task easier. These techniques are frequently valuable; they allow us to make accurate perceptions rapidly and provide valid data for making predictions. Conversely, they can and do get us into trouble. An understanding of these shortcuts can be helpful toward recognizing when they can result in significant barriers or distortions. They are given in Table 12-1.

PERCEPTION AND TEAMWORK

To perceive accurately is to think accurately. And to think accurately gives us the basis for thinking *teamwork*. If we're misperceiving others, we are likely to refrain from interdependence and maintain our independence. Can you imagine a highly successful basketball team that functions on miscues and misunderstandings, that fields five independent players? The road to teamwork starts with perceptual accuracy. The midpoint is *training*.

TABLE 12-1 Shortcuts in Perceptions of Others

Shortcut	Definition
Halo effects	A tendency to allow the traits exhibited by people to influence our impressions of their other traits.
Stereotyping	A tendency to assign attributes to people solely on the basis of their class or category.
Intuition	A tendency to have an intuitive picture of what other people are like that colors how we see them.
Selectivity	A process by which we systematically screen or discredit information we don't wish to hear and focus instead on more salient information.
Projection	A tendency to ascribe to others those negative characteristics or feelings we have about ourselves.
First impressions	A tendency to consider the first impressions we have of others to be their enduring characteristics.
Defense mechanisms	A tendency to distort or ignore information that is either personally threatening or culturally unacceptable.

Training

As a trainer (or developer of human resources), you influence an officer's values, attitudes, perceptions, learning, motivation, job satisfaction, stress, and wellness. Furthermore, as a trainer, you sway group dynamics, communications, and followership (your leadership). Likewise, as a trainer, you affect goal setting, planning, MBO, performance appraisal, discipline, conflict resolution, community relations, labor relations, and one's professional success. Pointedly, then, much of your success or failure as a supervisor hinges on your ability to *train*—especially teamwork.

ROLE OF THE POLICE SUPERVISOR

The police supervisor is in a most advantageous position to influence personal and organizational development in a local law-enforcement agency. Hence our basic premise—the police supervisor has a responsibility for the improvement of the human resources within his or her purview and in line with attaining the goals of the agency.

Some police agencies have established a training officer's position. This officer is usually provided with some form of incentive to "coach" a newer officer in the performance of his or her duties while on the job (on-the-job training, OJT). We are, in turn, proposing that the supervisor be assigned the responsibility for training his or her subordinates. Similarly, the supervisor should become involved in decisions affecting his or her team members' education, career progress, and organizational development. It is recognized that all of these concepts are, if not vague, certainly overlapping in their very nature.

Some clarification of these concepts will be attempted in subsequent sections of this chapter. To reemphasize, the supervisor should have *the* primary charge for personal and organizational development of his or her work unit.

TRAINING GOALS

Training, as we see it, has two fundamental goals: To make lasting *improvements in the performance* of one's organizational role and to *develop one's capacity* for handling higher levels of responsibility. In other words, training ought to help a person do her or his job better, while at the same time prepare her or him for more challenging duties. Consequently, training means a change, that is, a change on the part of the individual and the organization. Both are interdependent partners in any process of change. Furthermore, training means integration, that is, unifying people and the organization in a concerted attempt to more effectively achieve assigned goals.

Underlying its goals and characteristics is a certain philosophy, or perhaps better, attitude, of what training is. Five key attitudes underscore police training goals today.

1. Motivations attached to skills lead to action. Skills are acquired through practice.
2. Learning is a complex function of the motivation and capacity of the individual, the norms of the training group, the training methods and the behavior of the trainers, and the general climate of the police organization.
3. Improvement on the job is a complex function of individual learning, the norms of the working group, and the general climate of the organization. Individual learning, unused, leads to frustration.
4. Training is the responsibility of three partners: the organization, the trainee, and the trainer. It has preparatory, pretraining, and posttraining phases.
5. Training is a continuous process and a vehicle for consistently updating the skills of the individual human resources.
6. Training is also a continuous process and a vehicle for consistently improving the capacity of the individual officers to behave as a team.

These goals and attitudes, in turn, have produced the following set of training objectives:

1. Required entry-level information of a technical and a social nature
2. New information on a sustained and planned basis
3. Developmental learning and training experiences for all members in the department that promotes and reinforces teamwork
4. Required work experience and training for upper levels before the person is promoted

5. The police supervisor has the major responsibility for training and developing his or her subordinates
6. The police training officer has the responsibility for planning a total program including all members—officers, supervisors, and managers—of the police agency in a set of learning experiences both within and without the organization

Note again the fifth objective. Essentially we are saying that if you, as a police supervisor, separate training from the rest of the work experience and are concerned only with its contribution to the output of the police organization, the chances of effective training are sharply reduced. This latter point is extremely important. Nothing contributes so much to job satisfaction and morale as a sincere interest on the part of the first-line supervisor.

The preceding is not intended to ignore or challenge the viability of the field training officer (FTO) program. Agency after agency has found the FTO program most helpful in assisting a new police officer to quickly build proper job attitudes and behavior. Briefly, an FTO program provides close coaching and monitoring of a new officer's demeanor by a senior officer who has received *special instruction* on doing so. Untrained FTOs can create as much damage as benefit to a department. An FTO program should be used by a police supervisor as one of many training methods for ensuring the agency that his or her assigned staff are peak performers.

TRAINING: THE PROCESS

For thousands of years people have been talking about improving teaching—to no avail. It was not until the early years of this century, however, that an educator asked, "What is the end product?" Then the answer was obvious. It is not teaching. It is, of course, learning.

—Peter F. Drucker
The Effective Executive (New York: Harper and Row 1957), p. 30

At the focal point of training is the trainee. The changes in her or his behavior are the measure of the effectiveness of training. To produce needed behavioral changes, training subjects the participant to a process of change that includes three overlapping and circular stages: preparation, implementation, and evaluation (follow-up and repreparation). Naturally, participants other than the trainee are involved, that is, the organization and the trainer. The three partners—organization, trainer, and trainee—in the training process and their interrelationships are shown in Figure 12-4. The presence of all three is required to identify their relevant training needs. To put it another way, far too often organizations dictate to trainers what knowledge and skills should be imparted.

Many of us have experienced a lag in our attention to a training session. In most cases, this lag in attention is caused by a lack of trainee need fulfillment.

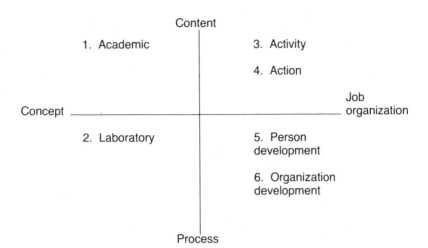

Figure 12-4 Six Training Strategies. (Rolf P. Lynton and Udai Pareek, *Training for Development* [Homewood, Ill.: Richard D. Irwin, Inc., 1967], p. 40. Reprinted by permission.)

This lag can be avoided by involving the trainee in deciding which needs should be met through both formal programs and developmental experiences.

The trainee and the organization are subjected to the same stages in the process but with different purposes in mind. The function of the trainer relates to her or his style. In regard to the trainee, we find (1) preparation: the trainee identifies needs and develops certain expectations and levels of motivation concerning the program, (2) implementation: the trainee selects the items she or he feels she or he must learn, and (3) evaluation: the trainee transfers the learning to application. Concerning the organization, we find (1) preparation: the organization identifies its needs and selects and motivates the trainees, (2) implementation: the organization provides an environment conducive to learning, and (3) evaluation: the organization provides support for the transfer of learning into application.

EFFECTIVE TRAINING

In practice, the aims of training are external to the process itself; that is, the goals to be achieved are modifications in organizational performance or capabilities. Furthermore, the results obtained from training are ultimately assessed in terms of organizational criteria and not by standards that are an inherent part of training itself. In short, *the common quality of training is its intended aim of moving something from an initial state in which problems or needs exist to an end state in which the problems have been solved or the needs met.* In all cases the action involves modifications in humans—the trainees—whose knowledge, skills, and attitudes are the targets. Moreover, there is an expertise of training, comprised in part of systematic knowledge and in part, too, of an empirical technology expressed in principles derived from experience. Thus one finds in this section various strategies now practiced in the field of training. However, the consideration of strategies for training involves the broader issue of effectiveness. In other words, the desire for effective training structures the entire program, including the employee strategies. Hence, we turn briefly to an examination of what is meant by effective training.

First, effective police training requires proper selection of both courses and trainees. This means that all concerned, trainees and their supervisors, should know the objectives of the course. It also means that the selection decision should consider the employee's training needs in his or her present job and in his or her career development.

Second, to be effective, police training must support operations. In other words, both trainees and supervisors should be able to specify in advance how the employee is expected to use the training in his or her work. Furthermore, if the training has been effective, they should be able at some later date to point to ways in which the trainee has used it.

Third, effectiveness of police training depends on positive action, not only by the trainee but also by the police supervisor. The aim of training is to change a person's behavior. However, the effects of training evaporate unless supervision and management are prepared to accept the changed person and have changed the work situation to accommodate him or her. As has been pointed out more than once, the organizational climate must reinforce the training experience, thereby increasing the probability that the employee will apply the training in his or her work.

How Do We Know?

Effective training calls, therefore, for clarity of objectives and means. Both the ends and the means must be appropriate to the purpose. Relating them demands clear specifications for each part of the training task, including the time, skill, and facilities required to complete it. Ensuring this clarity is a primary responsibility of the police supervisor. Unless this task has been accomplished, a new police training program is launched into a void, doomed to problems and failure.

The delivery of pre- and in-service training programs is being significantly enhanced by advanced technology. Telecommunications, and audiovideo (AV) cassette recorders, and a wide range of AV tapes are available today. Singularly or in cooperation with other agencies, police departments are in the process of building far-ranging and high-impact AV libraries. More and more police training and conference rooms include a VCR and monitor as regular equipment.

One final question remains, however, "How do you know when we have succeeded in providing an effective training program?" The answer is obvious —by evaluating the training effort! In summary, then, effective training calls for (1) establishing relevant training objectives, (2) defining training specifications, (3) selecting the appropriate strategy, (4) creating suitable structural arrangements, and (5) evaluating and improving the program.

Establishing Training Objectives

Since any training objective is based on the objectives of the police department, the main question is whether the department's objectives are realistic. Furthermore, is the training input of the program envisaged also realistic? Or is training in danger of being misused? For example, is it too little and too late? All this is to say that (1) the training objectives must support organizational activities, and (2) the training objectives must be realistic. These two basic needs suggest that four steps are necessary to ensure that departmental and training objectives are met.

1. Be certain that a needed change calls for training. What many police organizations need is not training, at least not immediately, but lots of detailed operational planning and implementation of plans. Training at this stage would be a disservice if it deprived the organization of skilled people currently needed for action.
2. Define the part that police training can play in the change. What new competences does the department require and which of these can be acquired through systematic training? Training strategy determines which goals can reasonably be achieved through a training program and which cannot. And, vice versa, the goals determine which training strategy is most appropriate.
3. The third step is more taxing and worthy of the most careful consideration; it concerns questions of quantities and levels of police personnel to be trained, and of timing and training as well.
4. The fourth step involves training for teamwork. *People who work together should be trained together.* The truly effective work groups are trained like any successful sports team. All members know what their job consists of, and what they should provide and can expect of others.

Training Strategies

Any attempt to train, that is to change, an individual automatically means a *freezing-up of relations* between people. The freezing-up of relations involves three stages: *unfreezing, moving,* and *refreezing.*

Unfreezing is necessary because the police officer (and his or her organization, family, and locality) comes up with habits, values, and practices, the very opposite of a clean slate. To affect him or her through training, normal habits have first to be questioned and disturbed, or unfrozen.

Training can do this by focusing on needs that police trainees cannot satisfy by habitual behavior. The supervisor then introduces other events that allow participants to try new ways of behaving, that is, changing. If the police trainees find the new behavior more useful in meeting the "new" needs, they can then be helped to make it habitual. Each officer thus gains a new set of behavioral patterns, which he or she then freezes.

The guiding principles for training strategies lie in these dynamics of the development process and in the minimum critical concentration of effort required at each stage of it. Training differences occur along two axes. The first axis delineates the subject matter that police officers are to learn. At one extreme it points toward learning about a specific task or piece of knowledge, such as the pros and cons of using certain investigative techniques. This kind of knowledge is *content*. At the other extreme are general understanding and insight into how people and things function. This kind of knowledge is *process*. For example, participants could learn how investigative techniques are developed and the principles that underlie them. This first axis then has content for one extreme and process for the other.

The second axis shows the basic function of police training. Is it to be used for constructing new concepts and theory? That would be one extreme, which we call *concept*. Or is it to improve action on the job? That extreme we call *job*. Along these two axes are six major training strategies, as shown in Figure 12-5.

The selection of a strategy depends on a number of factors. One is the training goals. Once the police department is clear about its goals, it can choose a strategy that leads to them. The second consideration when choosing a strategy is the resources (human, physical, and financial) available for training.

Your Delivery of Training

As a police supervisor, you are responsible for the delivery of needed training to your personnel. While the style may vary from a stand-up, roll-call lecture to ride-along coaching, train you must.

It is not sufficient to make police training supplemental to work; police work must be organized to facilitate training and development. Several factors support this conclusion. First, any help in training provided by the police agency must be welcome because the training demands are ever expanding in local law enforcement. Second, we live in an age of revolution in processes, systems, and products in public and private organizations. The training burdens are great. Increasingly, training must be part and parcel of the work itself, and it should be increasingly supplied and directly monitored by the immediate supervisor.

If your department is astute, they are rating your performance as a police supervisor, to a major event, on your ability to *deliver* timely and useful training to others. Trainers and supervisors are one and the same. Effective trainers and effective supervisors build teams.

Evaluating Your Accomplishments

The evaluation of training frequently falls prey to its becoming a popularity contest and/or merely an entertaining event. The key questions are, or should be,

- What, precisely, did you learn?
- Why is it important to you and your agency?
- How do you plan to use it?
- When and where will the new learning be applied?

WORK-GROUP-EFFECTIVENESS INVENTORY

Work Group: _____
Date: _____

Circle one number for each statement:

	Strongly Disagree	Disagree	Undecided	Agree	Strongly Agree
1. I have been speaking frankly here about the things that have been uppermost in my mind.	1	2	3	4	5
2. The other members of this team have been speaking frankly about the things that have been uppermost in their minds.	1	2	3	4	5
3. I have been careful to speak directly and to the point.	1	2	3	4	5
4. The other members of this team have been speaking directly and to the point.	1	2	3	4	5
5. I have been listening carefully to the other members of this team, and I have been paying special attention to those who have expressed strong agreement or disagreement.	1	2	3	4	5
6. The other members of this team have been listening carefully to me and to each other, and they have been paying special attention to strongly expressed views.	1	2	3	4	5
7. I have been asking for and receiving constructive feedback regarding my influence on the team.	1	2	3	4	5
8. I have been providing constructive feedback to those who have requested it-- to help them keep track of their influence on me and the other team members.	1	2	3	4	5
9. Decisions regarding our team's operating procedures and organization have been changed rapidly whenever more useful structures or procedures have been discovered.	1	2	3	4	5
10. Everyone on the team has been helping the team keep track of its effectiveness.	1	2	3	4	5
11. Members of this team have been listening carefully to each other, and we have been paying special attention to strongly expressed values.	1	2	3	4	5

Figure 12-5 Team-Building Evaluation

	Strongly Disagree	Disagree	Undecided	Agree	Strongly Agree
12. We have been speaking frankly to each other about the things that have been uppermost in our minds.	1	2	3	4	5
13. We have been speaking directly and to the point.	1	2	3	4	5
14. We have been helping our team keep track of its own effectiveness.	1	2	3	4	5
15. Our team's internal organization and procedures have been adjusted when necessary to keep pace with changing conditions or new requirements.	1	2	3	4	5
16. All members of this team understand the team's goals.	1	2	3	4	5
17. Each member of our team understands how he or she can contribute to the team's effectiveness in reaching its goals.	1	2	3	4	5
18. Each of us is aware of the potential contribution of the other team members.	1	2	3	4	5
19. We recognize each other's problems and help each other to make a maximum contribution.	1	2	3	4	5
20. As a team, we pay attention to our own decision-making and problem-solving processes.	1	2	3	4	5

Figure 12-5 (Continued)

Asking these pointed questions demands follow-up and feedback on your part. A final critical and, at times, risky question is, How can I, as your supervisor, improve as a trainer?

TEAM BUILDING

I've always found that the speed of the boss is the speed of the team.

—Lee Iacocca

As an internationally acknowledged successful manager, Iacocca is quick to underscore the importance of training for *teamwork*. Furthermore, he stresses that as the boss goes (in this case a supervisor), so goes the team.

You are likely to find that training for teamwork is one of your most difficult and intriguing chores. But the results will far offset your efforts. As you mold a group of individual officers into a cohesive team, you will find out why.

Briefly, you'll discover that the term "team" means:

T ogether
E veryone
A chieves
M uch

A team is a group of individuals who must work interdependently in order to attain their individual and organizational objectives.

The most obvious example of a team is an athletic team. The members have a purpose, which gives them an identity. Each player has a unique function (position) that must be integrated with that of the other members. The players are aware and supportive of the need for interdependent interaction, and the team usually operates within the framework of a larger organization (a league). A few years ago the Boston Celtics won the championship of the National Basketball Association. During an interview, the coach was asked, "What was the major difference between your team and the one you defeated?" He responded, "We had alignment!"

Not all working groups, however, are teams, nor should they necessarily be. The faculty of a department in a university is a good contrast to an athletic team. Other examples of work groups that are not teams are committees, in which the purpose is representation, rather than interdependence, and training groups, for which no charter exists.

There are several necessary assumptions concerning the nature of teams. The first assumption is that all the talent necessary to allow the team to be anything it wishes is already present within the group. The second is that everyone already knows what he or she wants to do; the prime focus is on how the members are stopping themselves from doing what they want. Third, the team's maximum potential for strength and effectiveness is limited only by the limitations each individual member sets on his or her potential. And, fourth, the work itself is potentially exciting. Clearly, police work fully meets or comes close to meeting these four assumptions.

Team Effectiveness

Team building and effectiveness occur through your leadership and the facilitation of group dynamics.

Leadership. Much has been written and spoken advocating the participative leadership approach as the one best way to manage team development; currently, the participative approach is highly favored in public and private business settings. Nevertheless, autocracy or any other particular leadership style is not precluded from being effective: one has only to look at the sports team to see that this is true. It is highly unlikely that the Miami Dolphins football team would vote as a team, prior to each game, on what plays will be run.

More important than the particular leadership style is your ability to combine individual efforts into group output, provide the necessary liaison between your team and the total police organization, and accomplish this in a manner consistent with professional values.

Group dynamics. The very nature of teamwork depends on the effectiveness of the interaction among team members. The concepts of contact, role, and values are elements of effective team interaction. Good *contact* is based on authenticity among team members. It implies that each individual is aware of his or her individuality and is willing to state views and ideas clearly and to support the principles of openness and conscious choice. An environment that encourages the open expression of disagreement, as well as agreement, accepts the reality that an individual may like some co-workers more than others. This is legitimate as long as openly stated preferences do not result in discriminatory, unfair, or task-destructive behavior.

Two elements, function and relationship, are combined in the concept of *role.* Function is the specific task each member is there to perform; relationship relates to the interaction necessary to get the task completed—with whom each member must interact and how the interaction occurs. In the well-functioning team, role clarity is evident. The team's objectives are clear and agreed on, and each team member knows each member's unique contribution to those objectives, thus eliminating any duplication of effort. Usually, the effective team is comprised of individuals who have complementary, rather than similar, talents and approaches.

All decisions, whether made by individuals or by groups, are based on *values.* Three specific values seem to identify good working police teams: (1) task effectiveness, (2) dealing in the present, and (3) conflict viewed as an asset.

1. *Task effectiveness.* The well-functioning group of police officers places a high value on task effectiveness, with greater emphasis on *doing the right things*, rather than on doing things right. The value implies that the team

also focuses on the objective, or end result, rather than only on the team's ongoing activity.

2. *Dealing in the present.* The effective team focuses on "right here, right now," an emphasis that allows a flexible response to changing conditions within the team itself and within the larger organization. The team can make more appropriate decisions when it is concentrating on *what* is happening rather than *why* it is happening.

3. *Conflict viewed as an asset.* Conflict provides two very necessary elements to the effective work group. First, it is the prime source of energy in systems, and, second, it is the major source of creativity. Since conflict is absolutely unavoidable, in any case, an effective team's approach to dealing with it is to use it rather than to try to resolve, avoid, or suppress it. More potential for ineffectiveness and marginal performance exists in avoiding conflict than in conflict itself. When conflict is seen as an asset, the preferred approach is to deal with it through collaboration, although competition or even compromise is not precluded, when called for by the situation.

Why Teams?

Although establishing teams frequently involves much hard work, the effort provides three important factors to group effectiveness: (1) synergy, (2) interdependence, (3) and a support base. What energy is to the individual, synergy is to groups. The synergy of a group is always potentially greater than the sum of the combined energies of its members. Thus, it is not infrequent in laboratory exercises that a group effort results in a better performance than that achieved by the group's most competent member. If you doubt it, have three people independently make a bed. Then have them make three beds jointly.

Effective teams are made up of highly independent individuals who must combine their separate efforts in order to produce an organizational result. The focus of the team effort is on combining, rather than on coordinating resources. *Interdependence* in today's organizations is a simple reality. Police services are too complex and the respective technologies too specialized for any one individual to accomplish alone. The team concept provides the necessary link to approach departmental objectives from a position of strength and creativity.

It is no overstatement that we spend most of our waking hours in a work setting. It is also a reality that the individual carries all his or her needs with him or her at all times, regardless of the location or situation. From this perspective, the quality of life must be attended to in the work setting as much as in the home setting. And the supervisor shares a responsibility for doing so.

The police team constructed for alignment has the potential to provide social and emotional support for its members, producing a more satisfying and work-productive environment. It is important to note that, for a group truly to function as a support base, the group norms that emerge for any specific team *must* originate from within the team itself and not represent a set of "shoulds" from the behavioral sciences or other social institutions. Sometimes, also, it is simply more fun to work with someone else than to work alone!

SIMPLY DO IT!

Despite the potential advantages to creating a shared-responsibility team, many managers express strongly negative sentiments about teams, groups, committees, and meetings. They associate teams with delays, endless talk (or false, constrained politeness), avoidance of responsibility, and other unpleasant outcomes. Indeed, too few management teams now function in ways that could produce enthusiasm and encourage emulation.

Suppose, however, that your direct subordinates could function as a team with the following characteristics:

- Everyone knows his or her own and others' tasks well enough so that nothing falls through the cracks; everyone knows who is, and who should be, doing what.
- Trust is so high that the group does not need to meet on every issue. Each member is confident that no one, including the boss, would act without consultation unless there was a good reason — such as prior general agreement, special expertise, legitimate time pressures, or unavailability of affected parties. And the person who does act would know that others would back any action.
- Such a group would not be very "groupy" or clingy, and would not waste time meeting on trivial issues or limiting those who had taken individual initiative.
- Members who were clearly more expert than the others, in certain areas, would be given great latitude to make the decisions on those matters.
- Nevertheless, if issues cross several areas or affect the department as a whole, members would seriously address the issues together, fight hard and openly for their beliefs, insist that their concerns be addressed, yet also pay attention to the needs of the department as a whole. Everyone would be comfortable wearing at least two hats, one for their area and one for the department.
- Although skilled at persuasion and willing to fight hard over important differences, members would feel no obligation to oppose automatically initiatives from other members or the manager. There would be no competition for competition's sake. Members would enthusiastically support the positions or ideas of others when they happened to agree.
- Despite members' willingness to fight when necessary, the climate is pervasively supportive, encouraging members to ask one another for help, acknowledge their mistakes, share resources (people, information, or equipment), and generally further everybody's performance and learning.
- The group pays attention to successful task achievement and to individual member's learning; members are not restricted to areas where they have

total competence and hence can't acquire new expertise, nor are they so overloaded with learning experiences that group performance seriously suffers.

- Perhaps most important, the group has self-correcting mechanisms; when things aren't going well, all members are ready to examine the group's processes, discuss what is wrong, and take corrective action. Whatever the problems—overly lengthy meetings, inappropriate agenda items, unclear responsibilities, lack of team effort, overly parochial participation, or even poor leadership practices—the group takes time out to assess its way of operating and to make midcourse corrections. Individual members as well as the manager feel free to raise questions of team performance.

Does this team profile sound too ideal? Is the well-developed team a fantasy projection that will remain frustratingly out of reach in the real world of petty politics, indirection, waffling, and hushed-corridor cabals? It could be but not necessarily. We've seen police teams achieve this level of alignment. If you want a team effort, develop one. Simply do it!

KEY POINTS

- What we perceive as reality, as compared to actual reality, may be considerably different.
- Human learning or conditioning will either change or reinforce our attitudes and behavior.
- The police supervisor plays a key role in both because she or he (1) can influence the accuracy of one's perceptions, and (2) is responsible for reinforcing proper behavior and changing that which is dysfunctional.
- A large number of factors and properties influence the quantity and quality of our perceptions.
- We are prone to take perceptual shortcuts, which can aid or hinder us in picturing reality.
- Training is a key responsibility of a police supervisor.
- An FTO program does not diminish or detract from a supervisor's training function.
- The training process incorporates three essential partners: department, trainer, and trainee.
- Effective training is defined by the clarity of objectives *and* means of delivery.
- Training objectives should be set according to (1) is training really required, (2) what part is it to play, and (3) how many and who should participate?
- Your training style will emphasize one of four behaviors: (1) excellence, (2) power, (3) efficiency, and (4) affability.
- Your training strategy depends on goals and available resources.

- Your delivery of training should be subjected to constant evaluation by your boss and yourself.
- The most difficult of all training goals for the supervisor is that of building and maintaining a work *team*.
- The main purpose for teamwork is that through alignment synergy is produced within the work group.

DISCUSSION

1. In your own words, define human perception.
2. Select one personal factor and one external property that you have recently experienced. Discuss how each affected you.
3. Select one of the described perceptual shortcuts that either you or a co-worker has used in the past few days. Discuss it in terms of its departmental implications.
4. How is a FTO program related to a supervisor's training responsibility? Are they compatible? Why or why not?
5. In your opinion, what are (in rank order) the major training needs of a police officer today?
6. "Feedback is the breakfast of champions." Why?
7. Why is team building important? What specific steps should be taken to form a team of independent employees?

STRUCTURED EXPERIENCES

This section is comprised of a case pertaining to learning and an exercise dealing with perception.

1. Case: The General

Yesterday the Chief was notified that a citizen was in the lobby waiting to see him. After a brief delay, an elderly gentleman was admitted to his office. The man was obviously in a highly emotional state of mind. His first words were, "My wife is dead!" The Chief asked him to be seated and to please elaborate. He began by relating that he had lived in the community for twelve years, his name was General (retired) Quotidian and that he was eighty-four years old.

The General went on to report that his wife had suffered a stroke the day before and had been rushed to the hospital in an ambulance. The ambulance crew instructed the General to follow their vehicle to the hospital. While en route, Patrol Officer Tortous observed Quotidian pursuing the ambulance. Tortous stopped the General who, with considerable difficulty, confusingly informed him that his wife was gravely ill. The officer listened and then officially admonished the General for violating the state vehicle code (following an emergency vehicle too close under critical response conditions). Next, Officer Tortous issued a moving citation to the General. Stupefied, General Quotidian asked if the officer knew to which hospital the ambulance had taken his wife. Tortous replied that the General ought to start telephoning the various hospitals in the immediate area. The officer then resumed routine patrol activities.

The Chief told General Quotidian that he would give top priority to this complaint. Further, he stated that he would provide the General with a detailed account of the findings of his pending discussion with the Officer.

Early the following morning the Chief instructed Officer Tortous to see him in his office. Once in his office, the Chief prudently and completely detailed the events of the preceding day. The Chief then inquired if the allegations were accurate or not. Tortous replied that they were.

The Chief continued the conversation by asking if Tortous had considered using any alternative approaches. The response was a firm and cold "no." The Chief then posed what he believed to be viable options. For example, "Officer Tortous, had you assessed placing the senior citizen into the police vehicle and taking him to the hospital?" After having explored three additional problem-solving approaches, the Chief asked a leading question: "Based on our discussion, would you handle a similar incident in the same manner?" Tortous quickly stated, "Yes, sir. I did my duty!" He stood, and with respect, left the room.

The Chief perused his personnel folder: (1) age, thirty-three; (2) law enforcement experience, eight years; (3) married; and (4) master of science degree in Criminal Justice.

1. What type of learning school would you assign the officer to? Why?
2. As the chief, what would you do, if anything, at this time?
3. What are your feelings and intuitions about this situation?

2. Exercise: Evaluating the Source of a Message

The objectives of this exercise are to

1. Provide a realistic application of perceptual filtering by examining the influence of the source of a message on its reception and interpretation.
2. Give you some insight into the process by which people evaluate the source of a message.

How to Set up the Exercise

1. Break the group into three-member groups for a role-playing session. There will have to be at least two different groups for this exercise: (1) a "negative" group and (2) a "positive" group.
2. There will be three roles in each group: (1) a police supervisor, (2) a neutral observer, and (3) an officer. Assign roles at this stage.

Instructions

1. Group A, the "negative" group: The *officer* must read the following instructions: "Relationships with your boss are extremely bad. He (she) is always hassling you and coming up with last-minute things to do, usually at the end of the day. In addition, he (she) never bothers to thank you when you do a good job."

   The police *supervisor* must read the following instructions: "You will call your subordinate on the phone in a few minutes and make the following request [be sure to read the words *just* as they are written]: '[name of subordinate], I'm sorry to be calling you so late in the day, but something slipped my mind. I've got a budget meeting tonight, and I wonder if you could stay behind thirty minutes after work to help me calculate some figures I'm going to need. I'll let you come in a half-hour late tomorrow morning if you will.'"

2. Group B, the "positive" group: The *officer* must read the following instructions: "Relationships with your supervisor are extremely good. He (she) has never hassled you and is very understanding and considerate in making job assignments to you. Very rarely has he (she) come up with a last-minute request, and when he (she) does, you know it's really an emergency."

   The police *supervisor* must read the following instructions: "You will call your subordinate on the phone in a few minutes and make the following request [be sure to read the words *just* as they are written]: '[name of subordinate], I'm sorry to be calling you so late in the day, but something slipped my mind. I've got a budget meeting tonight and I wonder if you could stay behind thirty minutes after work to help me calculate some figures I'm going to need. I'll let you come in a half-hour late tomorrow if you will.'"

3. Have each group role-play the phone call with the neutral person observing.

4. Regroup the class and have the neutral observers report back what occurred. Have the class discuss and draw conclusions about any differences between the two role groups.

3. Training Practices

Purpose

This activity is designed to discover how police personnel feel about current training practices in the police organization or your work group.

Process

1. Distribute a copy of the Learning Needs Questionnaire to each police employee in your work unit or department (or, if you have a large outfit, to a percentage of employees), and ask them to return the questionnaires anonymously. If you use a percentage of employees, make certain that it is

a fully representative group (i.e., from captain to typist, ten of thirty officers, etc.).

2. Summarize the information on the completed questionnaires (if they are not returned, something is being said about the climate in the police agency).

3. Circulate a copy of the data to each employee and ask him or her to comment on the relevance of the results of his or her section.

4. You can then establish training goals and begin working on the important issues.

4. Team-Building Evaluation

Apply the following questionnaire to critique your team process.

Learning Needs Questionnaire

Directions. Circle the number that you feel best represents your experience.

I am not well prepared for my job.	1	2	3	4	5	I am fully prepared for my job.
I lack essential skills for my job.	1	2	3	4	5	I have all the necessary skills for my job.
I was not carefully introduced to my job.	1	2	3	4	5	I was carefully introduced to my job.
I found it difficult to learn my job.	1	2	3	4	5	I learned my job with minimal difficulty.
I have no opportunities for development.	1	2	3	4	5	I have good opportunities for development.
I have far too little proper training.	1	2	3	4	5	I have sufficient training.
My boss is not concerned about training needs.	1	2	3	4	5	My boss is concerned about training needs.

Paul Whisenand, POLICE SUPERVISION: Theory and Practice, ©1976, p. 284. Reprinted by permission of Prentice Hall, Inc., Englewood Cliffs, N.J.

RESPONSIBILITY THIRTEEN

Community Oriented Policing: A Focus on Effectiveness

A competing model of community-based policing has developed and gained increased acceptance in the 1980's and is seen by many as the preferred policing style of the future. The community policing model treats service to the public and prevention of crime as the primary function of police in society. Proponents believe that the police, the public, and other government agencies must form a working partnership to have a meaningful impact on crime. Officers at the patrol level are required to spend less time in their cars communicating with other officers and more time on the street communicating with the public.

Report of the Independent Commission on the Los Angeles Police Department (1991)

What is the difference between supervision and leadership? Supervision looks through its glasses and does the work, but leadership looks at the lens and asks, "Is this the correct frame of reference?" Supervision functions within the standard operating procedures. Leadership deals with direction, vision, principles, and people development, culture building, personal satisfaction, and teamwork. Supervision deals more with external controls, logistics, and efficiency. *Supervisors emphasize efficiency (doing things right). Leaders stress effectiveness (doing the right things).* Both leadership and supervision, effectiveness and efficiency are necessary! Responsibility Thirteen concentrates on effectiveness. (Responsibility Fourteen addresses efficiency.)

MORE ON EFFECTIVENESS

Effective police supervisors lead their lives and manage their relationships around values; ineffective supervisors attempt to manage their time around priorities and their tasks around goals. *Think effectiveness with people; efficiency with things.*

Effective police supervisors carry their agenda with them. Their schedule is their servant, not their ruler. They organize weekly, change daily. However, they're not fickle in changing their plan. They exercise self-discipline and proactivity, and do not submit to fads and moods. They allocate blocks of prime time for high-priority planning, projects, and creative work. They work on less important activities as time allows.

By now you may have wondered why we have placed this opening emphasis on individual effectiveness. Well, personal effectiveness must precede organizational effectiveness. And, *community-oriented policing (COP) totally hinges on effectiveness*, and doing the right thing with your community, customer, citizenry, and client.

UNIVERSAL MISSION STATEMENT

At the very beginning, we previewed a "universal mission statement." It went as follows:

> To improve the economic well-being and quality of life of all stakeholders.

Please reexamine it now. Does it attempt to encompass, in a brief sentence, the core values of an organization? Is it comprehensive? Does it deal with all aspects of a person's responsibility, with the long term and short term? If your answers to these questions are "yes," then it appears to be an appropriate mission statement. If your responses are "no," then it isn't.

Three Parts

Let's assess the three parts that comprise the universal mission statement.

1. *Economic well-being.* Employment is the way we make our livelihood. Police work consists of police jobs. The sworn and civilian employees produce services, and, ideally, receive enough money to make home payments, pay bills, take a vacation, and more. Sometimes we lose sight of this simple fact.
2. *Quality of life (employees).* This part covers both the quality of life of employees and stakeholders. We'll address the police employee first. We believe that police employees should find in their work (1) a sense of belongingness and acceptance; (2) intellectual challenge and professional growth; (3) a known purpose and a meaningful contribution; (4) consistent fairness and numerous opportunities; and (5) alignment—the economic rewards are balanced by the professional and psychological rewards. For example, if police employees have fairness regarding economic income, but they lack challenge and meaning in their work, they'll press for more money and seek their intrinsic satisfaction away from work.
3. *All stakeholders.* The best way to discover who is a stakeholder is by asking, "Who will suffer if the department fails?" It takes a lot of insight, foresight, and sense of stewardship about all stakeholders—all who have a stake in the welfare and success of the police agency—including citizens, noncitizens, policy makers, clients, community, and the police profession

at large. When we use the word "stakeholder," we mean *everyone* who will suffer if the department fails. Even the clients or consumers we would label as criminals or scofflaws stand to lose if the police are inept. Even they become more susceptible to being victimized.

We see the universal mission statement as the prime choice for a COP program. It doesn't preclude the need for a department-wide and perhaps more specific mission statement. Every department needs one of its own.

The mission of a COP program is, therefore;

To improve the economic well-being and quality of life of all stakeholders.

SOME SPECIFIC MISSION STATEMENTS

We thought Tiburon's mission or value statement reflected a concern for COP (see Figure 13-1). Chief Herley wrote that it "is very important as it was developed by all levels of the Department—both sworn and non-sworn personnel. The process was actually more important than the product—though I am very proud of the final product. The values statement is given to and discussed with all new employees, part of the Field Training Officer program, included in the Department Manual, and used as a criterion for personnel evaluation."

Earlier you saw (Figure 5-2) the overall mission statement of the Los Angeles County Sheriff's Department. Figure 13-2 presents that mission statement for the numerous cities that contract for police services from them. Can you find its reference to COP? Figure 13-3 provides evidence of the department's commitment to COP. The department was aided by a market research company to study the attitudes of their employees. Nearly 11,000 questionnaires were distributed with a return rate of 38 percent (10 percent is considered good for such a survey). We think the results were most encouraging. What do you think?

CENTRAL MISSION

The central mission of the police is to control crime. Crime fighting enjoys wide public support as the basic strategy of policing precisely because it embodies a deep commitment to this objective. In contrast, other proposed strategies such as problem solving or community policing appear to ignore this focus.

Professional crime fighting now relies predominantly on three tactics: (1) motorized patrol; (2) rapid response to calls for service; and (3) follow-up investigation of crimes. The police focus on serious crime has also been sharpened by screening calls for service, targeting patrol, and developing forensic technology (e.g., automated fingerprint systems, computerized criminal record

ORGANIZATIONAL VALUES

TIBURON POLICE DEPARTMENT

We of the Tiburon Police Department recognize our contribution to the quality of life and a safe environment in our community through the provision of professional law enforcement services. We will meet the challenge of providing these services by basing our thoughts and actions on the following shared values as the foundation of our organization:

SERVICE TO OUR COMMUNITY

We value the opportunity to provide fair, courteous, responsive and effective law enforcement in order to continually improve the quality of life of the community. We value the members of our community as partners and indispensable resources in a combined policing effort.

INTEGRITY

We value candor, honesty, and ethical behavior in the members of our department. We are committed to uphold our positions of trust by maintaining the highest ethical standards as set forth in the Code of Professional Conduct for California Peace Officers and the Law Enforcement Code of Ethics.

RESPECT FOR DIVERSITY

We are aware of and value Human Diversity, respecting the Dignity and Rights of all we serve. We are committed to ensure that persons are not discriminated against because of race, religion, culture, disability, gender or sexual orientation.

RESPONSIBILITY and ACCOUNTABILITY

We value and accept the full scope of our responsibilities and are accountable for our own actions -- being willing to admit our errors and learn from them. We have a responsibility to the department, community, and our profession to ensure our behavior earns their support and trust. We will make maximum effective use of resources and demonstrate fiscal responsibility.

PROFESSIONALISM

We value the spirit of professionalism, having a clear sense of commitment, perspective and direction through constant self-evaluation. Our professionalism is reflected by our demeanor, personal and organizational competence and excellence in caring for our community. We are dedicated to achieving the highest standards of the law enforcement profession.

RECOGNITION AND REWARD

We value an atmosphere which recognizes, rewards, and encourages creativity, innovation, teamwork and mutual respect. We acknowledge and appreciate commitment to quality performance and recognize the accomplishments of both our department and each individual who contributes to its success.

PRIDE IN AND ENJOYMENT OF OUR PROFESSION

We value our work and believe it to be a source of enjoyment and satisfaction. We take pride in being an integral part of the community. We do not take ourselves so seriously that we fail to have some fun doing what we choose to do -- serving the Law Enforcement Profession with the Tiburon Police Department.

Figure 13-1 Organizational Values of the Tiburon Police Department

CONTRACT LAW ENFORCEMENT MISSION

THE LOS ANGELES COUNTY SHERIFF'S DEPARTMENT'S CONTRACT LAW ENFORCEMENT MISSION *is to provide cost-effective municipal law enforcement services responsive to the varied characteristics of the cities served. Our guiding values are:*

SERVICE TO CITIES: *We recognize contract cities as the ultimate focus of our municipal law enforcement activities. We are committed to understanding each city's vision, underlying values, and specific needs and to administer/develop law enforcement services that respect the desires of the cities.*

ETHICS: *We recognize our badge as a symbol of public trust and expect exemplary behavior from our employees both in the performance of their duties and in their personal lives. We monitor adherence to Department rules and standards to insure the highest level of law enforcement service and the respect of our contract cities.*

QUALITY: *We strive for kind, understanding, and courageous professional service in the delivery of community-oriented law enforcement.*

ADAPTABILITY: *We accept change in meeting the specific needs of contract cities. We encourage questions on established practices and suggestions for doing the job better.*

TEAMWORK: *We work as partners with our contract cities. We share our plans and strategies, providing on-going honesty and candor in communications. We require individual accountability.*

INTERNAL OPERATIONS: *We aggressively pursue the internal efficiencies and flexibility necessary to deliver quality services at a reasonable cost.*

Figure 13-2 Contract Law Enforcement Mission (Reprinted with permission of the Los Angeles County Sheriff's Department.)

Respondents were asked how community-oriented the Department is, as well as how employee-oriented it is. They responded on 1-to-9 scales extending from "not at all" to "extremely."

The Department is clearly seen as community-oriented. Almost two-thirds of the respondents (63%) use 7, 8 or 9 on the scale, while only 8% circle 1, 2 or 3. When averaged across all respondents, these scores fall at 6.6 on the scale. There is a slight difference between sworn and civilian employees on this measure, with sworn personnel more enthusiastic about the Department's community orientation than are civilians. (Of course, sworn personnel are far more likely to have contact with people in the community than are civilian personnel.) Among sworn personnel, there are small differences in the Department's perceived community orientation as a function of assignment. People on custody duty and in administration (i.e., those with the lowest contact with the community) see the Department as less community-oriented than do others.

How Community-Oriented is the Sheriff's Dept.:

Mean Values

Sworn	Civilian
6.63	6.34

(Based on 9-point scale:
1 = not at all;
9 = extremely)

Figure 13-3 Community-Oriented Policing

files, etc.). Although these tactics have scored their successes, they have been criticized within and outside policing for being reactive rather than proactive.

Reactive tactics have some merits, of course. The police go where crimes have occurred and when citizens have summoned them. They keep their distance from the community and thereby retain their impartiality. They do not develop the sorts of relationships with citizens that could bias their responses to crime incidents. The reactive tactics do have preventive effects—at least in theory. The prospect of the police arriving at a crime in progress is thought to deter crimes.

Finally, many police forces have developed *proactive* tactics to deal with crime problems that could not be handled through traditional reactive methods. In drug dealing, organized crime, and vice enforcement, for example, where no immediate victims exist to alert the police, the police have developed special units that rely on informants, covert surveillance, and undercover investigations rather than responses to calls for service. In the area of juvenile offenses, the police have created athletic leagues, and formed partnerships with schools to deal with drug abuse, gang activity, truancy, and so on. *It is not accurate, then, to define policing as entirely reactive.*

The greatest potential for improved crime control does not lie in the continued enhancement of response times, patrol tactics, and investigative techniques. Rather, improved crime control can be achieved by (1) diagnosing and managing problems in the community that produce crimes; (2) fostering closer relations with the community to facilitate crime solving; and (3) building self-defense capabilities within the community itself. Among the results may be increased apprehension of criminals. To the extent that problem-solving or community strategies of policing prepare the police to use local knowledge and capacity to control crime, they will be supportive of the future of policing.

CASE FOR QUALITY

In the 1980s, police agencies began to explore the crime-fighting effectiveness of tactics that build on previous approaches. At the same time, they sought to extend them by looking behind offenses to the precipitating causes of crimes. They endeavored to build closer relations with the community and enhance the self-defense capacities of the communities themselves.

Their guiding theory was that the effectiveness of existing tactics can be enhanced if the police increase the quantity and *quality* of their contacts with citizens (both individuals and neighborhood groups) and conditionally include in their responses to crime problems thoughtful analyses of the root causes of the offenses. The expectation is that this will both enhance the direct effectiveness of the police and enable them to leverage the resources of citizen groups and other public agencies to control crime.

The 1980s saw, therefore, many police agencies attempting to "work smarter and not harder" and to "do more with less." What still remains unanswered is the consequence of shifting a whole department to a different style of policing. For example, if officers are taken from patrol and detective units to do problem-oriented or community policing, it is fairly certain that response times would lengthen—at least until the problem-solving efforts decreased the demands for service by removing the problem that was producing the calls for service. And even though longer response times do not necessarily indicate a loss in crime-fighting effectiveness, it would be *perceived* as such because the public and the police consider rapid response to crime calls as crime-control effectiveness.

What is inviting, of course, is to avoid deciding between these strategies, and to adopt the strengths of these various approaches while avoiding their weaknesses. This could be seen in decisions to create special units to do COP within existing organizations whose traditions and main forces remained committed to traditional patrol and investigation tactics. But this means more resources, which means more money, and more money is darned difficult to acquire.

COP is not merely a matter of budget dollars. It is, likewise, a matter of administrative *style* and *structure*. COP requires a greater degree of decentralization than does the current policing strategy. It depends more on the initiative of the officers. And they reach out for a close rather than a distant relationship with the community. It is very different from the current administrative posture that stresses centralization, control, and professional separation from the community.

Most basically then, COP includes a likelihood of a need for more money and certaintude of a need for administrative change.

WHO'S REALLY RESPONSIBLE?

If we believe that the police are the first line of defense against disorder and crime, and the source of strength for maintaining the quality of life, what should its strategy be? The traditional view is that the police are a community's professional defense against crime and disorder: Citizens should leave control of crime and maintenance of order to police. The COP strategy is that police are to promote and buttress a community's ability to create livable neighborhoods and protect them from criminals.

What about neighborhoods in which criminality prevails—where, for example, drug dealers take over and openly deal drugs and threaten citizens? Clearly, our police must play a leading role defending such communities. Should they do so on their own, however?

Oddly enough, when the police move in to attack dangerous street crime aggressively, the very neighborhoods plagued by disorder reject their approach. The citizens are not ready to surrender control of their neighborhoods to remote police who show them little respect. Are police the first line of defense in a neighborhood? No—citizens are!

WHY COP?

There are three driving forces pushing COP.

- Citizen frustration with police services
- Research conducted during the 1970s
- Dissatisfaction with the traditional role of the police officer

Frustration with Police Services

Citizens respect most police officers. Most people enjoy contact with police. However, some people continue to be frustrated by police who whisk in and out of their neighborhoods with little sensitivity to community norms and values. Regardless of where one asks, people want both the familiarity and accountability that characterize foot patrol. More and more people are demanding increased participation with police in the determination of police priorities in their neighborhoods. Community crime control has become a cornerstone of their sense of neighborhood security and a means of opting for different police services.

Research

Research in the 1970s showed that preventive patrol in patrol cars had little effect on crime, citizen levels of fear, or citizen satisfaction with police. Rapid response to calls for service likewise had little impact on arrests, citizen satisfaction with police, or levels of citizen fear.

Role of the Patrol Officer

Finally, patrol officers are frustrated with their traditional role. Despite the lip service that patrol is the "backbone of policing," every police officer knows that, at best, patrol is what officers do until they become detectives or are promoted. Patrol officers have the most important mission in police departments—they handle the public's most pressing problems and must make complex decisions almost instantaneously. Even so, police administrators continue to treat patrol officers as if they were the "butbone"—not the "backbone"—of the agency.

WILL COP HAPPEN?

There are four reasons for believing that COP will continue to grow among police agencies.

- Citizen response thus far to the new strategy
- Ongoing research on police effectiveness
- Recent experiences the police have had with COP
- Values of the new generation of police managers and supervision

Citizen Response

The overwhelming public response to community and problem-solving policing has been positive, regardless of where it has been instituted. Police and citizens alike are now able to say yes or no to COP based on documented experiences in such places as Boston, Massachusetts; Flint, Michigan; Kansas City, Missouri; Houston, Texas; Arapaho County, Colorado; and Santa Ana, California.

New Research on Effectiveness

Research conducted during the early and mid-1970s frustrated police executives. It generally showed what did not work. Research performed during the 1970s and early 1980s was different. By showing what new tactics did work, it fueled the move to renovate policing. This research provided police with the following guidance:

- Foot patrol can reduce citizen fear of crime, improve the relationship between police and citizens, and increase citizen satisfaction with police.
- The productivity of detectives can be enhanced if patrol officers carefully interview neighborhood residents about criminal events, get the information to detectives, and detectives use it wisely.
- Citizen fear can be substantially reduced by police tactics that emphasize increasing the quantity and improving the quality of citizen–police interaction.
- Street-level enforcement of heroin and cocaine laws can reduce serious crime in the area of enforcement, without being displaced to adjacent areas.
- Problem-oriented policing can be used to reduce thefts from cars, problems associated with drug trafficking, and household burglaries.

Experience with Innovation

The desire to improve policing is not new with this generation of innovators. Before COP there were two major efforts to form a police–community partnership. In the 1960s, it was labeled "police community relations" (PCR). It went down the drain when the citizens saw it mainly as a public relations scheme. The 1970s gave birth and death to "team policing." The early team-policing programs were burdened by a lack of documented successes and failures. Those who experimented with team policing were not aware that elements of team policing were simply incompatible with preventive patrol and rapid response to calls for service. It would be implemented, officers and citizens would like it, it would have an initial impact on crime, and then traditional habits would overwhelm it—the program would disappear.

Moreover, the lessons about innovation and excellence that Peters and Waterman brought together in *In Search of Excellence* were not available to police administrators. The current innovators have an advantage: They have seized the opportunity to learn from the proven successes and failures of the past. They're looking for facts and are not content with merely studying innovation and management in policing.

New Police Leadership

The new police leadership is unique in the history of American policing. Unlike the tendency in the past for chiefs and sheriffs to be local and inbred, chiefs and sheriffs of this generation are knowledgeable and sophisticated. In our opinion, they are every bit as skilled and creative as their private-sector counterparts. With growing criminality and a worldwide drug problem, they've been compelled into *thinking smarter*. And, with an ever-greater competition for budget dollars, they've been forced into *doing more with less*. Our police leadership, in every way, is looking better each and every day.

COP IMPLEMENTATION

Lee P. Brown, while chief of police in Houston, wrote about his experiences with COP in a paper entitled, "Community Policing: A Practical Guide for Police Officials" (National Institute of Justice, U.S. Department of Justice, 1989). By trial and error, he discovered that COP is best approached in two phases. The following is based, in part, on his experiences and recommendations.

Phase 1 of COP is the implementation of programs designed to provide the public with ways to participate in policing efforts. The initial phase does *not* require a total change in the organization's operating style. Phase 2, conversely, *does* require the organization to make such a change.

Because phase 1 includes only the implementation of individual programs, the systems that support the organization's policing style—such as recruitment, training, performance evaluation, rewards, and discipline—do not change. Therefore, individual and separate programs do not affect the entire department or the entire community.

Phase 2, however, encompasses more systemwide changes. It is not merely programs that are being implemented—it is the department's *style* or culture that is being restructured. Unlike individual programs, style affects the total department and the total community.

Two Phases: From Program to Style

Commissioner Brown indicated that COP is best seen as a three- to five-year installation endeavor. It is not a quick fix. Long-standing ways of doing police business must be undone and new ones implanted. Habits are not easily unlearned. COP requires patience, persistence, practice, and a lot of perspiration.

Phase 1 lays the groundwork for phase 2. By implementing one program at a time the department is able to accomplish the following:

- Break down barriers to change
- Educate its leaders and line employees on the merits of COP
- Reassure the line employees that the COP concepts being adopted had not been imported from outside the department but, instead, were an outgrowth of existing programs
- Address problems on a small scale before making the full transition to COP
- Demonstrate to the public and elected officials the benefits of COP
- Provide a training ground for COP concepts and strategies
- Free up a willingness to experiment with new ideas

Shift in Attitude

Although it is an *operating style*, COP also is a *set of attitudes* about police work that contain several interrelated components. All are essential to the COP concept and help distinguish it from traditional policing.

Results versus process.   The first component of the COP attitude is an orientation toward *problem solving*. Embracing the pioneering work of Herman Goldstein (see Responsibility Fourteen), COP focuses on *results* as well as process. Incorporated into routine operations are the techniques of problem identification, problem analysis, and problem resolution.

Values.   COP also relies heavily on values that incorporate citizen involvement in matters that directly affect the safety and quality of neighborhood life. The culture of the police department becomes one that not merely recognizes the merits of community involvement, but moreover organizes and manages departmental affairs in ways that are consistent with such beliefs.

Accountability.   Because different neighborhoods have different needs and priorities, it is necessary to have an adequate understanding of what is important to a specific neighborhood. To acquire such an understanding, officers must interact with residents on a routine basis and keep them informed of police efforts to fight and prevent neighborhood crime. This ensures accountability to the community, as well as to the department.

Decentralization. The decentralization of authority and structure is another component of COP. Roles are changed as the authority to participate in the decision-making process expands significantly. The expansion of such empowerment makes it necessary to adjust organizational functions throughout the department.

Power sharing. Responsibility for making decisions is shared by the police and the community after a valid *partnership*—one that encourages *active* citizen involvement in policing efforts—between the two groups has been established. *Passive* citizen involvement will not suffice. Power sharing means that the community is allowed to participate in the decision-making process unless the law specifically gives that authority to the police alone.

Beat redesign. Beat boundaries are drawn to coincide with natural neighborhood boundaries rather than in an arbitrary fashion that meets the needs of the police department. Individual neighborhoods are not placed in multiple beats.

Permanent assignments. Under COP, shift and beat assignments are issued on a permanent, rather than a rotating, basis. This allows the beat officer to become an integral part of the community that he has been assigned to protect. When a beat officer is reassigned to another area, his replacement is required to participate in an orientation period with the outgoing officer.

Empowerment of beat officers. Rather than simply patrolling the streets, beat officers are encouraged to initiate creative responses to neighborhood problems. Beat officers must become actively involved in the affairs of the community. They must be given the authority to make decisions, based on the circumstances of the situation. This empowerment reflects the trust that police leaders have in their officers' ability to make appropriate decisions.

Investigations. Neighborhood crime is best solved with information provided by residents. COP makes it necessary to decentralize the investigative function and focus on neighborhood, or area-specific, investigations. Centralized investigations, however, cannot be eliminated entirely as these are needed to conduct pattern- or suspect-specific *citywide* investigations.

Supervision and management. *Under COP, the role of persons at all levels within the organization changes.* For example, the patrol officer becomes the "manager" of his beat, whereas the supervisor assumes responsibility for facilitating the problem-solving process by training, coaching, coordinating, and evaluating the officers. Management's role is to support the process by mobilizing the resources needed to address citizen concerns and problems.

Training. Under COP the attitude toward officer training is changed. At the recruit level, cadets are provided information about the complexities and dynamics of the community and how the police fit into the larger picture. Cadet training also enables the future officer to develop community-organizing skills. Supervisory training is designed to provide the skills needed to facilitate the problem-solving process. This is accomplished by training supervisors to solve problems, coordinating officers' activities, planning community-organizing activities, and mapping out criminal investigation. Management training focuses on leadership, vision, and values.

Performance evaluation. With the modified roles for all personnel comes the need for a revised system for evaluating officer performance. Rather than simply counting numbers (e.g., number of citations issued, number of arrests made, number of calls handled), performance quality is based on the officer's ability to solve problems and involve the community in the department's crime-fighting efforts.

Managing calls for service. Inherent in COP is the understanding that all police resources will be managed, organized, and directed in a manner that facilitates problem solving. For example, taking of incident reports over the telephone, by mail, or in person at police facilities; holding lower-priority calls; and having officers make appointments with an individual or a group. This provides the officer or deputy more time to interact with "their citizens."

Philosophy of Supervision

COP is a way of thinking about how to supervise one's self and others to

- Ensure mutual support among various departmental functions
- Ensure alignment between officers and citizens so that a consensus can be reached on what needs to be done to improve the quality of neighborhood life
- Integrate the expectations of citizens with the actions taken by the police to identify and address conditions that have a negative effect on the quality of neighborhood life
- Ensure that all actions are designed to produce intended results

WHO BENEFITS

If done correctly, COP will benefit both the public and the police. Some of the benefits to the public are

- *A commitment to crime prevention.* Unlike traditional policing, which focuses on the efficient means of *reacting* to incidents, COP strives to confirm that the basic mission of the police is to *prevent* crime and disorder.
- *Public scrutiny of police operations.* Because citizens will be involved with the police, they will be exposed to the "what," "why," and "how" of police work. This is almost certain to prompt critical discussions about the responsiveness of police operations.
- *Accountability to the public.* Until the advent of COP, officers were

accountable for their actions only to police management. Now officers also will be accountable to the public with whom they have formed a partnership.

- *Customized police service.* Because police services will be localized, officers will be required to increase their responsiveness to neighborhood problems. As police–citizen partnerships are formed and nurtured, the two groups will be better equipped to work together to identify and address *specific* problems that affect the quality of neighborhood life.

- *Community organization.* The degree to which the community is involved in police efforts to evaluate neighborhood problems has a significant bearing on the effectiveness of those efforts. The success of any crime-prevention effort depends on the police and citizens working in concert — not on one or the other carrying the entire load alone.

The benefits of COP to the police are

- *Greater citizen support.* As people spend more time working with the police, they learn more about the police function. Experience has shown that as people's knowledge of the police function increases, their respect for the police increases as well. This increased respect, in turn, leads to greater support for the police.

- *Shared responsibility.* Historically the police have accepted the responsibility for resolving the problem of crime in the community. Under community policing, however, citizens develop a sense of *shared* responsibility.

- *Greater job satisfaction.* Because officers are able to resolve issues and problems within a reasonable amount of time, they see the results of their efforts more quickly.

- *Better internal relationships.* Communication problems among units and shifts have been a chronic problem in police agencies. Because COP focuses on problem solving and accountability, it also increases cooperation among the various segments of the department.

- *Support for organizational change.* COP requires a vast restructuring of the department's organizational structure to ensure the integration of various functions, such as patrol and investigations. The needed changes are new management systems, new training curriculums and delivery mechanisms, a new performance-evaluation system, a new disciplinary process, a new reward system, and new ways of managing calls for service.

CONCLUDING REMARK

Commissioner Brown wrote the following, and we totally concur with his proposition.

Because community policing is relatively new as a style of policing, questions have been raised about its effectiveness. Any doubts, however, should be put to rest. Experience has shown that community policing as a dominant policing style is a better, more efficient, and more cost-effective means of using police resources. In the final analysis, community policing is emerging as the most appropriate means of using police resources to improve the quality of life in neighborhoods throughout the country.

We would, in closing, underscore that COP means a change in

- Departmental programs
- Departmental style (culture)
- Officer attitudes
- Supervisory philosophy

KEY POINTS

- There is an important difference between supervision and leadership. The supervisor is intent on doing the work right or efficiently. The leader seeks to do the right thing or be effective.
- The leader thinks and acts to be effective with people, and the supervisor thinks and acts to be efficient with things.
- A universal mission statement of a police agency could be: "To improve the economic well-being and quality of life of all stakeholders."
- The central mission of a police agency is to control crime.
- In the 1980s a movement began to increase the quantity and especially the *quality* of police contacts with the public.
- The *citizens* are the first line of defense to criminality in a community.
- The three driving forces behind COP are citizen frustration with police services; research findings from the 1970s; and dissatisfaction with the traditional reactive role of the police officer.
- There are four reasons to believe that COP will continue to grow in number and improve in results: ongoing favorable citizen response; continuing action-oriented research; experience in what works best; and the effectiveness of police leadership.
- COP is best installed in two phases. The first phase encompasses singular programs, and the second phase involves a systemwide change in style of policing.
- COP is dependent on the two preceding phases plus a shift in attitudes and philosophy.
- A successful COP will generate benefits for both the public and the police.

DISCUSSION

1. What is your opinion of the "universal mission statement"? Is it comprehensive enough? Should anything be added or deleted in it? Does it or could it apply to your department?

2. Do you agree, or not, with the premise that the central mission of a police agency is to control crime?

3. Is your agency mainly "reactive" or "proactive"? List your reactive programs. Next, list your proactive ones. Do you see any trends emerging?

4. Where is your agency today in terms of *quality* of services? Is your agency evaluating its quality? If so, how?

5. Review the four reasons for believing that COP is likely to occur (in some cases continue). Do you see any of them operating in your department?

6. One cornerstone of COP is "a shift in attitudes." What should the new attitudes be? How is this best accomplished?

STRUCTURED EXPERIENCES

Exercise 1

This is a group exercise for six to eight people. Draft a memorandum for your chief or sheriff to sign that explains his or her reasons for installing a COP program.

Exercise 2

Again in a group setting, attempt to add more benefits to the list for the police and the list for the public.

Exercise 3

Commissioner Brown wrote about a phase 2 implementation that stresses a change in style. (We refer to style as organizational culture.) Discuss with one another what this style should look like. What are its key characteristics?

RESPONSIBILITY FOURTEEN

Problem-Oriented Policing

If you're not a part of the solution, then you're definitely a part of the problem.

Anonymous

Responsibility Thirteen covered one strategy for improving police services. Responsibility Fourteen likewise deals with a strategy for doing so. You'll soon learn how the two strategies complement one another. Adopting one does not preclude the other. In fact, where you find one, you'll often find the other.

In summary, COP stresses the key role that a working partnership between the police and the community can play in solving crimes, reducing fear, and resolving situations that lead to crimes; these are the challenges that define the future of policing in the next decade.

Problem-oriented policing (POP) emphasizes the value of being able to diagnose the continuing problems that lie behind the repeated incidents that are reported to police employees and to design and implement solutions to those problems. Herman Goldstein, one of the foremost thinkers in the police field, defines a police department as practicing POP when it

- Identifies substantive community problems
- Inquires systematically into their nature
- Analyzes community interest and special interest in each problem
- Assesses current responses
- Conducts an uninhibited search for tailor-made solutions
- Takes initiative in implementing solutions
- Evaluates the effectiveness of solutions

Many police departments concentrate on one incident at a time as they respond to calls for service. They neglect to assemble into a single picture the separate symptoms they treat. A neighborhood may be experiencing a flood of troubles—street fights, insults to passersby, solicitation by prostitutes, pick-pocketing, and drunken driving—but the department does not recognize their sources in a sports bar. When the sole police response to a community problem is to arrest the current troublemakers, that department is not engaging in POP.

DEPARTMENTAL STRATEGY

Assuming your department has a mission statement, then a strategy, or strategies, for pursuing its attainment becomes paramount. In other words, you know where you want to go, but now the issue is how do you most effectively get there? A strategy includes unique operational programs and particular management-supervisory style for fulfilling your mission.

The strategy that guided policing during the last half-century is captured by the label "professional crime fighting." This strategy helped the police. It carried them from an arena of amateurism, lawlessness, and political vulnerability to an arena of professionalism, integrity, and political independence. The driving forces include

1. Increased concentration on crime control as the central mission of the police
2. Modification in organizational structure from decentralized, geographical units to a centralized structure with subordinate units determined by function rather than by geography
3. Large investments in modern technology and the training of officers

Experience with the professional crime-fighting strategy eventually revealed two flaws. First, the tactics are basically reactive. They depend on someone noticing a crime and calling the police. That leaves many crimes—those "invisible others" that do not produce victims or witnesses who are willing to mobilize—beyond the reach of the police. Such crimes include drug dealing, bribery, extortion, often rape, frequently child and spouse abuse, embezzlement and fraud, and even gang violence. Second, the tactics often fail to prevent crimes. Analyzing and eliminating the causes of crime under this strategy is seen as not doing "real police work."

Remember, a police agency is not constrained to one strategy for accomplishing its mission. It is important, however, that if two or more strategies are adopted, they are compatible and not confrontational. Compatibility of strategies offers the possibility of "synergy" of results. Confrontational strategies hold promise of wasted effort and lost opportunities. It so happens that COP and POP are friendly strategies.

PROBLEM-ORIENTED POLICING

The practice of POP seeks to improve on the professional crime-fighting model by adding proactiveness and thoughtfulness. It differs from COP by the emphasis of an analytical effort. It differs from professional crime fighting, which focuses on discovering offenders and apprehending them. The crime-fighting model assumes that this alone prevents crime. Also, it assumes that the police can position themselves to see offenses and quickly respond to them.

Problem-oriented policing takes a different posture about crime. In POP, it is not automatically accepted that crimes are caused by predatory offenders. (True, in all crimes there will be an offender.) But POP makes the assumption that crimes could be caused by particular, continuing problems in a community such as drug dealing. Hence, crimes might be controlled, or even prevented, by actions other than the arrest of particular individuals. For example, the police might be able to resolve a chronic dispute or restore order to a disorderly street. Arrest and prosecution remain crucially important tools of policing. *But ideas about the causes of crime and methods for controlling it are substantially expanded.*

In POP, the applied imagination of police employees—sworn and civilian alike—is galvanized as a crime-fighting tool. "Problem identification" and "problem definition" are essential steps in POP. The superficial symptoms of crime are avoided while the root causes are fervently sought. The common linkage of POP, COP and the professional crime fighting-model remains the same however—*crime control!*

The subtle but fundamental switch in perspective requires police and sheriff agencies to broaden their methods for responding to crime beyond patrol, investigation, and arrests. For example, the police can use negotiating and conflict-resolving skills to mediate disputes before they become crime problems. Disputes (between parents and children, landlords and tenants, merchants and customers, and between neighbors) might be resolved without waiting for a fight to occur and without immediate recourse to the criminal law, arrests, and prosecutions. Moreover, the police can take corrective action the second time they are called to the scene rather than the sixth or seventh time, thus making timely savings in the use of police resources.

The police can use their civil licensing authority and other municipal ordinances to enhance neighborhood security. Bars can be cautioned on excessive noise, merchants urged to comply with traffic regulations, and children cautioned on curfew violations to reduce situations that require police involvement.

Further, other local government agencies can help to deal with existing or potential criminal offenses. The fire department can be asked to inspect "crack houses" for fire-safety regulations. The public works department can be asked to inspect buildings and property for code violations. (Perhaps this is one of the least explored areas of assistance.)

A shift to POP has implications for the structure of police organizations. *To the extent that problem solving depends on the initiative and skill of officers and civilians in defining problems and devising solutions, the administrative style of the organization must change.* Because POP depends on individual initiative, the agency must decentralize. If not, local awareness and knowledge are curtailed.

Once again, an attempt should be made to give full recognition and enhanced rewards to the job of patrol officer. Bluntly, the notion of patrol as a staging area for better career opportunities must be erased. Patrol work has to be seen as a springboard and not a mill stone. Recognition and rewards will promote this goal.

Both COP and POP strive for greater crime control. The techniques are sufficiently different, which necessitates separate coverage. COP depends more on community involvement while POP relies more on police-employee problem solving. One strategy obviously contains portions of the other. The crime-fighting strategy targets crime control. COP and POP also target crime control but add a strong commitment to order, maintenance, and prevention by analysis.

WHY POP?

At first blush POP may appear to be another label for crime prevention. Or, it may look like several clever tactics for "cracking down" on a specific police problem. POP is much, much more than this. In fact, it involves an organization-wide and in-depth shift in policies, practices and thinking. In a few words —*POP places effectiveness first and efficiency second.*

There are eight reasons for POP.

1. *Lack of success.* There is an old adage that, "Nothing succeeds so much as a successful failure." The professional crime-fighting strategy, although not a disaster, has not proven itself effective in crime control. Herman Goldstein and a few others pointed this out, and in 1979 started their quest to refine an alternative policing approach.

2. *Efficiency has been inefficient.* Police management has been preoccupied with the internal operations and "doing things right." "Right" statistics, "right" training, "right" procedures, and looking "right." POP addresses the highly value-laden question of "why?" Or, rather than simply doing things right, "Are we doing the right things?"

3. *Scarce resources.* Whatever the budget, there is never enough to do the *entire* job. Hence, some demands for service may go begging. POP seeks to establish police priorities. If drug trafficking is the most significant problem, then the first allocation of resources goes to that, and so on. POP means priorities!

4. *Reaction.* It seems that everyone today is talking about, and doing little about, *proactivity.* POP requires self-initiative on the part of the police to prevent or reduce community problems.

5. *Community partnership.* POP encompasses COP or vice versa. The past has seen this partnership attempted in a random or haphazard way. POP is based on a systematic and continuing working relationship between the police and its public.

6. *Brain power.* POP depends on the thinking of everyone in the department (sworn, civilian, part-time employees, whatever). Once more, we return to

the need for *empowerment*. Unfortunately, many police agencies function as if the only "good ideas" come from the top. POP operates on the premise that good ideas can come from anyone, and must be encouraged and rewarded.

7. *Culture.* POP requires that the old ways of doing things be carefully replaced with a different organizational structure and management ethic. This is difficult because most new ideas or systems are suspect of being grossly inefficient or plainly stupid. Usually, the first reaction to POP is—"Big deal, we've been doing this for years." The POP culture is keyed to effectiveness and not efficiency.

8. *Expanded mission.* POP envisions an altered and much better articulated police mission. Earlier, we discussed the police mission and mission statements. It is vital to POP and POP to the department that everyone is "reading off the same music sheet." In other words, the police employee, the department, the policy makers, and the community must understand and, it is hoped, appreciate what the police are accountable for doing.

For many agencies, the mission is no longer limited to the efficient control of street crime. It also includes (1) a strengthened attack on dangerous offenders, organized criminal groups, and white-collar offenders; (2) a more determined effort to resolve the problems that underlie incidents reported to the police; and (3) a heightened concern for fear, disorder, and other problems that communities designate as high-priority issues. The mission at times includes police action on community problems such as drugs in schools, drunk driving, public drunkenness, unsupervised children, and other medical and social crises. Although it is by no means easy for a chief or sheriff to create an organization that can accommodate these diverse purposes, there does not seem to be any fundamental contradiction among these missions. Indeed, many departments are already pursuing these diverse missions with encouraging degrees of success.

EXAMPLE OF POP

As mentioned earlier, a successful POP program depends on decentralization of decision making, management style, analytical ability and more. But, most of all, it requires *empowerment* (see Responsibility Nine). Everyone is the department must be mentally engaged in assessing the existing crime problem and, from their assessment, conceive of tactical methods for solving it. In a few words,

The one way to get a good idea is to get a lot of ideas.

Of the many POP programs, we have selected one to illustrate its key characteristics. Typically, working examples are presented later. We thought it prudent to include one early to comprehend better the various steps involved in moving toward POP.

The Oxnard Police Department commenced its POP operations in 1987. The city is nearly 130,000 in population with a highly diverse ethnic and income composition. In many ways it is a microcosm of our nation—a lot of change, some wealth, some poverty, increasing cultural diversity, and guarded optimism.

Aleric Street

A few years ago, residents of Aleric Street were afraid to let their children play outdoors. Prostitutes turned tricks in abandoned cars. Drug dealers sold their wares in the neighborhood park. And gang members covered the walls with graffiti.

The police responded nightly to reports of beatings, stabbings, and robberies. POP helped Oxnard officers clean up the four-square-block neighborhood. "We have gone months without having a robbery," one officer said. "It used to be we wouldn't go a week."

However, all the problems did not disappear. One can still see graffiti on the walls and youths wearing gang colors. "The best you can say," Police Chief Robert Owens said, "is it's a shadow of its former self." Indeed, Owens said he soon plans to begin evaluating officers during their biannual reviews on their problem-solving and analytical skills.

Officers begin by identifying a problem area. Then they take a survey of the neighborhood, asking residents and business owners about their concerns and how they think police can help them. The approach has been applied to several other neighborhoods in Oxnard.

But it is the project on Aleric Street, which cost the department $123,000, that Owens calls a textbook example of POP.

Crime in the low-income neighborhood, where a two-bedroom apartment rents for about $500 a month, became worse and worse for about fifteen years, officials said. Traditional police strategies—such as beefing up patrols and running undercover vice operations—failed to conquer the problem because they were used only for a set amount of time. Once normal patrols resumed, so did the crime.

Eventually, some people concerned about the area complained to the City Council. A task force from city departments was created in 1987 to look into the crime problem in the neighborhood. During a walking tour of the area, police department, city council, and public works officials saw a prime example of the broken-window phenomenon. "If you have a broken window and it goes unrepaired, it symbolizes a lack of interest and lack of concern," Owens said. Dilapidated furniture and refuse were piled high in the alleys. Needles and cocaine wrappers littered the ground. And the apartment buildings were in need of repair.

So the city departments, local businesses, landlords, and residents got busy. The police department increased foot patrols so officers could meet neighborhood residents and gain their trust. Graffiti-covered walls were repainted. Bright lights were added to the neighborhood. Police arrested prostitutes and their customers. And conditions of probation did not allow those convicted to return to the area.

Landlords were encouraged to evict drug dealers. Then they put up wrought-iron fences to guard interior courtyards and alleys between buildings so criminals would not have places to hide. Even the street got a new image. The name was changed from Aleric Street to Cuesta del Mar Drive.

Now children play in the streets, and families use the park. When officers chase criminals, residents point out where they are hiding. "The nice thing about this is that it solves the problem," Officer Struck said. "We don't have to keep coming back to it."

One lady, who co-owns eighteen apartment buildings in the area, said the neighborhood has changed drastically since her brother complained to the city council about conditions three years ago. "When I first came down here, you couldn't walk down the street without a drug dealer tapping you on the shoulder," she said. Now she feels safe in the area at night.

Gangs

Youth gangs are a growing problem for a number of midsize cities across the country. According to the FBI, the Crips and the Bloods have now spread to more than one hundred cities and count more than forty thousand members. Similarly, the U.S. Drug Enforcement Agency has confirmed the presence of Los Angeles street gangs in at least forty-nine other cities.

The gang presence in large cities can be traced back over two hundred years, rising in prominence in England with the spread of the Industrial Revolution. During the nineteenth century, as European immigrants flooded the United States, they brought gang members with them to emerging population centers. The White Rabbit gang, for example, flourished in New York City during the mid-1800s. In fact, the decision to arm New York City police officers was due, in some part, to the criminal reign of the White Rabbits. But they, like most gangs, confined their activities to major metropolitan areas.

Following changes in the immigration patterns of Europeans, the influence of gangs in the United States diminished during the 1940s. This trend continued through the late 1960s by which time the power and influence of gangs had waned substantially. Regretfully, in the last decade, street gangs have grown both in size and sophistication. Once only a problem in large cities like Chicago and Los Angeles, youth gangs are rapidly spreading to midsize cities and appear to be encroaching on small towns as well.

Gang migration. The continued decline of core cities has displaced urban populations, which, in turn, have moved further out into suburbs and surrounding towns. Similarly, the growing transportation network of interstates, bridges, and highways facilitates gang movement to outlying areas.

High unemployment and the decline of heavy industries have also contributed to the decline of urban areas. And, of course, the growing influence of the illegal drug trade in suburbs and small towns has expanded the traditional territories of street gangs. For many youngsters, an organized gang fulfills social needs otherwise lacking in their lives. The gang provides structure, prestige among peers, defined rules, security, and a sense of belonging.

Traditional response to gangs. Because gangs have historically been a large city problem, most law-enforcement techniques used to combat gang violence are based on departments with substantial personnel and other resources, and usually involve formation of a special gang unit.

Although such an approach may be appropriate for very large departments, according to the Bureau of Justice Statistics, 91 percent of the twelve thousand police agencies in this country employ fewer than fifty officers. For midsize and small law enforcement agencies, there are two major difficulties with the formation of gang units. First, smaller departments lack the personnel needed for special units. There simply aren't enough officers to create these units and still adequately cover the streets. Also, a special unit may require 3 or 4 percent of an agency's total human resources. Too often this is the "cream of the crop" talent, which further depletes the overall effectiveness of the agency. Once the unit is formed, the gang problem "belongs to the unit," and the rest of the department tends to leave it alone. They no longer consider themselves part of the problem or the solution. Hence, much of the critical information gathered on the street may be lost.

Also, as more and more agencies adopt COP or POP, the need for a strengthened street force increases. Departments across the country are currently restructuring to increase the number of officers out on the street.

One city's solution. For several years there have been organized groups of youngsters within the city of Oxnard, California, but there has not been enough organized illegal activity to warrant a specialized response on the part of law enforcement. Recently, however, the police began reevaluating signs of such activity and determined that the gangs had become a threat to the safety of the community. Not only were gangs gaining new members in neighborhoods, but they had also begun recruiting in neighborhood schools.

Since 1983, the Oxnard Police Department has been participating in the U.S. Office Juvenile Justice and Delinquency Prevention's (OJJDP) Serious Habitual Offender Comprehensive Action Program (SHOCAP). The SHOCAP program is aimed at juveniles who pose a chronic, serious threat to the safety of the community. Through SHOCAP, the police department works with other juvenile-related agencies including prosecutors, courts, corrections, the schools, and human resources, to ensure a comprehensive and cooperative information and case-management process resulting in informed sentencing dispositions. SHOCAP enables the juvenile and criminal justice system to focus additional attention on juveniles who repeatedly commit serious crimes yet may somehow "fall through the cracks" of the system. The SHOCAP program has been so successful in dealing with Oxnard's serious juvenile offenders that it was used as the basis for addressing the emerging gang situation.

With a $75,000 grant from the OJJDP, Oxnard developed a Gang Offender Comprehensive Action Program (GO-CAP) component for the SHOCAP program. The program is based on active participation of uniformed patrol and uses the Integrated Criminal Apprehension Program philosophy of data collection, analysis, planning, service delivery, and feedback. Thus, a gang analyst is critical to the process. The major function of the analyst is to provide for the careful, diligent collection and analysis of information to recognize patterns and linkages of gang activity. The gang analyst serves as the central clearinghouse for all gang intelligence information gathered or received by any law enforcement or juvenile-related personnel. Using that information, the analyst builds the strongest possible case file on each gang member involved in serious criminal activity.

Unlike the traditional large city-specialized gang units, Oxnard's gang approach is grounded in the belief that "intelligence" information should be gathered and analyzed for the tactical purposes of the *entire* department. Gang suppression then becomes a shared department responsibility focusing on the strength of patrol resources as the major tactical response to gangs.

Implementation. To address implementation issues, a gang steering committee was formed. Reflecting program strategy, the steering committee is based in operations, thus providing direct communication links with the rest of the department. The committee is chaired by a sergeant and includes the gang analyst, representatives from patrol, a school representative, and an investigator, all of whom sit on the committee while continuing their regular duties.

Last year, during the first phase of the program, the steering committee established the criteria for classifying gang members and gang-related incidents. Once committee members determined the needs of patrol officers, they created a comprehensive data base to aid in the investigation of gang-related crimes and to guide in selective enforcement activities. The committee chose a hardware and software system to store intelligence information on gangs and created a system for disseminating the information to all officers in a usable form.

It is also the responsibility of the steering committee to encourage the cooperation of other juvenile-related agencies such as probation, the schools, and the district attorney, in seeking informed dispositions for gang-related cases.

Tracking gangs and gang members requires a specialized type of analysis. Territorial graffiti, tattoos, symbols, and specialized clothing are all visual images used by gangs in Southern California. For a gang response to be successful, there must be some way of identifying and tracking these visual gang symbols. The department purchased a hardware and software system that combines visual images with a data base, thus providing a new dimension in identification abilities. Using the system, the visual images become part of the data base and can be displayed on demand along with any other stored information. This visual identification feature provides patrol with critical information on the ever-changing movements and activities of gang members.

Conclusion. Like the SHOCAP program, the gang approach uses case management actively to pursue vigorous prosecution of all gang offenders via the Street Terrorism Act. Because of diligent case management and interagency cooperation, this approach enables the probation department to place strict, nonassociation terms on gang members, thus further breaking the bonds between gang members. Uniformed patrol, who are kept apprised of probation terms, assist in enforcement.

As a developmental component of SHOCAP, the GO-CAP program shows promising applicability for most jurisdictions in the United States, and complements and strengthens the city's Community-Oriented Problem Solving (COPS) program.

Problem Analysis Report

We've included a police employee initiated report. It may originate from an officer, dispatcher, cadet, reserve, whatever. It is the basis of proactivity, problem identification and analysis. Thus, it also serves as the basis of POP (see Figure 14–1).

Thanks Chief Owens

Just before his retirement in 1992, Chief Owens spent considerable time with us explaining his COP and POP (COPS) programs. Chief Owens was a member of the Los Angeles County Sheriff's Department when he resigned as a lieutenant and assumed the chief's job in 1960 in San Fernando Valley, California. He was next selected to be the chief in Oxnard in 1971. (The city then had a population of forty-two thousand.) All told, he was a police professional for thirty-four years.

Most of what we've written about, the Fifteen Responsibilities, he subscribed to and daily sought that they were practiced. We can be thankful that he, and others who are now succeeding him, manage and lead our police and sheriff organizations. At all times, Chief Owens sought to "place the ladder against the right wall."

BASIC COMPONENTS

This section covers the essential components of a POP program. Later we'll show you how they fit together.

Component 1: Grouping Incidents as Problems

Police incidents are usually dealt with as stand-alone, unique events. Hence, the first component of POP is to move beyond just incident handling. It requires that incidents be looked on as *symptoms of a problem*. The police have to probe for relationships (how do incidents connect with one another) and conditions (what is the real cause of the problem).

Component 2: Focus on Substantive Problems

Reoccurring problems are substantive problems—or what we think of as *police work*. Police are prone to identify substantive problems in terms of internal

OXNARD POLICE DEPARTMENT
PROBLEM ANALYSIS REPORT

1. SUBMITTED BY: <u>B. Kelley</u>   ID# <u>3399</u>
2. Date Submitted: <u>07-03-94</u>

A. PROBLEM IDENTIFICATION (SCANNING):

3. Describe the Problem: (Who, what, when, where, how, and why)
   Drug usage and dealing from a location historically known as "The Fence".
   Actual address is 232 Avenida Gaviota.

4. Problem Reported by ____ Officers on patrol ____
5. Location of Problem (circle) BEAT 1 ② 3 4 5 6 7
6. Date(s) and Time(s) Problem(s) Occurring <u>Problem has existed in</u>

   various degrees for 30 years.

B. PROBLEM EXAMINATION (ANALYSIS):

7. Shifts affected: (Circle)   I   II   III   IV
8. Division affected: ____Patrol   Investigations____

9. Information Sources: (This list does not include all possible information sources.
   There may be other places where you can get information.) Please indicate <u>all</u>
   sources.

   [xx] Crime Ananlysis Unit   [xx] Parole Office
   [xx] Vice   [xx] Investigations
   [xx] Crime Watch   [xx] Neighborhood Canvass
   [ ] Literature Search   [xx] Citizen Complaints
   [xx] Personal Observations   [ ] Surveys
   [xx] Police Informants   [ ] Churches
   [ ] Schools   [ ] Media
   [ ] Central Records   [xx] Community Leaders
   [xx] Local Businesses   [ ] DMV
   [ ] Other Law Enforcement Agencies
   [ ] Government Agencies, list _____

10. Findings: (Based on the information you have collected, describe the problem.)
    Historically a location that is a gathering point for those persons
    involved in narcotic usage, dealing and other illegal activities.
    Suspects gather on private property behind a wooden picket-type fence
    for purposes primarily to illegally use and deal controlled substances.
    These persons gather with the consent of the resident. Assaults, muggings,
    etc. have occurred to passerbys at the location. Numerous arrests and
    selective enforcement has not eliminated the problem.

Figure 14-1   Problem Analysis Report

C. STRATEGIES (Responses):

11. Goals and Objectives: (What do you expect to accomplish?)

    Eliminate the gathering of persons for illegal activities at the location.

12. Recommended strategies: (how do you expect to obtain the above result?)

    The non-resident owner of the rental property has been located and has agreed to abate the problem. Officer Kelley, the property owner, and the resident have met and the resident has agreed not to allow loiters,

    placed a lock on the gate and to

13. Date and time for implementation: __08-15-94__

    (con't)

14. Expected date and time for termination: _____continual_____

15. Expected number of officers needed: _routine patrol to monitor_

16. Expected number of vehicles needed: __same__ Types: _____

D. SUPERVISORY REVIEW OF STRATEGIES:

[ ] Approved   [ ] Disapproved

Recommendations:

Date: __08-17-94__   Supervisor: _RKelly LT_____

E. EVALUATION (Assessment):

17. Did you get the results you expected?

    [ ] Yes   [ ] No   [ ] Partially   [ ] Temporarily

18. Actual number of Officers Used: _Routine patrol_

19. Actual number of Vehicles Used: _____

20. Actual Number of Hours Used: _____

21. Describe the results of what happened.

22. Is any further action required? If yes, explain.

    Continued monotoring of activities at the location.

23. Additional comments:

    (12) con't.

    sign complaints against trespassers.

Figure 14-1   (Continued)

management (e.g., not enough staff, poor training, malingering officers, low pay). Simply, but importantly, substantive problems are those very problems that justify establishing a police agency in the first place. Making this happen is not easy. The "internal management" habit is tough to break. It takes time and practice. As a supervisor, you're responsible for making the transition.

Component 3: Effectiveness First

Some would attempt to define effectiveness in terms of solving a problem—making something stop or go away. To do this in police work is ridiculous and even counterproductive. After all, zero crime is impossible. Some agencies point with pride to statistics that reveal a reduced increase in crime rates over last year. Effectiveness is defining for a specific agency, in a particular community, what ought to be tackled and in what order of priority.

Component 4: Setting up a System

Once the seemingly random incidents have been categorized into groups, a system for the collection of pertinent facts and their analysis must be designed. Crime and service statistics are helpful but much too limited. Systematic analysis includes (1) telephone questionnaire and individual surveys of those who might know something about the problem (e.g., citizens, victims, officers, offenders, other governmental personnel); and (2) literature searches of government and private sector repositories. Essentially, social scientific tools are applied at this juncture.

Component 5: Redefining Problems

What at first blush may be a traffic problem on further analysis should be categorized as a drug problem. *Problem definition can make or break a POP program.* Is there any doubt that attempting to solve a traffic problem versus a drug problem involves different methods and training? Additionally, there is an enormous difference between thinking tactically about dealing with burglars from a legal viewpoint and coping with burglary as it exists in the community. How we perceive and label a problem ultimately determines how we go after it.

Component 6: Who's Interested (or Should Be)?

Simply viewing conduct as illegal is not efficient in constructing a response to a problem. Because we mentioned gangs earlier (Oxnard), let's consider it as one example. To determine who is or ought to be interested in gang activity, we'd ask: Why is the community concerned? What are the social costs? Who is being harmed and to what degree? There are obviously many more questions of a similar bent. For the police to invent a successful plan to deal with gangs (or any other problem), they must find out who is interested in it. From this set of multiple interests will emerge a plan of attack.

Component 7: What's Working Now

We have witnessed police agencies discard successful operational practices. They tend to leap from one fad or technique to another. Frequently, the officers have the answer, but management fails to ask them. It is here that POP surfaces one of its major strengths—"If it's not broke, don't fix it." If the agency's approach to "espousal abuse" is successful then, unless some other tactic can nearly guarantee an improvement, don't fuss with it.

Component 8: Customized or Canned?

In the 1970s, the criminal justice system was filled with talk of "technology transfer." If a piece of equipment or a program functioned well in one organization, then it could be easily lifted and inserted into another. Many departments borrowed or purchased "turn-key" computers, helicopters, modified work weeks (4-40, 3-12, 5-9, and so on) and a variety of operational programs (e.g., team policing, neighborhood watch, Drug Abuse Resistance and Education). Most found that canned approaches when incorporated in an agency had to be retrofitted, redesigned, and restudied. POP relies on a tailor-made response. Problems are specific to an agency and any method of resolving them must be specific. POP is not saying, however, that agencies should shun the innovations of others. On the contrary, they should be avidly sought out and rigorously examined for potential use. At the same time, POP would caution the interested user—if it appears helpful, then test it and modify it in strict accordance with your department's particular problem.

Component 9: Take the Offensive

Taking the offense is accomplished in three ways. First, the initial identification of problems must be constant and systematic. Second, the police must be active in educating the public and placing choices before it. Third, the police should be advocates for the community (reporting if garbage is uncollected, potholes are unfilled, or vehicles are abandoned).

Component 10: Decision Visibility

More and more we're seeing the officer educating the public on why certain things are or are not done. Decisions are explained. It assists the public in understanding that the police do not have as much authority as they think, and they'll take risks and sometimes fail—they're not infallible.

Component 11: Evaluation and Feedback

Evaluation and feedback are not a concluding POP step. They are designed to support all of the other components in making incremental adjustments and improvements. For example, a reliable evaluation should be able to inform the department if its original grouping of problems was valid. Without this component, POP is likely to fail.

IDENTIFICATION OF PROBLEMS

The identification and definition of police problems encompasses components 1 to 3. It has been often stated that problem identification is two-thirds of the effort in getting a solution. We concur. We also agree that if an option exists, problems ought to be explored as close to the operating level as possible (e.g., Oxnard, California).

Who Identifies Problems

In general, problems will be surfaced by (1) the community; (2) police management; and (3) line employees.

Community. Community involvement in problem identification has benefits and downsides. On the one hand, community members will express their needs and frustrations. On the other, their problems may not involve situations that the police are equipped or obligated to handle. Bluntly, it may be someone else's problem. For example, a needed traffic signal near a senior citizen home is not likely to be something the police can resolve. They may help—but some other agency is actually responsible for installing it. This is where candor and openness count.

Police management. Police managers and supervisors are in a position to see the so-called big picture. We covered the importance of vision earlier. The perceptive, the aware, manager and supervisor can supply vital input to POP.

Line employees. Of the three, the line employees are in the best position to identify problems. We spoke of empowerment earlier. Employees should be not only encouraged but also *rewarded* for their observations and ideas. When we use the term "employees" we include everyone working—paid workers and volunteers, sworn servants and civilians—for the agency.

Problems Are Limitless

Typically, more problems will outcrop than time or resources can address. Once a list has been created, then the problems must be rank ordered. Some of the criteria for achieving this are as follow:

1. Is it really a police problem or not?
2. What is its impact (size and cost) to the community?
3. How much support can be anticipated from the community in tackling it?
4. Does it in any way threaten our civil rights?
5. How much enthusiasm do the police employees possess in combating it?
6. Is it indeed something that can be solved with existing resources?

ANALYSIS OF PROBLEMS

This phase involves components 4 to 7. The analysis of problems includes (1) types of information; (2) sources of information; and (3) scientific rules.

Types of Information

Those who identified the problem in the first place are likely to be the best resource for deciding what kinds of information are needed to solve it. Brainstorming is an excellent technique for arriving at what's required.

Sources of Information

Some of the sources are

1. Existing literature (research reports, current journals, and the like)
2. Police files
3. Knowledge of line employees
4. Victims
5. Community
6. Perpetrators
7. Other agencies (general government and criminal justice)

Scientific Rules

By their very nature, our police are "applied social scientists." They are constantly being challenged to think, act logically, and be objective. Long and detailed reports are turn-offs to many people. POP doesn't demand time-consuming and profound reports. A page or two is sufficient—if it adheres to the facts, and is objective and logical.

The police employee must be alert to such deficiencies as inadequate police files. The current responses to a problem may be confusing and very hard to describe.

OPTIONS

The development of optional choices encompasses components 8 to 10. All right, we've found and analyzed the problem—what now are the options for hammering it? Obviously, the choices are infinite. To gain some focus here, we'll lump them into nine groups while emphasizing that there is a lot of leakage and overlap.

1. *Frequent offenders.* Those few who create many incidents.
2. *Interagency cooperation.* The problem can be handed to another agency or jointly handled.

3. *Conflict management.* "Getting to yes" via mediation and negotiation.

4. *Process of making "public" public information.* This is an underused but potentially highly potent problem-solving tool. Here are some of the uses: (1) reduces fear; (2) helps people solve their own problems; (3) educates people about their rights and responsibilities as citizens; (4) warns possible victims; (5) develops cooperation and support; and (6) indicates what the police can and cannot do.

5. *Galvanizing of citizens.* POP depends on it! It goes beyond informing them to include organizing their support.

6. *Existing controls.* Means authority figures deploying their influence. Examples are teacher-student; apartment manager–renter; parent-child; employer-employee.

7. *Defensible space.* Denotes attempts to fortify our physical environment in some fashion, thus making crime and undesirable behavior more difficult, if not impossible. Alarm systems, antitampering packaging, lighting, and locking systems are a few examples.

8. *Increased or expanded regulations.* Requires a lot of imagination and risk taking. Some police agencies have used city building codes and land-use regulations to combat drug and prostitution problems. One city (Monrovia, California) enacted an ordinance that specifically prohibits loitering in drug-trafficking areas.

9. *Legal intervention.* Also requires experimentation and a willingness to take a chance. For example, some police agencies are placing public inebriates and the mentally ill under "temporary detention." Some are using decoys and sting operations. Some may target or saturate a crime problem such as gang violence. Some may intervene without making an arrest (traffic violations) or making an arrest without intending to prosecute (civil disturbance violations, e.g., "right to life"). More and more police agencies are aggressively confiscating property that aids in, or is the result of, a crime ("asset forfeiture").

CONCLUDING THOUGHT

If POP is approached as a method for improving the police, it will fail. If, however, it is looked on as a way to *solve community problems*, it has a chance of working. The agencies now using POP have demonstrated a willingness to cooperate with others in solving community problems. Further, they've resisted dwelling on the internal shortcomings of their organization. Quality and effectiveness are being redefined, thanks to POP, from "response times" and "crime rates" to *getting solutions*.

KEY POINTS

- Although not identical, POP and COP are highly complementary of one another.

- A strategy encompasses the operational programs and management style for achieving the department's mission.
- A police agency can adopt more than one crime-control strategy—but they must be compatible.
- POP improves on the professional crime strategy by adding *protectiveness* and *thoughtfulness*.
- The common linkage between POP, COP, and the professional crime-fighting model is crime control.
- Patrol work has to be given enhanced status and rewards for POP to be successful.
- POP places effectiveness over efficiency in importance.
- POP is comprised of nine component parts that commence with the *grouping of incidents together* and ends with *evaluation and feedback*.
- Problems should be identified and defined as close to the line level as possible.
- Those who identified the problem are probably in the best position to decide what kinds of information are needed to solve it.
- There are at least nine options for handling a problem.

DISCUSSION

1. What are the similarities and differences between POP and COP?
2. The professional crime-fighting strategy contained two significant flaws. What are they? How does POP avoid them?
3. How does POP differ from the professional crime-fighting strategy?
4. What type of structural changes must be made in an organization as it moves toward POP?
5. What can be done to make patrol work more appealing and prestigious?
6. Which one of the several ingredients of POP is the most important?
7. Eight reasons for POP were listed earlier. Rank order them in terms of their influence on causing POP to happen in police work today.
8. What are "substantive problems"? Can you cite some examples of such a problem?
9. What are the benefits and disadvantages to having the community involved in problem identification?

STRUCTURED EXPERIENCES

The exercises that follow are best handled in groups of six to eight persons.

1. *Problem analysis report.* Return to the "Problem Analysis Report" (Figure 14–1). Identify a problem that your agency is confronted with and complete it. If you do not work for a police agency, then seek to secure the cooperation of a department in completing it. (You may be doing them a big favor.)

2. *Rank ordering problems.* We listed six criteria for rank ordering problems. Apply the criteria to the following problems: (1) armed robbery; (2) drug trafficking; (3) homeless; (4) child abuse; and (5) police corruption. What does your ranking look like?

3. *Options—A.* Earlier we conceptualized at least nine avenues or options for coping with a problem. Can you add one or two more options to our list?

4. *Options—B.* Imagine that you work for a very honest, bright, and outspoken sheriff. His demeanor has irritated your major newspaper to the extent that it blasts him at every opportunity. When he gets the chance, he hits them back verbally. He is in charge of the highly successful regional drug-enforcement team.

   The captain that manages the unit has just informed him that three supervisory employees of the paper are trafficking in cocaine (estimated sales $7,000 per day). The users identified so far number thirty-four, most of whom work for the paper.

   What options does he have? Which one is the best?

5. *Options—C.* Now imagine that you work for one of the leading police chiefs in your state. He reveals to you and a few others that the city manager and city council informed him that the graffiti problem had grown to the point that the city is losing revenues. In the last three years, he has used POP to decrease all part 1 crimes. Nonetheless, they've indicated that his job hinges on him stopping the graffiti. What are his options? Which one is best?

RESPONSIBILITY FIFTEEN

Total Quality Services: A Focus on Excellence

Each day, each product or service is getting relatively better or relatively worse, but it never stands still.

Tom Peters*

We'll commence this, our concluding Responsibility, by returning to our "Overview." You may recall that we referenced Tom Peters, who is an authority on excellence (or the lack of it) in an organization. Except for a few "exceptions," he asserts that our national work ethic does not include quality as a top priority. Large-scale production does, being efficient does, and being the biggest does; however, quality and service are relegated a low priority in his opinion. Service (versus productivity) and quality (versus quantity) began to percolate in the mid-1980s.

For those who would push for a "back to the basics in policing," it would mean a continuation (not a return) of more output at less cost. Alternatively, we see a "new basic," one that accepts nothing less than the provision of total quality police services.

SOME BACKGROUND AND DIRECTION

Please re-read the opening quote by Tom Peters. Obviously, we can point to pockets of excellence in our country. We've seen excellence being successfully pursued by some local law enforcement agencies. The excellence and quality in service movement in our nation did *not* originate here. It started overseas and

---

*Tom Peters, *Thriving on Chaos* (New York: Random House, 1987), p. 80, Reprinted with permission.

much too slowly spread to our borders. Two nations in particular, Japan and Germany, shocked us in "excellence consciousness."

How did this happen? Bluntly, they pummeled corporate America. Do you remember when the word "SONY" meant junk and the Japanese automobiles fell apart? Today, SONY denotes "quality," and the Japanese hold about 30 percent of our car market. (Soon all Japanese automobiles will be manufactured in North American plants.) Incidentally, who manufactured the car you're driving today?

In the late 1940s, a Dr. Deming (an American) harangued American businesses to produce top-quality products and services. Basically, we ignored him. He went to Japan, and they listened! Today the Japanese and Germans are devoted to total quality management (TQM). Some of us are catching on to his message—people want quality—quality this, quality that—and certainly quality police work.

We would note that the Japanese have shifted gears from TQM to zero defects management. The Japanese are attempting to get out in front of their competitors. A few years ago IBM created a senior vice-president position of "market-driven quality." Where are we now in local policing? Are we in front of the burglars, the drug dealers, the juvenile offenders? Can you, can your agency, get out in front of the social problems that daily confront and confuse you?

We acknowledge that this section focuses on that other "sector"—the private sector. We hope you can discern the parallels. Quality is in, quantity is out.

Our hope is that top-drawer quality services will be demanded in your police management. As a supervisor, if it's not, you are still *responsible* for doing so!

To get the best, you've got to give your best. As a police supervisor, to get excellence, you've got to live excellence.

ACCENT ON EXCELLENCE

A few years ago, Thomas Peters and Robert Waterman co-authored a best-selling book *In Search of Excellence* (1982). It captured the attention of millions of readers around the globe. Briefly, they first documented and then revealed how one hundred successful business organizations got that way! Their scientific findings merit your attention. As a police supervisor, you can and should practice the right key principles or basics in your assigned work unit. In doing so, you will be pursuing "excellence." Successful supervisors have an accent on excellence.

Incidentally, a few of the one hundred firms studied fell on hard times. Further research discovered that they had either forgotten or chose to ignore the basic principles that caused their success. Let us now examine the eight ways for you and your co-workers to achieve excellence.

1. *Action.* In their research they found that, although the successful organizations may be analytical in their approach to decision making, they are not

paralyzed by that fact (as so many others seem to be). In many of these organizations the standard operating procedure is "Do it, fix it, try it." Hence, one primary step toward excellence in your work unit is a bias for action, for getting on with it.

2. *Client–citizen–community.* The effective organizations learn from the people they serve. They provide unparalleled quality, service, and reliability—things that work, help, and last. Everyone gets into the act. Many innovative organizations got their best product/service ideas from clients. That comes from listening, intently and regularly. The message here is clear: Get to know your community and the people you serve. Stay close to the community.

3. *Practical risk taking.* The innovative companies foster many leaders and many innovators throughout the organization. They are a hive of what we've come to call champions. They don't try to hold everyone on so short a rein that he or she can't be creative. They encourage practical risk taking and support good tries. Getting results automatically entails risk taking. Thus, exercise your autonomy and risk taking.

4. *Results through people.* The excellent organizations treat the rank and file as the root source of quality and productivity gain. They do not foster we/they labor attitudes or regard raw output as the fundamental source of efficiency improvement. Remember the definition of a TEAM: *T*ogether *E*veryone *A*chieves *M*uch.

5. *Values and MBWA.* Thomas Watson, Jr., chairman emeritus of IBM, said that "the basic philosophy for an organization has far more to do with its achievements than do technological or economic resources, organizational structure, innovation and timing." Watson and Hewlett–Packard's William Hewlett are legendary for walking the plant floors. During his tenure, McDonald's Ray Kroc regularly visited stores and assessed them on the factors the company holds dear—quality, service, cleanliness, and value.

   The point here is to manage (supervise) by walking (or driving) around (MBWA). When doing so, continually emphasize the underlying values of your department. Hands-on, value driven!

6. *Keep to the basics.* Robert W. Johnson, former Johnson & Johnson chairman, repeatedly told his managers: "Never acquire a business you don't know how to run." In other words, concentrate on your basic police mission. Stick to the knitting!

7. *Simple form, lean staff.* The underlying structural forms and systems in the excellent organizations are elegantly simple. Top-level staffs are lean: it is not uncommon to find a management staff of fewer than fifty people running multimillion-dollar enterprises. Police work is performed by the line sworn employee. Everything and everyone should view their job accordingly. Your job is to make their job as easy as possible. Unfortunately, some police supervisors opt to take the opposite approach.

8. *Centralized values, decentralized decisions.* The excellent organizations are both centralized and decentralized. For the most part, they have

pushed autonomy down to the line level. Conversely, they are fanatic centralists around the few core values they hold dear. The point being: make certain that the police personnel are (1) making decisions, and (2) making decisions in accordance with professional and departmental values. Simultaneous loose–tight properties!

ALIGNMENT

Have you ever driven a vehicle that is out of alignment? Typically, you can feel it in the steering wheel. Soon you'll observe uneven wear in the tires. Your gas consumption usually increases.

Have you ever worked in an organization that is out of alignment? Typically, you can detect it in the steering. Soon you'll observe uneven wear in the staff. Your energy consumption becomes excessive.

Organizations, like cars, require alignment to achieve excellence. This exercise will reveal how much alignment you believe your organization has.

To Begin with

We're quick to acknowledge that the eight points from the Peters and Waterman study on excellence did not include police organizations in their research base. However, we'd argue that organizations are just that—organizations. Plainly, it doesn't matter!

There are some who would allege—we're different, we're unique. In some ways, we concur. Yes, the local bank does not resemble the local police department. Yes, the regional discount store is vastly different from the county sheriff's department.

Nevertheless, in many significant ways they're alike. They have values, they have goals, they have ethics and standards, they have managers and supervisors, and they have much more in common.

Consequently, we're convinced that the eight dimensions or standards of excellence for private organizations equally apply (or should apply) to their public sector cousins. Let's now apply them to your organization and, in turn, gain a perspective on its degree of excellence.

Eight Dimensions of Excellence

Figure 15–1 depicts a "hub of excellence" and eight "spokes." Imagine this as a wheel of a bicycle. The more round, the more expanded or inflated the wheel, the better your trip. Conversely, if the outer rim is uneven and lacks symmetry, then a rough ride is awaiting. We'll briefly describe each dimension. Afterward make a mark on the specific spoke that pertains to that dimension. For example, if your police organization is (in your opinion) fairly active, then you'd place an *X* halfway or more out on that spoke.

Evaluation of Organizational Excellence

Bias for action
*

Client-citizen-* community		*Values and MBWA
Practical* risk taking	0	*Keep to the basics
Results through* people		*Simple form, lean staff

*
Centralized values, decentralized decisions

Figure 15-1 Evaluation of Organizational Excellence

1. *Bias for action.* Some police organizations creep along, some speed along, some don't move at all, and some move perhaps too fast. Where is your police agency today on the action dimension? Does it take appropriate action? Does it recognize and cope with incoming challenges? Do you have a sense of movement, a sense of taking the initiative, a sense of taking the lead? Think and make a mark on the "action spoke."

2. *Client—citizen—community.* We'll paraphrase the preceding comments about this dimension. "Effective police departments learn from the people they serve. They provide unparalleled quality, service, and reliability—things that work, help and last." Further, these police agencies "get to know their community and the people they serve. They stay close to their community." Does your agency, do the officers listen to its citizens (clients)? Is it open—better yet, eliciting ideas—about how it can improve services? Does it really want to know what the citizens want? Do you see the police officer or deputy sheriff candidly interact with people on a daily basis? Are they in touch? Are you in touch? Do you really know what is going on in the minds and hearts of the people you work for? Place a mark on the spoke that pertains to this dimension. (In doing so, keep your department in focus—not yourself.)

3. *Practical risk taking.* We've heard some police managers inform their staff, "Go ahead and take a risk. That's a part of your job. If you make a mistake, I'll be back you." One person, then, makes a risky decision that fails. And, guess what? The manager chews him out. (The manager would probably refer to his reaction as "constructive criticism.")

   In thinking about risk taking, an up-and-coming IBM vice-president made a decision that cost the company $10 million. Even for IBM, that's a lot of money to lose. The young vice-president was summoned into the chairman's office—Thomas Watson, Jr. He asked the vice-president to explain the reasoning behind his failed decision. Watson then pointed out a few flaws in his logic and indicated he was free to leave. The vice-president spoke out, "I thought you were going to fire me." Watson retorted, "Fire you. Hell, we've just spent $10 million in educating you!"

What is the degree of support for taking risks in your department? Does management have a high or low tolerance for mistakes? Do people believe that they'll be supported in making decisions that include some type or level of risk? Or, do you see the staff comfortable in making only the routine, the easy, the safe decisions? Place a mark on the spoke that pertains to the amount of practical risk taking that you see occurring in your police agency.

4. *Results through people.* Do you recall the episode involving Maynard and his chief (Responsibility Eight)? He has on the front of his desk a placard that reads "When I want your opinion, I'll give it to you."

We were talking to a sheriff one day about his management style. He commented, "I'm a believer in participative management. I'm going to manage, and you're going to participate!"

Years ago, a newly appointed lieutenant walked into his roll call. He introduced himself to the twenty-plus officers and sergeants who were seated. He went on to say, "If you wonder what I think about you people, I look at you as a bunch of warts." Until his retirement, he was referred to as Lieutenant Wart.

Conversely, we can cite many situations in which organizations have realized the importance of teamwork; have realized the importance of empowerment; have realized the importance of stewardship delegation. Moreover, these organizations are *behaving* likewise. They're not merely stating that their human resources are their most vital asset. They're living it on a daily basis—they're doing it.

We know of police organizations in which the managers and supervisors are out of their offices, away from their desks, and interacting with their staff. They provide witness to the fact that each person counts, what they think counts, and what they need counts. They treat everyone as a part of the team. No second-class personnel! The detectives are not smarter than or better than the patrol officer. When transferred into patrol, you're not "going back to patrol." The civilians attend roll-call training with the sworn personnel. In fact, they're not referred to as civilians but as "general government employees." Simply put, *everyone is on the team.* Everyone has a part to play.

Place a mark on the spoke that will indicate the amount of emphasis your department places on the human factor and teamwork.

5. *Values and MBWA.* Many pages ago, we started our journey into this book by emphasizing that supervisors must first know their own values, then the values (mission) of their department, and finally the values of each individual who works for them. The very work of the department depends on such a three-part understanding. Without it both communica-

tions and trust will suffer. Hence, any attempt at excellence will be severely undercut.

We see more and more mission statements being displayed in police facilities, radio cars, and neighborhood locations. We know of deputy sheriffs and police officers who have committed all or most of their mission statement to memory. They *believe in it* and are *behaving accordingly.* If you're looking for an example of what we're seeing, write the Sheriff of Riverside County, California, and ask to borrow their audio-video tape that in five minutes clearly conveys what the agency stands for.

Peter Marshall best summarizes what we're driving at when he said, "Help us stand for something, lest we fall for anything." Mission Statements, which are acted on, serve this cause.

Do you know the mission of your agency? Do you know its values? Are the managers and the supervisors doing MBWA? Place your mark on the appropriate spoke where you believe it should be at this point in time.

6. *Adherence to the basics.* Your mission statement should help you and others adhere to the basics—pursuing your intended goals as compared with false or useless goals. On occasion we've seen police agencies take on goals and prospects that are out of their purview. For example, one agency set up an elaborate AV studio when it could save money and staff time by using an outside professional resource.

As we view police work, it is primarily intended to keep us from being victimized, and, when victimized, to apprehend the perpetrator and return anything stolen from us. Anything else should be weighed carefully before being included as service. Are there staff and are there projects that are questionable in line with your basic mission? You might go so far, if you're accredited, to ask of yourself, "Is it really worth it? Who has benefited? How much does it cost us in real dollars and staff time? Has accreditation helped us 'stick to the basics'?"

Go to the proper spoke and place a mark on it now.

7. *Simple form, lean staff.* Years ago one of us played on a community college team that went to the Junior Rose Bowl. The day before the game, we attended a luncheon with our opponents. Our head coach introduced his six assistants and forty-one players. Their head coach introduced his two assistants and twenty-six players. The next day we lost 13-7!

Typically, sergeants and above in rank are an "overhead" expense. Although important, they usually *do not produce police services.* Police officers produce police services. As a consequence, police officers are easier to justify. For example, one can calculate the number of police services produced per budget dollar and per citizen. When it comes to sergeants and police managers, this formula or any other formula (such as eight police officers per sergeant) becomes highly subjective. *There must be a definitive and defensible argument for adding or retaining overhead in any organization.*

It is most common for police managers to want to add supervisory and managerial positions. How many chiefs and sheriffs have volunteered to reduce the number of captains or lieutenants? We know of a few; most others will vigorously defend their overhead positions. It's a natural instinct on our part to want to build or expand rather than curtail or decrease.

We know of one police agency which overreacted to the challenge of downsizing. The chief announced that the numerous tiers in the department severely impaired communications. His decision was to eliminate the sergeant's position. That's right, the first-line supervisor! All sergeants were immediately promoted to lieutenants. As lieutenants retire, the newly created positions would be reduced to the original number. The number of captains, majors, and deputy chiefs remained constant. It took only three months for the chief to learn his mistake. He nearly lost his job over his decision. (The sergeant's job was restored after six months.)

Look at your organization, look at the structure, and look at the staffing of overhead positions. Is it lean, is it simple? Go to the right spoke and make your mark as you see it.

8. *Centralized values, decentralized decisions.* Here the police agency is challenged to link centrally shared values to dispersed decision making. Much like a superb orchestra, everyone has the same music sheet (values) but are performing different functions (decisions) with it.

Think of commonly held values as a guiding navigational star. The steersman of a ship sights the star and follows it. He may steer starboard, straight ahead, port, or even reverse engines. The star serves as the core value system and thereby determines if the decision maker shifts right, moves forward, bears left, or backs up.

The real trick to establishing centralized values and decentralized decisions surpasses values and decisions. The real challenge is to *bond* them. For example, if my police agency has a core value of integrity and it is linked to my decisions, then anything other than a totally honorable act on my part just won't happen. My "integrity star" automatically steers my decision in the direction of morality.

Forging core values to one's decisions takes a great deal of effort. It can be done, it is being done, but all fifteen responsibilities must be activated. We're reminded of the military drill sergeant shouting at the new recruits, "Move, move, move!"

In the early 1970s, one of us was driving too fast in a city that had just elected a reform government and appointed a new chief who pronounced an anticorruption administration. The police officer walked up to my car and asked for my operator's license. I handed it to him. He commented, "O.K., forty-five miles per hour in a thirty-five per hour zone. You can pay the court or you can pay me." I was surprised and asked, "I thought your new chief was against this practice?" He replied, "What he does is his business; what I do is my business." Clearly, the centralized values were not resulting in the correct decentralized decision—at least for this officer.

If you know your department's core values, are they influencing your decisions and the decisions of others? Place a mark on this particular spoke now.

How Do I Look

Many years ago Steve McQueen played a French criminal nicknamed "Papillon" who was sentenced to Devils Island. His rebellious behavior resulted in his being assigned to solitary confinement for six months. A new prisoner was being put into a solitary cell. He looked out of his bars after five months and gasped, "How do I look?" He did not know what he looked like—he had no mirror, no reflection instrument. The exercise you've just finished informs you on how your organization (not you) looks. Or, what *you* think it looks like, and that counts a lot.

Now connect the eight spokes by drawing a straight line from one to another. You're probably seeing a jagged wheel in front of you. If your wheel has deep indentations, obviously it will mean a rough ride, low excellence. If your wheel has a fully expanded circle, then it will produce a smooth or excellent ride. Those supervisors and managers who are dedicated to excellence are constantly seeking to perfect the circle—make it fully round, make it *excellent.*

Action plans are most useful in defining and promoting excellence. Let's now take a look at action planning.

DEVELOPMENT OF ACTION PLANS FOR EXCELLENCE

Excellence does not happen by random chance. You must plan for it. And once planned for, acted on. Action planning includes the following interrelated steps:

1. Area of concern
2. Objective
3. Action plan

- What
- Who?
- When?
- Resources required?

Let us flush in these steps with the example in Table 15–1.

BUILDING OF EXCELLENCE

The building of excellence requires work—a lot of work. Some of us tolerate mediocrity. After all, it doesn't require a lot of work. Do the accepted minimum and get by. Our private-sector counterparts did so for a couple of decades

TABLE 15-1. Sample Action Plan

Area of concern
Employee orientation: Police employees do not think that important information about the department is accessible to them.

Objective
Develop a method to transmit important information to police employees in a timely manner.

Action plan
What:	Produce a thirty-minute video tape on a quarterly basis, where key police supervisors discuss what is going on in the organization. Give police employees an opportunity to view the tape and ask questions abut the presentation or on any other items of interest at one-hour departmental meetings.
Who:	Police chief and management team.
When:	First tape by July 15, 1996, budget.
Required:	1996 budget, $100.00.

and look where they are today. Fortunately, we see more and more police organizations awakening to the growing citizen demand for *quality* police services.

Police chiefs and sheriffs are realizing that their citizens have policing alternatives. For one, if the chief and sheriff are guilty of sloppy leadership and inept police practices, they can be removed from office. For another, if a police agency proves to be constantly deficient, the community leaders can disband it and contract for services from another police department or the sheriff. The days of "take my police services or lump it" are on the wane.

As a consumer, when you buy a product, you want it to perform up to its proclaimed standards. A forty thousand–mile tire should last at least forty thousand miles. The hotel room you rent should be clean and the staff courteous. The police officer, deputy sheriff, or state patrol officer should adhere to professional standards, be courteous, and furnish quality services.

Quantity of services isn't being rejected; we need productive officers. However, *quality of services* is being added as an equal participant in pursuing excellence.

Building excellence requires, in addition to the eight standards discussed earlier, the use of the following six tools. All six tools are actually offshoots of one or more of the original standards. The original standard is listed after its subsidiary. The original eight axioms are still valid; only in the past few years we've seen a few new twists to them.

• Customer responsiveness (client–citizen)
• Customer feedback (client–citizen)
• Fast-paced innovation (bias for action)

- Employee empowerment (results through people)
- Urgency to change (bias for action)
- New systems (simple form, lean staff)

Customer Responsiveness

The people needing police services can be referred to as customers, clients, citizens, criminals, and more. We prefer the term *customers*. Granted, these customers encompass such people as murderers, spouse beaters, hate criminals, and drug abusers. Nonetheless, they deserve the same quality of service that the major, judge, superstar athlete, or medical doctor expect.

The excellent police organizations seek to add value by developing services that truly satisfy the customer. The organization knows its community and what it wants. It is constantly open to, and actively listens to, its customers. The line personnel—sworn and civilian—are recognized and treated as its "marketing" arm. The entire organization displays a wholesale external orientation. Customer whims are converted into customer support. A linkage is forged between the police and the customer.

Fast-Paced Innovation

Police departments have been typically reactive. A traffic problem occurs, and it creates a traffic enforcement unit. A drug abuse condition emerges, and it constructs a drug enforcement program. Our earlier discussion of problem-oriented policing suggested such an approach. Only the reaction was *swift, immediate, concentrated,* and *creative.*

In this instance, we would add one more ingredient—*innovation.* The organization not merely permits but demands creative approaches for meeting customer interests. Our files contain thousands of highly imaginative ideas and actions on the part of police personnel. If asked, there's no more imaginative group of people than police employees.

Employee Empowerment

This tool is obviously a part of "getting results through people." Responsibility Nine covered this subject. Please peruse it and refresh your memory.

Customer Feedback

Ken Blanchard, the co-author of the celebrated *One Minute Manager,* has frequently underscored feedback by stating that, "Feedback is the breakfast of champions." We know a few police chiefs and sheriffs who do not want to know what is on the mind of their employees, let alone their customers. Basically, they operate in a vacuum, hoping that customer indifference will allow them to stay in office. And, unfortunately, our apathy often fosters their lack of caring about people—customers and employees alike.

Alternatively, we know of many chiefs and sheriffs who energetically solicit feedback. They want—no demand—evaluative feedback. They probe for their successes and their failings. They're convinced that the customer and employee count! Hence, they're asking the key question, "How do I, how do we look?"

Urgency to Change

This relates to the standard of "a bias for action." This tool, however, stresses "change" as compared with action. Action can mean more of the same, only at a faster clip. Conversely, change denotes a lot of movement—only it is "newness centered."

The effective sheriffs, police chiefs, other managers, and supervisors are always seeking a new way, a better way, for getting the job done. Why the urgency to change? Plainly, if you don't, you'll discover your *effectivity* is devolving into *ineffectivity*, and your *efficiency* is devolving into *inefficiency*.

We know of a police manager who at staff meetings asks, "What have you changed lately?" *We're not advocating change for the pure sake of change.* That would be stupid and wasteful. We are, however, recommending that everything be put up to scrutiny. Every rule, every procedure should be questioned as follows: "Is it practical? Is it productive? Is it dependable? Is it efficient? Why do we have this rule, procedure, or way of doing police work?"

New Systems

"New systems" is a catchall. It means everything should be changed (as indicated earlier). The difference is that any change should result in a new way of doing things. Creating change without a replacement system for conducting one's work is dangerous. It's like, "Let's completely change the regional narcotic task force! Regretfully, I have no idea about what it should be changed to."

New systems should seek to promote the "right stuff" (e.g., quality, innovation, flexibility, and especially bureauracy bashing).

Trust is the bonding agent that holds a police agency together in times of turbulence and gives the necessary stability to encourage constant reconfiguring. All of this requires a *system* for getting from *A* to *B*.

ON YOUR WAY: THE EXCELLENT SUPERVISOR

We have tried to avoid detailed, step-by-step advice; we have drawn your attention to a lot of things at once. In fulfilling the 15 responsibilities, it might be best for you to use the Zen tennis approach: Focus on the ball going back over the net and where you want it to land. Your swing and positioning will follow naturally. Only in this case, you are focusing on the responsibilities. At first this may seem awkward or even overwhelming. Don't be discouraged. Maintain your focus and the rest will happen. The responsibilities will become an integrated and very natural part of you.

Remember, the road to excellence is always under construction. Have a happy trip—the journey will be well worth it.

Index

A

Aberdene, Patricia, 58
Accountability:
  and COP program, 306–7
  and integrity, 39
Achievement, need for, 121
Ad hoc meetings, 85
Adjudication, 229
Affiliation, need for, 121
Age, and job satisfaction, 130
Alderfer, Clayton, 121
Alignment, 334–39
All I Really Need to Know I Learned in Kindergarten (Fulghum), 89
Alpha II suggested regulations sheet, 209–10
Altruistic egoism, and stress reduction, 263
Ascribed attributes, 275
Attitude shifts, and COP programs, 306–8
Authority, 47–48
  and rewards, 48
Avoidance, and conflict resolution, 217
Awareness, and police work groups, 206

B

Barriers to communication, 89–90
BARS, *See* Behaviorally anchored rating scale (BARS)

Beat officers, empowerment of, 307
Beat redesign, and COP program, 307
Behaviorally anchored rating scale (BARS), 179–80, 181, 183
Behavioral theory, 51
Bennis, Warren, 58
Blanchard, Ken, 341
Body language, 76–78, 275
Brown, Lee P., 305
Budgets, 143

C

Category II supervisor, 105–10
  action/flexibility of, 110
  goals of, 108
  mission statement, 105–7
  roles of, 107–8
  schedule of, 108–10
  See also Time management
Central-tendency errors, 166
Channel blockage, coping with, 91–92
Citizen complaints, 223–29
  adjudication, 229
  complaint receipt, 223–28
  investigation, 228
Citizen relations, 220–23
Civilian personnel, 55

Communication, 5, 60–61, 68–97
  barriers to, 89–90
    removing, 90–92
  communication networks, 86–87
  and decision making, 69
  definition of, 69–71
  downward communications, 78–80
  formal communication channels, 72
  horizontal communications, 80–81
  informal communication channels,
    72–75
  and leadership, 60–61, 68–69
  messages, 81–86
    types, 82–86
    volume, 82
  nonverbal communication, 76–78
  oral communication, 75
  structured experiences, 94–97
    empathetic listening, 96–97
    group communications, 95–96
    mutual understanding, 94–95
  and technology, 87–89
  and trust, 69
  upward communications, 80
  written communication, 75–76
  See also Messages
Communication networks, 86–87
Community-oriented policing (COP), 7,
    296–311
  benefits:
    to police, 309
    to public, 308–9
  central mission, 298–301
  citizen response, 304
  continued growth of, 304–5
  effectiveness, 296–97
  first line of defense, 302–3
  forces driving, 303–4
  implementation, 305–8
    attitude shifts, 306–8
    phases of, 306
    philosophy of supervision, 308
  innovation, 305
  new police leadership, 305
  quality, case for, 302
  research on effectiveness of, 304
  specific mission statements, 298–300
  structured experiences, 311
  universal mission statement, 297–98
Compromise, and conflict resolution, 217

Conflict-Management Climate Index,
    242–44
  scoring and interpretation sheet, 244
Conflict resolution, 6, 19, 213–44
  conflict:
    as plus/minus, 215–16
    sources of, 216
    value of, 216
  internal consequences of conflict,
    215–18
  intervention, 231–34
  negotiations, 230–37
  police supervisor role, 214
  problem employees, 218–23
  structured experiences:
    case studies, 239–42
    Conflict-Management Climate Index,
      242–44
  tactical routes for, 217–18
  See also Citizen complaints;
      Intervention; Problem employees
Conformity, and police work groups,
    206–7
COP programs, See Community-oriented
    policing (COP)
Counseling, 183
Covey, Steve, 7, 58, 271
Culture building, 40
Custom-designed wellness programs, 267
Customer feedback, 341–42
Customer responsiveness, 341

D

Decentralization, and COP program,
    306–7
Decision making, 34–38, 69, 85
  fast vs. slow decisions, 102
  and police work groups, 207–8
Delegation, 191–96
  benefits of, 192–93
  context setting, 193–94
  letting go, 192
  lonership delegation, 194–95
  ownership delegation, 195–96
  purpose of, 191
  and trust, 196–97
  See also Empowerment
Deming, W. Edwards, 2–4

Departmental goals, 57–58
Diseases of adaptation, 248
Dissatisfaction, and value changes, 16–17
Dissatisfiers, 122
Distress, 253
Downward communications, 78–80
Drucker, Peter, 58

E

Education:
  in ethics, 41–43
  of work force, 54
Electronic mail (E-mail), 87
Emotions, as personal form of stress,
    250–51
Empathetic listening, 76–78
Employee orientation, 51
Employee-oriented supervision:
  conflict resolution, 213–44
  empowerment and participation,
    190–212
Empowerment, 3–4 316, 341
  of beat officers, 307
  definition of, 190–91
  and delegation, 191–96
  and participation, 6, 190–212
  police work groups, 206–7
  quality circles, 199–206
  structured experiences, 209–12
    Alpha II suggested regulations sheet,
      209–10
    delegation, 210–11
    empowerment, 211–12
  See also Delegation; Participation;
    Quality circles
Endocrine system, and stress, 249
Environment, and job satisfaction, 130
Environmental stress, 251
Equity theory, 123–24
ERG theory, 121
Ethical competence, 42
Ethical issues, anticipating/recognizing,
    42
Ethics, 33–46
  and decision making, 34–38
  enhancing, 39–44
    collaboration, 40–41
    education and training, 41–43

  inspiration, 39–40
  integration, 43–44
  and ethos, 33–34
  integrity, fostering, 38–39
  structured experiences, 45–46
    dealing with citizens, 45–46
Ethnicity, 54–55
Eustress, 253
Excellence:
  achieving, 332–34
  action plans for, 339
  building, 339–42
    customer feedback, 341–42
    customer responsiveness, 341
    empowerment, 341
    innovation, 341
    new systems, 342
    urgency to change, 342
  dimensions of, 334–39
Expansion of resources, and conflict
    resolution, 217
Expectancy theory, 126–28
Expert power, 48–49

F

FAX machines, 87–89
Feedback:
  customer, 341–42
  of police supervisor, 24
  and SBO, 151
Field training officer (FTO), 280
Filtering, 89
Filters, 18
Forcing, and conflict resolution, 217–
    18
Formal communication channels, 72
Front-line bias, 57–58
Fulghum, Robert, 89

G

Gangs, 318–21
  migration of, 318–19
  SHOCAP program, 319–21
    implementation, 320
    traditional response to, 319
Gender, 54–55

General adaptation syndrome (GAS),
    247, 249
Global rating scales (GRS), 166
Goal setting, 6, 138–55
    definition of, 139–41
    and job satisfaction, 132
    and management by objectives (MBO),
        143–48
    multiplicity of goals, 140
    and planning, 141–43
    police supervisor role, 139
    real vs. stated goals, 140
    structured experiences, 153–55
        case study, 153–54
        goal setting exercise, 154–55
        goal substitution exercise, 155
    supervision by objectives, 148–51
    See also Job satisfaction; Management
        by objectives (MBO); Planning;
        Supervision by objectives (SBO)
Goal-setting theory, 124
Graves, Clare, 16–17
Group dynamics, teamwork, 288–89
Group unity, 41
Guidance, 26, 27
Guidelines, specifying, 41
Guilt-trippers, 252

H

Halo errors, 166
Herzberg's motivation-hygiene theory, 122
Horizontal communications, 80–81
Hyperstress, 251–52, 253
Hypostress, 252, 253

I

ICMA Code of Ethics, 37
Imprinting, as source of values, 15
Independence, and police work groups,
    206–7
Individuality, acceptance of, 132
Informal communication channels, 72–75
    personal nontask-directed, 74–75
    personal task-directed, 74
    subformal, 73–74
Information, and communication, 71
Information overload, 89–90
Innovation, 305, 341

Inquiry, 84
In Search of Excellence
        (Peters/Waterman), 332
Integrity, 26–27
    fostering, 38–39
Interdependence, 289
Intervention, 231–34
    and conflict prevention, 233–34
    supervisory attributes, 233–34
    where/when/how, 231–32
Intrinsic rewards, and job satisfaction, 131
Investigation:
    of citizen complaints, 228
    and COP program, 307

J

Job analysis, 162–63, 181, 183
Job satisfaction, 128–33
    causes of, 129–30
    and environment, 130, 131
    and goal setting, 132
    individuality, acceptance of, 132
    and intrinsic rewards, 131
    matching people to jobs, 132
    and monetary rewards, 131–32
    and morale, 129
    and rewards, 132–33
Job Satisfaction Questionnaire, 136–37
Job-Time Analysis Form, 112–13
Johnson, Robert W., 333

K

Kroc, Ray, 333

L

Lateral communications, 80–81
Laws/rules, limitations of, 40
Leadership, 5, 47–67
    authority, 47–48
    behavioral theory, 51
    by example, 39–40
    definition of, 49–50, 65
    goals, 57–58
    leadership challenges, 54–56
    leadership paradigm, 58–64
    power, 48–49

self-management, 58
situational theory, 51–54
structured experiences, 66–67
  leadership characteristics, 67
  questionnaire, 66–67
and teamwork, 288
trait theory, 50–51
Leadership paradigm, 58–64
  communication, 60–61
  positioning, 61–63
  positive self-regard, 63–65
  vision, 59–60
Legalistic misconduct, 221–23
Leniency errors, 166
Listening skills, 71, 76–78
Lonership delegation, 194–95
Los Angeles County Sheriff's Department,
  mission statement, 298, 300
Loyalty, 54

M

McClelland, David, 121
McCormack, Mark, 102
Management by objectives (MBO), 2,
  143–48, 183–84
  definition of, 143–44
  dynamics of, 145
  goals vs. objectives, 144–45
  objective-setting, responsibility for, 146
  obstacles to, 151–52
  performance measurement, 146–47
  philosophy of management/supervision,
    147–48
  specific objectives, 145–46
  supervisor assumptions, 147
  See also Supervision by objectives (SBO)
Managing by wandering around
  (MBWA), 104, 333, 336–37
Marshall, Peter, 337
Maslow's hierarchy of needs, 120
Matching people to jobs, 132
Meetings:
  purposes of, 85
  types of, 85–86
Memorandum, 84
Mental discipline, and stress reduction,
  262
Message blockage, reducing, 91
Messages:
  types, 82–86

oral, 85–86
  written, 83–85
volume, 82
Misconduct, 221–23
  legalistic misconduct, 221–23
  moralistic misconduct, 223
  professional misconduct, 223
Mission statements, 105–7
  specific, 298–300
  universal, 7, 297–98
Modeling, as source of values, 15
Monetary rewards, and job satisfaction,
  131–32
Morale, 129
Moralistic discretion, and integrity, 39
Moralistic misconduct, 223
Moralizing, about ethics, 41–42
Motivation, 6, 20, 117–37
  definition of, 118–19
  and job satisfaction, 128–33
    morale, 129
  need theories of, 120–23
    achievement, power, affiliation
      needs, 121
    ERG theory, 121
    Herzberg's motivation-hygiene
      theory, 122
    Maslow's hierarchy of needs, 120
  police supervisor role, 117–18
  process theories of, 123–28
    equity theory, 123–24
    expectancy theory, 126–28
    goal-setting theory, 124
    reinforcement theory, 125–26
  structured experiences, 134–37
    Job Satisfaction Questionnaire,
      36–37
    motivation factors in the job, 134–35
  and work performance, 128–33
Moving, as training strategy, 283

N

Naisbett, John, 58, 249
Need theories of motivation, 120–23
  achievement, power, affiliation needs,
    121
  ERG theory, 121
  Herzberg's motivation-hygiene theory,
    122
  Maslow's hierarchy of needs, 120

Negotiations, 230–37
  analysis, 237
  discussion, 237
  hard vs. soft approach, 235–36
  interests, concentrating on, 236
  objective criteria, adopting, 237
  options, generating, 236–37
  planning, 237
  positional bargaining, 235
  principled negotiations, 234–35
  separating people from conflict, 236
  See also Conflict resolution;
    Intervention
Nervous system, and stress, 249
New systems, 342
Nonverbal communication, 76–78
Nonverbal cues, 90

O

One Minute Manager (Blanchard), 341
One-way communication, 71
Operational planning, 143
Oral communication, 75
Oral messages, 85–86
  meetings, 85–86
  telephone conversations, 86
Organization:
  and job satisfaction, 130
  values of, 24–27
Organizational/social stress, 251–52
  hyperstress, 251–52
  hypostress, 252
  problem personalities, 252
  uncertain conditions, 252
Organizational values:
  guidance, 26
  power, 27
  security, 24–25
  self-esteem, 25–27
  wisdom, 27
Otherness, and stress reduction, 262–63
Owens, Robert, 317, 321
Ownership delegation, 195–96

P

Participation:
  and empowerment, 6, 190–212

misconceptions about, 198
and police work groups, 207
purpose of, 198–99
Participative supervision, 207–8
Perception, 70–71, 272, 273–78
  characteristics:
    of perceiver, 275–77
    of person perceived, 274–75
    of situation, 275
  definition of, 273–74
  perceptual shortcuts, 277, 278
  police supervisor role, 273
  and teamwork, 277–78
  and training, 277–78
Perfectionists, 252
Performance, and value clarification,
  22
Performance domain rating scale
  (PDRS), 166–78, 181, 183
Performance evaluation, 6, 146–47,
  156–89
  complexity of, 158–59
  and COP program, 308
  counseling, 183
  definition of, 158
  job analysis, 162–63, 181, 183
  management by objectives (MBO),
    183–84
  methods of, 164–80, 181
    behaviorally anchored rating scale
      (BARS), 179–80, 181, 183
    global rating scales (GRS), 166
    performance domain rating scale
      (PDRS), 166–78, 181, 183
  police supervisor role, 157–58
  purpose of, 159–84
  and quality, 156–57
  raters, 181–82, 183
    evaluating, 182
  reliability of procedure, 160–61
  significant (critical) incidents
    database, 182–83
  structured experiences, 185–89
    case study, 185
    performance appraisal practice
      session, 185–89
  system design/implementation, 181–
    84
  validity of procedure, 161–62
Permanent assignments, and COP
  program, 307

Personal forms of stress:
emotions, 250–51
power, 251
Personal goals, 57–58
Peters, Tom, 2, 58, 102, 104, 305
Physical appearance, perception of, 274–75
Planning:
definition of, 141–42
and goal setting, 141–43
and negotiations, 237
purpose of, 142
types of, 142–43
Police Code of Conduct, 36
Police supervisor:
conflict resolution, 214
feedback of, 24
goal setting, 139
motivation, 117–18
organizational-environmental values, 22–23
perception, 273
performance evaluation, 157–58
performance of, 23–24
position and person, 22
responsibility of, 23
stress, 246–48
training, 278–79
as value driven, 22–24
Police work groups, 206–7
POP programs, See Problem-oriented policing (POP)
Position:
and authority, 48
and person, 22
Positioning, 61–63
Positive self-regard, 63–65
competency, 63
other-regard, 63
three sides of, 64–65
Wallenda factor, 64
Power, 27, 48–49
need for, 121
as personal form of stress, 251
Power sharing, and COP program, 307
Principled negotiations, 234–35
Proactive tactics, 301
Problem employees, 218–23
citizen complaints, 223–29
citizen relations, 220–23
helping, 219–20

misconduct, 221–23
preventing, 229–30
recognizing, 218–19
supervisors/managers as, 219
worker relations, 218–20
See also Citizen complaints
Problem-oriented policing (POP), 7, 312–30
components of, 321–25
departmental strategy, 313
example of, 316–21
Aleric Street case study, 317–18
gangs, 318–21
problem analysis report, 321, 322–23
options, 327–28
problem analysis, 327
problem identification, 326
purpose of, 313–15
reasons for use of, 315–16
Problem personalities, and organizational/social stress, 252
Problem solving, and COP program, 306
Process intervention, See Intervention
Process theories of motivation, 123–28
equity theory, 123–24
expectancy theory, 126–28
goal-setting theory, 124
reinforcement theory, 125–26
Professional misconduct, 223
Programs, 143
Proposal, 85
Public affirmation, and value clarification, 22

Q

Quality circles, 199–206
benefits of, 204
building, 201–3
components of, 200–201
definition of, 199–200
failure, causes of, 203
history of, 199–200
problem-solving procedure, 204–6
workshop, 203
Quantitative/qualitative input overload, 251–52
Query, 84–85

R

Raters, performance evaluation, 181–82, 183
Rating manual, 182–83
Reactive tactics, 301
Receiver blockage, combating, 92
Recruitment/hiring, 55–56
Referent power, 49
Refreezing, as training strategy, 283
Reinforcement theory, 125–26
Reorganization, and conflict resolution, 218
Rewards:
    and authority, 48
    intrinsic, 131
    and job satisfaction, 132–33
    monetary, 131–32
Role ambiguity/conflict, and job satisfaction, 130
Routine meetings, 85
Routine report, 83–84

S

Sanctions, and authority, 48
Satisfiers, 122
SBO, *See* Supervision by objectives (SBO)
SBWA, *See* Supervising by wandering around (SBWA)
Security, 24–25
Selective perception, 89
Self-acceptance, 26
Self-concept, 276
Self-esteem, 25–27
    roots of, 26–27
Self-interest, 118
Self-management, 58
Self-responsibility, 26
Sender blockage, overcoming, 91
Serious Habitual Offender Comprehensive Action Program (SHOCAP), 319–21
Sermonizing, about ethics, 41–42
SHOCAP program, 319–21
Significant (critical) incidents database, 182–83
Significant emotional events (SEEs), and value changes, 16

Single-use plans, 143
Situational theory, 51–54
Situation identification, 41
Smoothing, and conflict resolution, 217
Socialization, as source of values, 15–16
Social stress, *See* Organizational/social stress
Stakeholders, 297–98
Standards, and values, 19
Standing plans, 143
Strategic Planning: What Every Manager MUST Know (Steiner), 143
Strategic planning, 142–43
Stress, 245–67
    converting into wellness, 260–63
        affixing responsibility, 260
        altruistic egoism, 263
        measuring life change units, 261
        mental discipline, 262
        otherness, 262–63
        reading/relaxation/recreation, 263
        supportive relationships, 261–62
    as demand for change, 246, 248–50
        medical findings, 249
        turbulent change, 249–50
    Episodic Nonwork-Related Stress Evaluation (table), 257
    Episodic Work-Related Stress Evaluation (table), 255
    general signs of, 254
    Long-Term Nonwork-Related Stress Evaluation (table), 259
    Long-Term Work-Related Stress Evaluation (table), 258
    police supervisor role, 246–48
        individual implications, 246–47
    organizational implications, 247–48
    sources of, 250–52
        environmental, 251
        organizational/social, 251–52
        personal, 250–51
    specific signs of, 254–60
    structured experiences, 265–67
        custom-designed wellness programs, 267
        laughter, 266–67
        stress-control formula, 265–66
    types of, 252–53
Stress management, 6
Strictness errors, 166

Subformal communications, 72–75
Superordinate goals, and conflict
    resolution, 217
Supervising by wandering around
    (SBWA), 104
Supervision:
  and COP program, 307
  transformation of, 3
Supervision by objectives (SBO), 6,
    148–51
  alternative strategies, 149–50
  evaluation, 150–51
  feedback, 151
  implementation, 150
  objective statement, 149
  obstacles to, 151–52
  See also Management by objectives
    (MBO)
Supervisors, total quality leadership, 2–5
Supportive relationships, and stress
    reduction, 261–62
Sworn personnel, 55
Symbol blockage, decreasing, 91

_T_

TBA, *See* Trust bank account (TBA)
Team building, 61, 287–90
Teamwork, 271–95
  group dynamics, 288–89
  and group effectiveness, 289–90
  leadership, 288
  and perception, 272, 273–78
    police supervisor role, 273
  and police work groups, 207
  structured experiences, 292–95
    case study, 292–93
    evaluating source of message, 293–94
    team-building evaluation, 295
    training practices, 294–95
  team building, 61, 287–90
  team profile, 290–91
  See also Perception; Training
Technology, and communication, 87–89
Tenure, and job satisfaction, 130
Tiburon Police Department, mission
    statement, 298, 299
Time management, 5, 98–113
  and Category II supervisor, 105–10

fast decisions, 102
  generations of, 102–5
  and interaction with staff, 99–100
  and mission, 99
  overloads, 101–2
  and productivity, 100–101
  structured exercises:
    Job-Time Analysis Form, 112–13
    sources of wasted time, 111–12
  time dimension, 100
  time-management matrix, 103–4
  time wasters, 104
  See also Category II supervisor
Time pressures, and communication
    problems, 90
Total quality leadership, 2–5
  and empowerment of people, 3–4
  leadership and people paradigm, 2–3
  transformation of supervision, 3
    foundation for, 4–5
  See also Leadership
Total quality results (TQR), 1–3
  knowing your job, 5
  knowing your staff, 5–6
  putting yourself to work, 6–7
Total quality services, 7, 331–42
  alignment, 334–39
  background/direction, 331–32
  excellence:
    achieving, 332–34
    action plans for, 339
    building, 339–42
    dimensions of, 334–39
TQR, *See* Total quality results (TQR)
Trained raters, 182–83
Training, 7, 43, 277, 278–87
  and COP program, 307–8
  delivery of, 284
  effectiveness of, 281–82
  ethics, 39–44
  evaluating, 284–87
  goals of, 279–80
  objectives, establishing, 283
  and perception, 277–78
  police supervisor role, 278–79
  process of, 280–81
  strategies, 283–84
  Work-Group-Effectiveness Inventory,
    285–86
Trait theory, 50–51

Trust, and delegation, 196–97
Trust bank account (TBA), 61–62, 69
Type A behavior, 252

U

Unfreezing, as training strategy, 283
Universal mission statement, 7, 297–98
  economic well-being, 297
  quality of life (employees), 297
  stakeholders, 297–98
Upward communications, 80

V

Value orientation, 40
Values, 5, 11–32
  changing, 16–17
  and conflict resolution, 19
  and COP program, 306
  definition of, 14
  as emotional indicators, 19
  as filters, 18
  and generation gaps, 18
  and imprinting, 15
  and individual differences, 18–19
  and MBWA, 333, 336–37
  and modeling, 15
  as motivators, 20
  of organization, 24–27
  overview of, 12
  police supervisor, as value driven,
    22–24
  and socialization, 15–16
  sources of, 14–16
  and standards, 19
  structured experiences, 28–30

supervisor value priority rankings,
    31–32
  value-clarification exercises, 28–30
  as thought provokers, 19
  understanding and respect, 12–13
  value clarification, 20–21
  See also Organizational values
Verbal communication, 275
Verbal intonations, 76
Vision, 59–60

W

Watson, Thomas Jr., 333, 335–36
Wellness programs, 260–63
  custom-designed, 267
Winners, 252
Win-win attitude, 77
Wisdom, 27
Words, 89
Worker attitudes, 13
Work force:
  education of, 54
  gender/ethnicity of, 54–55
  ladder of professional success, 56
  loyalty of, 54
  selection of, 55–56
  type of, 55
Work-Group-Effectiveness Inventory,
    285–86
Worriers, 252
Written communication, 75–76
Written messages, 83–85
  decision, 85
  inquiry, 84
  memorandum, 84
  proposal, 85
  query, 84–85
  routine report, 83–84
WSM (Whining, Sniveling, Malcontent),
    214, 218, 252